Other books by Herbert Warren Wind

THE STORY OF AMERICAN GOLF

THIRTY YEARS OF CHAMPIONSHIP GOLF
    (Co-Author with Gene Sarazen)

THE MODERN FUNDAMENTALS OF GOLF
    (Co-Author with Ben Hogan)

ON THE TOUR WITH HARRY SPRAGUE

THE COMPLETE GOLFER
    (Editor)

TIPS FROM THE TOP
    (Editor)

GREAT STORIES FROM THE WORLD OF SPORT
    (Co-Editor with Peter Schwed)

THE GILDED AGE OF SPORT

HERBERT WARREN WIND

SIMON AND SCHUSTER
NEW YORK . . . 1961

PUBLISHED BY SIMON AND SCHUSTER, INC.
ROCKEFELLER CENTER, 630 FIFTH AVENUE
NEW YORK 20, N. Y.

FIRST PRINTING

THE ARTICLES "THE BOUNCING BALL"; "THE MULBERRY BUSH"; "IN FRONT
OF THE OUTBACK"; "MAY THE MAGPIE FLOURISH"; "MAURICE RICHARD";
"BOB COUSY"; "BEN HOGAN"; "SAM SNEAD"; "YOGI BERRA"; AND "ON THE
VERANDA WITH JAMES MICHAEL CURLEY" APPEARED ORIGINALLY IN Sports
Illustrated.
THE ARTICLES "PEE WEE REESE" AND "G A M INC." APPEARED ORIGINALLY
IN True.
THE ARTICLE "A DISQUIETING ROUND AT THE ROYAL CALCUTTA GOLF CLUB"
APPEARED ORIGINALLY IN Town & Country.
THE ARTICLES "ST. ANDREWS" AND "THE LURE OF GOLF" APPEARED ORIGI-
NALLY IN Holiday.
THE ARTICLE "HARVARD NEVER LOSES AT HALF TIME" APPEARED ORIGINALLY
IN Collier's.
THE ARTICLE "XCEED XPECTATIONS, YELL YOURS, ZIP ZIP" APPEARED ORIGI-
NALLY IN The New Yorker.
THE ARTICLE "THE BEST SINCE KLEM" APPEARED ORIGINALLY IN The Satur-
day Evening Post.

LIBRARY OF CONGRESS CATALOG CARD NUMBER: 61–12863
MANUFACTURED IN THE UNITED STATES OF AMERICA
BY GEORGE MC KIBBIN AND SON, INC., NEW YORK

For my brother Jack,
the poor man's Billy Werber

ACKNOWLEDGMENTS

The articles in this collection first appeared in Collier's, Holiday, The New Yorker, The Saturday Evening Post, Sports Illustrated, Town & Country, and True, and I should like to thank those publications for their courtesy in permitting their use in this book. A large percentage of these articles were written for Sports Illustrated, and so I am especially indebted to that magazine for its co-operation.

In preparing the rather extended preface it was of enormous value to me to be able to talk over certain points with persons who know these aspects of sport far better than I do. I am particularly beholden in this respect to Kyle Rote, Richard S. Tufts, Herbert Goren, Shelley Mayfield, and William Talbert for their interest and knowledge. This is also a very good moment to express my genuine appreciation to a number of friends and colleagues who were, in one way or another, of exceptional assistance in my research on the preface and the articles: Bruce Addison, John Gardiner, Camil DesRoches, Morton Sharnik, James Finger, Al Mengert, Jane Corcoran, Seymour Sioff, William Rae, Michael Steinberg, and Professor John Pelzel. Professor Edwin Reischauer of Harvard, now our Ambassador to Japan, was generous enough to go over the pieces on Japan, and his suggestions, as need hardly be said, were remarkably helpful. I am grateful to Gerald Holland for our many zestful conversations, to Frederick L. Keefe and J. M. Flagler for their attentive reading of the manuscript, and to Peter Schwed for his considerate counsel.

H. W. W.

CONTENTS

7

III PERSONS AND PLACES

PREFACE

When sports historians get around to writing their books about the fifteen years following World War II—and I would imagine that even now a few are in the process of collating their old notes on such half-forgotten luminaries as Billy Cox, Chuck Davey, Billy Vessels, Shirley Fry, Gene Bearden, Mal Whitfield, Mac Speedie, Fanny Blankers-Koen, Sam Urzetta, Gretchen Fraser, and Bevo Francis (who once scored over a hundred points in a basketball game)—they will probably be at wide variance in selecting an over-all name to designate the era. Those in tempo with the calculated romantics of Madison Avenue, for whom the beat must always be up-up-up, will deplore the fact that such a lustrous image as "The Golden Age of American Sport" has already—and properly—been bequeathed to another period, the decade of the Twenties. Since no other mineral or precious stone readily connotes a superiority to gold, this group may have to settle for "The Real Golden Age" or "The Second Golden Age." In some ways this would not be wrong, either. While its spirit was neither as simple nor as soaring, the stretch of years between 1945 and 1960 certainly produced athletic virtuosos comparable to Ruth, Jones, Dempsey, Tilden, Weissmuller, Grange, Paddock, and other heroes of the Twenties. And financially, of course, it was far more golden.

Other historians, listening to a different drum and viewing the period somewhat more dourly, will be tempted to call it something less indicative of solid value, perhaps "The Chrome Age." Indeed, purposeful excesses and applied glitter frequently carried the day, and as sport became bigger and bigger business, quite often the heart went out of things when the veneer of Big Sport went over them. (This past autumn we were offered a literally stunning example of the spirit of the age when the New York Yankees, in what surely must be a new low freezing point in that organization's warmhearted reverence for baseball, dismissed Casey Stengel on the grounds that at seventy he was too old for the job of manager. This was an opinion that no one else in baseball had arrived at while watching Casey whip his team down the stretch to fifteen consecutive victories and the pennant, perhaps his finest bit of managing over the dozen years in which the old maneuverer led the Yankees to ten pennants and seven World Series championships.) However, to characterize the whole period that cynically would be to distort its character. Neither the best of times nor the worst of times, it was a complicated compound of many distressing and many inspiriting elements. It was the age of the professional. It was the age of the specialist. Above all, as future chroniclers will surely note, it was an age of enormous expansion which not only brought about a dramatic revival and extension of international competitions but also ushered in at home a new concept of sports for everyone, what with the shorter working hours, the easier transportation, and, above all, the advent of television, the greatest boon for the sports fan since the discovery of movable type. The only danger, perhaps, is that if the predicted day arrives when each of us has at home a color television set with a screen the size of a wall, carrying sports events originated on all continents, we may never get outdoors again.

These ruminations on the general state of sport are one of the by-products of the happy task I have been bending to in recent weeks: assembling for this book a number of the magazine articles on sports and sports personalities that it was my pleasure and assignment to write between 1945 and 1960. The articles are arranged in three sections. The first is made up of two fairly lengthy studies of sport in Japan and in Australia, dealing in the first article with the factors behind Japan's surprising but utterly genuine orientation toward western sports, and in the second with a continent so young that it has yet to evolve a true culture of its own but has established itself as the most sports-minded nation the world has ever seen. (This, on second thought, may be the path of Australian culture.) The second section contains studies of six remarkable athletes of the period: Bob Cousy, the greatest of all basketball players, a thoroughgoing genius at his game; Maurice Richard, "The Rocket" of Les Canadiens, the most prolific scorer in the history of hockey and as intent, embroiled, and hopelessly magnetic a performer as any sport has ever produced; Ben Hogan and Sam Snead, who are presented jointly, the latter the ablest golfer who has never won our National Open Championship, the former an outright wonder, as peerless in his period as Bobby Jones and Harry Vardon were in theirs; Yogi Berra, possibly the last of baseball's wonderful characters and quite possibly, too, one of the last members of that almost extinct race, nature's noblemen; and Pee Wee Reese, over a span of nineteen years the Brooklyn Dodgers' shortstop and, for many of us, the personification in this age, as Jones was in the Twenties, of the ideal American athlete. The third section is a gallimaufry of eight pieces of assorted types: an essay on golf; a close-up of Al Barlick, the National League umpire; a profile of the Queen Mother of Tennis, Hazel Hotchkiss Wightman; a brief look at Gussie Moran, tennis's gift to lingerie, or the other way around; a short visit to the Royal Calcutta Golf Club; a rather involved portrait of St. Andrews, the cradle of golf; an investigation of that perennial star of the Harvard football season, the college band; and a reminiscence about the late James Michael Curley, an old friend.

Time moves so quickly, in sport as in every phase of life, that these pieces already have about them the patina of another day. Several of the subjects who were in their prime or not too far past it at the time the articles were written—Berra and Hogan, for example—are now nearing the close of their careers. Several others, such as Reese and Richard, are already in retirement. There would have been some advantages, granted, in rewriting the articles and bringing them up to date, but it was decided that it would probably be best in the long run to leave them as they were and to supply each with a short introduction sketching in, among other things, any significant data between the date of publication and the present. In a few cases, notably in the articles on Australia and on Mrs. Wightman, some new material—or, more precisely, original material which the limitations of magazine space made it necessary to omit—has been included. Aside from this, however, only minuscule changes have been made. In addition to the central personalities named before, the articles offer glimpses of quite a number of the memorable figures of the postwar period (including Branch Rickey, John Landy, Jackie Robinson, Casey Stengel, Herb Elliott, the Konradses, and Joe DiMaggio), so while this collection cannot begin to approximate even an impressionistic history of sports over the past fifteen years, perhaps it will evoke some of the singular flavor and the temper of the times.

On the other hand, when the histories of that period are written, major attention will be given to many events, persons, and trends that are conspicuous by their absence in a collection of this kind. For instance, the closest these articles come to football is the story on the Harvard band, which is not close at all if you live south of Dedham. Furthermore, as far as the authentic champions go, there are, for example, only passing references to Ted Williams and none at all to Rocky Marciano, respectively the best left-handed hitter and the best right-handed hitter of the age. As a native of Brockton, Massachusetts, Marciano's home town, and by reason of the propinquity of Brockton to Boston a careful observer of Williams' career in the majors since his debut in 1939, I would have very much enjoyed doing articles on them. For one reason or another, I never did. When you write for magazines, either as a contributor or as a member of the staff, it will frequently happen that way, of course. Sometimes the magazine has already run a story on that particular subject and other times you have all you can carry to complete your regular assignments on time. In any event, I would like to avail myself of this opportunity to make a few tangential remarks about Williams and Marciano that may clarify certain things about them.

I do not know Ted Williams well at all, having been in his

company on only two occasions. The first was in the winter of 1956 when I had gone to Miami to do a story on Snead and discovered that Sam, not too uncharacteristically, was up in Palm Beach engaging in a two-day sailfishing contest with Williams. What struck me most about Williams at this meeting was the extra dimension of everything he did. When he laughed, he laughed more loudly than most people do. When he was annoyed, he was vehemently irritated. When he was serious, he was somber. When he was engaged in thought, he was impenetrable—and so on. He was, in truth, like a figure by Michelangelo, a little larger than life-size. Two winters later in Boston, when I saw him for a second time, he was much more at his ease. On this occasion I spent two exceedingly pleasant hours with him and his manager, Fred Corcoran, an old friend of mine, in Williams' suite in the Somerset Hotel where Ted was relaxing between the afternoon and evening exhibitions of fly-casting at the Sportsman's Show. As most people in baseball have known for a long while, Williams is a man of restless vitality, unusual natural charm (when the spirit moves him), unusual natural stubbornness, a candor which borders on overhonesty, and, as you would expect, a considerable egotism, this last being a trait common to all but a few of the leaders in every field. A perfectionist who knew his stuff and could produce, Ted never found it easy to suffer fools gladly. A very goodhearted man who needed appreciation, he was ruffled by the fickleness of the fans, for, additionally, he possesses the kind of ever-ready sensitivity which can make life extremely trying for a public figure and which, indeed, led him into several unfortunate displays of temperament. Fate was generous to Ted in one way. His gifts as a batter were so extraordinary that he was able to carry on for the astonishingly long period of twenty-one years, coming back as few men could have from two wars and a series of lingering injuries and successfully taking up where he had left off. At length, in his final years he was a living legend. The old flare-ups were forgotten and he was accorded the admiration due a bona fide giant who belongs in the exclusive company of Ruth and Hornsby as a batter who hit with great regularity and with great power over a long period of years.

On the evening I refer to, Williams felt like talking and I was

certainly glad he did, for otherwise I would have had no idea of
his impressive intelligence. He began, as I remember, by identifying the airplanes in a movie about the Korean war on TV. Then
he switched off the set and described with more preciseness the
performances of several of these planes which he had flown. After
that, I am not sure how we got from one topic to the other or the
order in which they came, but I recall that he discussed the difficulties of investing wisely; the ways and means of making fishing
tackle better than it is; why he occasionally played tennis during
the off-season; his awareness of his inability to be tactful toward
certain types of fans despite his resolutions to be; several over-the-
years correspondences he had kept up with faithful fans; the
incidents in which he would now admit he had been wrong in the
way he had behaved and the incidents about which he still felt he
had been right and saw no reason why he should say otherwise;
his long, long thoughts on what he might do when his playing
days were over; some laconic references to his boyhood in southern California; the failure of many sports reporters to measure up
to even a moderate standard of accuracy; the sportswriters whose
work he liked; some of the players he liked; the instructional films
he was making for a large industrial firm; why he was saving golf
for his doddering old age; and the general enigmatic state of the
world. Few of his statements stick with me in any detail, which
is a pity, since Williams is a hound for exactness. When he spoke
of the inaccuracy of sportswriters, he could quote passages practically verbatim. When he spoke of baseball statistics, his figures
were not approximations—they were the correct figures, sometimes to the fourth decimal point. I do remember somewhat more
clearly his answer to the last question I asked: Was the pitching
better in 1957 (when he had batted .388 in 129 games) than it
was in 1941 (when he had batted .406 in 143 games)? "Better in
'57," he said after a moment's thought. "There aren't many more
real good pitchers today than in 1941, but the staffs are better
balanced. Today there are far fewer really poor pitchers. The
quality of the relief pitching—that particularly has improved.
About comparing my averages those two seasons, I think I had
more well-hit balls that went right at some fielder in 1941 than
last year. Last year, too, I was lucky in the reverse way: I got many

more base hits on balls that weren't well hit but got through the infield or fell safe one way or another."

There is a Williams story I should like to tell, a light vignette, a view of Ted on one of those not infrequent evenings when he was bestirred by his chronic restlessness. It took place early in the spring of 1958 and was told to me by a friend who had never met Williams previously and was tagging along with an old crony of Ted's. There were about six fellows in all assembled that evening in Williams' suite at the Somerset a couple of hours after an afternoon game when, no longer able to abide the fruitless, drawn-out discussion as to where they might eat dinner, Ted grabbed his sports jacket and said, "Come on, let's get out of here." Without waiting, he opened the door and was gone. The rest of the group reached the main lobby in the next elevator in time to spot his tall, angular silhouette plowing out into Commonwealth Avenue. They caught up with him and, as they struggled to match his long strides, it was hastily decided that they would try a restaurant situated a long block away. The moment Ted walked in he was, of course, recognized by nearly everyone in the place. Anxious at the prospect of a constantly interrupted meal, he glanced around the restaurant and then instructed the group in a quarter-roar, "Let's get out of here." On the sidewalk a middle-aged fan congratulated him on the base hit he had made in the afternoon's game. Williams, who had gone 1 for 5, told the fan somewhat impatiently that he had hit that ball lousy, practically on the handle. Still pacing the group with his long strides, he headed for another restaurant two blocks away. Inevitably, since no one else looks quite like Williams, a loud buzz of recognition again followed his entrance. "O.K., O.K. Let's get out of here," he said in that quarter-roar. With the group strung out behind him, he retraced his steps back toward the Somerset. He had decided that it would be best after all if they ate in the hotel in the privacy of his suite. He was starting across the lobby, shaking his head fretfully at his own folly and the folly of mankind in general, when he was intercepted near the sanctuary of the elevators by a nice old lady.

"You're Ted Williams, aren't you?" she said excitedly.

"Guess again, madam," Williams snapped. He had tried to be

very gruff but had failed to carry it off at all well. It was very funny. He was into the elevator in a flash.

Where Williams was intensely complicated, Rocky Marciano was simplicity itself. There is an adage to the effect that no man can be the hero to the people in his home town that he is elsewhere, that the home towners who "knew him when" will insist on chopping him down to their own size. Marciano was an exception, then. The only criticism I have ever heard of him by Brocktonians were references to his moments of Sneadian frugality. For the rest, he was and is held in exceptional regard and affection, and he was deserving of at least this. In an era when the fight racket was plunging to new lows in the Norris regime—today it is only a few rungs above wrestling—Marciano's steadfast decency was something. He was no fool. He had the practicality to accede to being managed by Al Weill, for Weill could get him the fights he needed in order to move to the top. However, in all his dealings and in his actions in the ring and outside it, Marciano was a man to admire: straight, modest, sensible in the face of idolatry, ever the same warmhearted, unaffected fellow he was before he became champion. I was always astounded by the gracious sense of sportsmanship that characterized his panting remarks when the microphone was thrust into his face only seconds after a bruising fight was over—a moment, if there ever was one, when a man could be excused if his words caught the tone of the raucous crowing of the weathercocks around the ring. But Marciano's never did.

The one hundred and one ways in which the people of Brockton reacted to the spawning of a champion in their midst were, to say the minimum, interesting. Early in Rocky's professional career, when he was still fighting four-rounders in Providence, I learned on visits to Brockton that old friends of mine who had never followed boxing before attended all his fights. He had the unmistakable stamp of a winner, and they liked him. Long before he defeated Joe Louis and established himself as more than just another young fighter with a punch, his impress on his home town was ubiquitous. His photograph, duly inscribed, hung in the place of honor in every self-respecting bar and grill. Each shoe manufacturer in town confided proudly that Rocky's father had worked in *his* plant. When people had five minutes on their hands and didn't know what to do, they would drive past the Marchegiano's small house near Edgar's Playground—and later past Rocky's new home in a development behind the old Fair Grounds—in the hopes of catching a glimpse of him. From the Louis bout on, he was greeted on his return to Brockton after each fight by crowds estimated between 25,000 and 40,000, an astonishing turnout considering that the population of Brockton is only around 65,000. However, I think the most amazing thing of all was the thousands of Brocktonians who regularly poured into New York to attend his fights. They had some distinction now. They were not just anonymous visitors to the big city, they were personal friends of the champion. People I had known since boyhood as hard-working fellows who had to watch the old budget, I'd obviously pegged wrong. You found them on the day of the fight luxuriating like sultans in their hotel suites, fondling their ringside tickets and their fancy drinks and talking about following Rocky to Europe if the rumors of his fighting on the continent materialized. Fellows I'd always thought of as having no interest in sports were in town, too—in hordes. Somehow they had become veteran fight fans overnight, and now they talked authoritatively of Kid Chocolate and Tommy Gibbons and the rest as if they roomed with Nat Fleischer. Not once did the thought of Rocky's being defeated ever seriously cross their minds. They came expecting the victory he always provided, and when the electric moment came they converged on the ring in a howling body to greet their boy. Since Rocky's retirement, the tang has gone out of the lives of many Brocktonians, but it was something unforgettable for them to have been struck by lightning and to have come from the same town as the heavyweight champion of the world.

Of all the Brocktonians who knew Rocky and told anecdotes about him, no one was closer to him than a friend of mine named Albert Doyle. They had gone to grammar school together and had attended the same YMCA gym classes on Saturday mornings when they were nine or ten. With a young boy's generosity, Al, who was given a dime each Saturday—a nickel for a soda and a nickel for carfare—had split the dime with Rocky at the soda fountain and walked home. Al had long forgotten about this, but Rocky, those many years later, had not. Whenever he was training for a big fight, for one thing, he would always invite Al to come up to the camp and be his guest. One time, when Al showed up at Grossinger's, where Rocky was training for the second La Starza fight, Rocky grabbed his bags and led him to a large room in the main house at the camp where there was a bed against the window and one against the far wall. Rocky asked him which bed he wanted. Knowing Rocky to be a fresh-air fiend, Al pointed to the one against the wall. When they got up the next morning, Rocky inquired if Al had had a good night's sleep.

"Perfect," Al answered.

"I knew you would," Rocky said. "That's my favorite bed."

Between fights Marciano kept in the strictest training. This included daily roadwork. He invariably punctuated these runs by visiting some sick youngster or some bedridden fan he had been told about who lived near his route. He never mentioned these things. Rocky disciplined himself into a fantastic conditioner, and in time he came to assume that long-distance running was a natural means of transport for everyone. One year when the Brockton High football team was playing an old rival, Quincy, at Quincy, some fifteen or twenty miles away, Rocky and Al made tentative plans to go to the game together. The day before, Al asked him what time he thought they ought to start over.

"No later than nine, Al," Rocky said. "That's a long run to Quincy."

As I say, I never did get to meet Rocky on my visits home, but one evening when some of us were having drinks at a tavern on the outskirts of the city I met his sister Betty. What I remember most vividly about that evening was the way she handled what had all the earmarks of a very awkward situation. As she was leaving the tavern, a fellow who had obviously broken training with a vengeance many hours before yelled over to her obstreperously, "Why doesn't your brother fight any Irishmen? He's scared of them. You know that. They'd knock his block off."

"That's why he doesn't fight them," Betty said easily—and nothing more.

Since none of the pieces in this collection is about professional football, I should like to take advantage of the freewheeling nature of this preface to air some opinions about it, inasmuch as pro football undoubtedly made the greatest advances of any game in the period between 1945 and 1960. I am thinking not so much of the steady annual increases in attendance and gate receipts racked up by the National Football League or of the way that watching a program on TV, if one isn't at a stadium, has become an ingrained national habit on autumn Sundays. I am thinking more of the game itself, the astute way it was brought along with sound rule changes so that football developed into a better game than it had ever been before—a much better game, in fact, than many of us ever dreamed it could be. The heights of precision which National Football League play has now reached were summed up very well, I believe, in a random remark by a friend of mine who was nurtured on the ambivalent pleasures of Ivy League football: "In college ball whenever a pass is completed it is very exciting—you really don't expect the completion to be made. In pro football, you're surprised when a pass isn't completed."

Before World War II, pro football had matured into a good game. It had discovered and refined the beauties of the passing attack, and the renaissance of place-kicking was also well under way. It had its superbly drilled teams, such as the Chicago Bears, the Green Bay Packers, the New York Giants, and the Washington Redskins. It had its majestic individual stars, such as Sammy Baugh, Don Hutson, and Bronco Nagurski. At the same time, pro football had not wholly left behind some of the muddier aspects that had been part and parcel of its genesis in the 1920s as a game played largely by tramp athletes on the grassless gridirons on the tough side of town, principally in the hard lands of the Middle West. As late as the mid-1930s some NFL games still degenerated into saturnalias of grisly force, the science of football only fleetingly observable as one watched the thudding clashes in the line with real awe, wondering if the contests at the Roman Colosseum could have been much more violent. There was an unfinished quality about much of the routine play. In the first NFL game I saw, the Green Bay Packers versus the Brooklyn Dodgers in 1936, Paul Schissler, the coach of the Dodgers, had come up with an ingenious triple shift that was designed to throw the Packers off balance. The way it worked out, it didn't bother the Packers but it ruined the Dodgers. The majority of the backs didn't know where they were supposed to go on the second shift, and by that time linemen were bumping into each other left and right—those who had not forgotten that a final shift had to be made and were still on side. Half the plays had to be called back or were whistled dead before they started for one infraction or another. It made you wonder if there had been many, if any, serious practice sessions.

For all this, that game had its undeniable moments. For one thing, there was the end play of Don Hutson; for another, there was the kicking of Ralph Kercheval, the Brooklyn specialist. Kercheval, as a matter of fact, was the reason I had gone to the game. Earlier that autumn I had come down from college to New York on a Sunday and, riding in a taxi, I had turned on the radio in back. This was a new advance in civilization that had just arrived and it ranked as a "must" on any visit to the big city. The station I tuned in was carrying a broadcast of a pro game at Ebbets Field. The announcer was saying in a dry, dramatic voice, "Yes, the Dodgers are going to try for a field goal. Wilson is kneeling just past midfield and Ralph Kercheval is back to try and kick a fifty-yard field goal. Yes, you heard me correctly, fans—a fifty-yard field goal. There's a snap from center . . . the kick is in the air . . . it's a high kick that doesn't look like"—the crowd roared—"it's good, it's good. Ladies and gentlemen, Ralph Kercheval has just kicked a fifty-yard field goal." I couldn't believe it. I had read about successful kicks of over forty yards and I couldn't believe them either. The longest field goal, placement or drop kick, that I'd ever seen in college ball could not have been more than twenty-seven yards.

On a weekend not long after this, I went to Ebbets Field to see for myself. As I remember it, in that game against the Packers, Kercheval kicked no field goals, but I recall clearly that he put on the finest exhibition of punting I had ever watched. This was exciting, and so, too, in a rather offbeat way, was the play of Don Hutson, the Packers' famous pass-catching end, whose feats every sports fan had been aware of since his debut as a national celebrity in the 1935 Rose Bowl game between Alabama and Stanford in which he had caught passes all over the field. How did Hutson get free so often when he was a marked man? This was what I wanted to find out. Whenever the Packers had the ball I focused on him. On their first marches, as I remember, he contributed nothing. Arnold Herber, the Packers' passer, never threw to him, and Hutson, for that matter, always seemed well covered. As the game went on, it became easier and easier to follow Hutson's moves. Everyone else's uniform had become begrimed with the mud of the wet field, but his mustard pants and green jersey were almost as unsoiled as when the game began—a state of affairs that was simply explained. On offense, on the plays when he was not going out for a pass, Don did the most perfunctory kind of blocking, just brushing his assigned man. Then, when the Packers went on defense, though this was years before the two-platoon system arrived, he usually trotted off the field and his lean, easy-gaited, well-groomed figure was not observed again until the Packers regained possession of the ball.

I was still wondering why Hutson was so renowned when he caught his first pass—good for a touchdown, incidentally. It was one of the least spectacular catches I had ever seen, or perhaps it just seemed so because I had been visualizing some picture-play in which Don, leaving the defenders behind with a burst of speed and a subtle fake, would glance up over his shoulder and pull the ball in with his finger tips. Instead, he scored like this: with the ball on about the Brooklyn twelve-yard line, he ran straight ahead until he was a yard inside the end zone, where he suddenly stopped, whirled around to face the passer, and fell to his knees in the same motion. At this precise second the ball arrived from Herber, a low, fast pass that wasn't more than two feet off the ground when Hutson grabbed it. Far from a picture-play but a smart one, for the defenders, waving their arms behind and high above Hutson, were yards from the ball. Later in the game Hutson and Herber worked the same play for another touchdown, and not long after this, with the game now a rout, Hutson called it an afternoon. His uniform was still as spotless as ever except for a daub of mud on each knee.

The picture-play I had been hoping to see Hutson and Herber execute I saw many years later in the late 1940s in a preseason exhibition game for charity between the New York Giants and the

Los Angeles Rams. The Rams at this period had one of the most varied passing attacks of all time. Bob Waterfield was the quarterback. In Elroy Hirsch and Tom Fears he had two talented ends, and in Vitamin T. Smith and Glenn Davis, his halfbacks, he had two more fine receivers. The team, as you would imagine, operated beautifully out of spread formations even when it was deep in its own territory. On the play I am referring to, the Rams had the ball on about their own fifteen and Davis was positioned as a flanker wide to the right. As every sports fan remembers well, Glenn had the speed of a sprinter; indeed, he was a sprinter. As Waterfield took the ball from center and faded back, Davis took off straight down the field like a hare. No one had checked him at the line of scrimmage and as he fled over the five-yard stripes he veered only a foot or so out of his line to avoid the safety man, who had come over presumably to pick him up on about the thirty-five-yard line. As Davis hit the forty all by himself, he looked back over his left shoulder, saw the ball coming, kept racing at full speed, reached up with his right hand like an outfielder as he hit mid-field, plucked the ball out of the air with that fully extended hand, and gathered it in without breaking stride the faintest fraction. In a few stupefying seconds he was over the goal line. At that instant the nearest defender may have been a full fifty yards behind him. The play had struck with the speed of lightning and it was at least fifteen seconds before the spectators had digested what they had witnessed and rose to their feet with a roar of tribute. And then—I suppose it had to happen—there was a huddle of the officials, the Rams were penalized five yards for some illegal procedure, and, for all intents and purposes, the play had never happened. In my experience I have never seen a pass play to compare with it for flawless, thrilling execution.

Every professional football fan's selection of the best plays he has seen will necessarily vary, depending on the games he has watched and, to some extent, on his rooting affiliation, but there is no question that pro football's basic stamp is the beautifully clear-cut patterns and the synchronized timing of the attack. Play after play, even those that are stopped, develop in front of the spectator with the fascinating clarity of an animated cartoon. (The newly organized second professional league, the American

Football League, which at this writing has just finished its first
season, fell far short of approximating the NFL's proficiency and
reminded us in the process that one doesn't reach professional
standards simply by playing for money.) In the faraway days
when every town had its baseball team, major league baseball
built its immense appeal on the simple fact that the skills of its
players were so apparent that the athletes seemed a different breed
entirely from even the most outstanding minor league players. It
really was the Big Time. When you set your foot inside a major
league park, you vibrated all over at the realization that you were
only seconds away from watching baseball played as it never came
close to being played outside a major league park. The National
Football League has succeeded in doing the same for professional
football. NFL football is so markedly superior to even the best
college football that it seems unbelievable that not too long ago
some informed sports fans could declare that they preferred the
collegiate game.

The adroitness with which the NFL brought along its game
after the war came as a surprise to many of us. Bert Bell, the
League's commissioner from the resignation of Elmer Layden in
1946 until his death in 1959, hardly gave the impression of a keen,
vigorous intellect stewarding the enlightened growth of the game.
Bell's major concern seemed to be protecting the interests of the
owners. Many of the owners, for that matter, appeared to be out-
and-out house-counters who lived less for football than for the
publicity that came to them in the daily papers and at the weekly
press luncheons. (In today's jargon a man who buys an athletic
team automatically becomes a "wealthy sportsman." The current
definition of an All-American you probably know: any fellow
who played some college football and has been out of school seven
years or more.) Be that as it may, in Commissioner Bell's regime
pro football made one excellent move after another. It came up
with the right answer where baseball and other sports frequently
did not in its handling of television, generating national enthusiasm for its product by making it available in all areas except those
in which the games were scheduled but never budging from a
firm policy of local blackouts. (A particularly incisive example of
how well this worked took place a few Decembers ago when thou-

sands of San Francisco Forty-Niner fans, unable to buy tickets for a key game that was completely sold out, jumped in their cars and drove to the Nevada border where the blackout zone ended and the telecast was available.)

The NFL's most significant wisdom, however, was nursing the game itself into an increasingly better expression of football. Back in 1933 when the league was gaining its first foothold, it had recognized the importance of passing and kicking in attractive, wide-open football. In that year it brought the goal posts back to the goal line and so brought back the field goal; it also decreed that the forward pass could legally be thrown any place behind the line of scrimmage. After the war, the NFL kept moving in the right direction. Its decision not to draft or assign college players until their class was graduated upgraded the game and the caliber of the persons playing it. The league arrived at a just method of handling the player draft, realizing the intention behind it of equalizing the teams and making the competition more even. As for the game itself, freedom of substitution afforded room for the offensive and defensive specialists. Unnecessary piling on and needless injuries were arrested by ruling that a ball carrier could not get up and run again once his knee touched the ground after he had made contact with a defensive man. Stricter calling of the fifteen-yard penalty (and automatic first down) for roughing the kicker or the passer eliminated much of the thuggery which frequently had seen a team stop its opponent by deliberately banging up the rival star so that he had to leave the game. (One official's primary duty today is to watch the passer.) The officiating in general became sterner and clearer, and in the long run this was to prove of incalculable value despite the intermediate frustration of attending certain games, as every fan did, in which on play after play one or more officials tossed a handkerchief to the ground to signal an infraction.

At the present time—and I am speaking not as an expert but as an ardent fan, which is indeed the vantage point from which all these prefatory remarks are made—there are only two or three rules that might be changed or better administered. Defending backs, invariably players who aren't able to do the job capably to begin with, still get away far too frequently with breaking up a forward pass by tackling the receiver before he receives the ball. Admittedly, this is sometimes a hard play to call (particularly at field level) because, at its core, it is a judgment decision: did the defender make contact in a legitimate effort to intercept the pass or was this not his intention? Personal fouls still occur more persistently than they should. From the players' point of view, in a game as rugged and hard-fought as pro football you must expect some personal fouls to be part of its complex. You can't have one without the other. The players further believe that considering the severity of the contact and the heat of the fray, the percentage of fouls is remarkably low. I am sure that they are right and that only a few of the fouls are gratuitous, but since fouling, whatever its extenuation, detracts so mightily from the game, it strikes me that it might be a helpful measure to name the individual offender (not simply the team) over the public-address system and to call a match penalty on the offender—i.e., put him out of the game—with much more alacrity when the foul obviously had nothing to do with normal self-protection. In a different direction, there is something to be said for moving the point of the kickoff back five or ten yards to either the thirty-five-yard line or the thirty now that the kicking tee has made kickoffs into and through the end zone an almost common occurrence. A rule is also needed, in the opinion of Kyle Rote, that clear-eyed student of the game, to protect the man who kicks off, making it illegal for the players on the receiving team to make contact with him for three seconds after the kickoff or until he has moved five yards downfield from the line of the kickoff.

By setting higher standards for itself after the war and maintaining them, professional football opened the way for the coaches in their turn to advance the game. Football brings out in all of us the lurking strategist, the Walter Mitty commander of armies, and so it is not in the least surprising that the imaginative coach should be as old as football itself. (No one, for example, was ever more inventive than Pop Warner.) The postwar coaches, typified by Paul Brown, have naturally gone far beyond their predecessors in infusing power, speed, and deception into the attack. They have worked on their offensive and defensive patterns with such perfectionistic detail and with such an outpouring of mentality that it made one almost regret, in his semi-reflective moods, that persons capable of this total commitment of their talent and energy were not down in Washington devoting themselves to more serious affairs. Today these coaches have "the horses" to execute their sinuous blackboard mosaics. In addition to wonderful backs and ends, who have always been plentiful, there is a whole new race of linemen, mastodons with the quick reflexes and mobility of small men.

The fortunate thing thus far has been that the carefully schooled offenses have not run away with the game. There have been stretches when it looked as if they would, but at those times corresponding advances in defensive techniques were devised (by specialists like Steve Owen and, later, Tom Landry of the New York Giants) and the balance was restored. For example, in 1950, when everyone was wondering how Otto Graham and the Cleveland Browns could be contained, the Giants, after defeating them 6–0 at Cleveland, held Graham to ten short completions and the Browns' rushing attack to a total of twelve yards when the two teams met in New York three weeks later. As for the champion Detroit Lions teams of the middle 1950s, the offensive unit (led by Bobby Layne) did its job very well, but there was at least an equal pleasure in watching the way the defensive unit (and particularly defensive backs led by the peerless Jack Christiansen, Doyle Lary, and Jim David) took care of things. The Lions' splendid record was really built on what happened when the team was trying to regain possession of the ball. At the present time, when two top-notch pro teams meet, there is often so true an equipoise of power between one offense and the opposing defense that the first quarter is spent with the two teams probing for one slight defensive deficiency (like a slow-starting corner man or a line backer who is "red dogging" too regularly) and then keying the attack to exploit that small, improperly defended area.

All in all, professional football has made itself into a superlative game, both rousing and full of subtlety, and it is presently hard to conceive how it can improve on itself in its main proportions. It is just where it should be.

Football, it seems to me, is the only major game that has changed for the better over the past fifteen years. All games, of course, remain in a fairly constant state of flux. In many, higher levels of excellence in techniques are periodically reached. Sometimes they result from improved equipment: the stronger shafted clubs in golf; the slimmer, more passable ball in football; the steel pole which supplanted the old bamboo pole in vaulting; and so on. Sometimes these advances come about when a cluster of players by sheer hard work and good coaching carries the techniques of earlier decades to new plateaus of proficiency—the fuller exploitation of the big serve and the big volley in tennis, for example, or the phenomenal accuracy that basketball players have acquired with the one-hand jump shot. By whatever route these increases in skill come about, when they do arrive they alter the pattern and tactics of the games. If they are properly understood and handled by the powers regulating that sport, they can enhance its appeal considerably, increasing its vocabulary, as it were. If they are misunderstood and maladroitly handled, they bring on a sort of Gresham's Law of sports: obliquely effective and only superficially exciting new styles of play drive out the essentially superior old styles that lay at the meaningful heart of that sport and made it fun to play and a treat to watch. The responsibility—and it is the principal one—of the men governing each sport is to see that the proper balance is maintained in the game. To achieve this, they must be open to innovation, but they must make certain that a new technique or tactic which can change a game is correctly integrated. The right elements must remain dominant. Higher scoring must mean better scoring and must not be simply a euphemism to describe a wayward trend that has abused innovations and taken the game to the point where it has lost much of its fiber and will soon lose most of its finesse.

In sports the governing bodies must be watchdogs as well as promoters, for it is amazing how quickly people and institutions can alter their scale of values, their appreciation of quality. A friend of mine—if I may illustrate with a non-sporting example which happens to be the first that comes to mind—used to stop regularly at the old Ritz-Carlton on his visits to New York. That really was an elegant hotel in the best international tradition. The rooms were comfortable and tastefully furnished, the service was immediate, some genius had lighted the Oval Room restaurant in such a way that the sun forever seemed to be shining softly, and ducks swam under the red bridges in the restaurant in the outdoor Japanese garden. The establishment was quiet but animate, and even the elevators smelled good. "This hotel belongs to a vanished era," my friend used to say. "I wonder how much longer it can last?" Well, it did linger on a few more years, and then in 1950 it was torn down to make way for a much taller office building which would naturally return a much greater revenue. On his trips to New York after this, my friend elected to stop at the Ambassador. It was, he realized frequently and at length, a definite cut below the "Old Ritz" in décor, service, and general atmosphere, but he felt that it came as close as anything that remained to what he wanted in a hotel. He set about making his adjustment to it. By the time 1960 rolled around, he had succeeded so well in this respect that the Ambassador—or the Sheraton-East, as it had been renamed—had come to loom for him as a last stronghold of gracious metropolitan hotel living. "At times I almost forget what the 'Old Ritz' was like," he was musing not long ago. "Everything is comparative, you see. One forgets and one gets conditioned to things, without even realizing it. My son never saw the 'Old Ritz.' This hotel will be his standard of elegance."

Today, though they are often equipped with a very meager background, young sports fans are convinced that anyone who believes, say, that baseball was in many ways a better game in the old days is a senescent devotee of nostalgia who would always damn the present and contend that American civilization reached its peak in the merry reign of Chester A. Arthur. In some respects —and nostalgia has nothing to do with it—baseball was a more enchanting game in the old days when the ball didn't have so much rabbit in it. There was more baseball to baseball. I doubt if even the extreme purists would argue that the advent of the first home-run era following the livening of the ball in 1920—the introduction of Australian yarn made tighter winding possible— was not a good thing for the game. The "long ball," the home run over the fence or the double off the fence, did create a new dimension of color and drama without twisting the fundamental proportions of the game out of shape: only an exceptional hitter like Ruth could reach the bleachers with any regularity; the line-drive hitter's value was hardly impaired; the audaciously stolen base, the well-executed sacrifice or hit-and-run play, and other such ancient means of coaxing a big run around remained intrinsic parts of the fabric of the game. In 1947, however, the ball was given a new injection of rabbit—or perhaps, since the officials denied that any change had taken place, it would be more correct to say that it appeared that a still more lively ball had been introduced. That year the New York Giants set a new team record for home runs, 221, which included 51 by Johnny Mize, 36 by Willard Marshall, 35 by Walker Cooper, 29 by Bobby Thomson, and 17 by, of all power hitters, Bill Rigney. It was a bad mistake. Every player, even the pitchers, could now hit a few out of the park, and when the home run became that cheap it lost much of its special character.

It might be well to point out, moreover, that the everyday home run—the high fly ball that lands in the no longer distant bleachers as opposed to the blasts that Mantle unloads—is not the incomparably spectacular feature that contemporary legend would have us believe. When the ball drops into the stands or clears the fence, the play is over then and there. The action halts. On the other hand, the old-fogy school of baseball fan, to which I belong, contends that more of the essential thrill of baseball is present when, with men on base, the batter lines the ball, let us say, toward the hole in right-center or left-center. The action is continuous, the suspense builds to a climax. The number of bases the hit will be good for depends on how well the outfielders play it . . . the runners whirl around the bases . . . the throw comes in . . . there's a close play at a base or at the plate . . . the ball is in play all the way. The home run, nevertheless, has been so glorified that every youngster with his eye on a career in baseball knows at the tender age of thirteen that the clubs pay the big money to the power hitters, and many boys work on becoming nothing else but that. As a result, the all-round ballplayer—a Reese or a Robinson who can field, throw, hit, run, bunt, hustle, and think—instead of becoming more numerous, is becoming a rather rare bird, this despite the fact that the number of young men with high athletic ability was never as great as it is today. Incidentally, much as I dislike finding myself in Frank Lane's corner, it struck me that he showed a brilliant suspicion of the current inflated valuation of the spasmodic long-ball hitter when, just prior to the start of the 1960 season, he traded Rocky Colavito, the league's reigning home-run champion, for Harvey Kuenn, a far less explosive but more reliable batter.

One of the most eloquent persons at describing what has gone out of baseball is Ty Cobb. In Cobb's day, the men who played baseball pondered its niceties with the same endless attention to detail that the professional golfer gives to his game today, with Cobb, like Hogan, a good step ahead of the others. "You thought long and hard about the small ways in which you could gain a slight edge over the pitcher," Cobb reminisced not long ago over some cups of coffee following a breakfast in New York. "If you kept your eyes open, you made some valuable discoveries. For instance, I don't know when it was in my career that I learned an almost sure-fire way of drawing a walk when you had three balls on you against a good control pitcher you weren't certain you could hit and when getting on base was important. What I learned was this: if you started to fall back from the plate just as the pitcher was getting ready to release the ball, nine times out of ten he'd throw the ball so that it followed you as you backed away. It would be way inside. Why that happens, I wouldn't know exactly. It's some psychological pattern you set up, of course. But nine times out of ten, as I say, you'd make the pitcher follow your move and you'd get that pass.

"When I watch the batters today, with few exceptions they just go up there and take a big cut at the ball. They never exploit the advantages the hitter has over the pitcher. We were always thinking about those things. To give you a concrete example, let's say I'm a left-handed batter and I want to hit the ball down the left-field line in this particular situation. I don't want a pitch that's in tight, that's for certain. How do I get the pitcher to give me the sort of pitch I want, one that's a little on the outside? Well, I take my stance up there as if I've got my mind on nothing else but pulling the ball into right field. I know the catcher and pitcher will notice this and they'll probably try to cross me up by pitching me a little on the outside. Get it? Then, when they're all set to go, when the catcher has gone into his crouch, at this last moment I change my stance, move that front foot up, and when that ball comes in on the outside, it's just where I want it to punch it into left field." Cobb paused a moment to see if this had registered with his guests at the table. "I could go on and on with examples," he resumed. "It was full of subtlety, baseball was, full of skill. It was a charming game. That game won't return, and if it did I wonder if the fans today would like it or appreciate it, they've been so educated away from the fine points."

Compared to the other popular games, baseball is an old one and a strong one which went through a lengthy period of development between 1845 and 1895. Its devisers worked out a masterful set of checks and balances, not unlike the American Constitution, until they had it right. (It is a marvelous thing to me that the ninety feet between the bases, which Alexander Cartwright defined in his master diagram in 1845, still functions as the ideal distance: if an infielder makes a proper play on a ground ball, he gets the runner at first; if he plays the ball just a fraction wrong, usually he will miss the runner.)

Because of its careful genesis, baseball hasn't been as drastically affected as have the later-born games by the principal trend of the last fifteen years, the emphasizing of the offense and scoring to the detriment of the best expression of the game. There are many of us who especially question the soundness of the direction in which basketball has been moving. As we all know, in a game in which the object is to project a ball through a hoop ten feet above the floor, there is bound to be a huge premium on height. Twenty-five years ago a man who stood six-feet-two was regarded as a tall man on the court. Fifteen years ago he became a middle-sized man. Today, when the tall men in pro ball are around six-feet-eleven and the middle-sized men average about six-feet-six, the man who stands six-feet-two is now regarded as "the diminutive playmaker." (In college ball

he is a sort of smaller middle-sized man.) Each season the
number of giants who are co-ordinated athletes and not awkward hulks increases, but, for all this, the drift toward taller
and taller and bigger and bigger players (populating a court
that has become too small for them) has resulted in stereotyped
offenses. Time after time the ball is fed into the big man in the
pivot who, if he is unable to get a shot away or to draw a foul
in the process, feeds the ball mechanically back to the backcourt men or occasionally to the corner men moving across.
Then the ball comes in again. However, it isn't the sheer altitude
alone of the present players that has brought on the semi-planted
offense. The improvement in shooting has also been a conspicuous factor. Today the offensive star doesn't have to get free or
get set in order to get off a scoring shot. His back turned to the
basket, his dribble concluded, his man covering him, the modern star is still a threat, for these paragons have developed unstoppable shots—hooks and jumps and fall-away twisters—which
they can somehow get off and make when they are apparently
as tied up as Laocoön. Tommy Heinsohn, who, it should be
remarked, is one of the most mobile of the middle-big men, is,
for illustration, far less dangerous shooting when set than when
he lets one go hurriedly and off balance, his right hand pushing
the ball on a line as he jumps and his left seemingly groping
for something to hold onto, like a man falling down a staircase
and grabbing for the banister rail.

To master their unstoppable shots, today's stars have worked
on them hour after hour in high school and college, and, one
would deduce, neither allotted themselves the time nor felt the
inclination to work on the other facets of the game. In the lopsided imbalance of their skill they resemble the average pitcher
in baseball who, having practiced nothing but pitching, looks
as if each trip to the plate is his maiden voyage on a strange sea.
The offensive star who has a well-founded understanding of defensive play before he enters the professional ranks is the exception, and many never truly learn to play defense. As a result,
unless a Bob Cousy or a lesser playmaker is directing the team,
professional basketball can frequently bog down into a game
that is 90 per cent shooting and rebounding, with ball-handling

and team movement, the true essentials, relegated to such sporadic appearances that when a simple give-and-go, that staple of back-yard basketball, is neatly executed, it has the mark of high artistry. Today only when a pro team is hitting on its shots does it look like a good team. When it isn't hitting it will look like no team at all, and during the stretches when both teams are off in their shooting the result is a shambles. It is easy to understand why a growing percentage of the game's faithful, while admiring the magnificent new moves that the intuitive technicians such as Cousy and Baylor and Robertson have introduced, regard the last fifteen years as a period in which much first-rate talent has been wasted on a rudderless sport that has lost its way.

Pro basketball affects all basketball. All pro sport exerts a magnetic influence on all the "lower orders" of that sport. If the men directing the course of pro basketball had been as intelligent as their counterparts in pro football, we might be watching a superlative brand of basketball in which, by thought and study, by experiment and thoughtful revision, the modern game had been molded into a blend of the finest of the old and the new. For years now, many of the sport's best minds (while accepting the reality that pro basketball is bound to be a game for the very tall just as pro football is a game for the very sizable) have been meditating on the changes which might curtail the excessive advantages of height and so speed the return of some of the desirable aspects of the old game. Some of these men believe that the present maximum court size of ninety-four by fifty feet, while adequate for high-school and college players, should be enlarged both in width and in length for professional ball. Their thinking here is that the big man who is not a fairly natural athlete would have more trouble staying with the pace, that the standard pick-off for the corner man would be less effective if the corner were further from the basket—in sum, that mobility would be encouraged and court clogging diminished. Other interested critics have propounded these various suggestions: the height of the basket should be raised; a different scoring system should be introduced that would divide the court into zones, with a field goal scored in the close vicinity of the basket counting less than one from farther out; an offensive team should be limited to one rebound and then should be required to take the ball beyond a certain line before launching another shot and getting another rebound. It has also been proposed that the problem of the tall man might be dealt with by regulating that the collective height of a team of ten men could not exceed some total—say, 780 inches (which, in this example, would mean that the average height of the players would be six-feet-six)—so that a team carrying a number of men well over that average figure would have to carry several men under it in order not to exceed the maximum collective team height.

It is hard to know which of these suggestions would actually work out. Raising the baskets two feet, for example, might, as Pete Newell advances, produce rebounds that carry much further away from the basket area, which would help a lot. Of course, it would be ideal if it were feasible to try to get more basketball back into basketball without resorting to any legislation, direct or indirect, governing the height of the players. In this connection, it has occurred to many observers that the simple measure of enforcing the "floor rules" more strictly would enable the game to settle down. If palming, traveling or running, moving the pivot foot, charging, and the other basic floor rules were called as rigorously as they were twenty-five years ago, a fair amount of the current solo offense work (such as the reverse backing-into dribble and the forced drive) would have to be abandoned. The majority of the players could not pull it off then and would have to rely more on working with their teammates. Whenever one watches Adolph Schayes, for example, he must remark that the Syracuse veteran is an excellent rebounder, has a beautiful set shot, and is a spirited competitor, but it is difficult not to remark also that on many of his drives toward the basket he seems to be guilty of traveling before he starts his drive, of taking too many steps before releasing the shot, and sometimes of palming the ball and charging en route. Schayes is not the only offender by any means, but one singles him out since he is the leading all-time scorer in the National Basketball Association. The ineptness of the referees in pro ball—and with few exceptions they are a very sorry bunch—makes it too easy for a man to be an offensive threat without earning it by his skill.

Since one cannot foresee which changes will benefit the game until they are tried out, the National Basketball Association should be conducting experimental clinics to determine these things during the off-season with the aid of its best players and a committee of experienced basketball men. This is also the atmosphere in which someone may arrive at some simple prescription which, like Beardsley Ruml's revolutionary concept that income tax payments should be geared not to the previous year but to the current year, will afterward loom so obvious that all of us will wonder why we never thought of it ourselves. Unfortunately, President Morris Podoloff and the other men at the helm of the NBA seem delighted with their game just as it is. If scores climb so that teams pour in two hundred points apiece a game, the NBA will no doubt view-halloo this as further proof that basketball is getting better—just so long, that is, as attendance also increases.

While no other game has gone awry as badly as basketball has, a few short comments on the present state of ice hockey, golf, and tennis might not be amiss. In each of these sports, for different reasons, certain skills which were at the core of the game's fascination have become less and less in evidence. In hockey, for example, stick handling, poke checking, and plain good passing are now hardly practiced at all. A principal reason behind the disappearance of these old skills, unlike in basketball, has been a new approach to defensive play.

Up to the late 1930s, about a decade after hockey entered its modern phase, when forward passing was permitted within all three zones, it was more or less accepted procedure for a team that had lost the puck after an attack to skate back into a set defensive pattern. The defending center tried to break up the offensive team's rush by poke-checking the puck away from the man carrying it up the middle, usually the opposing center. The defending wings skated along close to their men, looking to prevent or intercept a pass. The two defense men were stationed at the blue line ready to dish out a stiff body check to the puck carrier. The point that should be underlined is that very little body checking was undertaken by the defending forwards and almost all of this was confined to their own end of the rink when the opposition had poured in dangerously close to the goal and extra measures were called for.

The pattern began to change in the late 1930s. The New York Ranger teams of this period, instead of falling back when they lost the puck in their opponents' zone, kept pressing in after it, buzzing around the cage trying to regain possession or, if they were unsuccessful in this, at least harrying the other team so effectively that it was difficult for them to clear the puck and to form a clean counterattack. (Those Ranger teams and the Boston Bruins of that period were, by the way, probably the finest hockey teams ever assembled.) This departure from the old pattern of defense led to another that came into the game just before World War II. It worked like this: to break up an offensive rush, the defending forwards came to rely less and less on stickwork and more and more on body checking. As soon as the player he was covering got his stick on the puck, the defending forward cruised into him, rode him off the puck, and broke up the play that way. Before the counter-rush was under way, it was often stopped this same way—checking the puck carrier in the neutral zone or wherever he was. When the center red line was adopted, what with the more than occasional inability of either team to get a play neatly organized in the melee in the neutral zone, it became common procedure to relieve the confusion by scaling the puck from just behind the red line all the way to the backboards behind the rival goal and then to mush in after it.

As I remember it, the Detroit Red Wings just before the war were the first to employ this general body-checking tactic. Later it became part and parcel of the kitty-bar-the-door hockey which the Toronto Maple Leafs used to sit on a lead. Today it is the standard mode of defense in the professional leagues. In nearly all contact games the players have become bigger, and perhaps the heavy, bruising forward would have become the rule and not the exception in hockey anyway, but certainly the shift to body checking all over the ice hastened his arrival. In any event, the present-day forward, forever aware that he must be braced against a check, has become less adept in his stickwork generally and particularly in spotting his line mates and feeding them passes at the right time.

With all this milling around, the game has taken on a certain indistinction except when the solid forward lines or when the superstars are on the ice. Then it can be a prodigious game, for there are few sports in which the action can compare with the best hockey action—when Gordon Howe, without seeming to be expending an ounce of juice, glides away from the puffing defense and, without appearing to have glanced in that direction, whips a perfect rink-wide pass to a teammate at goal mouth; when Andy Bathgate, absorbed in sifting his way with tiny steps through a muddle of players, quickly backhands a little lead pass just where his wing can collect it at full stride (and, incidentally, reminds you in a twinkle how seldom the average player can lead a teammate with an accurate pass at the right speed); or when Jean Beliveau, having collected an only adequate pass so crisply on his stick that you think the tape must still be tacky, guides the puck with a series of feints past his check and comes stick-handling in on the goal all heft and grace. Good hockey action is so thrilling, Stanley Cup play-off hockey especially, that the National Hockey League has continued to prosper despite an antiquated, synthetic administration that has often been more diffident, vague, ingenuous, and invisible than the game has deserved.

To change the pace, before discussing the current state of golf—the excellent things that have come into it, the noteworthy things that seem to be going out of it—I would like to present the illustration first and to tell you about an unforgettable morning on the Brackenridge Park course in San Antonio during the first round of the 1955 Texas Open. In a stroke-play tournament, with so much going on all over the course simultaneously, more often than not an observer finds himself stationed intently just where nothing is happening. As he hovers behind the third green, let us say, a distant roar informs him that something of consequence has obviously just taken place on the sixteenth. He dashes to the seventeenth and arrives just in time to hear a volley of applause emanate from the tenth hole. Off he rushes to the eleventh, where he is met on his arrival by another galvanic roar from the vicinity of the third green, bringing him the happy news that again an extraordinary shot he should never have missed has just been made, and so on and on. Something went wrong that morning. For once I was at the right place at the right time, although I wasn't to be aware of this until sometime later. I had left the clubhouse—which is modeled after a farmhouse that Louis XVI built for Marie Antoinette, what else!—and had made my way with no definite object in mind past the rubber-matted tees and across the scabrous, dark-brown fairways, dotted here and there with stray blades of grass, wondering whether this beat-up layout was the true pearl of the winter tour or whether that distinction really belongs to the El Rio course in Tucson. A small band of spectators was congregated behind the fifteenth green and I drifted over to watch the parade go by. I had been there some five minutes when a light tickle of applause from the crowd around the nearby thirteenth green drew my attention to that spot. A ball was rolling to rest about five feet from the cup. Mike Souchak, one was soon able to piece together, had set himself up for an eagle on that hole—a par 5, 520 yards long—by flying a three-wood second right to the flag. I watched him hole the five-footer and then belt a long drive off the fourteenth tee. Then I thought no more about Mike until some twenty minutes later. At that moment, approaching the fifteenth—a short par 4, 385 yards long—he lofted a lovely wedge shot about eight feet from the cup. When he holed this putt for his birdie, I decided to follow him in. Mike probably had a very hot round going.

On the first day of an ordinary seventy-two-hole circuit tourney such as the Texas Open, there were, as you would expect, no mobile scoring standards proclaiming how the players stood with par. Souchak had driven off the sixteenth and was halfway down the fairway when I learned from an official that he had not only a good round but a terrific one under way. He had gone out in 33, which is not exceptional for the pros on a short course like Brackenridge Park, and after starting back with a birdie and two pars, he had gone eagle, birdie, birdie. On the sixteenth, 375 yards long, he followed his drive with a tidy pitch seven feet from the cup. He holed that birdie putt and was now six under par after seven holes on the back side. On the seventeenth, still another abbreviated par 4, 360 yards in length, Mike was way down the fairway with his drive and had only a flip with his wedge left. He didn't hit it exactly right, catching the ball a shade high. Instead of being up there snug, the ball finished eleven or twelve feet past. He made that putt, though. Now he was seven under coming in with the home hole to go, a difficult par 3, 155 yards long, to a plateaued green, the pin set to the left of center. A swirling wind had come up and a first-class shot was required to hit the eighteenth, since the left half of the green sits above a high bank that falls sharply down to a creek. Souchak's tee-shot, a five-iron, had a bit too much draw on it but it was firmly hit and it carried over the bank and ended up at the back left-hand corner of the green about twenty-five feet from the cup. It left him a very slippery putt. Mike went for it boldly and got it. When the ball fell, he jumped a couple of feet in the air, and well he might have, for this birdie gave him not only a 60 (which tied the PGA record for eighteen holes) but an incredible 27 for the second nine, the lowest score ever made for nine holes in an official competition. In this day when most records have such infant mortality that many are eclipsed before they even reach the record books, Souchak's 27 for nine holes still stands as a PGA mark, as does his Texas Open four-round total of 257 (60–68–64–65), and they may be around for some time to come. What he did on that historic nine-hole stretch probably can be made clearest in chart form.

Hole	Par	Distance	Souchak's Score	Clubs and Putts
10	3	180	2	6-iron, 14-foot putt
11	4	365	4	driver, pitching wedge, two putts from 20 feet
12	4	375	4	driver, pitching wedge, two putts from 25 feet

13	5	520	3	driver, 3-wood, 5-foot putt
14	4	370	3	driver, pitching wedge, 1-foot putt
15	4	385	3	driver, pitching wedge, 8-foot putt
16	4	375	3	4-wood, 8-iron, 5-foot putt
17	4	360	3	driver, pitching wedge, 12-foot putt
18	3	155	2	5-iron, 25-foot putt
	35		27	

The point is no doubt self-evident: you cannot handle a circuit course any better than Mike Souchak did that morning, but circuit golf has become a different kind of game than golf used to be. Essentially it is, as it has often been described, a game of three clubs—the driver, the wedge, and the putter. Major championships, to be sure, are played over longer and far more demanding layouts, but, in truth, the players, with their increased skill, have simply outgrown all but a few classic tests, such as Pebble Beach and Merion. (Even Merion no longer looks as enduring as we used to think it was after Jack Nicklaus' four rounds under 69 in the 1960 World Amateur Team Championship.) Playing with improved golf balls and equipped with more powerful steel shafts, which have enabled them to develop their late-hitting techniques, the modern stars consistently crack their tee-shots so far that they carry the old fairway-flanking hazards and are in a position to get home with a medium or short iron even on lengthy par 4s. They understand the properties of the wedge and regularly perform wonders with it. On putting surfaces which refined grass strains have now made much truer than greens used to be, the leading professionals and amateurs putt so marvelously well that one wonders if the best golfers a century hence will have advanced that phase of the game one iota. However much the leaders of modern golf have been helped by improved equipment and better course maintenance, it should be noted that they have been unremitting in their pursuit of dependable methods. I have been closer to golf than to any other sport, but I do not think it is myopia that leads me to the opinion that no other group of athletes studies and practices with anything comparable to the discipline with which the modern golfer approaches his game.

It is ironic, then, that the strength and proficiency of the current tournament golfers have rendered obsolete many of the subtleties of shotmaking which separated the men from the tourists in the old days when golf was not such a point-to-point game, when a player could not simply drive the ball to a point on the fairway and then fire it to a receptive green, and when he had to take into consideration the vicissitudes of the intervening terrain and hazards plus the dangers of a resilient green. A few reasonable purists of my acquaintance persist in wondering whether or not golf actually became a better game when the rubber-cored ball replaced the gutty, when steel supplanted the hickory shaft, when the flanged wedge was accepted, when the well-watered green succeeded the harder, touchier surface. But these are not foolish men, and rather than pine for what is not going to return, they would gladly settle for getting back into golf some of the game's former articulations by making the championship courses testing for today's leading golfers to the same degree that championship courses were for their predecessors in earlier decades. They want to see courses of challenging design which compel the players to control the ball all the way— hitting it high here, low there, fading it down this fairway, now drawing it, feathering it to this green, punching it into the next, and so on. As we remarked earlier, few of our courses remain this exacting. The shot values of some obsolescent courses can be restored by adding new back tees, revising the trapping, and remodeling the green areas, but as we have learned at several of the recent National Opens, not all layouts have the space and not all holes have the malleable character to respond to wholesale remodeling. A current device of the U. S. Golf Association, which conducts the National Open, is to toughen up a course for the championship by bringing in the rough to narrow the fairways and by using high rough as a tight collar around the greens. As the U.S.G.A. appreciates, this is at best a stopgap expedient. We see the champions and the challengers called upon to play all the shots on far too few occasions.

To make golf the complete game it should be, what we need in this country—along with the thoughtful remodeling of fading courses—is the construction of superb new courses not only of sufficient length but also embodying the best principles of strategic design. Each year dozens of new courses are constructed, but only 5 per cent of them have any worth. Nevertheless, most of them claim to be "championship courses" under the mistaken notion that a course measuring over 6,750 yards from the back tees is, perforce, a championship test simply because it is almost as long as, say, the Augusta National. Most golf architects have had so much business during the present boom years that they do not devote to any of their jobs one-quarter of the time and attention that is needed. The exceptional architect who still burns to build great courses is hamstrung eleven times out of twelve by the specifications set down by his clients who insist on a course that can be "economically maintained." What they really mean —and what they get—is a flat, hazardless, electric-cart course made to order for the sunset member who has bought a lot adjoining a fairway and is dreaming of a green Christmas.

What is upsetting about this trend is that two important truths are being forgotten. First, as the Augusta National demonstrates, it is not at all impossible to build a course that is simultaneously a stimulating examination for the experts and yet a fair, scorable, and eminently enjoyable test for the average player. Second, the average golfer has the ability, if he is forced to call on it, to score just about as well on a fine golf course as he does on the bunkerless lawns he craves. In the Twenties, when the average player had to learn the shots necessary to cope with legitimate rough, an occasional lipped bunker, downhill and side-hill lies, and racy green areas, he found he could manage it. He scored no worse, really, than the average golfer does today when all the fight and back-talk have been taken out of the holes. The modern golfer has reduced the amount of satisfaction and delight that the game can give him. Without knowing it, he is like the

man who reads only the boiled-down digests of the books of his
favorite author.

In tennis in recent years the chief controversies in that chronically embattled world have centered around the creation of
"open" tournaments (in which both the pros and amateurs
would compete, as they do in golf) and the merits of the now-
dominant "big game" with its recurrent sequence of the big
serve, the rarely forcing return, and the put-away smash or volley.
The first of these matters requires little elaboration. Since first-
class amateur tennis today is seldom first-class and hardly amateur, the open tournament will arrive just as soon as the official
national governing bodies, which control the "tradition" and the
clubs, work out a suitable balance of power and prestige with
Jack Kramer, who controls the professional stars. The second of
these matters, for our present purposes, is worth some inspection.

When players decades ago began to leave the base line during
rallies to smash and volley up at net, they were described as ex-
ponents of the "all-court game." The circle has now come full
turn. The serve-and-volley artists today play the reverse of an all-
court game, appearing in the backcourt (apart from serving) as
infrequently as a Wills or Lacoste was seen in the forecourt.
Gone are the moderately long and the extended rallies which as
recently as the age of Budge were the rule and not the exception,
since the leading players then depended on their ground strokes
for the most part to open the court and came to net only after a
genuinely forcing shot. For many fans, this was tennis as tennis
was designed to be played. Accordingly, after a decade and more
of the big game, they believe the time has come to modify certain
rules in the interests of getting tennis back where it becomes
once again fundamentally a game of maneuver.

The advocates of the big game go along with none of this,
naturally. They don't feel that tennis has taken the wrong fork
in the road and has become less exciting for both the player and
the spectator. Quite the opposite, they assert: the fans love the
incisive tempo, the thunderous hitting. In sum, they contend that
the power game has taken over because it is the better, more effective, more modern game. It had to come.

The fascinating thing about the rise of the big game after the war is that it had no assistance from any relaxation of the rules or from any substantial improvement in equipment, although every old tennis hand, I would venture, has experienced afternoons when he would have sworn that the ball was faster than in Tilden's day. The top players simply learned how to serve better and to exploit the full advantages of the big serve. Hitting the ball at least as hard as anyone did before World War II, they learned to get a power serve in consistently and, on their good days, they could put the ball precisely where they wanted to, with tremendous spin on it. Where the big server in earlier decades had saved his cannonballs for crucial games and points lest he wear himself out with a profligate expenditure of energy, the postwar player discovered that, in top physical condition, he could serve at top speed, or close to it, during an entire match. He knew before he adopted the big game that after delivering an attacking service he would have all the time he needed to follow it in and volley the return, but he also learned something new. If he had to, a well-conditioned athlete possessed the stamina to move into this volleying position on serve after serve. It was, in fact, less of a drain on a man's reserve than being trapped into long, exhausting rallies.

If any one player deserves the credit for breaking down the old you-can't-put-a-big-service-in-regularly-and-you-can't-come-up-to-net-after-each-service barrier, it was Jack Kramer. After Kramer showed that it could be done, then, in much the same way that miler after miler bettered four minutes once Roger Bannister had cracked that barrier, other tennis players began copying Kramer's style of play. Most players, lacking the talent needed, did it poorly. A few did it well. The man who did it best was Pancho Gonzales, who, to risk a purely personal opinion, may be at least the peer of any and all the great players since Tilden. As a matter of fact, though I appreciate that this borders on the sacrilegious, Gonzales on many occasions made one suspect that his genius for tennis was superior to that of Cochet and Budge and the equal of Tilden's. Gonzales was (and is) an astonishing athlete who commanded the full repertoire of strokes. All but three, however, were irrelevant to the simplified power game he built: a careful, steady return of service; the sharp volley in which his eye and touch were complemented by his phenomenal footwork—he moved like a jaguar; and a serve so explosive and yet so controlled that in the Meadow Club invitational tournament in 1948, back when he was an amateur, he scored half a dozen aces on his second serve in his match against Gardner Malloy.

I trust that it is clear that no one is criticizing Gonzales and the other practitioners of the big game for gravitating to that type of play. Today it is the winning game. You hold your serve and concentrate on breaking the other fellow's once for the set. Anyone who can play it plays it. I do not think that even the most intransigent foes of the big game can claim in all honesty that they disliked it at first sight and instantly read the handwriting on the wall. For myself, the first times I saw Kramer and, later, Gonzales, the sheer power they could unfurl was positively thrilling to behold. It was a number of years after this before the complaints of the traditionalists, which were beginning to be heard in the land, started to make sense to me. I had watched too many stirring matches, such as the battles between Lew Hoad and Tony Trabert, to agree readily with their contention that the limiting, repetitive format of the power game was making for boring tennis.

I believe I know the exact day when it became clear to me how much had slowly been going out of tennis. It was the afternoon of the quarter-final round in the 1956 championships at Forest Hills, and it brought together Ken Rosewall and Dick Savitt, two of the few remaining stars whose game was built on ground strokes. Rosewall, as you will remember, was an adept volleyer, as he showed in his doubles matches. In singles, while he was not averse to coming to the forecourt, he relied principally on the steady production of well-placed ground strokes to set up his placements or to force his opponent into error. Though not an attacking weapon, his service was stronger than it looked. His forehand, which was supposed to be his major weakness, seldom was as vulnerable as his opponents hoped it would be, but it is true that there were periods in every hard-fought match when he would start overhitting his forehand and would have to weather several erratic games before calming it down. His backhand, as need hardly be pointed out, was his finest stroke. It was probably

the best backhand since Budge's and he used it well, concealing
until the last moment whether he would be crossing it or hitting
it down the line or playing some other shot. Rosewall could
think on the court. He had courage in the tight spots and played
untimid shots at critical points. While he never dramatized himself, this small, slim, poker-faced Australian was a most attractive
player. His style made for interesting matches. As I write, I have
been remembering the many gripping battles in which he was
involved, including one nightmarish match with Pancho Segura
(after Rosewall had turned pro) where he waded through five
sets in heavy, enervating, ninety-degree heat before he finally
pulled out a marathon fifth set in which both players were nearly
out on their feet and played from memory. Rosewall that afternoon barely made the dressing room when, as untheatrically
as he did everything else, he collapsed.

On that balmy September afternoon in 1956, when he was
scheduled to face Savitt, the young Australian—he was only
twenty-one then—was supposed to win. How easily he did would
depend on what Savitt showed. This was unpredictable, for Savitt
had been in semi-retirement for four seasons and no one could be
sure whether he was in good enough form to get off on the right
foot and not lose his jarrable concentration before he had fortified
it by playing a run of games encouragingly well. One knew that
there would be stretches in which Savitt, as burly and strong as a
Percheron, would awe you with that big, flat, rocketing service
and his hard, flat, deep hitting off both sides from the base line,
but one remembered his temperamental volatility and knew that
it would be a matter of waiting and seeing whether he would
merely produce intermittent flashes of his 1950 form or really dig
himself into the match. If he could, he might even win it.

It is rare in tennis to find both players in a match at the top of
their games, but Rosewall and Savitt were that afternoon. This
was patent from the beginning, and there was lots of rousing stuff
in the first set. Rosewall won it or, you might say, Savitt lost it
just about the way one guessed he might. After moving into a
4–2 lead, Dick blew two service games and, with them, the set,
6–4. He digested his frustration manfully and went to work on
the second set. It followed somewhat the same pattern as the

first. Savitt got off in front, 2–0. Thereafter, there was little to choose between the two men until the tenth game when Dick's control again went off the slightest bit. It was enough, nevertheless, to allow Rosewall to take two crucial games and the set, 7–5. It is asking too much of most men to expect them to pick themselves up again after two bitter blows of this kind. All of us felt that Savitt would never be able to muster his resolve once more. We were simply thankful, I think, for the excellent play we had seen.

We couldn't have been more wrong about what was in store for us. With a wonderful effort, Savitt reknitted his will and, if anything, began to play a shade better than before, accelerating his pace and lengthening the depth of his drives, pasting the ball so hard at times that in the exchanges he began to score regularly even off Rosewall's backhand. Rosewall, for his part, now started to try and move Savitt off the base line. He lobbed him more often and tucked in a number of drop shots. Sometimes he was successful with these new tactics, sometimes he wasn't, but Ken scored often enough to lead 3–4 in games and to sweep the first three points on Savitt's serve in the eighth game. Savitt didn't yield. He fought his way up to deuce and went on to take the game. At this juncture, instead of impatiently blasting for winners with miraculous shots, which had been his mistake in the first two sets, Savitt bravely waited for the right opportunities. He made them himself and broke Rosewall's service in the ninth game. Exhilarated by this, he tapped a new well of reserve and, serving harder than he had yet, held service and ran the set out, 6–4.

Because of the way the match was pitched, the gallery was viewing it in terms of the immense fight Savitt was putting up. During the intermission, when you thought about the fourth set, you did so in terms of Savitt. Would he be all played out now? Was one set his psychological quota? When you looked at the match in terms of Rosewall, you knew he would return as fresh as ever. In dropping the third set he hadn't really faltered at all. He had, in fact, played as well if not better in this match than ever before in the United States.

The fourth set produced even grander tennis than the third— Savitt still energetic and hopeful, Rosewall biding his time, moving his man around, waiting for the fire to go out of Savitt's racket, coming to net more and more often behind his own thrusts. Then, as the set wore on, 6–6, 7–7, 8–8, there came a point that epitomized the quality of play of the entire match. It came, if I remember correctly, after Savitt had overcome a 30–0 deficit (on Rosewall's service) with a staggering series of passing shots and had arrived at game point. Rosewall put the ball in play and after that I have no idea how many times it crossed the net. In the first exchanges Savitt was in charge, but when he underhit a drive, Rosewall pounced on this chance to seize command of the rally. At length he cross-courted a deep forehand, took the defensive return near mid-court, and whipped that stinging backhand of his to Savitt's backhand corner. It looked as if the shot had Savitt beaten clean, that the ball would be by him before he could get his racket to it—or, if he did hit it, that he would never be able to get around on the ball and would merely foul it off, as it were, into the left-field stands. In a way, Savitt never did get in position to hit that ball. The best he could do was to reach out desperately with his arm, or, rather, with just his forearm. With that powerful wrist of his, he not only got around on the ball but also pulled it on a line across the court. The ball ducked sharply as it crossed the net, whistled by Rosewall on his backhand side, and fell well in court for an absolutely stunning placement. You should have heard the applause! Rosewall, as a matter of fact, joined in. For a moment he stood transfixed, and then, in a charming and spontaneous gesture I have never seen before or expect to see again, he let his racket fall to the grass and solemnly clapped his hands three or four times. Then he smiled at himself and the two went back to work.

Though obviously tired, Savitt had gained just the lift he needed. He put every bit of fire he had into his own service game. He won it. The set was his, 10-8. The sets were now 2-all.

This, as it transpired, was to be the climax of the match. Unruffled, still remarkably fresh, and as workmanlike as ever, Rosewall continued to play impassively and well. As for Savitt, it was immediately apparent at the beginning of the fifth set that he had gone as far as he could. There was nothing he could do about it. He was so nervously exhausted that he could not get his tired body and his drained concentration to work together. For a cluster of points he would play cohesive tennis, but his errors became more pronounced and the clusters came further and further apart. The steadiness of Rosewall's play blasted the one hope that remained for Dick, that his opponent's errors would enable him to get back into the match once again. Rosewall moved to 4–1, to 5–1, and took the next game handily for the set and match. (He went on, by the way, to win that championship, defeating Hoad in four sets in a wind-swept final.)

Acknowledging that the hospitality of circumstance played at least as large a part as sound ground strokes in making this encounter between Savitt and Rosewall the classic it was, the match impressed on many of us the comparatively terse pleasures of big-game tennis where most of the points are won or lost before they are really under way. No one wants to eliminate the volley and thunder of the power game, but how much more enchanting tennis would be if certain changes could be effected that would somewhat lower the effectiveness of the power game and open the way for a return of the more eloquent all-court game! A good many people have thought deeply about this. One teaching professional I know is of the opinion that making the ball less lively would rectify all the excesses then and there. He may be right. Whether he is or not, I am inclined to think that there is sense and acuteness in the recommendations advanced by James Van Alen, that old sports stalwart who, among other things, is the chairman of the Newport invitational tournament. Mr. Van Alen proposes two changes aimed at restoring a proper value to the serve. First, the size of the service boxes (presently thirteen and one-half feet in width by twenty-one feet in length) should be reduced half a foot in width and a foot in length, thus giving the server a smaller target area. Second, a new service line would be ordained three feet behind the base line to reduce the sharpness of the angle of flight of the service. This new service line would additionally make it a bit more difficult for the server to race in to volleying position. There is another school of thought, which, while thinking highly of Mr. Van Alen's proposals, believes that the best way of getting the old game back is to teach the young players better ground strokes. Bill Talbert, the former Davis Cup captain, maintains that if young players practiced their ground strokes with the same application with which the devotees of the big game practice their serve and volley, they could handle the big game, as all but a few play it, with little trouble. In this regard, Talbert recently mentioned the reaction of Don Budge when he found certain opponents coming to net after very ordinary shots and rendering themselves easily passable: Budge felt insulted by their reckless temerity.

There may be merit also in the suggestion, which several groups have made, that would curtail the serve-volley sequence by regulating that the server could not play the return of service until the ball had bounced. It was typical of Jack Kramer, a most personable fellow, a resourceful promoter, and a perfect child of mid-century America, that he responded with his best anything-for-the-good-of-the-game zeal to this one-bounce suggestion and then proceeded to parody it slightly. Jack's fundamental interest, of course, is in selling the virtues of the big game, which all his professional stars play—Rosewall, too, now, alas!—but he scheduled experimental preliminary matches at many stops on one of his recent winter tours in which the players had to let the ball bounce the next two times it crossed the net after the service before they were allowed, if they so wished, to volley it. Kramer conscientiously reported that the spectators seemed to prefer the big game. If Jack were a tailor trying to protect the two-button jacket against the dangerous inroads of the three-button jacket, I am sure he would produce a five-button jacket to show the folly of departing from the *status quo*. In a professional championship tournament that was played at Cleveland a few years back, Jack not only tested the twenty-one-point game, which many had advocated as worth a trial as a replacement for the conventional set, but also chose this occasion to test simultaneously the extreme device of limiting the server to one serve, a fair enough experiment in Kramer's mind to adjudge whether or not the critics of the big serve and big tennis were right. Jack conscientiously reported that the spectators seemed to prefer the old scoring and the big game. This communiqué had all the shock impact on serious tennis people as would an announcement by Kramer that he did not intend to sign Adlai Stevenson, able player that he is, for his next professional tour. For all his vagaries, however, Jack Kramer has approached tennis with vitality and imagination, and this is far more than can be said for the United States Lawn Tennis Association.

It was not my intention at the start of this preface to go into this degree of detail in commenting on the present shape of some of our major games. It is a subject, though, which calls for more than abstract generalizing, and once you leave that safe province, the going becomes involved. If you touch on one thing, you must touch on another, and so on and on. A conscientious study would, to be certain, go far deeper, but it is my hope that this once-over-lightly survey has brought out the not unimportant central facts: through one impetus or another, games keep changing, and it is the job of the men in charge to make the proper periodic adjustments so that the new developments become extensions in the right direction, secondary skills do not replace the superior skills at the heart of the action, and the changes and modifications instituted make each game a better and not a poorer expression of the essence of that game.

This survey will have missed its mark if it has produced the impression that all recent developments have been injurious and that the old was automatically idyllic. At the same time, in sports as in many other phases of our culture, we have displayed in this country a costly penchant for becoming so beguiled by the faddish and the promoted that we forget to make use of some of the choicest parts of our inheritance. Granting that each generation comes up with many necessary improvements on the past and that much that results is notable and enriching, we somehow fail to "pass the baton" properly from one generation to another in this country so that what was, and remains, worthy is perpetuated and becomes a base for the new ideas, new tastes, and new techniques that each ensuing generation creates. We deprive ourselves of so much that is pleasurable and fruitful this way. In popular music, for example, the postwar plague of rock-and-roll would not have been so hard for everyone over nineteen to countenance if one had felt that it had not been commercially contrived and that the kids had been given some exposure to the charms of ragtime, the Tin Pan Alley tunes of the 1920s and

1930s (which were just the right weight for popular songs), the
Goodman brand of swing and the earlier forms of jazz, and the
"show music" from the turn of the century on. This same process,
moving six steps forward but somehow taking four to seven steps
back at the same time, continues all around us. To cite one example everyone is aware of, we get frozen food and all the other
kinds of modern packaged food, and it seems a step forward
until we discover on a trip to the country how much more flavor
is packed into a fresh piece of fish or a fresh tomato. The abundant
has become a luxury. We get television, and at the dawn of what
should be an era of more intelligent entertainment we enter
instead a new Dark Ages of massive banality with such a concomitant drop in some aspects of the national I.Q. that fewer and
fewer people can distinguish between a synthetic "personality"
and a person of genuine substance. In this so-called age of communication there is less communication. Wealth is misused with
such regularity that the projects of the Rockefeller Brothers,
with their taste and thoroughness and their fine regard for both
the past and present, stand out like metal upon sullen ground.
We have made laudable strides—let us not forget that, for all
the chances that have been thrown away and for all that remains
to be done, millions of men and their families, who forty years
ago had nothing, today have good homes, ample food, adequate
clothing, and access to many of the pleasures of life—but it does
seem a pity that while gaining much that is beneficial, we also toss
away so much that we should have carried along. We don't pass
the baton well at all, and it is the loss of each generation.

In sports, and they are anything but singular in this respect,
one of the main troubles in recent years is that they have become
very big business. Sports were always business, of course. In most
instances, however, the amount of profit a sports enterprise returned was not inviting compared to an investment in some
other commercial venture, and men who were primarily interested in making money seldom turned to sport. After the last war,
this altered. It soon became apparent to many shrewd businessmen that there was big money to be made in sport in a country as
large and as prosperous as ours, with a built-in television audience
that could be counted on, and they proceeded to buy out the old

owners. Many of the new entrepreneurs have proved to be splendid additions, but at least as many rapidly made it clear that, despite their well-phrased assertions to the contrary, they felt no real responsibility to sport or to the public.

All of us would agree, I believe, when it was that we finally came to realize that the old unwritten law that the public possessed a vested interest in publicly supported sport no longer obtained. This was in October of 1957 when Walter O'Malley, the president of the Brooklyn Dodgers, received the official go-ahead from organized baseball to move his franchise to Los Angeles. This was a wholly different case than the previous resettlements of the Boston Braves in Milwaukee in 1953, the St. Louis Browns in Baltimore in 1954, and the Philadelphia Athletics in Kansas City in 1955. It was different as well from the Giants' move from New York to San Francisco in 1957, which was tied in with O'Malley's hegira. None of these other clubs had been in sanguine financial shape. The weak and waning teams they had fielded had not been supported by the local fans. Once these teams had been transplanted, their old fans bewailed their loss, but it was hard to nurse a sympathetic tear since these were the same fans who had stayed away from the park in droves. The situation in Brooklyn, however, was not like that. Historically a vigorous baseball town, it hadn't changed. The Brooklyn franchise remained one of the most profitable in baseball. Mr. O'Malley talked a lot about needing a larger park and more municipal co-operation, but in the final analysis he wanted to move his team because he believed he could make more money in Los Angeles. It was as simple as that. The fact that the Coliseum did not have space for a left field did not deter him since it had seating accommodations for 94,600. Like everyone else, Walter O'Malley had been bedazzled by the unexpected prosperity that had rained down on the Braves after their move westward. (In Milwaukee, in contrast to the empty stands they had played to during their last moribund seasons in Boston, the Braves in their first year played to 1,862,397 customers, a new National League record. In 1957 the Braves broke this record by drawing 2,215,404 fans, a league mark.) In the opinion of a number of experienced sports observers, the National League and the office of the Commissioner of Baseball were delinquent in sanctioning the transfer of a well-rooted, healthy team like the Dodgers. The time was more than ripe to bring major league baseball to the West Coast, but only a team that was not being adequately supported should have been given permission to relocate itself.

From the day when Mr. O'Malley was given his way, major league baseball has never recovered its former equilibrium. This was revealed more brilliantly than ever before in the autumn of 1960 when the American League, breaking from its slumbers, could not make up its mind whether it should hurriedly try to set up one or two new clubs for the 1961 season or wait until 1962. Deciding to risk 1961, it decreed that the owners of the new franchises would create their rosters by drafting the unstellar players of the existing teams at the price of $75,000 per player. Talk about charity beginning at home! This implausible performance led Red Smith of the New York *Herald-Tribune* to one of his wriest observations: "The men who own baseball never weary of telling the public what a hazardous business they're in and how, if it weren't for their selfless dedication to the game, they would invest in something safe like breeding schnauzers and spend their evenings drinking champagne from slippers with two dozen girls giggling and throwing the dark meat out the window."

Wayward stewardship in professional sport customarily takes a less florid form than this example of closed-circuit philanthropy by the men who run baseball, but it is all around us. It arises essentially, I believe, from the fact that the owners of the clubs in a league also function as the governors of that league, and it is impossible for a man to wear both hats at the same time. If an owner has his choice between, on one hand, moderate profits and a long-range program for building a sounder sport with a sounder following and, on the other, a quicker buck, a faster profit, and the short-range view of let's-worry-about-that-when-we-have-to, he consistently goes for the latter. One time-honored means by which the owners-governors can enlarge their yield is to schedule as many games as the traffic will bear. The National Hockey League, which formerly played a fifty-game schedule, now plays seventy games—all this, by the way, to eliminate two of the six teams from the Stanley Cup play-offs. (While the NHL doesn't consider this strung-out season too much hockey, it has never gotten around to restoring the ten-minute overtime period for tie games which the fans have long clamored for. The overtime period was dispensed with during the war to enable the teams to make their tight railroad connections, but there is no such exigency today.) The teams in the National Basketball Association similarly knock themselves out over a frenetic, overextended schedule running from October to March. Then, in the middle of March, they move into the preliminary rounds of the play-off from which only two of the eight teams are excluded. During the seventy-nine-game regular season the teams meet each other so often that no one game has any significance. The league standings seldom have any meaning and the players seldom have any freshness left in their systems. (One bizarre effect on me of this clutter of games is that, glancing quickly at the morning's box scores, I often get the feeling that I must have picked up yesterday's paper by mistake—all these teams could not have played each other once again since last I looked.)

It is a curious thing, moreover, how certain administrative groups, which in many respects are on the ball, take their eye off it at the strangest times. I am thinking, for instance, of the Professional Golfers Association whose tournament bureau has done a very able job in developing the week-to-week schedule so that the players in 1961 are shooting at prize money totaling over a million and a half dollars. The jewel in the crown of the PGA should be its own annual tournament, which traditionally determined the national match-play champion. In 1957, after permitting this tournament to dwindle into a shadow of its former self, the PGA, instead of going all out to bolster it into the glamorous "prestige championship" it once was and should be, decided to switch to a format of a seventy-two-hole stroke-play event which would be an almost guaranteed winner at the gate. (In match play, as you know, there is no insurance that the big names will not have been eliminated early in the week; in stroke play, the stars are all but certain to be on hand on the weekend when the sizable crowds can be attracted.) Apart from believing firmly that a well-run match-play event would build up over the years into a more profitable fixture than a seventy-two-hole event, many of us are of the opinion that in a larger sense the PGA made a most unwise move. In effect, it lost a championship and gained just another weekly tournament. Match play, that basic form of golf competition, has now virtually vanished from the professional scene. The only occasions when the leading stars presently engage in the classic man-to-man duels arrive every four years when the Ryder Cup is held in the United States. If match play merely had the press of tradition to recommend it, like mounted cavalry or compulsory Latin, there would be no point in being concerned about its survival. Compared to a stroke-play tournament—which, in truth, is dramatic only on the last round when the outcome is determined—match play is rousing and decisive each day of the tournament, a wonderful form of golf to watch as well as to play.

While the operation of professional sports has left a lot to be desired, there have been no bouquets either on the way amateur sports have been conducted. The amateur sports which the country follows can be roughly divided into two major divisions: college competition and competition that is open to all amateurs. A word first about the collegiate scene.

As most of our colleges approach them, sports have been a princely business for a long time now, and not all of the excesses are the product of the last fifteen years by any means. It is extremely illuminating to learn—as I did quite accidentally by going to see a revival of the 1917 musical comedy, *Leave It to Jane*, and subsequently reading the play it was based on, George Ade's smash hit of 1904, *The College Widow*—that by the turn of the century the practice of recruiting talent for college football teams was already well established. ("Silent" Murphy, an inarticulate giant who comes to Atwater U. to deliver a piano, is induced to stay on and become a star lineman. Billy Bolton, the hero, pops in on the Atwater campus on his way to Bingham, Atwater's great rival and his dad's old school. This is a fatal mistake. He is a tremendous halfback, this Billy Bolton, and the task of seeing that he remains at Atwater is left to Jane, the dean's flirtatious daughter. Everything turns out splendidly in the end. A breath-taking touchdown run by Bolton wins the big game for Atwater, and Jane discovers that she has fallen in love with him.) Down through the decades the national extravaganza of college recruiting has provided such a wealth of humor that it seems ungracious to summon one's best sanctimonious attitude on learning, for example, that the favorite course of the members of the 1959 Syracuse football team was Canadian Geography, or that Dave Davis, the Olympic shot-putter who couldn't cope with the academic pace at the University of Southern California, had transferred to San Fernando State College and was doing very nicely, thank you, in all of his five courses: First Aid; Dance; Methods of Baseball; Methods of Track and Field; and Safety Education.

Nevertheless, we all appreciate that there is something faulty with helping the helpful athlete to the extent presently in vogue at all but a small percentage of our colleges. Today the most successful college coaches often are very capable technicians and teachers, but as a rule their true forte is recruiting. In this pursuit they have the support of the college itself and the rambunctious assistance of well-heeled alumni who, inexplicably, seem to find life without savor except on eight or nine Saturday afternoons in the autumn. Their concerted efforts sweep far beyond a sensible attitude toward recruiting, which, I suggest, might be defined as follows: By all means try to get outstanding athletes to attend your college in preference to others, but keep the number of athletic scholarships in a sane ratio with the other scholarships and, in every case, insist that the athlete be able to meet the same academic standards as the other students in order to get into college and stay in. There are a hundred and one ingenious ways by which colleges, while paying lip service to codes like this, circumvent them. Their agility has taken us to the point where we have almost forgotten that it is not in the least inconsistent for a young man to possess both a good mind and good athletic abilities. In any event, the young athlete is so catered to that he has inevitably come to regard himself as a privileged character who has the white convertible and the rest of the accessories coming to him. The most incisive comment in recent months on the present position of the college-bound athlete was made by, of all people, the Dean of Harvard College, John Usher Monro. The heart of it is worth quoting.

It does not matter how bad the high school, how poor the family, how dull the mind—the gifted athlete gets to college. We have to mobilize everybody for miles around to do it—coaches, schools, parents, neighbors, alumni, boosters' clubs, special tutors —no effort is too great for us. Indeed, there is apt to be remuneration: the athlete expects it; it is part of his All-American birthright. The colleges have learned to care about athletes, and to hunt them down, and treat them well. . . . The contrast between our success with athletes and our failure with merely able minds is a fantastic irony and a thoroughly unpleasant truth about American colleges and universities.

Why is the athlete so fussed about? In the final rubdown, it all goes back to the business side of sport. Along with the pleasure and pride a winning football team creates, it is not a bad thing financially. Let us say, for instance, that on an average 45,000 spectators are induced to purchase tickets at $4 a head for a college's six home games. This adds up to a take of over $1,000,000, a fair-sized figure in any league. A winning basketball team can also do all right for you. Furthermore, no one has yet invented anything to compare with a winning football team for reorienting the orbit of old grads closer to the college and rendering them that much more touchable during fund-raising drives for the new nuclear physics laboratory or, if you will, the additional faculty needed to teach the new course in Methods of Polo.

In the noncollegiate or general sphere of amateur athletics, the fathers of amateur sport have battled valiantly against the odds and have succeeded in building a stirring tradition of mismanagement. While continuously readjusting their halos with one hand and waving aloft with the other the gleaming banner of Sport For Sport's Sake, the majority of the career officials of amateur sport, either through naïveté or ignorance, have allowed our young athletes to grow up in an atmosphere permeated with commercialism where, as often as not, negotiation for the best possible price is the order of the day. (Even this does not explain the college basketball player's sad vulnerability to bribery.) In tennis and track and field in particular, as has long been pointed out, it has been standard procedure to insure the appearance of the star performers by paying them under-the-table "expenses" considerably exceeding what it costs the athlete to make the trip and maintain himself. Every now and then, in a show of righteous indignation, a national organization will crack down hard on some athlete, as the Amateur Athletic Union did on Wes Santee in 1956. The hypocrisy of this is infuriating. The time is long overdue for these organizations to stuff their false piety away and to take a good hard look at themselves. First, they must realize that the *raison d'être* of the amateur bodies is to produce the real flavor of sports so that participating in them is a valid pleasure and doing well is its own reward. They must admit to themselves, as they rarely do, that when they stage a big tourney or meet, they are trying to make a financial success of their promotion, no different from the men who run professional sport. If they find that professional sports have lured away their drawing cards and that their amateur events consequently cannot make money, they must find other ways of financing their activities. They must face the fact that the times have changed. In the past, many superlative athletes remained amateurs, technically anyhow, because they had no alternative: their sport was not organized professionally or, if it was, it teetered along feebly, offering little money and less prestige. Today there is an immense amount of money to be made in professional sport with no drop in status—the reverse of it, if anything. In this regard, the majority of the men engaged in administrating amateur sports must sincerely revise their philosophical outlook. They must come to recognize the simple truth that being an amateur does not per se make an athlete a higher cut of fellow than a professional or, for that matter, a truer sportsman, a more devoted teammate, or a sturdier pillar of his community. Today's professionals are the same fellows they were when they were yesterday's amateurs. Finally, the officials of amateur sport would do well to acknowledge the corollary condition that only a thin technical line frequently separates the model amateur from the amateur bum. A few years ago in golf, for example—and here let me interject that the U.S. Golf Association is far and away the best of all our national organizations—there was a great to-do when a prominent amateur was suspended for a year for accepting travel

expenses to certain tournaments. These were paid by his employer. Had his employer merely raised the player's salary so that
he technically could have paid his own expenses out of his own
pocket, nothing would have been amiss. It was strictly a matter of
bookkeeping.

If the national and sectional amateur organizations can come
to grips with these realities and see that amateurism is not a
special state of grace but simply an aspect of sport, then perhaps
they can get on with the job they should be doing now. It is a
most important job. In sports today, as we mentioned earlier,
the opportunity to make big money has attracted, along with valuable new blood, a number of wheelers and dealers who understand neither sport nor their obligations to it. Since the authentic
color and excitement of sport often leaves them cold, it starts
them worrying about the box office. Their solution quite often is
to inject their own arrant versions of "color" and "excitement."
Up to now they have not done too much damage, but they will in
time if they are allowed to proceed unchecked. It is the responsibility of the schools, colleges, and the sectional and national
amateur associations to see to it that boys and girls grow up with
a clear idea of sport at its best, a true understanding that goes
right in through the pores and stays with them a lifetime. This is
critical because many of these young people will continue in
sports all their lives as mature amateur athletes, professional athletes, coaches, broadcasters and writers, promoters, local and national officials of amateur and professional sports groups, and even
as sponsors. In these positions their well-founded knowledge will
be a mighty influence in seeing to it that sport degenerates neither
into vulgarized circuses nor into secluded exclusivity. At the
present time between these two extremes there is in many sports
an ever widening middle ground, for men of the best type who
have given generously of themselves over a long period have become so appalled by the successful inroads of the purely exploitive
interlopers in both the amateur and professional fields that they
have recoiled too far toward the opposite pole. Their approach
has become pallid and sometimes reactionary without their knowing it. Scornful of bogus promotion and the "wrong new fan,"
they are reluctant to admit that there is such a thing as construc-

tive promotion and have become suspicious of the "right new fan" in their preoccupation with keeping their own preserve untrammeled. This kind of retreating leadership hasn't helped much either.

Sports, in a way, are far less important than most of us who love them sometimes like to think, but for all this they are at least as important as many things which are held to be of grander significance. As William Hazlitt long ago said so memorably when writing of handball, "There are things indeed that make more noise and do as little good, such as making war and peace, making speeches and answering them, making verses and blotting them, making money and throwing it away." In the lives of most American men today, sports are an interest third only to their family and to their job, and in the lives of youngsters they are often paramount. No one sets out to make this so. Sports never needed to call on the good gray poets of Madison Avenue or to set up a lobby in Washington. Just why playing games and watching them, reading about them and talking about them, should be the endless avenue of fascination it is, no one really knows. They simply captivate mankind and they always did.

In America today, and in many other countries, one grows into sports as naturally as he grows into long pants. Sports are the great common denominator. There is nothing like them for bringing people together and for providing a mutual zone of informed interest for persons of far different ages and from quite separate walks of life. (To my knowledge, there is only one other medium of "popular entertainment" where the average man invites and distinguishes all the subtlety, all the intellectuality, and all the art that can be mustered, and this is the mystery or detective motion picture.) Sports are with us all day every day. We start the morning with the sports pages of the newspaper. We ventilate the working hours with one hundred and one conversations on sports. There is hardly an evening when we don't discuss them or play them or wish we had the time to do so. There is scarcely a weekend in which the focal point for tens of millions of us is not pursuing some athletic recreation or watching it either "in person" or on television. The "folk heroes" of our time, to use a phrase which can usually be counted on to clear an arena in two seconds flat, are the great athletes, the Mantles and the Mayses, the Unitases and the Palmers. Thanks to TV, we can all watch them even when they are in action thousands of miles away, and there is no need for ballad singers to travel the land from village to village, lute or electric guitar in hand, and to narrate for us in stately dissonance the wonders those heroes have performed.

With sports so closely interwoven into our lives—and, all things being equal, they will be commanding an increasingly large amount of our hours—it matters to us that we do not permit the air around them to grow stale. In the last fifteen years we have been somewhat remiss about this, not only in going along too docilely with the errata of the top echelons in Big Sport but also in not taking adequate care of our everyday sports. A participant is supposed to try to win at games—one of the deep satisfactions is doing your best to win—but we are currently inclined to put too much store by winning, as if there were nothing else to sports except the winning and losing. For many adults, the ordinary game of golf or tennis or the informal sailing race has become in our intensified civilization less a path of recreation than an expressway for releasing frustrations in a flashing display of superiority. Consequently, what should be a relaxing diversion can be very grim business, almost a test of who is the better man all the way through. Friendly competition has given way to purposeful gamesmanship. In another direction, as has often been noted, the frayed adult has gone about realizing his own dreams of glory through his kids. Little League competition, organized to a fare-thee-well, agrees with some youngsters but it imposes a strain on many others who are not old enough to shoulder the burden of winning or losing the big game. At the age when he would be ready to enjoy competitive sport, the overpushed youngster often has had his fill of it and is ready to hang up the old jersey and sweat socks and set up the bridge lamp.

In brief, we are allowing the spirit of sports to go out of sports. What made the sports field—the empty lot and the country club, the backyard and the school gym—so appealing when each of us first encountered it in our youth was that people were at their best there. It was as simple as that. They were full of humor and fun without even trying. They were spontaneous, as they were nowhere else. There were some crotchety types, of course, but there was also unfeigned companionship, and with no conscious effort you got to know people and enjoy them. In a deeper sense, it is not going too far to say that in a miraculous way the playing of sports somehow makes contact with something idealistic in our natures when we are young and that the poet in all of us blossoms wordlessly in a genuinely sporting atmosphere. These are the reasons, I would guess, why all our lives we go out to sports so wholeheartedly. It is a corner a man likes to keep green because he learns as he grows older that the world is not exactly a playground. More than is generally appreciated, it is necessary for most men (and wonderfully good for them) to have some enthusiasm like sports in their lives which they can approach with some of the direct idealism of youth. There is no need to do more than mention the complementary fact that physical exercise in itself makes a person feel good and disengages him from his problems and cobwebs as few other things can. To be very practical about it, then, as the world becomes more pressureful, which is where it seems to be headed, it is going to be more and more important for all of us to make sure that sports and the other Hyde Parks of our lives, those safety valves where we can let off steam, function for us.

At this point it might not be irrelevant to say a quick word about sportsmanship, a concept which in both the higher and lower reaches of sport has become somewhat confused. For many people today, sportsmanship is synonymous with artificial good manners, such as pulling up a chair for a boring aunt who has come for a visit at an inappropriate moment. More than this, for some people, any gesture of graciousness in competition is suspect, as if it betrayed a lack of determination and the old will to win. There are, granted, few things more disagreeable than calculated, theatrical "sportsmanship" but this is precisely the opposite of the real stuff. Sportsmanship is nothing more or less than considerateness for your opponent and respect for the game you are playing. One misunderstands the enormous influence that Bobby Jones had in the Twenties not only on golfers but also on all sports followers if one thinks that it resulted from a few isolated dramatic instances, such as calling penalty strokes on himself in the National Open when other men might have neglected to. Not at all. People responded to Jones because they admired the way he played golf. They knew he went all out to win, but they instinctively sensed that he saw the game in its entirety.

When you are distressed by your own bad play, for one thing, or when you are up against a hostile, grudging opponent, for another, it is anything but easy to act the sportsman, but I suggest that good sportsmanship at these trying times boils down to considerateness for yourself. Oddly enough, there is nothing like it for taking the sting out of disappointment and for putting thoughts and feelings into a shape where you can handle them better and quicker. Furthermore, I would go as far as to say that forcing yourself to observe the code of sportsmanship, even when you cannot own to one grain of the true feeling, is exceedingly important. If an atmosphere of sportsmanship is absent, a vacuum is created, and when emotions are flying out of hand, some pretty ugly things will rush in and fill it. In Great Britain it is customary to play the national anthem not before but at the conclusion of sports events. The idea behind this was not to provide players and spectators with a moment to redirect the high pitch of their feelings, but that is how it works. During the playing of the anthem you find that you slow yourself down and get things in a proper perspective. It would be a salutary practice for us to adopt.

While sports in their rudimentary form are about as old as man, it was roughly two centuries ago that they began to take the structure we know today. Modern sport seems to divide itself into three main periods: the English (or British) era, the American era, and the contemporary era of world-wide sport.

No handy date marks the commencement of the English era, but in the last third of the eighteenth century that bailiwick of the huntin'-fishin'-shootin' squire was stirred by a burgeoning of sports in general. Soccer, which goes back to the Roman occupation, achieved a more uniform expression. Cricket, another ancient game, took on its present-day lineaments in 1788. In horse racing the annual classics were inaugurated: the St. Leger in 1777, the Epsom Oaks in 1779, and the Epsom Derby in 1780. Other peoples in other countries played sports with skill and exuberance, but the English were the great games-playing people, and in the nineteenth century they originated many of our modern games and refined many others. Rugby, that descendant of soccer and ancestor of American football, was born accidentally in 1823 at the public school from which it took its name. Hard racquets was revived at another public school, Harrow, in about 1822, and a quarter of a century later the boys there invented squash. London, somewhat surprisingly, was the venue of the first swimming competitions in 1834. The Henley Regatta was launched in 1839, and in that year as well the first Grand National Steeplechase was run.

In the second half of the century, things really began to move. In 1851 the first international yachting race for the America's Cup was held off the Isle of Wight, with the American boat the victor. In golf the old feather ball was replaced by the gutta-percha ball, and after this change that old Scottish game spread like wildfire throughout England and then around the world. Polo came out of India to England in 1869 under the aegis of British Army officers who had witnessed the native version of the game in the Punjab. In 1872 bare-knuckle prize fighting, which had flourished from about 1700 on, gave way to boxing under the Marquis of Queensberry rules. The following year, 1873, in a quite different corner of the garden, Major Walter Wingfield conceived the game of Phairistike, the basis of lawn tennis, and in four short years the famous championships were under way at Wimbledon. Running, which had been gaining in popularity from the middle of the century on, grew into track and field, and in 1896 the Olympic Games were revived.

During the nineteenth century, the English were not only the most ardent practitioners of sports but also the best. At around the turn of the new century, the rest of the world, but principally American athletes, began to catch up with the English. The leading boxers were Americans, which, in fact, had been the case since the advent of John L. Sullivan in the 1880s. In the first two Davis Cup challenge-round matches in 1900 and 1902, the United States team defeated the British Isles—not that we immediately gained a supremacy in this sport by any manner of means. The remarkable May Sutton won at Wimbledon in 1905, but it was many years before an American man was able to win that championship. In golf an American-bred player, Walter Travis, broke through in the British Amateur in 1904, but Travis was Australian-born. It was not until 1912 that an American-born professional golfer won our Open, and that man, Johnny McDermott, did not face a field that included Britain's best. Francis Ouimet did, however, in the 1913 National Open, and this is what made his victory monumental. In track and field, where our roots went back to the founding of the New York Athletic Club in 1868, we were, however, already a power at the turn of the century. We were producing world record-breaking sprinters and hurdlers and were leading the way in the vault and other field events, faring so well altogether that in the 1904 Olympic Games at St. Louis we won twenty-one events. In the 1912 Games that consummate all-round athlete, Jim Thorpe, took both the pentathlon and the decathlon.

The greater part of our interest, however, was directed toward the games that had been devised in America—baseball, which started to develop in 1845 or thereabouts; football, which emerged from rugby around 1874; and basketball, which Dr. Naismith fathered at Springfield, Massachusetts, in 1891. Two other new games, which had been invented in Canada—lacrosse (circa 1834) and ice hockey (circa 1855)—were also played in the United States, if to a more limited degree. Horse racing had dug in near the close of the Civil War. The Travers Stakes was inaugurated in 1864, the Saratoga Cup in 1865, the Belmont Stakes in 1867, the Preakness Stakes in 1873, and the Kentucky Derby in 1875. We had quickly instituted our own national championships in sports that the British had pioneered and still excelled at. For example, the United States lawn tennis championship was first held in 1881, the United States Amateur and Open golf championships in 1895. While all these different sports thrived and spread, at the turn of the century and for many years after that, baseball occupied a position all by itself. It was the uncontested national pastime. The second sport was undoubtedly football and its flower was college competition. American boys played these different sports in set seasons, and versatility became the hallmark of the natural athlete. The ideal college athlete was the three-letter man. He usually played football and baseball and sandwiched in either hockey or basketball in the winter interval, although occasionally he picked up that third letter in track.

The American era arrived at the close of World War I. Where athletes from the British Isles had long dominated the scene, Americans now did, and the United States came to be regarded as the cradle of champions. In the Olympic Games our athletes were supreme not only in many track and field events but also in diving, swimming, and the eight-oared shell—the only areas in the many-sided Olympics in which our interest was strong and organized. Bill Tilden broke through at Wimbledon in 1920. Walter Hagen shattered the British monopoly in golf when he took the British Open in 1922 and later in 1924, 1928, and 1929 and laid the foundation for our continuing primacy in that game. Our polo players became world leaders. In boxing, American fighters held the championships in nearly all the divisions. This ascendancy in international sport was accompanied by a fantastic growth at home of the intrinsically American sports—baseball, football, and basketball—which few other nations played to any extent and most did not play at all.

What was at least as arresting was the type of athlete we had come to produce in America. The mere mention of Paavo Nurmi, Harry Vardon, and Suzanne Lenglen should be sufficient to offset any impression that our stars had an exclusive patent on grace, but it was a fact that the average American athlete was a new sort of breed and a remarkably "pretty" athlete. We had our truck horses and our sheer-strength men, but for the most part there was a suppleness and fluidness about the co-ordination of the typical American athlete that set him off from his more mechanical, less relaxed European counterpart. To an American eye, at any rate, our performers seemed far more natural. It is difficult to know exactly what the factors were behind the rise of the American athlete, and one can only speculate. The fact that a boy was bred on baseball, football, and basketball undoubtedly had something to do with it. The fact that he did *not* grow up on soccer, the national game of so many countries, no doubt contributed too, for soccer leads a boy to a far different concept of movement and balance. Substantial arguments, I would venture, could also be made out for the various influences of living in a new country with vast spaces, where the robust pioneer life was not many decades away, where there was no engulfing military tradition, where college was not for the few, and where the climate and diet were beneficent. There is no question, however, that the development of so many excellent athletes was hastened by the new progressive coaches, who were beginning to study sport quite scientifically and who regularly arrived at more functional techniques. In any event, our athletes emerged as attractive stylists with power and as hearty competitors, and where the British had formerly been the models, the American champions were now studied and copied around the globe.

When sports were resumed after World War II, our athletes continued to retain their leadership in many phases of international competition, but gradually there was a change and a new era began. Boys and girls in nearly every country, both the old ones and new ones, set their sights on attaining world-class standing, and many of them achieved this. Often they outdistanced our athletes in the diligence of their training, sometimes they refined American techniques more successfully than we did ourselves, and occasionally they evolved their own solutions to old enigmas and reached the top that way. There was an impressive renaissance of sport in Britain and on the European continent. Australia, long renowned for its hardy athletes, began to produce great ones. Seeking a place in the athletic sun to dramatize its new position as a world power, Russia undertook a colossal national program in which promising athletes, supported by the state, labored day in and day out perfecting their prowess. The 1960 Olympic Games furnished a very clear illustration of how these other nations had caught up with us in many events and closed the gap in others. Indeed, for the first time in decades our representatives were defeated in the high jump, the 100- and 200-meter dashes, women's diving, and the eight-oared crew race, which was something of a shock. It was not so much that our athletes had performed poorly. They had, on the contrary, done marvelously well. Rather, it was that most of our side-line experts—not for the first time, either—had grossly underrated the young men and women from other countries. In the years to come, American athletes will surely continue at the forefront of sports, but just as we realize that we have no monopoly on pretty girls, we must appreciate that superb athletes are blooming the world over and that they will often be better than our best. This is something not to regret but to look forward to, for a first-class international sports event can possess an almost incomparable dramatic appeal. Speaking for myself, I can think of few sports occasions over the past fifteen years as honestly thrilling as the U.S.–Russia dual track meet in Philadelphia in 1959 and the Olympic hockey games the following winter between Russia, Canada, and an inspired American team.

In the nature of a footnote to the above, it should be added that we must be intelligent about how we approach our competitions in the future with Russian athletic teams. We cannot ignore this rivalry which has been thrust upon us because it has come to have a curious importance in the eyes of a watching world. However, just because Russia has made its athletes state property is no reason why we should subsidize ours. There is also no need to hearken to the alarmists who became panicky when Russia won 103 medals to our 71 in the 1960 Olympic Games and who now advocate an all-out crash program aimed at the 1964 Games. We should remember that the program of events in the Olympics was essentially devised for European athletes and, as such, places considerable emphasis on gymnastics, Graeco-Roman wrestling, cycling, fencing, and other sports to which we historically have paid little attention. If a young American athlete should exhibit a real flair for one of these specialties, we should, needless to say, try to help him (or her) reach his full potential, but there we should leave it.

In other words, if we go along the way we have been going—encouraging the gifted but making certain above all else that the pleasure never goes out of sport—we will do very well indeed. We have made errors we should correct, but for the most part we have planted so well that each year a wondrous new crop of fine young athletes springs up in every corner of the country with the corn and the wheat.

HERBERT WARREN WIND

March 1961

I

REPORTS
FROM
ABROAD

THE RIDDLE
OF JAPANESE SPORTS

1. THE BOUNCING BALL

This two-part article on Japan was published early in 1958. About a year later it became much clearer than it had been at the time of my visit in 1957—to me, anyhow—that included in the plexus of modern Japan is a current of violent political feeling which manifested itself in the mass demonstrations against Premier Kishi and President Eisenhower and in the physical attacks on Japanese political leaders. I bring this up because there is more emphasis in these articles on the new poise of the Japanese people and the wise ways in which they have adapted themselves to the multiple hazards of modern living. Both these strains exist side by side, and I suppose the degree of ascendancy of one or the other varies with each person and each group among the ninety millions who live in Japan.

At Christmas this past year I received my annual card and report from one of my oldest Japanese friends, George Ozasa, whom I worked with in Tokyo during the Occupation. A few excerpts from George's report will, I think, serve to bring some pertinent aspects of the national picture up to date.

"Japanese newspapers have started to refer to 1961 as The Year of Leisure, as an advertising device. Nobody any more is interested in staying home. Everybody is too busy drinking or visiting friends, the hot-springs spas, or skiing. Tokyo is really

73

a mess now with a new building going up every day. The traffic problem grows worse, if you can imagine that. Oh well, they'll probably come up with something before the Olympics.

"Speaking about sports, baseball continues to be the big news in Japan. Last year's principal hot-stove-league story was about a Waseda University third baseman who is picked to be the top player to enter the pro ranks since Nagashima. Every one of the twelve major-league teams bid for his services and he joined the Kokuketsu Swallows for a reported fifty million yen, or about $140,000. The crowds are, of course, just as big as ever. How else could they pay such fabulous wages!

"Another sport that's making rapid inroads is boxing. That is entirely due to television. There's a televised fight every night now. During the past year several good men have sprung up in the lower divisions, fighters who pack a knock-out punch. Yes, the fans demand someone hitting the canvas now. And in the traditional sport of sumo wrestling there are two twenty-year-old youngsters who have monopolized the headlines. One called Taiho is unlike the usual potbellied sumo man. Standing 6'3", he is built like a Greek god and has the looks of a movie star. He has brought the women back to sumo.

"Incidentally, getting back to the term The Year of Leisure, yes, 'leisure' is the actual word they use, though I doubt that very many people know what the word means. Anyways, the stores all advertise leisure products, more cars, more golf bags, more fur coats, and they remind you to plan to take that leisure trip abroad."

The world, every corner of it, continues to spin a little faster each year.

No less than eleven daily newspapers devoted to sports— one with a circulation of over 400,000—are published in Japan today. These papers were never gobbled up faster than they were the last week of October 1957, when Japan's well-known passion for sports reached what was probably its most fevered pitch in a quarter of a century, the previous high having occurred in 1932 when the nation's swimming stars carried off five of the six big races in the Olympic Games at Los Angeles. The commotion last October was caused by two major events which took place simultaneously. The first of these was the Canada Cup golf match in which, as you may remember, Torakichi (Pete) Nakamura emerged as what might be called the "Francis Ouimet of Japanese golf." Nakamura won the individual competition by seven full shots from players of the caliber of Snead and Demaret, and he combined with his partner, Koichi Ono, to capture the team competition in which thirty nations were represented by two top players each. Before the four-day 72-hole stroke-play tournament began, the average Japanese sports fan was hopeful that Nakamura and Ono might finish among the first ten teams. When Nakamura's second round of 68 moved the home boys in front, and when they proceeded to hang onto this lead over the last two rounds, it really was more than a little like Brookline in 1913 when new-to-golf Americans came out to The Country Club to watch Vardon and Ray work their wonders and, once on the scene, were both flabbergasted and enraptured when the home-grown boy, who they hoped would not give too poor an account of himself, cleanly outplayed the masters from across the ocean to the east.

The second October event, the Japan Series, their World Series, was only of national importance, and one had to be in Japan to realize that it marked the dramatic end of an era. The Japan Series, like ours a best-four-of-seven affair, had barely started when it was all over. The Tokyo Giants, the Yankees of Japanese baseball, were unceremoniously knocked off in four straight games by the Nishitetsu Lions, a hustling young club from the island of Kyushu. In Tokyo, this humiliation of the home heroes was suffered through by millions of glum-faced fans congregated around TV sets in factories, offices, stores, bars, restaurants, shopping arcades, and cafés. I had hardly expected Japanese television to be in the same class with ours, and its quality so surprised me that I may be guilty of extravagance in thinking (which indeed I did) that they get a clearer and more defined picture than we do.

When one is visiting a foreign country, particularly a land like Japan where the unexpected similarities to the West are at least as striking as the spectacular oriental qualities, in a single week one naturally bumps into as many brief but eloquent incidents as one does in one's home park in six months. I would like to relate two of the many which occurred that last week in October, for I think they will serve as portals to an understanding of some of the ways in which the Japanese infatuation with sports expresses itself.

First, there was the pleasant talk I had with Mr. Sotaro Suzuki, a director of the vanquished Tokyo Giants, the day after his club had lost its fourth straight game and the Series. Compared to our current prototype of baseball executive, Mr. Suzuki is a mild, unflamboyant fellow. This may be because he has been around baseball longer than most of our shoguns. He got into the game in 1920. In that year, poor health forced him to leave Waseda University, and his father sent him to the States to study economics. In New York young Mr. Suzuki fell in with bad company— New York Giant fans. He became a close friend of John Mc-Graw, he got to know Connie Mack and the game's other major personalities. When he returned to Japan, he was the Japanese baseball expert.

It was Suzuki who sold Matsutaro Shoriki, the dynamic owner-publisher of the *Yomiuri Shimbun* newspaper, on the idea of sponsoring in 1931 a postseason barnstorming tour in Japan of two teams made up of our top major league stars. Aside from doubling *Yomiuri*'s circulation, the colossal success of this tour gave professional baseball in Japan the im-

petus that led, successively, to further postseason tours by
Ruth and other occidental legends, to the formation of the
Tokyo Giants as Japan's first pro team, and to the founding
in 1936 of a professional Japanese league and, in 1949, of a
second major league. Instrumental in every stage of the development of the game, Mr. Suzuki, who is now as bald as
Benny Bengough, is frequently referred to as The Father of
Japanese Baseball. Being a modest man and, moreover, an
experienced man who has spent a lot of time in the States, it
is his habit to dismiss any claim to this title with an easy
wave of his hand and to suggest that it properly belongs to
his boss, Mr. Shoriki.

During our conversation Mr. Suzuki reminisced about the
many American stars who had come to Japan (including such
half-forgotten stalwarts as Clint Brown, Larry French, and
Willie Kamm) and described in detail the attributes of the
four or five Japanese major leaguers who he believes could
possibly make the grade in our majors. There is nothing antique or quaintly honorific about the way Mr. Suzuki talks
baseball: "Inao has a pretty good curve and lots of poise."
"Nagashima is one of our few natural power hitters." "Toyoda is a sound all-round ballplayer." With Mr. Suzuki it is
always *ballplayer*, never *baseball player*.

"Well," he said as he stood up to leave, "now back to work.
This morning we had a meeting of the directors of our ball
club, a long meeting. You can't lose four straight and stand
still. I'm afraid most of our old Giant stars are past their peak
and good young players are hard to find." He paused a moment and a long assessing look came into his eyes. "There's
no use kidding ourselves," he resumed. "We have a tremendous rebuilding job in front of us."

I thought I'd never left home.

A few days earlier—this is the second incident, one which
I think illustrates another phase of the picture, the variations
the Japanese introduce in their approach to our sports—I

had dinner with an old friend, Charlie Tuttle, a fellow from Vermont who went through Harvard practically unscathed. I got to know Charlie when we were both stationed in Tokyo during the grim period of the Occupation. He stayed on after his tour of duty was over, opened his own publishing house, and married a charming Japanese girl. On the evening I refer to, with dinner behind us, the Tuttles were showing me through the Ginza district, the heart of Tokyo's teeming night life.

The Ginza is an incredible place—a grid of narrow lanes, each of them packed shoulder to shoulder on both sides with bistros, cabarets, supper clubs, penny arcades, beer joints, coffee shops, and dance halls, many of these structures so advanced in design and décor as to give the Ginza something of the feeling of a world's fair, all of them featuring eye-popping neon and electric signs and some very watchable girls to match. We turned a corner out of one of these fluorescent lanes into a somewhat wider and quieter avenue. Across the street, according to the comparatively hushed sign in front, stood the Fairway Café.

The café, it turned out, was situated on the second floor. The room below it was literally on the ground floor, there being no board flooring. Some of the earth had been shoveled up and packed into four small tees, and on them four golfers, shirt-sleeved and wearing that look of total divorcement from all outside life which is common to the dedicated, were whanging golf balls off mats into canvas-backed netting hung against the opposite wall. In this narrow arena the netting was set so close to the tees that the player's clubhead swept within two yards of the nets on his follow-through; the thud of the ball against the canvas occurred practically at the same moment as the click of contact. None of the entranced practicers seemed to be the least disconcerted by this, however. Returning to the front of the shop, the Tuttles and I hefted a few Japanese-made clubs—they are lighter than ours, the shafts are whippier, and the faces of the woods have more loft—and leafed through a few of the many American books on technique which have come out in translation to slake the nation's burning thirst for golf.

To Charlie Tuttle's knowledge, the Fairway Café is the only enclosed practice ground in Tokyo, but driving nets have been set up on the roofs of at least five downtown office buildings. Furthermore, in and around Tokyo no less than fifty-two outdoor driving ranges are now flourishing, and on one public course (where Nakamura, incidentally, is the pro) nine holes are illuminated for play at night. The victory of the Japanese team in the Canada Cup naturally upped this already formidable exuberance for golf a few more notches. Perhaps it was inevitable that, within a week of the event, copies of a pirated Japanese edition of Ben Hogan's *The Modern Fundamentals of Golf* began to appear in some bookstores.

A third incident comes to mind as I write. It has nothing directly to do with sports but it probably would be well to include it in these prefatory remarks, for its theme moves potently, if invisibly, behind any thoughts on Japan. It took place at the Kasumigaseki Golf Club on the second day of the Canada Cup matches. Nakamura and Ono were paired with Snead and Demaret that day and, as was to be expected, this foursome attracted just about all of the spectators and the full corps of sports writers. About thirty Japanese reporters were on hand, among them one Shorge Ohashi, a thickset, fortyish fellow who covers for *Asahi*. Ohashi ("I am really a Japanese-Irishman") has a most pleasant sense of humor and speaks English fluently. He was a wonderfully agreeable companion to walk and talk with. On the 17th hole—we had gotten to feel quite at home with each other by this time— Shorge spotted a friend of his in the gallery, a Maryknoll missionary, and the two soon were deep in a lively conversation.

"They're great fellows, those Maryknoll priests," Ohashi

said when he caught up with me further down the fairway. "I got to know them during the war when my outfit was fighting in China. They were very kind to us and we became good friends. They were short of food and we gave them whatever rations we could spare. We were very happy to. Do you know China?"

I told Shorge that I had been stationed there during the war.

"Whereabouts?" he asked.

"Kunming and Namyung mostly," I said.

"Namyung!" Shorge exclaimed. "Why, we were within seventy miles of each other!"

For a moment we stood wordlessly, our minds full of thought. Then we walked quickly up the fairway because Nakamura had a difficult shot to play and we wanted to be up close.

Since the conclusion of World War II, the peoples and governments of the United States and Japan have gone about building a new friendship with a genuineness of purpose and a spirit almost unique in the long history of nations and wars. However, there was a war and it ended less than thirteen years ago, and that is still much too short a time for human beings to have forgotten it.

The four islands of Japan—Honshu, the main island; Hokkaido, to the north of Honshu; Kyushu, which lies to its south; and small Shikoku, tucked in between Honshu and Kyushu—have a total square mileage a little smaller than that of California. Volcanic in origin, a sizable portion of this land—82 per cent or so—is not arable or livable. Since the beginning of history, the people have clustered in the pockets of the hills and mountains and in the two main coastal plains, the Kansai (around Osaka, traditionally the great business city) and the Kanto (around Tokyo, traditionally the seat of the ruling power).

Whatever aspect of Japan you are looking at, there are two significant points to keep in mind, for there is nothing they do not affect. First, Japan has always been densely populated. Today, over 90,000,000 live on the four islands (13,000,000 live in California). Second, it is only one hundred years since this island group, hermetically sealed off from the rest of the world and slumbering a long uninterrupted feudal sleep, was forcibly roused by Commodore Perry to face the complicated problems of the modern world.

Now here's a puzzlement—one of the many. How did this nation, in several ways the apogee of the Oriental, produce in so brief a time a "baseball adviser" like Mr. Suzuki and a Fairway Café and become, in short, such a hotbed of Western sport? By all logical rules of measure, the role of a country like Japan in the world of "modern sport" should be minor, tangential. You would expect one or two top-notch swimmers to be developed, an occasional serious contender in the Olympic hop-step-and-jump competition (or some such out-of-the-way event), a few indefatigable marathoners, a respectable but limited Davis Cup team, and maybe every now and then some individual star popping up in some very individual specialty like ice skating, flyweight boxing, billiards, or the parallel bars. Instead, among the "comparatively small nations of the world"—so goes a standard bit of locker-room punditry—the three which are head and shoulders above the rest are Japan, Australia, and Hungary. (The word *small*, of course, is quite inexact and applies properly only to Hungary, large neither in size nor in population. Australia is small in population only, 9,500,000 inhabiting the continent. When people refer to Japan as small—in population it is the world's fifth largest country—what they actually have in mind is that one would hardly expect any non-Western country's role in modern sports to be more than minor.)

Hungary a big sports nation? Not surprising, really. After all, it is at the junction where eastern Europe meets western

Europe, and a long sporting history lies behind its people's dashing performances in middle-distance running, field sports, soccer, water polo, and Rugby. Australia? Of course. A natural. A lusty young nation with blessed few other directions in which to channel its extra energies poured them into the pastimes it inherited from its British antecedents— tennis, cricket, track and field, golf, horse racing—and into sports like swimming and boating and Australian football which suited the rough-and-ready character of a new land and a new people.

But Japan? How come? From this vale of the meditative drinking-in of the fragile beauty of the cherry blossom, the unchromatic plink of the well-tempered samisen, the mannered ease of the kimono, from this plexus of the geisha tending her fan, the working girl her silkworms, the samurai his sword, and the farmer his Lilliputian rice paddy, how come that group of record-breaking swimmers who wrested away our domination of that sport in the '30s, and how come all those Class AA baseball players, the best track men in Asia, the reigning table tennis champions of the world, an Olympic skating champion, an outstanding skier (Chick Igaya), and now golfers of proved international caliber?

This is only half the riddle. What is truly astonishing is not the champions Japan has produced but the widespread participation in Western sports by people of all ages, the deep love of sport which nourishes all this activity. For example, it has long been the accepted thing to acknowledge in a marveling tone that the Japanese like baseball almost as much as we do. This statement is incorrect. The Japanese like baseball better than we do. No one ever gets enough of it. Their high schools and colleges play not one baseball season but two, the regular one in spring and a second in autumn. Thousands travel miles to Osaka for the All-Japan High School Championship. Over 45,000 annually turn out for The Game between Keio and Waseda, two of the oldest and Iviest colleges; it is precisely the equivalent of the Harvard-Yale game, only it is baseball, not football. The large industrial firms, taking a page from our book, sponsor baseball teams, corralling the best talent that isn't headed into the professional leagues and assigning the young men plushy jobs in their public relations department to give them something to occupy their time between games. Last summer, unnoticed by most of us, the nonprofessional (meaning semi-pro) baseball championship of the world, held at Detroit, was captured by the Kumagai Construction Company's team. Kumagai earned the right to represent Japan by winning the pennant in its regional league and then going on to defeat the five other regional champions in the annual elimination tourney at Korakuen Stadium in Tokyo.

As for major league baseball in Japan, as good an index as any of its vitality was the recent payment of 30,000,000 yen, or $85,000, by the rebuilding Tokyo Giants to procure the services of a standout college star. That is a lot of money—in Japan $85,000 would have a purchasing power perhaps three or four times as great as in the U.S., for though commodities are high, services are still very inexpensive. In this general connection, the half dozen or so top Japanese players who might conceivably make the grade in our majors are not interested in trying because of the financial loss that would be entailed. Say that Yasumitsu Toyoda, the splendid young shortstop of the Nishitetsu Lions, went to an American team's spring training camp and caught on (à la Willie Miranda) as a utility man, if not a regular. He might draw $9,000, or some figure in that neighborhood. Back home he gets quite a few thousand dollars more than that to begin with, and it goes three or four times as far. In addition to enormous stature, he has a car, a fine home, one or two servants, and, all in all, a much better life than he would have here as just another good ballplayer.

Perhaps the most eloquent comment on the Japanese

adoration of baseball is provided by a sound one hears wherever one travels in Japan: the light smack of ball meeting glove. In the cities you can always tell when it is noon without consulting your watch. Your ear tells you. At twelve sharp that distinctive spank of ball and glove starts to emanate from a nearby gas station, a shipping yard, a loading area. Lunch hour has arrived and the boys are out. This happens every day, this game of catch—*ketchiboru*, the Japanese call it—and it goes on not only during the lunch hour but, to a lesser degree, during all free daylight hours. If the renowned artist Hiroshige were alive today and developing his celebrated project, views of the fifty-three different stopover stations on the seacoast highway between Osaka and Tokyo, one can well imagine that in his backgrounds figures of boys and men tossing the baseball would appear almost with the regularity of Fuji.

The answer to the riddle of Japan (and what seems to a Western visitor to be a fascinating split-level culture) lies, of course, in learning more about this unusual people. They are decidedly different in many ways from the oversimplified stock conception we have dealt in for years. To my mind, the best introduction to a more correct view is contained in one sentence in a report written in 1814 by the representatives of the British East India Company who had been dispatched on a trade mission to Nagasaki by Sir Stamford Raffles, the English governor of Java. "The Japanese," went this clear-eyed sentence, "are a nervous, vigorous people whose bodily and mental powers assimilate much nearer to those of Europe than what is attributed to Asiatics in general."

This mission of the British East India Company was not successful. The Japanese did not want to do business. It was an old story. In 1638 Japan had embarked—or disembarked; that is more in the spirit of what happened—on a course of fantastic isolation. No Japanese was permitted to leave the islands, and contact with the outside world was limited to set dealings with the trade missions the Chinese and Dutch were allowed to maintain, the Chinese in Nagasaki, the Dutch on the island of Deshima, a spot of land off Nagasaki only 236 paces long by 82 paces wide. This "closed-door" policy had been decreed by the Tokugawa, the ruling shogunate. It was, in essence, a reaction to the troubles which had befallen Japan near the end of the sixteenth century largely as a result of the activities of Christian missionaries. The various missionary orders fought among themselves, which brought some disruption; head-on collisions between the missionaries and the long-entrenched Buddhist priests brought more. But more serious than these conflicts, in the Japanese view, was the problem of conversion, since it embodied the idea of a person's having a loyalty to something outside the borders of Japan. By expelling all foreigners from their land—at this time Japan was still a hodgepodge of feudal states ruled by military clans—the Tokugawa, the mightiest of the clans, hoped to prevent such divisions of loyalty, to perpetuate peace, and to ensure the succession of their family line.

From time to time some scraps of knowledge about the West slipped through the closed door via Deshima. Outstanding Dutch scholars in all branches of the arts and sciences were periodically stationed at the trading station, and individual Japanese who wanted to keep abreast of the world hied themselves to Deshima and received instruction in natural history, languages, medicine, agriculture and astronomy. From their Dutch teachers they learned of such epochal events as the exploration of the new world, the American and French revolutions, and the defeat of Napoleon. Save for this small body of the intellectually curious, however, the Japanese continued to view the foreigner as a potential molester and exploiter. Consequently, consternation seized the country when Commodore Perry steamed into Tokyo Bay in 1853 with four gunboats and the conspicuous intention not to take no for an answer to President Fillmore's request that Japan enter into trade relations with the United States, make coaling stations available to our ships, and take care of shipwrecked American sailors. The Tokugawa shogun tried to stall off negotiations with Perry, but when the commodore returned to Tokyo Bay the following year with ten gunboats, he capitulated to the American demands. Two ports, Hakodate on Hokkaido and Shimoda on Honshu (and later a third port in Kyushu), were opened to United States vessels. In 1856 Townsend Harris arrived at Shimoda, forty miles below Yokohama, to open the first American consulate.

The dike was breached, and now that it was, other nations wanted to trade with Japan. The hopelessness of stemming this influx became increasingly apparent to the Japanese. While the samurai (the privileged warrior class) advocated using force to expel the foreigners, the majority of the more responsible officials saw the folly of such myopic bravado and the benefits that might accrue to their country with the resumption of international relations—that is, as long as Japan's integrity as a nation was not abused. Reluctantly bowing to reality, the Tokugawa shogun stepped down and, in effect, turned his powers over to the emperor.

From the twelfth century on, the imperial house had been deep in the shadow of the military rulers—so deep, in fact, that Townsend Harris had been in Japan for several months before he even learned of the existence of an emperor. Traditionally, however, the imperial house had handled all Japanese external relations and, more to the point, it was felt that being represented by its emperor would be Japan's best insurance of being treated with proper respect by the outside nations. In 1867 the occasion was finally right for the big step. The old emperor died and was succeeded by his fifteen-year-old son, Meiji. Certain of the more powerful feudal clans rallied behind him. This new leadership brought the others into line, and, to make real their support, the clans returned their ancient feudal rights and hereditary lands to the young emperor and encouraged him to rule in actuality as well as in name.

There is no need to go into detail—and we shall not—on the dizzying speed with which Japan fledged itself into a modern nation, but there is one period of this transformation which cannot be bypassed. I am thinking of the first two decades of the Meiji restoration when the capable young emperor dispatched his country's most promising young men and women to the best European and American universities and to the world's other recognized centers of knowledge, there to absorb and bring back the best of Western thought and techniques. To expedite this program, outstanding men in all fields of activity were invited to Japan to instruct and organize. From this vast amount of new information, the leaders of Japan, very much like men compiling an anthology of contemporary civilization, attempted to pluck for their country's use the different and distinct fortes of the Western nations.

From the British, Japan took its legal system, railway organization, and the structure of its navy; from the Germans, the organization of its medical schools and its army; from the Italians, its concept of Western art; from the United States, its postal and its educational systems plus its farm program; from the French, its criminal code and its system of local government. In 1890, only twenty-three years after the ascension of Meiji, Japan held its first general election and seated its first national legislature, or Diet. All this in a country where, when Perry arrived, four-fifths of the population were farmers anchored back in the Middle Ages and where, as historian Marion May Dilts has expressed it so well, the main excitement in village life "was afforded by the eagerly anticipated first nightingale to return in spring, an evening's gossip in the light of a full moon, the festivals of local shrines and temples, or occasional wandering acrobats and storytellers."

Sports were a little different. Dutch instructors were invited to set up a course of gymnastics for the middle schools, but as far as games went, the usual pattern of planned overseas study and domestic digestion did not obtain. No one was sent to Boston to learn from A. G. Spalding how he gripped his curve ball; no one headed for St. Andrews to record old Tom Morris' true-tempered tips on cleek play; no one took a room in New Haven, the better to be close to Walter Camp, or rented a flat near Wimbledon to study how peerless Lottie Dod executed the backhand lob. Western sports just sidled into Japan. On one hand, young Japanese who had studied or worked abroad brought back the games with them, and on the other, teachers and businessmen and consulate employees from America and Europe brought their games over with them for their own pleasure.

Baseball, for example, caught on the way all things catch on: beginning in the 1870s, the members of the American colony in Tokyo found a field where they could play baseball on their days off, the Japanese watched them, they liked what they saw, and they began playing ball, too. Americans coached them. By the early 1890s, Japanese schools were organizing their own teams, and by 1905—as early as that— Waseda University sent its ball club to the United States to play our colleges. Today, as we know, Japan supports thirteen major league clubs, and there is hardly a schoolboy who cannot give you the regular line-ups of such gloriously named teams as the Nagoya Dragons, the Tokyo Swallows, the Hiroshima Carps, and the Kawasaki Whales.

Of the countless manners and measures the Japanese adopted in the nation's furious rush to leap into the late nineteenth century in one giant running broad jump, some they understood in part, others they understood not at all, some they half liked, others they really didn't care for but persisted with because these things were "Western," *i.e.*, modern and, so, desirable. Sports were the big exception. The Japanese really understood them and loved them instinctively. Why did they take to sports? And why with such a passion? Perhaps our brief glance at the nation's history has provided more than a clue, and the remainder of the answer is the old story of causes and effects operating on many planes. What follows is a quick compendium of the ideas on this subject advanced by scholars and laymen, both Japanese and American, with whom I've talked during my two visits to Japan and here at home.

To begin with, as the Raffles mission noted, the Japanese are a vigorous people. Up to a point, their vigor stems from the usual reasons. They live in a North Temperate climate. The crusty terrain of their islands yields only to hard labor, and then not generously. Additionally, the feudal character of the country necessarily placed great emphasis on military and physical prowess. Whereas a young Chinese growing up in that ancient and sophisticated civilization esteemed the scholar the flower of his culture and hoped that he, too, might some day grow a scholar's long fingernails and mark himself as a man of thought, a young Japanese was frequently visited with much shorter-nailed dreams of glory. His ideal was a leader who indeed had a strong spiritual fiber but who was also a man of action equal to the demands of any physical engagement. One very primary reason, then, why the Japanese took so avidly to Western sports (and were so good at them) was this fondness for the physical, which in feudal times expressed itself in such warlike games as judo, *karate* (a lethal relative of boxing), *yabusame* (archery on horseback), and *kendo* (dueling with bamboo staves).

In addition to their straight vigor, the Japanese possess a

second kind of vitality, a most un-Eastern nervous energy, a
real Vanderbilt Avenue brand of drive which has long differ-
entiated the Japanese from the Korean (from which stock he
is descended) and from the Chinese, both of whom are
energetic but not in this second or compulsive way. This
national trait derives from Japan's being an island country in
which isolation bred a highly complicated sense of uniqueness. "In premodern times," Professor Edwin O. Reischauer
writes in his superb and superbly readable book, *The United
States and Japan,* "no other important group of people consciously participating in the rich culture of the Eurasiatic
land mass lived so far removed from all other civilized peoples. The straits between Japan and Korea are five times as
wide as the Straits of Dover, which had had a significant influence in shaping England's history and the character of her
people. The distance between Japan and China, the home-
land of her civilization, is even greater." Because of this
marked isolation, Professor Reischauer continues, the Japanese early developed a self-consciousness which, among other
things, contains "a large degree of embarrassment and the
fear of inferiority," an attitude "strengthened by the painfully obvious contrast throughout most of their history
between small, backward and remote Japan as opposed to
China, the admitted home of civilization, which was far
larger, far older, and far grander than Japan could ever hope
to be." This intense awareness of a separate identity, as
Professor Reischauer points out, led to the early rise of Japanese nationalism, and it explains in a very considerable
measure the historic (and continuing) Japanese need not to
be depreciated by larger outside nations, to show the world
how well they do things—in brief, to excel and be admired.
Excelling at the sports the Western peoples set such conspicuous store by has long been one of the routes the Japanese
have taken in their chronic quest for this respect. Like
Europeans and Americans, they drive to stand out.

This pent-up, vigorous people—only the Germans, who have yet to discover the coffee break, are more industrious— has traditionally lived in small, crowded villages and in small, crowded dwellings. After World War II a few apartment houses, the logical semisolution to the eternal housing problem, were built for the first time, but the Japanese did not rush to occupy them. They far preferred the old way in which each family (sometimes inflicted with in-laws and other relatives) lives in its own one-story wooden structure, the familiar fragile Japanese house with rice-straw matting on the floors, rice-paper windows, sliding walls, and interior sliding partitions. Exceedingly gifted in domestic matters, the Japanese have long done wonders in making their small homes livable. By sliding the interior partitions out of the way, they combine two or more tiny rooms into one fairly commodious room for group occasions. At night, by sliding the partitions back, they redivide the space into private quarters for sleeping—*comparatively* private, that is, since several members of the large families generally share the same rectangle, there seldom being rooms enough for each to have his own. To give their homes some illusion of space, the Japanese encumber them with no set furniture apart from one or two low tables. When chairs are needed, pillows and armrests are taken from the closet and placed on the floor. The same thing with beds; when it is time for retiring, the quilts are hauled from storage and rolled out. The art of the Japanese garden, similarly, is to give the appearance of space where none exists. A trickle of a stream meanders through dwarf cedars, and a wide, wide world is created on a plot that could barely accommodate a one-car garage. By exercising exceptional restraint and honoring the other members of the household, the Japanese long ago learned to make their homes comparative castles of peace and pleasure. However, it has always been a physically cramping life, and a vigorous person feels it. He needs to get out and move. This

is true for the kids—you can't dive from the raised arms of
the sofa onto the cushions below when you don't have a
sofa—and it is no less true for the adults.

In overpopulated Japan the family ricewinner has always
been under terrific economic pressure. Today, for example,
the average farmer wrests his living from a piece of land about
two and one half acres in area. The average white-collar
man, engaged in keen competition for the rare chances at
advancement, is both frustrated by and thankful for a
monthly wage slightly over $50. When the man of the
house returns home, seeking relief from the crush and press
of the day, there are some evenings when he needs a more
active release than he can get by contemplating in solitude
the tranquil beauties of his miniature garden. Over the past
ninety years, he has found that release increasingly in sports.
If he isn't able to afford to belong to a club which has its
own facilities, well, he simply walks out into the street before
his house—often the only open space in town—and passes
the baseball with his neighbors.

The Japanese male, traditionally and currently, has been
under several other considerable strains. Because there was
no gradual evolution from feudal times to modern times, he
has been the heir of the hang-over cult of the hero man. He
has been expected to embody the valor, endurance, and
other mile-high traits of the heroes of Japanese mythology
and ancient history. In a tight corner he was supposed to
match the impossible dedication of the samurai. It has been
quite a load for him to carry. In his own mind he seldom
makes the grade. Western sports and their code of sportsmanship provided him with the kind of outlet he needed, a
life-sized environment in which he could get excited about
something he could control to some degree. If he played
them well, sports gave him strong individual satisfaction. He
felt like somebody for one of the few times in his life. If he
didn't shine, he wasn't exactly disgraced. Furthermore, he

was still in one piece, and frequently, if he was a devotee of one of the brutal, old-line native "sports," he wasn't. In *karate*, for instance, a combination of boxing with the open hand and kicking with the flying foot, the standard blow is known as the *sannen satsujin*, or "three years murder": the victim may not perish on the spot, but the internal damage he suffers will probably prove fatal within three years.

The simple fact that sports make a person feel better physically has been another important side of their popularity. The Japanese have historically valued good health with such intensity that they have been positively hypochondriacal in their efforts to avoid illness, and they remain so today. They rival us as purchasers of pills, powders, and other pharmaceuticals. Viewing cleanliness as the handmaiden of health, they have for centuries placed tremendous value on the manifold virtues of bathing. Some Japanese take three baths a day; nearly everybody takes one four time a week, at home or at the public baths. They soak—rather, they parboil—in deep wooden tubs. The bather first squats on a small stool on the slightly slanted floor outside the tub and soaps the dirt off. Then he enters the tub where the clean and extremely hot water engulfs him to above his shoulders. He stays there soaking and relaxing for about twenty minutes, sometimes longer. In Japanese inns at hot springs resorts, where a plentiful supply of hot water is available, the tub remains filled all day. Fresh hot water is fed in continually by a tap, the "old" surplus water softly overflowing the sides of the tub onto the tilted floor which channels it to the drain. All in all, in the art of the bath and the bathroom, the Japanese are at least the peer of Cecil B. de Mille, not to mention the Finns.

Western games also fitted in well with certain domestic diversions the Japanese were fond of. With no backyards at their disposal and such limited interior space, the Japanese had early developed a great taste for parlor games, little family entertainments built on the quickness of eye and the agility of fingers, the fun of variation, and the knack of out-guessing. This love of manual dexterity expressed itself also in the national fondness for playing with rubber balls. (A classic work of art by Harunobu, incidentally, depicts a geisha bouncing a ball. It is called "Bouncing Ball" and has recently been reproduced as a stamp, a most beautiful one.) No doubt this old familiarity with throwing and catching balls ac-counted for the fervency with which the Japanese embraced baseball rather than, say, soccer. Certainly the fact that base-ball was an American game contributed, too, for it was on the popular level that America exerted its biggest influence, an overwhelming influence.

And there was another reason, a significant one. As a people who had to find a way to live together harmoniously in huddled numbers, the Japanese placed their faith in the "ground rules" of social behavior. The articulated ground rules of Western sports in general made them attractive and made baseball especially so. Whereas soccer could easily de-generate into an unscientific skirmish, baseball was neat, defined, and decisive. Each pitch was either a ball or a strike. When a batter hit a fair ball, he was either out or he was safe. Additionally, the Japanese loved the variable tactics and strategies deriving from the ground rules, and they loved the dramatic moments when the tension built up and up and one man (bases full, two out, a full count) stood undeniably etched as a hero if he delivered in that unignorable clutch. The Japanese Walter Mitty is a baseball dreamer.

For all these reasons, it takes very little fancy to imagine the elation of the Japanese when they first saw baseball and began to piece it out. It must have struck them as something almost too good to be true, and they must have been stag-gered by the thought that foreigners could have devised a game that so perfectly expressed *their* ideas of what the ideal game should be. In any event, baseball is now deep in the

Japanese blood. When you toss a ball to a European boy, for example, his instinctive reaction is likely to be to try to trap it with his foot. Whether he knows it or not, he has watched older people playing soccer. When you toss a ball to a Japanese child, he tries to catch it. In my experience, this is the only place, except in the United States and the countries adjacent to us, where this occurs.

In their eagerness to learn, the Japanese copied the methods of the most proficient. This, of course, is what every young country from the beginning of time has done when it has set out to learn something new. At the turn of the century, for illustration, when we in America were first getting all steamed up about golf, we practically denuded Scotland of its pros. If a guy was named Willie and spoke in a cultivated burr, we told him to start packing and come on over. Same thing in the '30s when the skiing bug hit us: any fellow named Hans or Sig who could distinguish edelweiss from eiderdown—man, he had it made. We have all copied, but, I suppose, no one has ever copied quite as literally or as conscientiously or, for that matter, as well as the Japanese. There are thousands of amusing stories about their extremes of assiduity, my favorites being the ones which Gene Sarazen tells about his golfing tour in Japan in 1938. Sarazen, as you may remember, had developed the sand wedge not long before this, and his mastery of trap play was something to marvel at. The Japanese who turned out for his exhibitions didn't merely marvel and let it go at that. No, they carried umbrellas along, and as soon as Sarazen had played out of a trap, the gallery automatically formed a line; one by one, each student entered the trap, set his feet in Sarazen's footprints and his umbrella point at the scar in the sand, and sought to imitate the technique Gene had used. Sarazen's stay in Japan lasted three weeks. Before he left—not that anything else should have been expected—several sporting-goods houses had come out with exact copies of his wedge. (In the nature of a footnote, to underline how everything moves in cycles, it might be added that twenty years earlier, when he was a tyro and not a master, Gene had such a rough time getting a foothold in American golf—only Scots need apply—that he debated the wisdom of changing his name to MacSarazen.)

Granting that the Japanese have frequently carried their zeal for imitation to inordinate lengths, the cliché that types them as a nation of mere copiers is a bum rap. It overlooks the wonderful creativity of the native Japanese culture. It doesn't take into consideration the borrowings other countries have made from the Japanese—in the field of architecture, to name a notable example. It slides by the fact that all of Asia is at a stage where it borrows from the West and that, if we always focus on Japan in this respect, it is largely because the Japanese themselves frequently comment on this yen for importation. Furthermore, it doesn't take into account that the Japanese do things with what they take, ingenious and inventive things. (Ask any photographer.) They are sensitive, and with reason, about the endless repetition of this charge of being mere copiers. As proud of their country as we are of ours, they are hurt by the implied slur that there is nothing creative in themselves and their culture.

I didn't realize how easy it is to slip into this glib condescension until one afternoon on my recent trip. A Japanese girl, who had returned not long before from the United States, where she had gone to school, had been assigned to help me get my travel arrangements straightened out. As we were walking through the streets of downtown Tokyo it occurred to me to ask her to point out any Japanese-made automobiles, for I couldn't distinguish them from the other small cars.

"That black one," she said an instant later, "that's a Toyopet. It's very popular."

"Looks like an English Austin decked out with American styling," I ventured. I turned to see if she agreed. Her expression had changed and she looked troubled. I am not good at reading faces but it seemed to me that she was trying not to show how let down she was by the insinuation of my remark. We walked on and the situation repaired itself quickly, but some time later, when I was thinking it over, it struck me that we never give the Japanese credit for anything that at all resembles our products. Just what is a Japanese auto supposed to look like anyhow? A pagoda?

In recent years, though, things have been changing by and large. As we in America have begun to realize that we do not possess a monopoly of the world's talents and intelligence, we have acquired a new appreciation for the peoples of the Far East and we have certainly "rediscovered" Japan. Puzzled by the way life for us has become less meaningful and more wearing, we look across the waters and see the Japanese riding tougher bumps than ours with at least as much and probably more equanimity. The current vogue for Zen philosophy among American artists and writers is one of the more rarefied manifestations of this window to the East. A Japanese offshoot of Buddhism, Zen concerns itself with the individual's getting to know and feel his elusive true nature and releasing it in his activity. Incidentally, a slim book, *Zen in the Art of Archery*, was the spark that lit the fire in this country.

In a word, we now think the Japanese have something. And they do. Spelling it out is not easy, but for a starter it might be remarked (as it is by everyone sooner or later) that a large share of the credit for what is right with Japan belongs to the Japanese women. They are as gifted as any in the world at that difficult job of being essentially women. A far cry from the romantic stereotype that portrays them as little pitter-patterers with parasols self-effacingly mincing across the arched magenta bridge, they have always had a remarkable fiber, filling the home and the family and themselves with sound emotion even when the bewildered male was running off in three directions at one time. The war and the Occupation were the best things that ever happened to the Japanese female. It gave her more status, far more room to move in. Instead of changing, she just blossomed out. (This is one of the best things that ever happened to the Japanese male.) The fact that a flock of the modern Japanese girls have something of the looks and style of the Audrey Hepburn-Leslie Caron school is not exactly beside the point.

What is the Japanese woman's special gift? It would appear to be an unconfused understanding of where her true pleasures as a woman really lie, along with a remarkable understanding of what brings a man authentic self-respect and enjoyment. "They're on a different frequency entirely from our women and the Europeans," one correspondent at the Canada Cup matches commented. "I haven't as much as laid a finger on a woman here and yet I've never felt as manly in my life. It isn't that they cater to you. They don't. But they don't think they're lowering themselves when they do things for you and enjoy it. So what do you do? You find yourself responding as if you were a top-notch guy and, by George, you feel you are. You know," he added with a bittersweet smile, "when I get home I've a good mind to write out a list for my wife of the changes I want made and paste that list on the wall. I can see her ripping it down now and admonishing me, 'Now, just because you've had a trip to the Orient, don't think that you . . . and so on.' "

In this last decade Japanese women have entered the sports world in numbers for the first time—even the geisha. She has had to. As you undoubtedly know, the geisha is primarily an actress or entertainer or, if you will pardon the horrible but apt expression, a fun girl. Her traditional skill has been her facility in relieving the tired businessman of his worries, which she does by the superfemininity of her manner, her ability to talk merrily about the nonbusiness side of life, and her decorative songs, dances, and attentiveness. When golf erupted into a national passion after the war, she had a problem. Her clients frequently wanted to talk about their golf and they needed a thoroughly qualified listener. There was no other way out for the first-class geisha than to take up the game herself. Many of them, accordingly, joined golf clubs and met the game face to face. As a result, it is no trouble at all for them during office hours to proffer the most professional listening this side of Sandwich. "I can picture it well, Mr. Okamura," she says with just the right blend of sympathy and awe. "There you were, out in 53, due to the poor shape of the greens. You were 3 down at the turn to Mr. Watanabe. With nine holes to go, you indeed had your work cut out for you. But you were not downhearted, were you? As you whipped your driver out of your bag and strode to the 10th tee, I can well imagine you said to yourself, 'I can win this match and I can win the Texas press bet and the Yamanashi press bet, too. Just keep the old head down and supinate and let the rest take care of itself.' And, you know what, Mr. Okamura? I'll bet you won!"

2. THE MULBERRY BUSH

Even in this age of the airliner, when a flight from New York to London takes only twice the time of the train ride from New York to Boston, the islands of Japan are still quite a long way away. The average traveler from the eastern part of this country, if he is flying the southern route across the Pacific, needs a bit over three days to get there: one day to cross the continent to San Francisco; a second day in which he gazes for some nine hours at the featureless blue water of the Pacific and comes down at length in Hawaii; and then a last double hop, nine hours westward to Wake Island—nothing more than a long par 5 in the middle of nowhere—and a second stretch of nine hours from Wake to Haneda airport on the outskirts of Tokyo. Protracted as such a trip is by present-day standards, it has brought the Orient immeasurably closer than it was in the days of the weeks-long, Somerset Maugham-type cruise, and it has made Tokyo a favorite gathering point of the American traveler who has got Europe under his belt, the retired businessman who has always dreamed of Old Cathay, not to mention American conventioneers who have come to realize that an annual convocation frequently can go on the old expense account as a business cost so why limit themselves to some "local" spot like Mexico City.

When I was in Japan this last autumn I never quite got over how the country had changed, in this respect among others, in the eleven years since my previous visit. The Imperial Hotel, where we stayed, has, of course, long been known as a principal headquarters for foreigners in Tokyo, but it was still jarring to walk into the lobby so many miles from Main Street and see it densely populated with American conventioneers togged out with fezzes or blue arm bands and calling for ice.

There are a number of other sights and sounds which the traveler to Japan is quite unprepared for. In my case, I had barely made my way through customs and mispronounced "Kasumigaseki Golf Course" with a flourish for the benefit of the taxi driver when it became apparent that the Japanese immersion in sports today exceeds anything one has been told to expect. Turning out of the airport drive, the taxi slowed down for a chubby little girl of ten or eleven who skipped across, lugging a large tennis racket. We made a right turn, and in front of us a brightly painted signboard announced that the third annual Asian Games (track and field) would be held in Tokyo in the spring. As we started to cut across the rim of the city down a crowded thoroughfare, we passed some young auto mechanics—at any rate, three fellows in coveralls—throwing a baseball on the sidewalk in front of a garage. In a school playground a flock of little girls in white blouses and black skirts were playing basketball, using a volleyball and shooting at hoops set about eight feet from the ground. In the playground of another grade school not much farther along, the girls were playing volleyball, the boys were playing basketball, and a tennis game was in progress on a small-sized court laid out on the orange-brown earth. And that is the way it went: past another group of men in coveralls tossing a baseball; past two little girls batting a shuttlecock with metal-strung rackets in the narrow space between two stores; past a hardware store—rather, a store stocked with a variety of products all made of wood—where nine baseball bats were displayed in a wooden rack; on past another school playground with several slides as well as the usual facilities for tennis, volleyball, and basketball; past an eight-year-old striding up the sidewalk carrying a red rubber ball about the size of a grapefruit; and so on and on.

This first impression of sports on the right of you, sports on the left of you, sports on every side proves to be, on further examination, not an exaggerated introduction to their place in contemporary Japan. Life there today recalls the '20s in America in its frenetic pace on all fronts. Part of this is a reaction, I am told, to the enervating years of the war and the state of general fatigue, emotional depression and real apathy that overcame the country at the close of the war. Japan was just starting to stir slowly again when its economy received a terrific shot in the arm; all kinds of matériel were needed quickly when the Korean war broke out, and Japan roused itself to make it. When the war was over, this boom was expected to subside. It continued. Astute conversion of the wartime manufacturing plants built up, practically overnight, a new and thriving export trade. At home a self-nourishing cycle of prosperity began to spin—and is still spinning at a good rate—due largely, economists explain, to the increasing purchasing power of the burgeoning middle classes. The surge toward sports has been just one of the many aspects of this astonishing national recovery during which Tokyo has swollen to the largest city in the world (almost 9,000,000), rivaling New York in the incredible amount of new building construction, recalling Los Angeles in the smog that has arisen from so much concerted industry and the new domestic heating systems, replacing Shanghai (in some ways) as the good-time city of the Far East, and generally assuming (in a healthy way) a leadership of the infant nations in that sector of the world.

Going all out for Western sports is, to be sure, nothing new for the Japanese, who began playing baseball in the 1870s, held their first official track and field meet in 1886, and entered their first Olympics in 1912. During the gray days of the Occupation, when the Japanese did not know what they were allowed to do and were waiting to be told, Major General William F. Marquat of General MacArthur's staff had the acumen to realize that a revival of sports would be a good thing and ordered the country's baseball men to get the major league started again. This helped morale a lot. Shortly afterward, the general arranged for the nation's crack swimmers to compete in a meet in Los Angeles. This marked Japan's return to international competition, and it is impossible to overstate the effect this had on the people. They began to hold their heads up again. Today no one talks about the war in Japan or wants to be reminded either of it or of its aftermath, but the name of General Marquat is frequently mentioned. He is a man they have never stopped appreciating.

The traveler arriving in Tokyo a little over a century ago would have encountered no evidence at all that the West existed. When Japan, under the leadership of its perspicacious young Emperor Meiji, re-entered the world as the last third of the nineteenth century began, it did so with supernal ardor and application, adopting Western institutions and methods with such speed that it may possibly have skipped a whole phase in a country's normal development. At any rate, it looks like this to many Westerners, the contrast between the old and the modern being so sharp.

This is certainly so in sports. As the old order changed, most of the traditional Japanese games lost a great deal of their popularity and appeal. It is easy to understand how. These games, for the most part, were rough adaptations of

medieval military skills, designed originally for Eastern Ivan-
hoes and perpetuated in all their ceremony. There was judo,
which needs no introduction, and then there was kendo. In
this gentle samurai pastime, the two antagonists are attired
in ankle-length smocks, leather-and-bamboo breastplates,
and steel masks with protective leather padding which covers
the neck and shoulders. They go at each other with bamboo
poles, aiming at five body points: the abdomen, wrists,
throat, and the sides and top of the head. The man who first
scores two hits is the winner. Sometimes it doesn't take that
long. You can knock a man cold with a well-executed thrust.

Then there was karate, a kind of boxing with the open
hand and the kicking leg. Karate made its way to Japan from
China via the Ryukyu Islands. A conscientious karate man
hardens his fingers and knuckles, his soles and his toes by
continually pounding them or abrading them against hard,
rough surfaces. When he has got his mitts in shape, he can
split nine layers of cedar board with one blow—or kill a man.
Today, incidentally, the few karate masters who carry on
their old profession must get a license from the police, for
they are considered to fall within the same classification as a
man carrying firearms. (In the 1920s and '30s, when the military clique was increasing in power, karate, kendo, and the
other martial sports gained a great revival of popularity. At
the onset of the Occupation, General MacArthur prohibited
their practice and outlawed the Butokukai, the national organization which promoted them.)

Then there were archery and sumo wrestling, both of them
rooted in history and mythology from Japan's earliest days.
Archery took many nonmilitary forms down through the
centuries but none as skill-demanding as yabusame, an
equestrian variation devised in the Kamakura Era (1186–
1335) and continued down the years, with its original ritual
and trappings little disturbed, as an annual national event. In
yabusame each contestant is outfitted in splendid brocades

and silks, "chaps" of deerskin, and pointed black-lacquered hats with a center tassel of lustrous horsehair. Sitting a lacquered saddle astride his horse, he totes a seven-foot bow and a supply of blunted arrows tucked in his waist. What he attempts to do, as he grips his horse with his knees and gallops full tilt down a straightaway gravel runway 370 yards long, is to plant an arrow in three different target disks. These targets are set about four feet above the ground and are colored with concentric rings of black, green, red, and white. The targets diminish successively in size, the first being twenty-four inches in diameter, the third eight inches. Each contestant is allowed seven runs, or twenty-one tries. He is scored not only on his hits but on such technical niceties as the finesse with which he handles his bow, whips his arrows from his waist, fits the arrows, draws the bow. It takes a man about nine years of practice to become fairly good at yabusame.

Sumo, Japanese wrestling, dates back to the first century B.C. Among the traditional Japanese diversions, it unquestionably is the national sport. At present it is riding a crest of enormous popularity, one of the factors behind this being that it televises so well. Like those of yabusame, the roots of sumo were military, but the sport early acquired moral and religious overtones. It trained the heart and mind, so its ancient mystique asserted, and produced a type of man who was a mountain of virtue—courteous, sincere, faithful, considerate, and reflective. In any event, it produced physical giants, for in sumo the point is to topple your opponent to the mat. If any part of his body (besides his feet) touches the mat, you win. You also win in modern sumo if you force your opponent outside the curb of straw bags filled with sand which bounds the circular ring.

The actual bout in sumo usually lasts a matter of seconds and rarely longer than two minutes. It is the elaborate, theatrical prelude that makes the sport so fascinating for its aficionados. "Ten to fifteen minutes are consumed by the wrestlers' preparations," Frank Iwama, an old ringsider, has written. "Loosening up his muscles, he lifts his leg up sideways and brings it down with a resounding thud on the ring. He goes through this quite a number of times, rinses out his mouth several times, and follows this with a purification ritual. This is done by grabbing a handful of salt from a barrel placed in the corner of the ring for this purpose and throwing the salt into the center of the ring. Then with the referee standing in the middle—costumed in traditional brocade kimono and *hakama* (just like a Shinto priest) and holding a brightly colored fan—the big pot-bellied wrestlers crouch in the center of the ring facing each other. Just as they seem to be ready to spring at each other, one gets up leisurely to shuffle back to the salt barrel, throws some more salt into the ring, and then comes back. His opponent then does the same thing. This is repeated five or six times. As the deadline for time permissible for such antics approaches, the wrestlers get down to business and actually charge forward like two bulls. They meet in mid-ring with a smacking thud of quivering flesh, and the struggle is on."

Sumo stars have historically been human foothills weighing between 300 and 400 pounds. They amount to being a separate breed of Japanese and were consciously developed by selecting extra-large young boys for special training and feeding and by encouraging marriages between sumo champions and the daughters of sumo champions. Extremely aware that they are small in physique compared to the peoples of other nations, the Japanese have always taken immense pride in the sheer size of this home-grown species of giants, almost as if to say, "Look, some of our boys made it."

Forgetting about baseball—by the turn of the twentieth century Waseda and other college teams were almost on a par with ours—the Western sport in which the Japanese first earned world recognition was, surprisingly enough, tennis. In 1920 in Antwerp, when tennis was still on the Olympic agenda, the Japanese doubles team of Kumagae and Kashio went all the way to the final. In the early 1920s Japanese tennis players pulled off other stunning upsets, and in the Davis Cup Challenge Round in 1921, little Zenzo Shimizu, who could run all day, came within two points of defeating the lordly Tilden. That a Japanese could even stay on the same court with the likes of Tilden was frankly amazing, for they had very poor attacking strokes. The typical Japanese forehand drive, for instance, had the arching trajectory of a low lob; the players had grown up practicing not with regulation tennis balls but with high-bouncing rubber balls, and the only way to keep them in the court was to hit these looping top-spin drives. Furthermore, as the Japanese appreciated more acutely than anyone else, their physique was against them for tennis and, for that matter, for most modern sports. Compared to their competition, they were short and small-limbed. Moreover, they didn't pack as much strength and sinew in their arms, shoulders, and backs as did the Western athletes. What they achieved they managed by determination, discipline, and resourceful compensation. Centuries of squatting cross-legged on their rice-matted floors had bred a people with extraordinarily powerful thighs and legs. These they made the most of.

An ideal illustration is the story of Japan's first Olympic champion, Mikio Oda. In the 1924 Olympics, Oda came in sixth in the hop, step, and jump. This marked a new high for a Japanese track man. Twelve years earlier, when Japan had first entered the quadrennial international games, the two representatives sent over to Stockholm, a marathoner and a middle-distance man, had finished nowhere in sight. Eight years after that, a larger delegation, eleven track and field men (and two swimmers), had journeyed to Antwerp for the Games and had failed to place or come close to placing.

Hence, when Oda succeeded in capturing sixth place in the jump in '24, this mild enough triumph gave new heart to Japanese athletes and spurred Oda on to meticulous preparation for the next Olympiad. "My idea," he later wrote, "was to think out a method peculiarly suited to the Japanese physique, because I was convinced that there would be no sense studying Western methods of jumping by means of photographs and books." Thereupon he set about devising a new style based on the exceptional strength of his knee and ankle joints, deducing quite accurately that the national habit of squatting had developed these muscles to a degree that none of his foreign opposition could approach. In 1928, after three years of vigilant study and practice, Mikio Oda won his event in the Amsterdam Olympics. Four years later his countryman, Chuhei Nambu, employing the technique that Oda had pioneered, carried off the hop, step, and jump at Los Angeles.

That was in 1932, the summer the Japanese swimmers flabbergasted the sports world by winning five of the six major Olympic swimming events. (Buster Crabbe took the 400-meter free style, the single American victory in a sport we had dominated and expected to continue to.) The decisiveness of this Japanese sweep created the impression in the United States that Japan was historically an aquatic nation whose people were as much at home in the water as the Polynesians—they were simply just getting around to the Olympics.

This wasn't quite correct. Japan was a swim-minded nation but in neither a Polynesian nor a Western way. Endurance swimming and cold-water swimming were stressed, as was synchronized swimming in which a group performed certain movements in unison, like a shipwrecked Busby Berkeley chorus. The members of the line swam rhythmically while cloaked in heavy samurai armor, for example, or, floating in geometric patterns, they performed such stunts as fanning themselves, holding a parasol in the hand (and occasionally with the toes), or writing a Japanese poem on rice paper with a writing brush. When it came to speed, however, the Japanese were not in the swim. Their first two Olympic entrants, the duo who appeared in the 1920 Games, actually used the side stroke, and spectators watching their odd, maundering progress didn't know whether to laugh or to feel sorry for them.

Very much as Oda went about his problem, Japanese swimmers made themselves into champions by developing a style in which they used their major physical asset, their legs, to compensate for their lack of arm and shoulder reach. The key to this style was suspending the hips slightly lower in the water (in relation to the rest of the body) than conventional form ordained. With the hips slung in this lowered position, the legs were poised to unleash their fullest drive at hard six- and eight-beat kick tempos. This tremendous leg action powered the Japanese swimmers something like a jet: it created the basic momentum which the swimmer (eliminating the roll) augmented by driving his shoulders and arms through the water just as fast as he could, making up for the defect of his short arms by the very number and rapidity of his strokes.

One trouble with compensatory techniques is that the rest of the world does not stand still. Other athletes from other countries modify your ideas to fit their physiques or evolve new and sometimes more efficacious methods. If they are bigger and stronger than you to boot, you don't stay on top long. Brazilian track men, rangier than the Japanese, took the play away from them in their old specialty, the hop, step, and jump. Swimming, as we are all aware, has become an Australian province.

There are other troubles with compensatory techniques and, most assuredly, with the philosophy that this approach to sport regularly engenders. Training yourself into magnifi-

cent shape and using all the resourcefulness at your command—these are at the heart of sports, for pure skill by itself
only goes so far by itself. (When the Japanese fed their swimmers oxygen from tanks stationed at the poolside at the 1932
Games, old Olympic hands like Lawson Robertson, the veteran track coach, deemed this a quite acceptable extension of
resourceful preparation. Robertson had experimented as
early as 1908 with supplying Mel Sheppard, then our premier
half-miler, with oxygen.)

However, there is a point beyond which sport ceases to be
sport and becomes, in truth, almost the complete abnegation
of the spirit of sport. Sports are intended to be humanistic,
a source of real enjoyment for those who participate. They
are not supposed to be a morbid and ascetic realm in which
the athletes of different nations vie to see who can endure
the most punishing training, rationalizing that a winning performance may result and that the glory this brings to the
athlete's country more than justifies any hyper-Spartan extreme. Sometimes it is hard to draw the line, but there is a
decided difference between a reasonably dedicated athlete's
getting himself into peak condition and a halter-led athlete's
forcibly giving up the rest of his life and becoming a mere
vessel of sport.

This, of course, is happening in some respects in Russia
today and has happened in various countries at periods when
they wanted to cut a swath in the world of athletics and felt
that what they lacked in skill they could make up for by
drive, drive, drive. In this connection, Japanese swimming
coaches have frequently been under fire by education experts
and other Japanese for pushing their boys too hard, for applying the *tokko* or "special attack" approach to their training.
These methods, their critics claim, are the reason why Japanese swimmers burn out (in attitude as well as in performance) much quicker than Americans. (Kitamura, for one, the
brilliant fourteen-year-old boy who won the 1,500-meter

swim in the 1932 Olympics, was all done by the time the next Olympics rolled around.) If, they add, the Japanese technique is intrinsically attritive and can succeed only if the swimmer subjects himself to physical and emotional strain beyond the true measure of sport, well, it just isn't worth the effort. (It might well be interpolated here that while the apparent suicide of Jiro Satoh, the Japanese Davis Cup star of the '30s who vanished mysteriously from a transatlantic liner, has never been conclusively explained, most sports observers are of the opinion that the unrelenting pressure of representing his country well, even when he needed a respite from competition, is what pushed Satoh into his depression and over the edge.)

In any event, swimming is indeed a major Japanese sport and a highly organized one. The young boy with aquatic leanings gets into competition early, when he is still in grammar school. He competes for his junior high and his high school in official meets, and if he looks like he has the stuff to go to the top, he will probably be offered a college scholarship. Once on the varsity squad, he thinks swimming the year round. In the winter he works on his technique and conditioning (which, at one university, includes six different sessions of outdoor calisthenics daily during the squad's ten-day visit to a hot springs resort). In the spring when regular training commences, he works out two hours every morning and another two every afternoon, a usual order of procedure being to start with a couple of sprints followed by two or three 400-meter swims and winding up with the boys plowing 800 meters and 1,500 meters. The top Japanese stars never stop working on their styles and trying to find superior ones. To cite one example, Masaru Furukawa, the world's leading breast-stroke swimmer in 1955, changed his style radically that year to incorporate more underwater swimming; he decided he would swim the first forty meters underwater, submerged about a foot and a half below the surface.

Jiro Nagasawa, for another, the butterfly specialist, revolutionized that event in Japan by changing to the American dolphin kick. So it goes.

First-rank Japanese swimmers receive certain rewards that ordinarily do not come the way of swimmers. Cheered on by 12,000 to 15,000 fans at the big meets, they are talked about and lionized like football stars in America. When they must hang up the old swimsuit and bathrobe, they are sought after by the sports departments of newspapers and by radio-TV stations to serve as commentators and are pursued by industrial firms to coach the company swimming teams and do a little public relations on the side.

Undoubtedly the most popular Japanese athlete since the war has been Hironoshin Furuhashi, the marvelous distance swimmer from the Hamamatsu area, which has produced most of Japan's great swimmers. Called "The Flying Fish of Fujiyama"—a wonderful throwback to those good old alliterative sobriquets and one which went unchallenged for mouth-filling pleasure until Anderl Molterer, the Austrian skier, was knighted "The White Blitz of Kitz"—Furuhashi, though handicapped by having to live on the poorest diet imaginable for an athlete, broke records left and right in the years just after the war. It was his hard luck to have passed his peak before the Helsinki Olympics, and his performances there were a very bitter disappointment to the hopeful Japanese. Furuhashi came along, though, when Japan was hungry for an athletic hero and, being all of that, he remains a hero.

The national involvement in sport in Japan, as in our country, has increased year by year as more and more people have gained the money and the time for recreation. But the Japanese are not just avid participants. No other Asiatic people (and then some) compares with them as spectator sportsmen. Consonant with being the most modern of the Eastern nations, Japan long ago built excellent stadiums which in turn fostered an exuberant fandom. Besides, the Japanese simply love to look at things. (Sight-seeing amounts to a positive national mania.) During this last decade, the base of this pyramid of the sports-active and sports-minded has broadened as never before. The Kabuki actor, the traditional matinee idol of that slice of the female population which always feels incomplete unless it is carrying on a vicarious front-page romance, has been losing a lot of ground to the glamour men of sports. Radio and TV and the daily newspapers (which always played it big) have accorded sport wider and wider coverage. But the most telling tip-off on the boom is the existence today of *eleven* daily sports papers. Eight of these are not really major dailies, their circulations being less than 50,000. The big three, however, all have circulations of over 200,000, and *Hochi*, the largest, currently claims some 400,000 daily purchasers. *Hochi* was originally a straight newspaper, one of the oldest in Japan, founded in the early years of the Meiji restoration. In 1948, when it had lost much of its influence and many of its advertisers, its owners decided to turn the paper into a sports sheet, a sterling bit of Friday-morning quarterbacking as it has turned out. *Hochi* prints eight pages each day, six devoted to sports, one to radio and TV programs, and the other to amusements (stage plays, movies, concerts, night clubs). You can buy it for eight yen (about three cents) on the stands or subscribe to it for a month for 240 yen (about ninety cents).

The set percentages of space accorded the various sports in *Hochi's* six pages are a handy key to their relative importance and appeal. To begin with, three pages go to baseball the year round. One page goes to horse racing and all the other forms of racing in which betting figures as part of the scene. Bicycle racing, it is interesting to observe, is very much alive and may hold the equivalent position in Japan to harness racing here. Some sixty bicycle pits are spotted throughout the country, with the schedule worked out so that each pit gets six days of action a month. All the races, by the way, are sprints. One of the most surprising developments in recent years has been the success of hydroplane racing. This, some Japanese advance, is partially explained by the debut in recent years of women drivers, a phenomenon that epitomizes in one direction the total enfranchisement of the Eastern female and in another the up-up-up-beat of this kicks-happy postwar world. Except for the geishas, the female hydroplane racers are the highest-paid women in Japan. They make about $400 a month, almost eight times the salary of the average white-collar man.

The remaining two pages of *Hochi* go to sumo, swimming, table tennis, golf, mountaineering, skiing, and these other sports:

RUGBY AND SOCCER: The staple winter-season games, played in the months between the autumn baseball season and the spring baseball season by most of the high schools and colleges and some industrial teams.

TRACK: Besides the sprints, the Japanese are now concentrating on the distance events from 10,000 meters up through the marathon.

BOXING: Japan in 1952 produced its first world champion when Yoshio Shirai captured the flyweight title.

BASKETBALL: A coming sport most advanced in the state of Niigata, where the heavy annual snowfall prompted the building of good indoor facilities.

ICE HOCKEY: Not a coming sport at the moment, it is played only to a limited degree by schoolboys.

FIGURE SKATING: A surprising favorite. The six rinks in Tokyo are reserved months ahead down to their last practice square.

TENNIS: Perhaps the most patrician of games inasmuch as the clubs still pride themselves on their exclusivity, the ranking players invariably being the sons of ranking players of their generation.

JUDO: Still biggest in Kyushu, its historic home.

BOWLING: A new recreation that has caught on quickly but that is still a bit too expensive to fit into the budget of the average Japanese.

SAILING: High costs have been the chief factor in retarding what one would think would be a thriving sport but is surprisingly minor.

AMERICAN FOOTBALL: Like Rugby over here, it is played cavalierly by the smart set at some colleges and causes a wee public stir with its annual Rice Bowl game between the top college teams.

BADMINTON: The Japanese female has a traditional rapport with the shuttlecock, and the game should become almost as popular as it is in Malaya where there is a court in every back yard.

SOFTBALL: It is played by all ages and both sexes—so well, in fact, by the women that a team of Japanese girls broke even against male competition in a recent tour of Formosa.

Table tennis, golf, mountaineering, and skiing merit more extended comment. The latter two were nothing before the war, but, along with golf, they are now the sports which Japanese authorities (such as the editors of *Hochi*) believe have the biggest futures. To a considerable degree, the notable international successes of young Chick Igaya have contributed to the rush to skiing. Igaya, the former Dartmouth star, is the son of a skiing instructor from Nagano who saw to it that the boy was on skis as many months as possible, leading him progressively farther north, ultimately to Hokkaido, each year as the advent of spring melted the snow on the more southern trails. However, the main and commanding reason for the present boom in skiing is that, along with mountaineering, it has developed into a coed diversion, the newly emancipated girls joining their dates for weekend jaunts to the Japanese Alps and making the days on the slopes and the evenings around the old *hibachi* a lot more pleasant than they used to be. Though he likes to act the reserved, take-it-or-leave-it guy where women are concerned, the young Japanese male is very appreciative of the happy pretext that sports nowadays provide for enjoying the pleasures of mixed company. He has never fooled anyone anyhow. The super-flashiness he always puts on when he is having even a simple game of catch derives from his awareness that the girls may be watching—the same thing, really, as the American boy's trying to look like Joe Form as he passes a football on the beach. It is, to be sure, an old, universal and potent incentive—the women watching—and, as Jules Romains has written, it was probably one of the reasons why the French held Verdun.

We have earlier noted some of the exotic shapes the current Japanese infatuation with golf takes, and suffice it to add here that the game has made its advances in the face of the most discouraging of all obstacles, the paucity of free land in a country where nearly every available acre has long been used for the priority activities of living. Nevertheless, there are by the latest count 103 courses in Japan—ten are public—and twenty-five more are under construction, several along the margins of old river beds and not a few on land reclaimed from the ocean. The best Japanese courses are solid tests by the strictest standards and, what with their sculptured trapping and handsome trees, lovely to look at. They are beautifully cared for. It is not at all an unusual sight to look down a fairway in Japan and see a rough-to-rough line of women laborers, down on their hands and knees, moving toward the green like a slow wave as they pluck the weeds by hand. Since the 1957 Canada Cup match we know about the abilities of the winning Japanese team, Nakamura and Ono, and it should only be remarked in passing that they are not the only Japanese pros of tournament caliber. In the 1956 Canada Cup, which the American team of Hogan and Snead won at Wentworth in England, Hayashi and Ishii, who represented Japan that year, both shot 68 on the final round and finished a fine fifth, ahead of such reputable golfing nations as Scotland, Wales, and Australia.

Table tennis, a national passion for a long time, is more rampantly popular than ever these days now that the Japanese team has carried off the world championship two years in a row. The game was introduced to the islands a little over fifty years ago by one Seizo Tsuboi, a professor at Tokyo's Education College, who ran into it on a trip to England. Some five years later the game suddenly captured the Japanese imagination. Hotels set up tables in spare rooms, as they had earlier done for billiards. In factories and offices the employees chipped in to buy tables and played the game during lunch hour, which they continue to do today. In the late 1930s when Szabados and Kelen, the Hungarian masters, came over and were later followed by visiting American and Australian stars, the Japanese perceived with dismay that their best players were quite a few notches below championship level. There was interminable nationwide discussion as to whether the "penholder" grip (which they had always used) should be abandoned in favor of the "handshake" grip, and a new search for the right material for the paddle was undertaken. At this time the Western players were using rubber-faced paddles, the Japanese players cork, after having experimented with various kinds of wood including magnolia, paulownia, and Japanese cypress. Final decisions on these matters had to wait until after the war. The Japanese then decided they would stay with the penholder grip. As for the paddle, they have finally adopted a model that has a soft sponge-rubber face and produces fantastic spins. It is the ideal implement for the type of game the Japanese play, as their conquest of the table tennis world patently demonstrates. Today more than 250,000 addicts are registered with the Japanese Table Tennis Association, table tennis centers are everywhere (though thickest in the cold north), and the national pride in the sport is something to behold. "There is no money in operating a table tennis center," a not untypical owner of one such establishment declared not long ago, "but think of the honor of uncovering a potential world champion among my customers!"

In Japan's brimming world of sport, one meets up with the full roster of standard types each particular sport seems to nurture regardless of clime and circumstance. Japanese baseball, for instance, has its Stengels, its aging managers whose faces are lined like topographical maps and who speak with the rustic sophistication of men who have seen it all long, long ago. It also has its smooth young manager, the recently retired ballplayer who is on the verge of becoming a little too much the well-groomed junior executive and the television guest star. This vast vivarium of sports, from another point of view, brings forth every attitude imaginable and some singular extremes of emotion and deportment. Perhaps these extremes are really no more so than ours, but they are expressed differently and, consequently, they make a deep indentation on a Westerner.

There are, for example, moments when the turbulent Japanese heart, having kept itself in check till the last white line is passed, can restrain itself no longer and bursts forth in touching shows of absolutely honest sentiment. Such a scene took place a year ago last April when the victorious Japanese table tennis team assembled after the excitement of the final for its group picture. As the players shuffled into their positions before the camera, the captain, Ichiro Ogimura, drew from his pocket a photograph of Kichiji Tamasu, the young star who had died of a heart attack the previous January, and held the photograph before the trophy. Tamasu would have been a member of the winning team, Captain Ogimura felt, and it was only right that he be in the picture.

When orderliness is important, as it is in golf, where the

spectator is right on the playing field, the Japanese sports
fan can be the last word in co-operation. At the Masters in
Augusta, the best run of our annual tournaments, the huge
gallery behaves wonderfully well. At more than one presentation ceremony, Bob Jones has gone out of his way to tell
the patrons how much their conduct means to the players
and the tournament, pointing out with humor that there is
only one respect in which they fall down a bit: when a two-
some is on a green and the man in contention holes out,
some spectators begin to dash for the next tee instead of
waiting until the second player has also holed out. At the
Canada Cup matches last fall, the large Japanese galleries
comported themselves with all the savoir of Augusta veterans, although at least half of them were attending their first
big tournament. What is more, at every green they held
their places until each player—in this case, four—had putted
out. Then they walked quietly on to the next hole. I was
struck by this and asked one of the Japanese officials how in
heaven they had managed to achieve it. "Oh," he replied,
"on the back side of the pairings sheet the spectators receive
when they come through the gate, we asked them to do
that." That was that.

When he chooses, though, the Japanese sports fan can
make a lot of noise, and he generally chooses to when he goes
to the ball park. Professional as well as university baseball
has been accreted with the gala razzmatazz of American
college football. There is always at least one band in the
stands bursting periodically into some unlikely tune like
The Monkey Wrapped His Tail Around the Flagpole or
whatever that march is called. Between innings the cheer-
leaders for the rival sides, garbed in Music Hall costumes,
jump onto the tops of the dugouts and lead organized yells.
Individual players are exhorted hard and ridden hard, but
until a few years ago life was much easier for an umpire than
here in the States. On the field the ump was the constituted

authority and, brought up to respect authority, the players and managers rarely questioned his calls. Whenever a manager did, he bowed low and doffed his cap with a nice little sweep; he repeated these gestures and thanked his enlightener before returning to the dugout. In recent years, as we were saying, the sanctity of the umpire has been weakened. Having watched their idols, the barnstorming American stars, dish it out to the serfs in serge, the Japanese players have begun to make with the lip and to kick a little dirt around. Today when a manager bows low and doffs his cap, as often as not he does so with theatrically blatant mockery. It was better the old way.

When one looks down on the ball field from the stands these days, he notices a much deeper-going change. The players are a lot bigger than they were before the war, both taller and heftier. Where the average Japanese major leaguer once stood about five feet five inches or five feet six, today he is almost three inches taller. (Nagashima, the college bonus player whom the Tokyo Giants signed for over $85,000, is a strapping six-footer who weighs about 185.) This increase in size is not limited to the Japanese athletes. Most young Japanese are several inches taller than their parents, and there are more than a few lissome girls who have attained the hitherto unheard-of height of five feet six. A radical change in the national diet accounts for this, for the age-old repetition of rice and fish, fish and rice has since the war been replaced by a balanced diet emphasizing more fruits and juices, more meat, more green vegetables, more dairy products. In some schools milk is provided daily for the kids. Behind this drastic departure in diet lie the American Nisei, the sons of Japanese immigrants. When they arrived in numbers in Japan with the American forces, they shook the citizenry and made them question their thinking as did few other aspects of the unfortunate war. A Japanese, in his confusion and misery, might rationalize that the defeat had been brought about by the Allies' greater manpower and

productive capacity, and might buoy himself up temporarily
by retreating to the ancient propaganda that the Japanese
were a divine and superior race. It just wouldn't stand up,
though, when he saw the Nisei, tall, husky, hardy fellows, as
big as other American boys, a different breed from their
ancestors. "There is something wrong somewhere with our
ideas," the awed Japanese said to himself and to his neighbors, "if our own flesh and blood flourishes better in a foreign
country than at home."

Besides creating a taller people, the new diet is beginning
to nourish a stronger people. To cite a case in point, Japanese
baseball has always produced superb base runners and infielders, but in the other departments the standard has always
been definitely minor league. Even the best outfielders cannot make the long throw—they simply do not pack enough
tissue and sinew in their shoulders, arms, and hands. For the
same reason, their Bob Fellers do not own a real fast ball,
compensate as they will by unfurling the busiest leg action
you ever saw. This same deficiency explains to a good degree,
but not entirely, the chronic weakness of Japanese batters.
Most of the home runs are hit to the "opposite field"—right-
hand batters, for instance, dumping the ball into the stands
down the short right-field foul line. Even these hits are not
really well tagged as a rule. The batters, for some reason
or other, swing almost entirely with their arms and wrists,
rather stiffly, instead of taking a co-ordinated cut in which
the motion of the arms and the snap of the wrists are fluidly
tied in with the movement of the whole body. Nobody is
more aware of their deficiencies as batters than the Japanese,
and they are cautiously hopeful that the emergence of their
first natural power hitter in the person of Nagashima, the
bonus boy, is an auspice of the shape of things to come.

Happily, improving the national diet has not been the
only direction in which Japan has moved in its efforts to
salvage something constructive from its disastrous war. For

all of their abundant emotion and drive, the Japanese have steadied down appreciably and there are many evidences of a discernible new maturity. They have, for one thing, a better sense of selectivity and more confidence in their tastes. They are surer of what it is they like and admire in their native culture. They hope that outsiders will find appealing those things about it which they love, but it is almost enough for them that they themselves do. While their appetite for the Western and modern is greater than it ever was, their digestion has improved. The young people especially are now so thoroughly at home with many Western "institutions," like jazz, for example, that their knowledge is quite instinctive. In the old days a home-grown clarinetist who could copy Benny Goodman note for note was looked up to as a real musician. Today the kids can immediately spot an imitative performance and, having little patience with that sort of thing, they head for the coffee houses where they can hear someone like Toshiko Akiyoshi whose freshness they dig. The great thing is that they are also very much in tune with their own culture which, as the West is beginning to appreciate, holds so much that is wise and lovely and modern in any age.

You would have to look far for a better representative of maturing Japan than Torakichi (Pete) Nakamura, the stocky, forty-two-year-old hero of the 1957 Canada Cup match, the kind of self-possessed, unshowy and good-humored fellow you would like to have as your neighbor. He was extremely charming in victory, modest and very much himself. I remember best of all his appearance on a television show the following week, a program like the old *Home* show, on which he was interviewed by the local Arlene Francis. Replying to her questions, he told her how he had gravitated to golf: his family—his father was a woodcutter—had lived on a hill near a golf course; he had whittled his first club from the branch of a tree; he had started to caddie. . . .

"Well, it was certainly a marvelous triumph, Mr. Nakamura," the lady interviewer said. "It is very exciting to realize that our Japanese golfers are now the best in the world."

"I don't think that's quite accurate," Nakamura corrected her, breaking into an easy smile. "You see, everything was in our favor last week. We knew the course much better than the other players. We were used to the greens and many of the visiting players never got used to them. We were very lucky, too. Ono and I happened to be at the very peak of our games. Many of the other players weren't in their best form that week. That happens in golf."

"You mean that we cannot look forward to another victory next year in the Canada Cup?" the lady interviewer asked him with a twinge of disappointment.

Nakamura nodded. "That's much too much to expect," he said. "I think we will be doing very well if we finish among the first eight or ten teams next year. We're getting better, but there are many wonderful players in the world, you know."

Time was running out and the lady interviewer wrapped things up by again congratulating the man of the hour. "Thank you," said Mr. Nakamura, "it was a wonderful week. I never played that well before."

VISIT TO
A SMALL CONTINENT:
AUSTRALIA

1. IN FRONT OF THE
OUTBACK

This two-part article on Australian sports was written early in 1960 shortly after my return from a most edifying and enjoyable visit to that distant country. The reason for my going there in the first place was to cover, for *Sports Illustrated*, the Canada Cup match staged that autumn at the Royal Melbourne Golf Club and won most appropriately by the home team of Peter Thomson and Kel Nagle. Since golf was the sole subject of the dispatches sent home about the Canada Cup, it was accorded comparatively little space in this two-part article which followed, and I mention this because that game occupies a larger part in the Australian sports scene today than this study might indicate.

During the period I was in Australia, the beginning of the summer below the equator, the first concerted preparations were being made for the 1960 Olympic Games, then some nine months away. As it turned out, at Rome the Australian swimmers, though they did not pulverize their opposition as they had in 1956 at Melbourne, performed very well. John Devitt and Dawn Fraser took the 100-meter free-style races, Murray Rose took the 400-meter free-style, Jon Konrads the 1500-meter free-style, and David Theile the 100-meter backstroke. On the cinder track, Herb Elliott ran one of his greatest races in the 1500-meter run, knocking more than five seconds off the previous world record and finishing almost twenty yards ahead of his nearest pursuer. Some Australians, I am sure, had hoped for more sensational feats by their athletes, but, then, they have come to be as demanding of them as we are.

Sure enough, there was a slip in the corner of the basin; and on top of it two nice-looking lads in bathing clothes. . . . One of them said there would be no difficulty about a night's lodging for our boats; and the other, taking a cigarette from his lips, inquired if they were made by Searle and Son. The name was an introduction. Half a dozen other young men came out of a boathouse bearing the superscription ROYAL SPORT NAUTIQUE, *and joined in the talk. They were all very polite, voluble and enthusiastic; and their discourse was interlarded with English boating terms, and the names of English boat-builders and English clubs. I don't know, to my shame, any spot in my native land where I should have been so warmly received by the same number of people. We were English boat-men and the Belgian boating-men fell upon our necks. . . . But after all, what religion knits people so closely as a common sport?*

. . . And in the meantime we were led upstairs by our new-found brethren, for so more than one of them stated the relationship. . . . This one lent us soap, that one a towel, a third and fourth helped us to undo our bags. And all the time such questions, such assurances of respect and sympathy! I declare I never knew what glory was before.

"Yes, yes, the ROYAL SPORT NAUTIQUE *is the oldest club in Belgium."*

"We number 200."

"We"—this is not a substantive speech, but an abstract of many speeches—"we have gained all races except those where we were cheated by the French."

"You must leave all your wet things to be dried."

"O! Entre frères! *In any boathouse in England we should find the same.*" (*I cordially hope they might.*)

"En Angleterre, vous employez des *sliding seats,* n'est-ce pas?"

"*We are all employed in commerce during the day but in the evening,* voyez-vous, nous sommes sérieux."

These were the words.

—ROBERT LOUIS STEVENSON,
An Inland Voyage, 1878

AUSTRALIA is a sports-playing, sports-watching, sports-talking, altogether sports-minded country such as the world has never known before. As a result, when a person from a games-oriented nation such as the United States visits Australia and falls in with the local fandom and practitioners, the gentle rain of sports chatter falls on his ear from morn till night with only sporadic interruption. I have been back a while now from the trip I made to that friendly island continent this past autumn (for the primary purpose of watching the Canada Cup match in Melbourne), and even now I am hard put to recall any conversations in which sport was not the accepted subject or did not inevitably intrude and take over. I believe I can remember a few isolated questions not directly connected with sports: "How do you like our beer?" and "Your Marilyn Monroe—she's a good sort of sheila, isn't she?" (A sheila is a young woman in Australian slang, a lively congress of idioms which, for visitors who go jagging there, begins and remains pretty much of a brass razoo.) I think I can also remember participating in brief conversations on such nonsports topics as the merits of Australia's Holden automobile and why the government is doing a brilliant (or profligate) thing in tackling the mammoth Snowy Mountains project which will change the courses of rivers that start in the Australian Alps and send them flowing not eastward to the sea but westward into the countless arid acres of the interior desert that need water more than the Pacific does. It takes an effort, I repeat, to resurrect these interchanges, because if the other party is at all vulnerable, Australians will talk sport as if they existed for nothing else.

There is a lot to talk about. Until World War II placed it smack in the path of crucial circumstances, Australia was a sort of modern Atlantis, a lost continent. What did they have out there umpteen miles away? Kangaroos, sheep, boomerangs, and a few tennis players—so went the general conception. Beyond this, not a blessed thing, and nobody gave Australia much of a thought except in the stridently negative vein of Zero Mostel's famous far-out line in the post-Pearl Harbor night-club act in which he impersonated an isolationist senator who roared rhetorically, "And Hawaii! What was Hawaii doing out there in the middle of the Pacific Ocean in the first place?"

Since World War II, when the Allies' necessity to produce on the spot mothered an Australian steel industry and some attendant heavy manufacturing, Australia has come like the wind. Most importantly, because of the advances of the air age, the years of isolation from the rest of the world are finally over. Where Australians formerly grew up thinking in terms of London's being twenty-six days away—this was the usual length of time it took a ship to reach London from Free-mantle—today in the jet era Australia is less than twenty-six hours away from London or New York. At the same time, for all of this wondrous change, Australia remains a young country which is only beginning to investigate itself. Though it is approximately the size of the United States, only 10,000,000 live there, about the same number as in Pennsylvania. When, turning your attention to the gentler aspects of life, you then consider what the Australians have managed to do in the intensely competitive field of international sport

against nations drawing on huge populations, it simply stag-
gers your comprehension.

At the present time (the spring of 1960), for example,
Australia holds the Davis Cup, emblematic of world suprem-
acy in amateur tennis. In golf, it holds both the Eisenhower
Cup (the world's amateur team championship) and the
Canada Cup (the world's professional team championship).
It holds "the Ashes," which means that its cricketers defeated
England in the most recent test match. In women's swimming, nearly all the world's free-style records are presently
held by Australians. The country's male swimmers have
had an almost similar domination since 1956, the year of
Australia's sudden aquatic renaissance. In track and field,
its women athletes are unrivaled over the shorter distances,
and its men, since the arrival of John Landy in 1954 as the
world's second sub-four-minute-miler, have moved out in
front in the middle-distance events, such as the mile and
1,500-meter runs in which the current world's records (3:54.5
and 3:36) were set by the genuinely amazing Herb Elliott.

And what an array of individual stars, along with Landy
and Elliott, has been ushered forth! Peter Thomson, winner
of the British Open in 1954, '55, '56, and '58 . . . Frank Sedgman, that beautiful tennis player, two times a winner at
Wimbledon and Forest Hills . . . Lew Hoad, another two-
time winner at Wimbledon . . . not to mention Ken Rosewall, Mal Anderson, Ashley Cooper, and Neale Fraser, who
have all, in recent summers, won the United States championship and have made it four years in a row that an
Australian has done so . . . the two Konrads kids, Jon, now
seventeen, and Ilsa, fifteen, who between them hold over a
dozen world swimming marks . . . also in swimming, the
two record holders for the 100-yard free style, Dawn Fraser
and John Devitt, and that consummate stylist, Murray Rose,
who won the 400- and 1,500-meter free-style events in the
1956 Olympics. Let us mention just a few more and then call

a halt. Albert Thomas, the rising middle-distance runner, world's record holder at two miles and three miles. Merv Lincoln, the miler who has up to now been forced into the role of Elliott's shadow but who has five times broken four minutes. In auto racing, Jack Brabham, who ended his 1959 season as the winner of the FIA and world driving championship. This is by no means a complete catalogue, but there is no point in citing the heroines of women's track or the heroes of cricket and Australian Rules football in which our interest is, shall we say, somewhat less than white-hot.

Why are the Australians such superb athletes? Rather than jump headlong into listing the many factors of influence as formally as the ingredients of a pousse-café, perhaps it will be more meaningful to head there by somewhat slower stages, for there is a lot more to Australia and Australians than the conventional stereotype accommodates. "The romantic conception of the Australian," John Landy remarked this past autumn, "is a man on horseback on a dry flat plain. Frankly, he's pretty rare nowadays. We have been changing all along the line and at a very rapid rate. For example, up to recent years we haven't had too much of the automobile. Now we're certainly in the auto age. For another thing, we're fast becoming a race of city dwellers." Over a third of the 10,000,000 Australians, as a matter of fact, now live in two cities—2,000,000 in Sydney, the capital of New South Wales, and over 1,500,000 in Melbourne, the capital of Victoria. As good a way as any to become introduced to the country's unbelievable absorption in sport is to take a drive around either of these cities on a Saturday or Sunday. It soon becomes evident, even from this superficial vantage, why there is so much cream at the top of Australian sport: there is an enormous amount of milk at the bottom.

The Sunday after the Canada Cup match was concluded, I made my first extensive drive around Melbourne, weary of sports after four straight days of watching golf, quite unmind-

ful that I was setting up a classic appointment in Samarra, for
some friends had told me that on the weekend everyone
cleared out and went either to the beaches or to the handy
beauty spots in the Dandenong Mountains. Downtown,
true enough, there was no one around. On a Sunday—well,
let me put it this way—the residents of Sydney (who carry on
a feud with the residents of Melbourne akin to those between
Los Angeles and San Francisco, Montreal and Toronto) are
not far off the mark when they give you a mischievous little
wink and declare, "I spent a fortnight in Melbourne last
Sunday." All the bars are closed, no newspapers are printed
or sold, all the restaurants are closed, all the movie houses
are closed, all the sparkling new espresso shops are closed,
and it is even hard to get into the railroad station.

A little further out of town, though, in the large and
numerous parklands along and beyond the Yarra River, it
was entirely different: life was not only stirring, it was hum-
ming. (In keeping with the intercity rivalry, Sydneysiders
call the Yarra "the only river in the world that flows upside
down—the mud is on the top and the water is underneath."
The usual Melbournian rejoinder is to allude to the Harbor
Bridge, the pride and joy of Sydney, as "the world's largest
coat hanger.") In truth, I have never seen a comparable
smorgasbord of sports activity. In all the large parks every
tennis court was filled and track men were loosening their
fibulae on the periphery. However, the main activity was
cricket, December being the beginning of the Australian
summer. In one typical broad sweep of grassed land, no less
than seven cricket games were going on. The players in one of
these were clad, *comme il faut*, in white shirts and white
flannels, but in the other games they were dressed as hetero-
geneously as the line-ups in a Married Men vs. Single Men
baseball fracas at an old-fashioned factory outing. The children and wives of the players, strong-faced workingmen all,
lounged and ate sandwiches on the edge of the field or in

autos parked along the curb. In one of the vehicles there was invariably an eighteen-gallon keg of beer. The cricketers would adjourn their game every forty minutes or so, head for the keg and yield the pitch to the young'uns, and then, refreshed in mind and spirit, resume the battle.

"This is all very much like the United States at the turn of the century," I said to my cab driver after seeing this pattern repeated in park after park.

"That's what everyone says," he answered with a pleased smile. "America in 1895. Only our beer is supposed to be better. You put too many chemicals in yours. That's where the trouble is, isn't it?"

We drove past a stretch of the river clogged with families out boating, past a busy fly-casting club, and then past the Yarra Bend public golf course, thick with players. We slowed down at an intersection where a runner wearing a purple jersey and the marathoner's noble grimace was trotting in the wake of an automobile that was both pacing and protecting his progress through the traffic. Using the road that serves as the track for the Melbourne Grand Prix, we circled Albert Park Lake, where some were fishing and others sailing, and, after a quick inspection of an old Olympics building that is now headquarters for the local table-tennis set, headed up St. Kilda Drive and farther out of town.

In its uncluttered, livable, and leafy aspect, Melbourne resembles Boston perhaps more than any other American city. St. Kilda Drive, for sure, has much of the same look as Commonwealth Avenue. As the drive and the bay-front road that conjoins it ramble on far into the suburbs, they pass by or near the well-pressed grounds of a good sampling of the city's numberless clubs—tennis clubs, lawn bowling clubs, cricket clubs, football clubs, motor clubs, cycling clubs—which have arisen in response to the national thirst for sports, mateship, and alcoholic beverages, this last being available at the clubs' private bars at hours when the puritanical local laws have turned the public bars into deserts. On this Sunday nearly all of them seemed alive with some friendly competition, as did the swimming clubs and yachting clubs farther out of town along Port Phillip Bay. On this balmy December day the public beaches, too, were thronged. As we moved slowly inland to escape from the congested bay road, it occurred to me to ask the driver if the Australian bushman was a good swimmer.

"I don't know," he answered, "but some of those abos make pretty good jackaroos."

"Good-oh," I said. Later that day a kind bilingual friend explained that the driver meant to tell me that some of the aborigines make pretty good ranch hands.

Inland, albeit with a now tired eye after taking in this plethora of activity, we looked at a few of the dozen fine golf courses which occupy the Sand Belt country, including the new six holes which Dick Wilson, the American architect, is constructing for the Metropolitan Golf Club. Shortly after this, I decided to call it a day before I became completely sports-blind, and I explained to the driver, I thought, that this was why I wanted to return to the city and to be let off to recuperate at the Botanical Gardens.

"Oh, you don't see much going on on Sundays," he said, somehow missing my point. "Everybody and his brother shins off."

"I know," I said. "Out to Dandenong."

"Exactly," he said. "Saturday—now that's the day for sport here."

This is true, as I felt sure it would be and learned it was the next weekend. I will not weary you by describing in any detail what a summer Saturday in Melbourne is like. It isn't that many more people are engaged in sports, but the atmosphere is palpably more intense. The ambitious of all ages are competing in school, club, or more advanced competitions, and the young are out learning. At the Fawkner Park public

tennis courts, for instance, Don Tregonning, the head professional, and his aides were coaching several courtsful of kids
seven years old and up, quite a few of whom had come into
the city from over forty miles away for their Saturday lesson.
The Australian teaching pros think that mass instruction is
not particularly helpful, and certainly not as beneficial as
limiting a class to four youngsters, and the alacrity with
which their pupils pick up the elements of sound stroking
and hard hitting is extremely convincing.

In another section of town I looked in on a cricket school
run by Lindsay Hassett, for many years the captain of the
Australian eleven. That morning the students batting or
awaiting their turns at the stumps in three practice cages,
separated by rope netting, were working on the hook shot
which the batsman employs when a bowler has delivered a
short ball that bounces up high. (He should step across in
front of the wicket and slash the ball at a right angle to his
left.) Whenever Mr. Hassett or his assistants pealed forth,
"Let me see a big bold move with the right foot" or some
such fragment of instruction, there was appropriate attentiveness in the student body but never the thoroughgoing gravity
that tightened the faces of a group of middle-aged men seated
on benches to the rear of the bowlers. These were the fathers
of boys who were privileged to study with Mr. Hassett, and if
the nippers were perhaps too young to appreciate what a terrific thing that was, *they* knew.

Apart from being a day for purposeful tutelage, Saturday
is unlike Sunday in that the big spectator events, prohibited
on the Sabbath, take place. In the winter season, the whole
city turns out *en famille* at the six different stadiums for the
regular Australian Rules football matches between the twelve
professional teams representing different districts of Melbourne. The summer schedule is more diversified. On the
Saturday I am describing, for instance, the Victoria cricket
team was playing South Australia in the red brick stadium of

the Melbourne Cricket Club where, incidentally, the main events in the 1956 Olympic Games were held; the Victoria tennis championships were getting underway at Kooyong; Peter Thomson was in the process of wrapping up the ninety-hole golf tournament at the Victoria Golf Club sponsored by the Pelaco Shirt Company (whose more-English-than-the-English motto is, "It is indeed a lovely shirt, sir"); and, along with this, at Moonee Park the horses were running. Whenever they do it is a matter of more than feeble interest for Australians. They are the greatest bettors in the world, as a matter of record. In 1955, for illustration, pari-mutuel betting on horse races totaled $76,000,000 and betting with licensed bookmakers hit $467,000,000. Statisticians have worked out that this was tantamount to an average annual wager of $75 by every man, woman, and child. These figures, let me repeat, are now four years old and, in view of the rising national prosperity, they have undoubtedly been improved regardless of whether the breed has.

To describe the sports activities in Sydney on a typical weekend—Sydneysiders, naturally, would have you believe that Melbourne slumbers on as serenely as "Tazzie" (Tasmania) or "The Quaky Isles" (New Zealand)—would only proffer more of the same, and it would probably be best to touch merely on the salient respects in which Sydney is different. This it is for certain. To start with, it is situated about 450 miles northeast of Melbourne. While Melbourne has cold and damp spells in winter when the winds sweep up from Antarctica, Sydney has mild winters and long torrid summers which remind you that, for all the blocky, austere "architecture" that makes its outer suburbs reminiscent of the drab mill towns of the English Midlands, the city lies in a semitropical zone. From the point of view of climate it is accurate to say, as most people do, that Melbourne is like San Francisco and Sydney like Los Angeles, but it is

Sydney which *looks* like San Francisco. Lovely, sharp-pitched hills tumble down to the water on both the north and south shores of the glorious harbor, all the way from its narrow-necked opening into the South Pacific to its inner margin where it merges into the Parramatta River. Ferries painted green and mustard and trimmed with red ply across the blue water, but Sydney, liking to bustle and bubble and wanting no part of the ferryboat tempo (which, to a large measure, accounts for the magic that makes Hong Kong the most enjoyable city in the world today), began the erection in 1923 of the Harbor Bridge which, 1,650 feet in length, was the largest single-span bridge in the world at the time of its completion. Today downtown Sydney has, much to its delight, attained the thrashing pace of an American city complete with such flowerings of modern urban culture as department stores stocked with international goods, a shortage of taxis and constant fighting for those there are, and a Greenwich Village section called Kings Cross inhabited by artists, a local variety of beatniks, and young men who would like nothing better than to be mistaken for Americans and who are accordingly called "Kings Cross Yanks."

Above all else, Sydney is an aquatic city. On a warm, sunny Saturday afternoon, the harbor is crammed with sailboats, principally eighteen-footers, dragons, and V-J's (Vauclose Juniors), a class originated in Vauclose Bay. The boats capsize more frequently than over here, since it is the hallmark of the Australian sailor, who is nothing if not daring, to pile far more sail on his boat than it was designed to take. Everybody swims, even the Kings Cross Yanks, so puissant is the call of the water. They swim, body-surf, and surfboard in the breakers that cream up the yellow beaches at Bondi, Manly, and other outer districts that front on the ocean. They swim at the smaller strips of beach along the irregular inlets of the harbor and in harborside pools, wooden-frame rectangles which edge out into the water, some of them equipped with peripheral underwater netting to keep the sharks out. (On the ocean beaches the sharks come in close to the shore and there are casualties, but the Australian calmly accepts this risk as just part of the game, the way a Canadian accepts the probability of some broken bones as a possible price for the joys of hockey.) And they swim in orthodox pools, an ever-increasing number of them. "Swimming pools are becoming like service stations," Frank Guthrie, one of Australia's outstanding coaches, commented recently. "Every city council is putting them up. Five years ago in Greater Sydney we had three Olympic-length pools, fifty meters long. Next summer there'll be twenty." The need for more facilities becomes more explicit when you realize that during the first week of summer this year no less than 56,000 people paid their way into the Canterbury Municipal Pool, which Guthrie runs with the aid of five assistants. It is simply in the air in Sydney —learning to swim, to swim well, to swim superlatively. The first four girls ever to break five minutes for the 400-meter free style all lived in Sydney within eight miles of each other. At the present time there are 1,200 boys and girls around the city training seriously—that is, working with the idea that they are going to be champions like the Konrads kids.

The amazing Konradses, Jon and Ilsa, do their swimming at the municipal pool in the bleak industrial suburb of Bankstown. They started coming to the Bankstown pool in 1953 when Jon was eleven and Ilsa nine. Jon could swim forty yards and Ilsa could just about negotiate the width of the pool. Four years later, with little advance warning, first Jon and then his sister began smashing records left and right. Having been informed that the Konradses' early summer training schedule called for a daily session from six to seven-thirty A.M. and another session after school from four to six P.M., I went out to see them in action, for to be in Australia and not watch the top athletes perform is as unthinkable as to journey to Chartres and skip the cathedral. Being a typical red-blooded American tourist, I chose, naturally, to look in on a late afternoon session. In my mind a definite picture had formed of what I would see. The Konradses would have the pool to themselves, as befitted world champions training in this Olympic year. As they churned up and down, up and down, their styles would be carefully noted by dozens of openmouthed youngsters who had done their swimming earlier and were standing around toweling themselves off. Not at all! The pool was dense with the bobbing heads and splashing arms of 200 to 250 kids. Some were simply horsing around in the water, but many of them were churning up and down, up and down, the length of the pool, just like Jon and Ilsa were doing—once you located the Konradses in the tangle. None of the other swimmers seemed to be aware that they were the Konradses. At least, nobody bothered to get out of their way, and there in front of you, as you watched Jon, for example, was the curious spectacle of a world champion dodging a ten-year-old, barreling forth for five uninterrupted yards, cutting out and around two girls chatting as they dog-paddled, treating himself to seven yards of open water, breaking speed and swimming around a small body doing the dead man's float, and so on and on. I later mentioned to Don Talbot, the chunky young Bankstown coach who brought Jon and Ilsa along, that in the early morning sessions I imagined things were different. "No," he answered, looking at me with a mild expression but one which seemed to imply, nevertheless, that I didn't get the picture. "It's no different in the mornings. Everybody's here, the lot of them. Cold days, rainy days, windy days, they're all here."

Away from Sydney and Melbourne in the smaller cities and towns the pace is understandably less agitated, but the same mosaic of men in motion is generally true there, as it is in Brisbane in tropical Queensland, churchified Adelaide (the capital of South Australia), and the lovely city of Perth way out west on the rim of the Indian Ocean. I am sure it obtains as well in Alice Springs. One of the disappointments of my trip was not having the time to go out to "The Alice"—as the Australians affectionately refer to this cluster of 3,000 adventurous souls congregated in the very center of the continent in the heart of the broad, scarcely inhabited, bone-dry desert called the Outback—but something tells me that even there under the scorching sun there must be tennis courts, the rough lineaments of a race course, and some lonesome young Bradman noisily practicing his cricket strokes against the corrugated-tin walls of his house.

This terrarium of sport was the last major land mass discovered by Western man. For centuries before it "turned up," European geographers, much as they later had intimations that there could well be a northwest passage across the American continent to Cathay, used to inscribe the words *Terra Australis* (Southern Land) on their maps in the middle of the uncharted expanse of the South Pacific, for they had somehow picked up the notion that a continent existed there. Sure enough, it did. Dutch explorers were the first to hit it, William Janszoon reaching the north coast in 1606. Not unfittingly, it was Captain James Cook, that peerless navigator, who made the first considerable studies of the new continent. In 1768, when he was only forty years of age but already well known as an astronomer and mathematician as well as a marine surveyor through his work in the St. Lawrence River and the waters around Newfoundland, Cook was placed in command of the *Endeavor* which was to carry Sir Joseph Banks and other scientists of the Royal Geographic Society to the South Pacific to observe the transit of Venus expected to occur in that area the following June. These observations duly accomplished from Tahiti, Cook set sail westward, circumnavigated New Zealand, pushed further west, and struck the east coast of Australia in the spring of 1779. He charted the whole of that coast with his characteristic thoroughness and claimed it for Great Britain. Botany Bay was so named by the naturalists aboard the *Endeavor* and New South Wales by Cook himself because of its resemblance in his mind to the countryside around Glamorganshire. On a subsequent expedition, the second of Cook's three great explorations of the Pacific, he passed within the Antarctic Circle below Australia as he sought to determine the southern extent of that continent or the existence of another in those unsailed waters. On this trip, besides verifying earlier dim findings throughout the Pacific, discovering New Caledonia and Norfolk Island, surveying Tierra del Fuego, and recharting all of the South Atlantic, Cook also discovered how to cope with scurvy. He lost only one man of his complement of 118 despite being at sea for over 1,000 days on a voyage equal in miles to three circumnavigations of the globe.

The actual settlement of Australia was a left-handed result of the revolt of the American colonies. For 150 years prior to the Revolution, England, feeling the pinch of overcrowding and high unemployment even at that early date, had adopted "transportation" as a method of dealing with lawbreakers and political offenders, and thousands had been sent to America. With this traditional solution no longer available, William Pitt's government decided in 1786 to try out the new lands of New South Wales. Transportation to Australia began a year later and continued until 1838. The first settlement (initially at Botany Bay, then at Sydney) was commanded by Captain Arthur Phillip of the Royal Navy, a man of unusual size. Phillip made it clear from the outset that he conceived of Australia as no mere dumping-ground for prisoners but as the core of a colony, open to free settlement and to the rehabilitated, that could grow into an outpost of the empire. Some of Phillip's successors pursued this policy. Others were more sympathetic to the demands of the "exclusives," officers of the civil and military service (such as the New South Wales

Corps) who had received land grants and were anxious to acquire more land since it had quickly become obvious that fortunes could be made in sheep farming. The most affluent of these landowners was one John Macarthur, driving, voracious, reckless, and, withal, a man with a touch of genius when it came to sheep. Sent back to England to face court-martial for his defiance of the colony's economic policy, this early supersalesman got British traders all steamed up about the future of the infant Australian wool industry and eventually returned with breeding rams from the royal flock and authorization to purchase for himself 5,000 more acres of land. It was Macarthur who made the brilliant decision to import the fine-fleeced Spanish merino sheep to Australia, a climate in which he felt they as well as their owners would prosper, as indeed they have.

It wasn't too long, though, before Macarthur was locking horns with the new governor of the colony—of all people, William Bligh, the same severe, redoubtable character who some twenty years previous had been relieved of command of *H. M. S. Bounty* in the famous mutiny. Cast adrift in a small open launch off the Tonga Islands, Bligh and eighteen men finally landed at the island of Timor after a voyage of 4,000 miles. Governor Bligh's experience with Macarthur had a strangely similar echo to this earlier chapter in his ill-starred career. Macarthur provoked a showdown and Bligh retaliated by arresting him for trading irregularities. Macarthur was never tried, however, shimmying out of that trial with the aid of his friends who constituted the court. Re-arrested, he not only obtained his release a second time but persuaded Commandant Johnston of the New South Wales Corps to arrest the governor. Bligh was kept a prisoner for two years and then released only on his assurance that he would return to England. This he did but, true to form, he had the last word with Commandant Johnston if not with

Macarthur. The Commandant was ordered back to London, court-martialed, and dismissed from the service.

Though the dramatis personae were seldom this flamboyant, the formative years of Australia were replete with fractious disputes between the landed, who wanted more land, and the "emancipists" and small settlers who desired a more egalitarian society. Through it all, the compact colony slowly expanded. The formidable coastal mountain range was crossed and the plateaus and valleys beyond opened up. Large-scale free immigration at length commenced in 1832. Melbourne was founded at about this time and suddenly became the country's economic center when gold was discovered in 1851, the richest deposits around Bendigo and Ballarat. There were minor gold and silver rushes later and continual pastoral expansion but, for the most part, little stability in an economy that wavered sharply with the rises and falls in the price of wool. To challenge this unsatisfactory state of affairs, combative trade unionism grew up, but the great strikes of the 1880s and 1890s resulted in defeats for the unions. However, by organizing for political action in the years preceding the establishment of the Commonwealth of Australia in 1901, labor gained through political channels the points it had failed to bring off through its earlier methods. "If the middle class had stood neutral in politics in the latter half of the nineteenth century or turned solidly to the support of the oligarchists," C. Hartley Grattan, that acute observer of Australian affairs, has written, "political labor would have had a far harder and longer struggle for power. Labor recognized this, for obviously it formulated its early election programs to attract middle-class votes as well as those of its own normal followers. It was this discovery of the common ground between the workers and the small, liberal middle class that gave the democratic forces in Australia their head."

As far as the outside world was concerned, all this skirmishing was purely a storm in a billypot. It was not until World

War I that the northern hemisphere for the first time had a good look at the kind of men Australians were. Over 325,000 Diggers served overseas, and their outright bravery at Gallipoli and in other fearsome actions earned the admiration of a world that had not known what it had expected but certainly had not foreseen what the Australians had shown. After the armistice, everyone went back to look after his own back yard and Australians went back to theirs and to the same old bitter battle for political power between the conservative element, which believed that the country's prosperity lay in supporting a good measure of free enterprise, and the labor groups, which advocated a good measure of state socialism as the best means for making real the long-vaunted national ideal of mateship. Only when World War II broke out did Australia again emerge from obscurity, this time for keeps. Overseas the Australian soldier solidified his reputation and back home the country became far more industrialized, pushed forward into modern times over and past its own inertia by its technologically advanced Allies. Since the war Australia has been in the big leagues. It hasn't pitched very often, if you will pardon this sportified analogy, but it plays a very good left field—and, most important, it's been in the ball game.

Australia's continued prosperity since the war undoubtedly has had a lot to do with the splendid results of the new immigration program, its biggest postwar step, which has seen 1,500,000 people pour in during this last decade. These are the "New Australians," drawn from Italy and Sicily, from Hungary and other central European countries, and from northern Europe as well as from Britain. Their story comprises a heartening and almost unique chapter in the sad and often tragic annals of immigration. They are not only thoroughly accepted but are extremely popular. Many of the New Australians are employed in heavy and medium industry, where their zeal for work has been happily contagious, but their mark is most clearly visible in the changing cityscape of Melbourne and Sydney. Until quite recently the bulk of the downtown areas of these cities had all the charm of Glasgow, with the traffic lights the only spots of color. Today this cheerless sepia sea has finally been punctuated for fair. There are dozens of new restaurants, operated by New Australians, which bear no resemblance to third-class railway waiting rooms, dozens of new bakeries, new flower shops, new specialty shops, new pizzerias, new music stores, new delicatessens and hundreds of new espresso shops—nothing lavish, but each bequeathing a nice little note of gaiety and a whole new range of products to enjoy. "They taught us how to eat," an Australian public relations man I know blurted out one day as he toyed with his dish of cassata. "What do you think you could have got here in our restaurants five years ago? Fish and chips and a piece of steak with an egg on top of it. Then you'd had it." He paused to refill our glasses. "Look, we produce fairly good wines here and now we all drink it with our meals. Five years ago if you saw a bloke you knew drink a little plonk, you'd begin to wonder about him, the crazy plonko. The New Australians were just what we needed."

In the nature of a footnote, I would like to add an anecdote which amuses me when I think back on it. One Saturday when an Australian friend and I were taxiing around Sydney, we asked the driver, whose European accent and excellent English instantly established him as a New Australian, to tune in the radio to the sports roundup which goes on all afternoon, jumping from a track meet to a cricket game to a horse race and so on. At the top of a hill we left the cab momentarily to take in the panorama of the harbor, and, upon returning to it, we found that the broadcast had shifted from the account of the final of the Victoria tennis championship between Neale Fraser and Roy Emerson to the sixth race at Randwick. I asked the driver if he remembered the last score in the tennis match and he answered waveringly that he thought it was something like 20–20. I mentioned this to my friend when he got out at the next stop, remarking with my superfluous acumen that if the driver had got tennis scoring mixed up with some other game, it only went to show that the superadaptable New Australians were humanly fallible. The next morning, greeting the new day via the sports pages of the *Sydney Herald*, I learned that the second set between Fraser and Emerson had been a grueling, extended affair. Fraser had finally pulled it out 25–23.

From the beginning Australia was a land of hardy, outdoor men, but it was almost as slow in developing sports stars of the first caliber as it was in other directions. Australian sport seems to divide itself into three main eras: an early period from 1800 to 1920, a middle period from 1920 to 1946, and the present bonanza period from 1946 on. In the nineteenth century there was, as you would expect, sort of a frontier cast to recreation. The big game, as in the mother country, was cricket. (The first test match with England was played in 1877, the Australians providing surprisingly tough opposition from the start.) Horse racing most commonly took the form of "picnic races," held on makeshift tracks at someone's station (or ranch) as a feature of a weekend outing. In the cities the courses were hardly less primitive. Bullock trays made up the first grandstands and the tracks were marked off by saplings and rough palings. (The first running of the Melbourne Cup, the national classic, was held at the Flemington course in 1861. From the outset interest in it was considerable, but it did not presage that the time would come when the day of the race, the first Tuesday in November, would be an official state holiday in Victoria on which no one goes to school or to the office.) There was some track and field. An Australian by the name of E. H. Flack won the 800- and 1500-meter events in the 1896 Olympics but, significantly, he lived and trained in

London. Professional foot racing was far more popular. Its centers were the old gold-mining towns like Bendigo and Stawell where, long after the first rich strikes had been exhausted, the inhabitants were still possessed by the urge to plunge heavily and found an outlet of sorts in betting on foot races. The Bendigo Thousand and the Stawell Gift, a 130-yard handicap race, still go on today. Leading up to the Stawell Gift's final, which can be worth as much as $11,500 to the winner and his backers, are heats run on autumn weekends. The idea, of course, is to bring your runner along slyly under wraps so that while he manages to stay alive in the qualifying heats, he nevertheless disguises his full speed in the preliminaries and is assessed helpful handicaps by the officials, who allot the handicaps in much the same way that horses are assigned different weights. Even today, I am told—it is like a page out of Conan Doyle—in the months prior to this race you will find trainers who have come up with a good, fast lad hiding him away in some secluded hamlet in the bush where no one can put a clock on him and so ruin the chance for a big killing by backing him heavily and bringing the odds down.

The most celebrated of these early professional sprinters was Jack Donaldson, "The Blue Streak." The fastest human alive, Donaldson set a world mark for 100 yards (9⅗ seconds) and, in 1913, for 300 yards (29⅖ seconds) which stood for more than three decades. (Mel Patton finally cracked the 100-yard record in 1948 after Herb McKinley had bettered Donaldson's time for 300 yards in 1946.) However, the first national sports hero in the modern sense was Norman Brooks, the tennis player. A deliberate man of dour visage who could concentrate like a Hogan, Brooks was twenty-eight when he made his debut in Davis Cup competition in 1905, the same year he was defeated in the challenge round at Wimbledon. Two years later, with his rare instinct for half-court play backed up by an improved spin service, Brooks broke through at Wimbledon and then led the Australasia team—the other half was Tony Wilding of New Zealand—to its historic Davis Cup victory over the British Isles by taking his two singles matches in straight sets with the loss of only sixteen games. Australasia—it wasn't until 1923 that Australia and New Zealand fielded separate teams—successfully defended the cup against challenges by the United States in 1908 at Melbourne, in 1909 at Sydney, and in 1910 at Christchurch in New Zealand before falling before the British in 1911. This four-year reign confirmed the Antipodes as a ranking tennis power, and in 1914 they reconfirmed it, as airline terminology would have it, by wresting the cup back from the United States at Forest Hills. This was the occasion of the dramatic return match between Brooks and our young, hard-hitting star, Maurice McLoughlin, whom Brooks had outlasted in five sets at Christchurch. After a monumental battle in the opening set, McLoughlin finally won it at 15–13, and the next two came rather easily at 6–3. Brooks at this time was thirty-six. He was forty-two when he made his farewell to Davis Cup competition in 1920, losing then to both Tilden and Johnston but only after pushing these gifted young men to four sets. By this time, largely because Brooks's exploits had fired the imagination of his countrymen, other Australians, Gerald Patterson and Pat O'Hara-Wood among them, had followed in his path to the forefront, the first of a continuous line of superb players who would do so, and tennis had become rooted as a national game.

In the middle period (1920 to 1946), Australia was represented more regularly than before in international sports competitions but made only a secondary impress. This was due not so much to a decline in its own standards as it was to the new levels of excellence being reached by the athletes of other nations, in particular the United States, which in the 1920s entered upon an authentic Golden Age of Sport.

In tennis, for example, Australia was forced to take a back seat during these two decades while the United States, France, and Britain enjoyed successive Davis Cup dynasties. It was not until 1939, again on the eve of a great war, that Australia regained the cup, this time through the agency of John Bromwich and Adrian Quist. In track and field and in swimming as well, Australia all but dropped out of sight during this period. This was surprising inasmuch as Australia from the 1890s on had produced great swimmers, not to mention the term itself, "the Australian crawl." (Alec Wickham, a Polynesian, is credited by many authorities with being the first to use the double overarm stroke, moving both arms out of the water and employing a real leg thrash. When Wickham first performed in Australia, so one story goes, a pool owner, one George Farmer, exclaimed, "Look at that fellow! He's crawling over the water!") Nevertheless, after the 1924 Olympics, when one thought of swimming he no longer thought of Australia; instead, he thought of the Americans (personified by Johnny Weissmuller with his 6/3 crawl beat, the first swimmer with a modern balanced technique) and, later, he thought of the Japanese.

On the other hand, the golf got better. The first Australian golfer to attract attention was Joe Kirkwood who is remembered not so much for his tournament play as for being the pioneer (and the best) of the trick-shot artists. As for the more specialized sports, in sculling there was Bobby Pierce, the carpenter who won the singles sculls in the 1928 and 1932 Olympics, and in billiards Walter Lindrum, whom many Australians consider their "greatest ball-game master," a claim that seems grandiose until you realize that Lindrum gained the world's championship in English billiards in 1921 and held it undefeated until he retired in 1951. Lindrum, in fact, was so superior to his competition that he could get a match only if he spotted his opponents a handicap of 7,000 points. At the present time, this neat, clear-eyed little man, sixty-two years old, reminiscent of Willie Hoppe in his intuitive class, runs a billiard parlor in Flinders Lane in Melbourne when he is not on exhibition tours adding to the $6,500,000 his appearances have already raised for charities.

In the major sports the big exception to Australia's generally static position between the two wars was its ascendancy as a cricket power—*the* cricket power. The beginning of Australia's dominance was heralded when England went down to defeat in the first eight test games after the war. In 1930 the old country's dreams of regaining its former perch were dealt a smashing blow, for the matches that year witnessed the arrival of Don Bradman as the cricketer of the century. As you probably know, in cricket it takes the equivalent of a solid .320 hitter in baseball to score 100 runs, or a century, in top-flight competition. To give you an idea of Bradman's prowess, on his first crack at strange English wickets in the 1930 matches he reeled off successive scores of 254, 334, and 232. He won that series of games single-handedly and his batting probably decided the outcome of about half the test matches in which he appeared until his retirement in 1948. This wiry, average-sized, inexhaustible real-estate clerk was, it seemed, eternally at bat, staring gimlet-eyed at a succession of harried bowlers and then lashing the ball to all corners of the field with one decisive stroke after another, hour after hour—in fact, day after day. Now Sir Donald and a broker in Adelaide who rarely struts his stuff except at clinics for kids, Bradman remains very much alive in the memories and conversations of his countrymen. His special gift, it is almost unanimously agreed, was his unbelievably quick reflexes, the infallible union of eye and hand that enabled him to fathom what the ball was doing in the split second between the instant it bounced off the turf, spinning or breaking every which way, and the instant he dispatched it with the proper biting stroke.

Bradman was one of the two great heroes of this period.

The other was Phar Lap, the New Zealand-bred chestnut gelding, winner of the Melbourne Cup, the Victoria Derby, the Australian Jockey Club Derby, and many other races. In the spring of 1932 when Phar Lap, then a six-year-old, came to America to race, all of Australia was with him in spirit. The country swelled with pride when he won his first important start, the $50,000 Agua Caliente Derby. You can imagine the national shock when the tragic news came through a week or so later that Phar Lap was dead. The circumstances were mysterious, but for Australians it was hard fact and not conjecture that he had been poisoned, put out of the way by gangsters who had lost heavily on him. Phar Lap was carried back to Australia, his heart enshrined at the Institute of Anatomy in Canberra, and his body stuffed and mounted and placed in a signal position in the National Museum in Melbourne.

Most Australians have by now forgiven us for not taking better care of Phar Lap, but there are still a number of people, I was told, who find it hard to suppress their bitterness. On the afternoon I went to see him at the museum in Melbourne, I was wondering if perhaps I would hear any outbursts of recrimination. It was a rainy afternoon, and when I arrived there was no one else in the large hall where the big chestnut racer, magnificently mounted, stands enclosed in glass, extraordinarily lifelike, noble of eye, a snaffle bit in his mouth and black-and-white reins resting on his neck. I gazed at him for five minutes and then, awaiting the possible arrival of some Australians whose remarks I might overhear, studied the adjacent collections of bowerbirds and mollusks. At length two little girls, about twelve, I would guess, entered the hall and slowly made their way along the wall of exhibits leading to the corner where Phar Lap stands. I quietly drifted near them. For a minute or so they looked up at Phar Lap wordlessly. Finally one spoke up and said to her friend with that singularly breathless, liquid intona-

tion that children of English stock alone have, "He's lovely,
isn't he!"

There were few if any indications at the close of World
War II that we would soon be seeing Australia bursting forth
as a kind of super-California producing wonder athletes in
a wide field of sports. It did not happen immediately. We
are apt to forget that in tennis, for instance, so commanding
has Australia's dominance of the amateur game been in the
last decade, its first postwar Davis Cup teams were no
match for ours. But in 1950 Australian sports entered an age
every bit as golden as the Twenties were in the United States.
The Davis Cuppers led the way, the prospect of acting as
host to the 1956 Olympics spurred the nation on, Landy in
track and the late John Marshall in swimming astonished
their countrymen by their feats and their methods of training, and, before you knew it, Australia had established itself
as the land of the record breakers. Interest in sport, both
participant and spectator, has now reached such an exuberant
pitch that even the Australians themselves are sometimes
startled by it. I remember in particular the semi-soliloquy an
Australian friend who was marshaling at the Canada Cup
match addressed partly to the blue skies and partly to me
as he watched a gallery of 10,000 come pounding down the
fairway toward the green he was patrolling. "Quo vadimus?"
he exclaimed. "Golf today, tennis tomorrow, then the fights,
foot racing on Thursday, and so on and on, endlessly. What
the average Australian does when he gets to heaven and finds
there are no sporting fixtures, God only knows."

2. MAY THE MAGPIE
FLOURISH

THE MORE YOU GET TO KNOW about Australia, the more you appreciate that there is no other fact, except possibly its very isolation, quite as significant as the odd disparity of 10,000,000 occupying a land about the size of the United States. There is plenty of room for certain—only 3.5 people to the square mile, while in Europe there are 327. Since just about every aspect of life in Australia seems to be reflected in its sports, it should come as no surprise to discover that Australian Rules football, the one new game the country has invented, is played on an oval field roughly 200 yards long by 150 yards wide, about twice the size of an American football gridiron. A cross between Gaelic football and Rugby with some overtones of basketball—the eighteen players on a side are pitted in man-to-man duels—Australian Rules is too complicated to describe in a single paragraph. For our purposes, it is sufficient to note that it is a wide-open game which features rugged tackling (below the neck and above the knees), long and controlled drop-kicking, and a spectacular specialty called "high marking" in which a player will leap way off the ground to catch a ball booted into his territory and the man covering him will try to get up even higher, for if either succeeds in pulling the ball in on the fly and holding on to it, his team receives a free kick on the opponents' goal from that spot.

Though you would expect it to be and would foresee that it might yet be, Australian Rules football is not presently the national game. It is played only in the three states which front on the Southern Ocean—Western Australia, South Australia, and Victoria, with Melbourne its hotbed. This undoubtedly goes a long way toward explaining why Sydney (the capital of New South Wales, the most populous and influential state) has stubbornly stuck with Rugby, for the two metropolises are intransigent rivals, and for Sydney to take up something Melbourne is famous for would amount not to adoption but capitulation. In the southern Australian states, though, the Australian Rules season brings on a rampant fever of interest comparable to our annual autumn madness. Everyone roots for his or her team as ferociously as Brooklynites once barracked for the Dodgers long ago (see Herodotus, Chapter XXXI) and this applies to persons whose temperaments are otherwise noticeably restrained. I am thinking particularly of John Landy, that excellent young man. Talking about running and himself and Australian mores one evening last fall, he spoke in a lapidary manner, qualifying a statement here, painstakingly revising an opinion there, for he has a thoughtful, nay, a scholarly mind. Somehow the conversation swung to Australian Rules, and the instant it did, he became another man. Everything poured out with a boyish speed and he sat smiling at his own fervor as he rattled on about a memorable match ("Oh, it was a mighty game. Essendon was fit as a fiddle . . . ") or lamented the fact that no one who has not attended a grand final can imagine the excitement of "that moment just before the struggle begins when the mob of over 100,000, which has been absolutely quiet when they play 'God Save the King,' suddenly explodes with a mass roar, everyone shrieking a yell of allegiance to his team."

The lineaments of Australian Rules football had been outlined to me a few evenings before my session with Landy at an exceedingly pleasant dinner at the home of Joseph Wren who, among his other enterprises, runs the boxing in Australia. I had been "put onto" Joe Wren by Peter Thomson, an old golf friend, and I want to tell you about part of that evening because it seems to me to afford a convenient portal to understanding how sport is entwined in the lives of Australian families. The Wrens live in a district of Melbourne called Kew in an English-style house with a tennis court. Before dinner—we had shed our jackets, as is customary in Australia, because you are really meant to be at your ease—I was sitting with Mr. Wren and his wife Eileen over a good beer in the small den, awaiting the arrival of a couple named Galbally, when the Wrens' son, Christy, a strapping nine-year-old, made his entrance. With my usual flair for conversation, I remarked to Christy that he was a large boy for his age.

"I know," he answered proudly. "I'm a ruck man for my school team."

A ruck man, Mr. Wren informed me, has to be a big stalwart sort since his is the role of an enfranchised roving center.

"I hope I stay big," Christy continued. "I'd like to remain a ruck man."

"No, son," his father said in a tone of gentle admonishment. "All you are really aiming for is to get on the team."

"Yes," Christy agreed.

A minute or so later we were out in the back yard, the result of my inquiring if there was a football in the house. Father and son were kicking to each other. Christy confined himself to the conventional drop kick, but Mr. Wren was demonstrating the pass kick which calls for a technique in which you hood the ball as you boot it, in much the way you close the face of an iron in golf, so that the ball will fly on a low buzzing trajectory. Professional stars can whip these pass kicks in a twinkling to teammates forty to fifty yards away while on the run. The Galballys' arrival brought us back to the den. Jack Galbally, as I was to learn later, is a lawyer who is currently the Leader of the Opposition in the upper house of the Victoria State Parliament. As a young man he was a defense star for the Collingwood football team, a circumstance, he confided, which had done him no harm at all in getting started in his profession. That was some years ago, though, and he has to content himself now with golf (he holds two club championships), tennis (he lives across the street from the Kooyong courts), fishing, swimming, and surfing, not to mention rooting for Collingwood with an ardor that transforms simple watching into a virtual contact sport. Christy, who had momentarily disappeared, returned flushed with excitement, holding a framed photograph and a painting of a bird.

"Ah," said Mr. Galbally approvingly as we examined the photograph, which showed Christy standing with the captain and vice-captain of the Collingwood team, "that's the spirit, my boy. You're in good company there."

Christy then displayed the painting of a monstrous black-and-white bird. Puzzled, I asked him if nature study was also a hobby of his. "No," he said in a horrified voice. Then he added, "It's a magpie," as if that cleared up everything.

"The emblem of our team, the Collingwood Magpies," Mr. Wren explained. "And what would be the motto, son?"

Christy shook his head.

"*Floreat pica*," sang out Mr. Wren. "May the magpie flourish!"

"*Floreat pica*," Christy repeated after him.

"*Floreat pica*," Mr. Galbally intoned with a mystical gleam in his eyes as he placed his hand on the boy's shoulder.

Technically, my visit to Australia this past autumn was my second. In 1943, when my outfit was en route to China, the troopship anchored off Freemantle, the port for Perth, for three days, and we got ashore on two of them. I remember very little about that short stopover except that the Australian girls were as wholesome and unaloof as we had heard tell and that a troop of local entertainers put on a show at the dock climaxed by the inevitable rendering of "Waltzing Matilda" by the entire ensemble. This folk ballad, long a kind of unofficial national anthem, tells the story of a swagman who has stolen a sheep. Today there are quite a number of Australians who are of the opinion that it should be played far less often if at all, since, they contend, the subject matter presents their country in an incorrect and unfavorable light. A far more self-critical people than is generally recognized, Australians are the first to admit that this sort of touchiness stems from a kind of national inferiority complex as does, they add, their predilection for knocking themselves good-humoredly and the relish some of their countrymen take in being conspicuously and audibly Australian when in strange locales thousands of miles from home. They know as well that some of them can sometimes be direct to the point of abrasiveness. Better than anyone else, they understand their ambivalent attitude toward Britain—their resentment of anything smacking of stuffy colonialistic ritual and distinction and, conversely, the honest sense of security they draw from their ties with the mother country. (They are, for example, in no hurry to adopt a national anthem of their own to replace "God Save the King.") They are modest about their national virtues, which are abundant, to say the least, and are genuinely delighted when visitors comment, say, on their deep-going friendliness and their astonishing lack of all affectation, or when visitors simply remark that Australians today seem to lead a very good life.

There are no two ways about this. They do. Nearly every family has a nice little home, standing on its own plot of land, usually with a small garden. Few people are rich by American standards but then they do not have our extremes of poverty either. There are no slums as we know them. "The Australians did not play both ends against the middle but they are in a position today where they enjoy the fruits of both socialism and capitalism," Fred Hubbard, a well-informed American journalist who has spent the last decade in Australia, has said. "On one hand, one out of every four Australians works for the government, and legislation has provided the workingman with liberal sick leaves, long-service leaves, goodly pensions, and a generous medical setup which even includes a bonus for having a baby. On the other hand, one out of every four Australians now drives an auto (thanks to the hire-purchase or installment plan) and 60,000 are shareholders in the Broken Hill Proprietory Company, the vast steel combine."

Culturally, to be sure, Australia has produced and offered little. One of the reasons why sport has always loomed so large is this limited means of other diversion—few theatrical productions or concerts, hardly any light or jazz music, and a paucity of newspapers and lively periodicals. All in all, entertainment consists of going to English and American movies and watching television. (A high proportion of the feature shows on television, incidentally, are kinescopes or tapes of American series, and if you have missed a few stirring chapters of such classics as "The Bob Cummings Show" and "Sergeant Preston of the Yukon," this is the place to catch them.) The young person of talent often must go abroad to realize it. Compared to the large number of Australian athletes who have earned world-wide reputations—I would guess that a dinner table of knowledgeable

Americans might name as many as twenty—few have gained a comparable renown in other fields. The same dinner table would probably come up with Nellie Melba, the opera star; Henry Handel Richardson, the authoress; Errol Flynn (from Tasmania); Percy Grainger, the composer; Judith Anderson and Cyril Ritchard of the stage; Annette Kellerman, who popularized the one-piece bathing suit; Alan Moorehead, the writer; and maybe Ray Lawler, the author of that really splendid play, *The Summer of the 17th Doll.* After this, they would find the going hard.

But then, Australia is a young country, a very young country. Behind the cities in the partially settled scrubland fringing the Outback and in the parched wilderness of the Outback itself, life is not so different these days from what it was in 1860 when the government offered 10,000 Australian pounds to the first man to traverse the length of the continent from north to south. There are some alterations, though. When the first white settlers came, the aboriginal population was about 300,000. Today there are about 50,000 full-blooded aborigines and about 35,000 half-castes, the preponderate majority living in upper Queensland and in the government preserves in the Northern Territory. As the settlers moved westward onto the land suited for agriculture and for raising sheep and began to explore the Outback for gold and other minerals and oil (which has never been found), the aborigines were pushed back, leaving behind them all those lovely place names (like Wooloomooloo and Wagga Wagga) and, to be sure, the romantic lore of the spear, the stone ax, and especially the boomerang which some natives can throw a hundred yards or more away from them before it starts its curve to the left and its return flight to the thrower. Long before the bushman arrived, the wonderful animals, almost all of them unique to Australia, were already there—those sociable grass-and-plant-eating marsupials, the kangaroo, the wallaby (the small kangaroo), the tree kangaroo, and the koala (the sleepy-eyed, pocket-sized teddy bear which eats only the leaves of the eucalyptus and certain few gum trees). Additionally, there were the cassowary and the lyrebird and the kookaburra and the flightless emu, and those charter members of the animal kingdom, the duck-billed platypus and the spiny anteater, the only two remaining monotremes or egg-laying mammals in the world. Species as unadvanced and docile as the kangaroo and its pouched relatives generally perished eons ago, the victims of later developed, more savage breeds. Their mere survival is a fascinating story. As zoologists explain it, they were driven by the fiercer beasts to the ends of the land masses, Australia then being a part of the Asian continent. Then came the giant geological rumble in which Australia broke off from the continental mass; the sea swept in and cut off the bridge to the mainland. Only this fortuitous isolation saved the mild Australian animals from extinction. The sole carnivore on the continent, by the way, is the dingo, the wild dog which the bushmen brought over to help them with their hunting.

The most important animal in Australia, however, is the sheep. There are about 130,000,000 of them, more than in any other country—indeed, one-sixth of all the sheep in the world. Some are mutton sheep but the greater number, various strains of the curved-horn merino, are bred for their wool, the finest there is. Even today, when the development of Australian industry has introduced a long-needed balance to the economy, wool accounts for about 50 per cent of the total value of the country's exports. Some merinos are hardy enough to do all right in the scrubland areas where they may sometimes have to go two or three days before locating the next clumps of saltbush, but they thrive best in districts where the temperature is a moderate fifty-five to seventy degrees and where there is between fifteen and thirty inches of rainfall. Such a region is the cleared plateauland which rises up sharply behind the coast of New South Wales and runs off into the gentle western slopes, the wheat and cattle and fruit-growing country.

I don't know whether it was our wish to see the sheep country firsthand or the foreknowledge that we would probably see a real live kangaroo there that led Jerry Cooke, a peripatetic New York photographer who had just arrived in Sydney after ordering a few suits in Hong Kong, and me to arrange to go out to a sheep station. I suspect it was the latter. The station we visited was in Wollogorang, about five hours' drive southwest of Sydney, in the vicinity of Canberra (and, as Cooke kept on repeating as the fatigue of motoring overtook him, "probably not too far from the grand old Australian town of Yogiberra"). The drive out was on the dull side for the most part, though there were stretches where the road was lined with that lovely type of wattle tree that bursts out all over with soft yellow blossoms. On the outskirts of every town, moreover, there was a fenced-off plot of trees and shrubs, an unpretentious shrine to the nation's war dead, whom Australia seems to remember more truly than any other country. Just before Wollogorang, the character of the land changed. Wide vistas opened up and the hills rolled away, one after the other, under a high and deeply blue sky.

The owner and operator of the station was John Watson, a slim middle-aged man with a weather-lined face and a tendency toward laconic conversation—a perfect Texan, you might say. On his 12,000 acres there are 35,000 sheep. At the time of our visit, Mr. Watson and his hands were nearing the finish of their shearing season. They had been going at it for seven weeks. We spent a fair part of our two days at the station around the shearing sheds, but it was the fields we wanted to see and Mr. Watson was kind enough to understand this. As I remember those hours, we would bump along over the rocky ground from field to field in Mr. Watson's small truck, which he handled like a horse, sliding it down and across gullies and mushing it up the hills. Every now and then he would fix his narrowed eyes on his two greenhorn visitors and deliver a terse pragmatic statement.

"The job of the sheep is to turn grass into quid," I remember his saying characteristically halfway through the first afternoon.

We drove on past a small pond, and suddenly the air was filled with beautifully colored birds flying very fast, grass-green parrots and bright red parrots.

We drove past fields of huddled sheep, and Cooke, with the photographer's rare sensitivity, asked if sheep were as stupid as they looked. "Well," Mr. Watson replied as he made a cigarette with one hand, "they resist everything you want to do with them. It's understandable. You never do anything they'd like you to. You shear them, dip them, herd them. All unpleasant for the sheep."

High overhead a flight of Nanking ducks passed, having migrated that far from China. I thought I saw a kangaroo but it turned out to be a tree stump.

We drove over a stony field where Mr. Watson was conducting some experiments with clover. "This is what counts, this parasitic nodule," he said, fingering a twisted white knob on a clover root he had pulled out to check. "It fixes the nitrogen into the soil. Now we've learned that its distance below the ground is critical. We are just beginning to learn." He stared hard at us as if we, too, got up with the sun every morning and watched over 35,000 sheep.

Evening gradually came on and the solemn quiet of the fields was broken only by the noise the wind made in the eucalyptus and gum trees and the occasional whisk of the low-flying parrots. And then we spotted a kangaroo—four of them—grazing in the tall grass about 150 yards away. Sometimes they will let you get up close to them, within ten yards or so. These didn't. About as tall as a man, they stood, using their tails like spectator sports sticks, regarding us with their deerlike eyes until we were fifty yards from them. Then they took off. With no seeming effort they bounded in one leap across a broad gully and kept bounding with no slackening of pace across several fields and up the side of a long hill until they reached the top. Then they turned around and looked down at us in the safe distance. On the drive back to the main house we ran across two other small groups of kangaroos, and they behaved in much the same way. Friendly and gregarious, they customarily travel in larger bands and are generally not so shy of humans. Mr. Watson's surmise was that in recent weeks some kangaroo shooting must have taken place, as it does when their numbers become too numerous and they denude the pastureland of the grass that was meant for sheep. He appeared to be little less entranced by them than we were, though there are few days of his life when he doesn't see them. They are at least as arresting as you hope they will turn out to be, and what phenomenal athletes they are, bounding away on their toes twenty feet at a leap, always in perfect balance and as poised as if they were sitting in a rocking chair.

"Now you've seen a kangaroo," Mr. Watson said as he pulled some paper and tobacco from a pocket of his leather jacket and rolled one for the road.

Even in the sheep country, you cannot get away from sport for long. On the drive back to Sydney, we stopped for a beer in the bar of the Royal Hotel in Golbourn. I fell into conversation there with a fellow who turned out to be a warder at the local penitentiary. "I guess I can't ask you," I said to him, "the question I have been asking everyone else: why do you Australians produce such tremendous athletes?"

"Oh, that falls into my line," he said. "Application's the answer. The tennis courts at the penitentiary are always

filled. We've a couple of prisoners, too, who have been working hard on the 400-meter run, and I'm glad to be able to
report that they are beginning to turn in some very excellent
times."

Why indeed are the Australians such superb athletes?
Application is a part of the answer, as the warder suggested,
but if there is a fundamental reason beneath all of the
others, it is probably the climate. The lower two-thirds of
the continent, where the bulk of the people live, is con-
genially temperate. You can play sports nearly every day all
year round as you can in southern France or California. The
tropical upper third of the continent is too hot for sport
except in the winter (June–July–August). Now that there
is more money in the country these boom years, Australians
are beginning to utilize the Queensland coast during that
season as a sort of local Florida. The well-to-do are building
homes along the miles and miles of unbroken natural beach-
land. At Townsville, north of Brisbane, where the Australian
swimmers tuned up for the 1956 Olympics, they will be
encamped again for practice training before flying to Rome
for the 1960 Games. Not far from Brisbane in the area
called the Gold Coast, new resorts, such as Surfers Paradise,
are sprouting fast, not too impressive to Americans, since
they are reminiscent of a junior-grade Miami Beach, but
for the Australians paradise enow. While generally blessed
with mild winters, the country does have some snow. You
find it in the Australian Alps, a rugged little range—the
highest peak, Mt. Kosciusko, is 7,328 feet high—which lies
about halfway between Sydney and Melbourne. In the last
few years skiing has really caught on, and on weekends
an ever-increasing army of addicts heads for the snow
fields and the new camps, lodges, and chalets which have
gone up. Currently the country is also experiencing a boom
in gymnasiums. As soon as a small town or city has com-

pleted its Olympic-length swimming pool, the next project on its schedule is the community gym. In a slightly different direction, the marked improvement in travel and resort facilities has been a boon to the hunter and fisherman. Hare and fox and wild fowl can be hunted practically the year around, and for the more adventurous there are the water buffalo and the crocodile. The fisherman really has it good— in winter the game fish of the Great Barrier Reef, in summer the huge brown and rainbow trout of Tasmania and New South Wales and the celebrated shark fishing off Sydney and Narooma where giants of over a thousand pounds have been taken.

In the temperate zone, Australians play tennis and golf the year round although the championships are held in spring and summer. Horse racing also goes on around the calendar. For the rest, Australian sports fall into two main categories, summer and winter. The traditional summer team game is cricket, with most of the track and field, the swimming, the lawn bowling, and the sailing also taking place then. (The 680-mile Sydney-to-Hobart race, the glamour event of the yachting season, starts annually in late December.) In winter you get the football—Australian Rules in the south and west, Rugby (both Rugby League and Rugby Union) in New South Wales and Queensland—and some soccer, mainly in and around such centers of heavy industry as Newcastle and Wollongong, although with the advent of the New Australians the game is currently popping up all over. In addition, three comparatively new supplementary sports are making appreciable headway: basketball, squash, and baseball. Played indoors exclusively, basketball owes its growth to the coming of the gymnasium. Squash, off-season to tennis, is being taken up right and left, as you would expect it might in such a racquet-conscious land; in many gray city suburbs where no other new building has gone on, you often will see a new squash center, a simple two-story brick rectangle housing a dozen courts. Baseball is moving in as the winter or off-season game for cricketers. For all its charm, cricket can frequently dwindle into drawn-out soporifics that would try the patience of a registered Edwardian, and since the action in baseball is comparatively fast-coming and decisive, this accounts for the favor it is beginning to find.

The very fact that baseball is an American game, it should be interposed, also has had a great deal to do with its burgeoning popularity. At the present time, the United States looms heroically for Australia, as it does for other countries embarking upon their industrial age, for we are regarded as the trail blazers in modern technology. Furthermore, while they are not unmindful of the splendid endowment of their British heritage, Australians prefer the direction life has taken in our country. Americans, they feel, know how to enjoy life. (You are listened to with only half an ear when you try to temper their idealized picture with a cautioning word about our attendant rat-race or to point out the dangers in their too wholesale receptivity toward everything American, rock and roll included. Madison Avenue has succeeded so well that Australians envision every American heading for the beach in his convertible with an arm around Suzy Parker, and you can't fight that dream.) Their love affair with the United States actually goes back to World War II. While they don't like to say it in so many words, they do: they feel they were deserted by Britain. As the Australians saw it, the British general commanding Singapore gave up that strategic post without a fight and, on top of this, left the Australian soldiers to garrison the doomed city as the Japanese advanced. After that, miles from any ally, Australians waited apprehensively for the Japanese, who had overrun New Guinea, to invade and lay waste to their country. Instead, the Americans arrived. They viewed us as their rescuers. They still do, and you make very little indentation when you suggest that they are perhaps giving us a bit too much credit, that the circumstances of geography naturally influenced the Allies' decision that Britain should concentrate on the war in Europe and we should bear the brunt of the war in the Pacific, and, furthermore, that we were fortunate to have a base like Australia from which to mount our counteroffensive. Most countries whom we have helped, and gladly, over the last score of years don't think we've done anything like enough for them, and to be showered with more praise than we may possibly deserve is certainly a switch.

Along with a beneficent climate, in Australia there is, as we noted earlier, plenty of space for sports, and Australians have always found plenty of time to pursue them. The workingman and the small tradesman—and they are Australia—do not wait for the weekend. They are out playing their games on many of the weekday evenings, for Australians have never bought the nose-to-the-grindstone philosophy. They have had a short forty-hour working week for a long time now. They have habitually taken long weekends. There was, in fact, a danger at periods between the world wars that the nation would remain poor and floundering because the average Australian did only what he had to do to get by and took off the rest of the time for his sports. Currently, with the opening up of greater commercial opportunities and with the influx of New Australians who would work twenty-five hours a day if they could, the pace has speeded up, but the Australians have not appreciably cut down on the time they allot for recreation.

If Australians over the years had few other riches, they enjoyed superlative facilities for sport. The open country was handy and so was the sea: 75 per cent of the population lives within fifty miles of it. In the cities, broad expanses of parkland were at their disposal. For illustration, in Melbourne one-quarter of the city's total area of 7,767 acres is given over to public parks and gardens. (John Landy from boyhood on did his training on the seventeen rolling acres of Central

Park near his family's home. Herb Elliott, while attending Melbourne University, frequently worked out in the Domain and the adjacent Botanical Gardens, refreshing himself on hot days, to the consternation of peregrinating ladies' clubs, by running through the sprinklers.) In Adelaide there is even a larger proportion of green country. The city's commercial center is entirely separated from its suburbs by a deep belt of parkland reserved in perpetuity as public recreation grounds.

The quality of these facilities is also far better than one finds most places. Australia is lucky, for one thing, in having good grass for the many games which require it, and its people have inherited the British flair and patience for taking care of grass. The chief summer grass for both tennis and golf is couch. Its hardiness accounts for the sturdy fairways of Royal Melbourne and the other courses in the Sand Belt and explains why Kooyong and White City, while not up to the standard of the center court at Wimbledon, are not to be compared either with Forest Hills—they are that much superior. Another common grass for sports is a New Zealand browntop known to agronomists as *agrostis tenuis*. The researches of Sloan Morpeth, the secretary of the Australian Golf Union, reveal that this strain underwent a considerable odyssey before hitting the Antipodes. Originated in Germany and taken to Rhode Island, it was carried to New Zealand in 1860 by settlers from New England. This journey was quite accidental. Some of the seeds had gotten into the settlers' old traveling bags, and when they threw these bags away at Waipu, the ripened seeds germinated and spread like wildfire throughout New Zealand.

In a country as young as Australia where so much emphasis is placed on physical activity, where sports-loving parents get up in the middle of a winter night and sit before fires to hear the short-wave broadcasts of Davis Cup matches from Forest Hills and the cricket test matches from Lords (relayed from country to country by stations in the cricket

belt of Pakistan, India, and Malaya), a boy is born and bred
to sports. It is a sort of national ambition to become good at
one of them. The youngsters get a big push in this direction
at public school, for sports are a compulsory part of the cur-
riculum. (I can think of other countries where gymnastics
are but none where sports are.) From the time he is about
eight, a boy attends classes in athletics two afternoons a
week, usually on Wednesdays and Fridays, three hours each
day of cricket in the summer and football in the winter. The
kids who don't fit into those games are supervised in swimming and tennis. The whole enrollment, in short, participates in one sport or another. Interschool competition begins when the boys are twelve and thirteen, and juniors who
show promise early get an opportunity to find out how they
stack up against the best from other sections. For illustration,
annual Australia-wide track and field championships for
twelve-, fourteen-, and sixteen-year-old age groups and similar
swimming championships were inaugurated in 1951. "The
size of our population, I think, has a lot to do with the keen-
ness of our young athletes," Peter Thomson, the golfer, has
advanced. "Nothing helps you to climb a bit like a little success, and in Australia you can distinguish yourself without
too much difficulty. You don't have to make your way past so
many others. To get to the top in a country like the United
States with your 170,000,000, why, it must look insuperable
to a young boy, way beyond him."

Aside from the stimulus he receives at school, the young
Australian athlete gets enormous encouragement from his
family. There are some "stage mothers" and "stage fathers"
who push their kids, neurotically seeking to fulfill through
them their own ambitions, but their number is small. Australians by and large are a people with a healthy outlook and
they are healthy parents. They give their children considerably more elbowroom in which to find a normal individuality
than do their American counterparts, and they provide them

with an unstudied, friendly kind of support. Long before his rendezvous with golf, Peter Thomson had his heart set, like a million other Australian boys, on becoming another Don Bradman. " 'Go along and play your cricket, Peter,' my father would tell me when he saw me leave for a game. 'Stick with it and you'll make the Australian cricket eleven one day.' He wasn't too earnest about it. He just understood how I felt."

In this connection, I wonder if there ever were two parents more honestly helpful to an aspiring athlete than Alan and Bonnie Hoad were to their son, Lewis. Mr. Hoad had a feeling for sport, all right. In school he was a swimming and diving champion, and though a man of limited means—for fifteen years he worked as an electrician for the Sydney Transport Department—he found the time to be a first-grade ice hockey player, a good rifle shot, a skier, a three-mile racer with the Coogee Surf Club, and a competitor in the 100-miles-a-day jaunts of the Pedal Cyclists Association. The wonder is that a sports-saturated man like Mr. Hoad and his wife named their first son not after an athlete but after Lewis Stone, an actor they admired. The best way, I am sure, to bring out the unbelievably close and salutary sports communion the Hoad family shared is to quote a sentence here and a sentence there from the early chapters of the autobiography Lew wrote shortly after winning his second Wimbledon championship: "Because the war was on and there were few adults to play tennis with, my mother took up the game just to give me the opportunity to practice." "Every Sunday we Hoads packed up some sandwiches and went out to Wiley's Swimming Baths at Coogee for a day in the sun." "Always scheming to help my tennis, he [Dad] took me to all the Transport Department courts to give me experience on as many different surfaces as possible." "My brother, Larry, began to play tennis and my father habitually took us aside and told us not to become swell-headed. Today he thinks he may have overdone it and made me a little too reticent." "He [Dad] built us a kayak to sail in the local stormwater canal and made the exercises we did at night fun instead of hard work. . . . Mum joined a few sessions, too. She did backbends better than the rest of us." "We built our own [ping-pong] table in the club workshop, and my father acted as our coach." "My mother took me often to White City to watch the big names of tennis in action." "There was a time when I won the final of a New South Wales hard court title, and when I went home and entered the kitchen I asked, 'How'd you go, Mum?' She smiled and said, 'I won. How'd you go?'"

Australians consider themselves ungifted at organization. When they speak of the 1956 Olympic Games at Melbourne, for example, their fondness for self-ribbing often leads them to make wry comments on the order of "It was a miracle, you know, we got anything ready for the Games, but when they were actually held the same year they were set for—now, that was a shocker." There may be some areas in which the native administrative faculty may be retarded, but sports is not one of them. There they are organized to a fare-thee-well. Take swimming. The New South Wales Swimming Association, founded in 1889, is presently composed of 126 clubs with a total registered membership of 19,602. New South Wales, to be certain, is the swimming center, but Victoria is not exactly unbuoyant with its 13,000 registered club members or Queensland with its 10,206. (The oldest active competitor is a fellow seventy-two years old who still swims his leg of thirty-three yards in the handicap relay race for the Sydney Spit Diggers Club.) There is something for everyone. The current craze among the young girls, for example, is precision group marching, and there is hardly a town or village where teams of ten are not out in the evening practicing their routines for the next competition of the Australian Girls' Marching Association. Tennis, a workingman's game in Australia, has in the neighborhood of 300,000 registered tournament players and another 550,000 unregistered players; in other words, about one out of every dozen Australians is enmeshed in it. The figures for golf are not as overwhelming. Until recently it was hard for a youngster to gravitate to the game unless he was born into a well-to-do golf-playing family. Nevertheless, there are today some 1,000 golf clubs, counting the public courses, catering to some 100,000 golfers. (Golf in Australia, incidentally, is much less expensive than in any place except Scotland. The customary initiation fee is slightly over $100 and annual dues run to about $65. Green fees at some public courses start at a shilling, about eleven cents.) You find the same pattern repeated in every sport: low cost, high membership. There are twenty-six bicycle clubs with 4,020 members in New South Wales alone. There are 1,427 lawn bowling clubs with 171,687 members, and so on and on. Mateland is clubland.

While visitors to Australia are aghast at the extent of the competitions already on the schedule, the various sports organizations are grimly devoted to enlarging their operations, almost as if they felt that a moment's delinquence would put them a step behind a rival state or a competitive game. As incisive an example as any I know is the Lawn Tennis Association of Victoria with its 325 affiliated clubs and associations, 224 of them in the so-called country, 101 in the metropolitan zone of Greater Melbourne. In 1958, feeling that they were not doing enough to promote junior tennis, the LTAV inaugurated the Schoolgirls' and Schoolboys' Championships for under-seventeen and under-nineteen players. The entrants numbered 1,745, so apparently this tourney filled a need, for otherwise the state's juniors have a chance to engage only in school matches and club matches, the Victoria championships (on grass), the Victoria hard-court championships, interstate team matches (four on a side), interregional championships among the LTAV's fourteen regions, some interassociation matches, and either the Country Tennis Carnival at Kooyong (for those who live in the country) or the Metropolitan Winter Competition and Metropolitan Week at Kooyong. This, I believe, covers most of the authorized competitions, except for the junior divisions of the other state championships and the national championship. Mr. R. N. Vroland, the incumbent president of the LTAV, likes to think his organization has a progressive point of view, and he feels a yawning gap in its promotional program was filled when during six months of 1959 it provided planned instruction by accredited coaches for 1,400 young players between the ages of nine and fifteen. Well, it's a start.

A congenial climate, plenty of room, plenty of time, an inbred love of sports and the wish to excel at them, the lack of competing fields of interest, the worship of the physical idea which is part of a young country, the right pitch of support from one's family and friends, the splendid natural facilities, the relatively inexpensive cost of sport, the early orientation in school, the opportunity to develop in highly organized competitions—and, added to these, good food for growing bodies and the natural desire of the people of a small nation to do famously in fields which command international attention and respect—these in combination are the amalgam which has made Australia the most vigorous sports country of all times. It doesn't entirely explain, though, the emergence of its superathletes. If you add to the amalgam two other factors on which Australia places strong emphasis, it does. They are extremely able coaching and plain hard work.

These are more closely related than you might think at first. The basic ability must be there, of course, but, aside from this, every young boy (or girl) who is seized deep within himself with the unexpiring urge to become a champion, who burns with a different flame than Walter Pater had in mind but one that is nonetheless hard and gemlike—he will work toward his goal like a horse, he cannot stop working like a horse, until he gets there or is resigned to the fact that he can't. There are times, however, as there are bound to be, when every athlete, even the most extraordinarily gifted, loses that drive which is barely explainable to himself and begins to question his ability, the saneness of his desires, the whole damned exhausting business. In movies the hero's confidence in himself is usually renewed during these periods of depression by his wife or, preferably, his girl friend. They walk down by the brook near the campus and she looks up at him and asserts in cathedral tones, "I believe in you, Bruce." It makes all the difference. He goes out the next day and his fast ball has its old hop on it. In real life more often than not the person who helps him through the sloughs of despondency is his coach. The Australians, being an uncomplicated people, realize that the success of a potential champion's development depends more on how his personality fuses with his coach's than on the latter's technical skill as an instructor. The governing fathers in every sport may have their private ideas about which coaches are technically the best but, with the big picture in mind, they encourage their stars to go to whatever coach he or she enjoys working with.

There are many exceedingly well-qualified coaches in every sport but the best known—the ones whose pupils have made them renowned—are Harry Hopman in tennis, Percy Cerutty and Franz Stampfl in track, Norman Von Nida in golf, and Frank Guthrie, Harry Gallagher, Sam Herford, Forbes Carlile, and Don Talbot in swimming. The most controversial is Cerutty, Herb Elliott's coach, a garrulous, white-haired anti-traditionalist whose ideas include diets in which dried fruits, nuts, and rolled oats figure prominently, along with training runs over the sand dunes near his home in Portsea. Cerutty's yen for self-advertisement periodically gets out of hand, and there is no doubt that his interest in his charges can be excessive. He has a compulsion for wanting to take over not only their athletic careers but their whole lives. With a wisdom far beyond his twenty-two years, Elliott has learned how to ride with Cerutty's extravagances and sticks with him because he thinks Perc knows more about running than any other person alive. He also likes him.

In a land where everyone is an authority on tennis, Harry Hopman, naturally, has his detractors who query anything and everything he does, but most Australians have boundless faith in Harry. They should. Hopman was the coach of the team that in 1939 gained the Davis Cup for Australia after a twenty-year hiatus. He was called back again in 1950 to restore Australia's sagging fortunes and has succeeded so well that his teams have lost the cup but twice in the last decade. He is in a class by himself in developing players to step in and take over for stars he has lost to the professional ranks. In the spring of 1959, for example, after Ashley Cooper and Mal Anderson had turned pro, it was questionable if Australia could regain the Davis Cup since the best it had was Neale Fraser, an erratic left-hander who had never won a major title or ranked better than number three at home. In the months preceding the challenge-round match, Hopman worked on Fraser's second service and his backhand, which had hitherto amounted to a wild swipe at the ball. "Fraser found out," Harry recently said, "what could be done with his backhand, what strokes could be made." In August Fraser almost personally won the cup back with a brand of powerful all-round play that no one suspected he had in him. A somewhat puzzling man, easily direct at some times but all ambiguity at other times, Harry Hopman may not have some qualities but the many he has are precisely what the job calls for. Tactically his cardinal tenet is to put the other fellow under constant strain: i.e., when your opponent is behind 15–40 on his service, this is not the time you dally with the next point; this is the time you make sure to hit a forcing return of service and keep him cooped up. He is a bug on physical condition. When he first saw Frank Sedgman in a coaching class at Kooyong in 1940, he sent the slender boy to a gymnasium to build himself up. When Hoad used to go for conditioning runs in the park in London at night, Hopman went out and jogged with him. In the weeks and days directly before a major match, Hopman concentrates on sharpening his players' reflexes. Having been a doubles player of international caliber himself, he likes to warm the kids up personally. Perhaps this is one of his most important contributions, these sessions on the eve of the critical hour in which he evokes good stroking and builds valid determination. He is very close to his players.

The era of the swimming coach, a big man in Australia today, began in 1946 shortly after the idea of getting back into the competitive swim dawned concurrently on several of the sport's leaders, most notably the late Professor Frank Cotton of the University of Sydney, who was investigating the physiology of muscular exercises, and Marsden Campbell, a former backstroke champion, who advocated adopting the American methods of off-season body-building, as espoused principally by Bob Kiphuth of Yale. By 1950, Australians were approaching swimming as a sport that had to be worked on hard the year round. In the off-season the swimmer did his bodybuilding exercises—"Bob Kiphuth may have really made a bigger contribution to Australian swimming than he has to American," Syd Grange, the secretary of the New South Wales Swimming Association, has said—and during "the season" he worked himself up to top form via eight weeks of pre-water conditioning, six weeks of light preliminary workouts, eight weeks of intensified workouts, and a final two weeks calculated to bring him to the peak of his form. Now this is the kind of regimen from which a Spartan might recoil with an airy wave of his hand and the excuse that he had changed his mind and was going in for darts instead. As for the Australian swimmers, there is not one who wouldn't long ago have become the victim of mental fatigue were it not for the companionship and understanding of his coach, an alter ego indeed. An extreme case but not an atypical one is that of Dawn Fraser, the world record holder in the 100-meter free style. When her coach, Harry Gallagher, took up a new position in Adelaide, Dawn, a Sydney girl, changed jobs and moved to Adelaide. (She lives with the Gallaghers in their home which is right beside the pool.)

There is a wide range in personality among the coaches. Forbes Carlile, a protégé of Professor Cotton's and himself the holder of a master's degree who has lectured on physiology at the University of Sydney, is the most laboratory-conscious. His studies have led him to explore such phenomena as the effect of hypnotism on swimmers' performances. Frank Guthrie, who brought along Lorraine Crapp and Sandra Morgan among others, is erudite but in a different way. He is a realistic fellow who has studied international methods for twenty years. The least intellectual of the coaches is Sam Herford, the regent of the Spit Baths, a most unmodern domain. It is a weather-beaten wooden-frame "pool" that reaches out into the Middle Bay, the inlapping water decorated with bits of wood and some jellyfish, the ramshackle accommodations painted a loud orange and red which fail to conceal their age, the whole archaism punctuated with commanding signs, such as "Sand Throwing, Running on Decks and Concourse Strictly Prohibited." It was in this rugged environment that Herford developed his two greatest stars, John Devitt and Murray Rose. Don Talbot, the coach of the Konradses, a crew-cut young man who looks like a Big Ten blocking back, gives the impression of lacking the sensitivity of the older coaches, but he has done well with Ilsa and Jon, and they are highly intelligent kids. Jon, a seventeen-year-old with astonishing poise, is training presently to be the M.C. of TV rock-and-roll shows. It is like him, when he is kidded about it, to explain with a nice humor that he hopes you understand that his chief interest is folk music, you know. A good bit less outward-going than her brother, Ilsa, fifteen, has about her more than a suggestion of the charm of a young Ingrid Bergman. She is apple-cheeked, innately gracious, and her speaking voice has a lovely lyrical quality, something that stands out in Australia where vocal harshness is the rule. The Konradses are the children of New Australians, their father being a Latvian emigré who now works as a dental technician.

While a certain individuality exists in the approaches of the coaches of the various swimmers, there is, notwithstanding, a definite Australian style. It may have been best described in an informal comment which Bob Kiphuth made to an Australian friend at the 1956 Olympic Games: "You're swimming just like we used to." The explanation is quite interesting. After the 1924 Olympics, as we mentioned earlier, Australia stood still and the United States and Japan moved far ahead. As they did, they began to search out new methods of body-building and increasingly refined techniques. By 1936 the Japanese, for example, were experimenting with delayed breathing and the intricate timing of the overtaking arm action in the glide. "The Americans and Japanese over-experimented—that was the rock they tripped on," an Australian coach pointed out to me. "We avoided all of that simply by not being in the picture. When we returned to serious swimming just before the 1952 Olympics, we were lucky enough to make two decisions that have turned out to be right. In body-building we stressed a small number of exercises to develop gross power: body presses and work with the medicine ball and the weights. Kiphuth had over thirty exercises. He wanted to increase a swimmer's flexibility. We felt they didn't need that, that they were flexible enough. Our other correct guess was in style. We stayed with the classical technique." This, among other things, has meant using fewer strokes than was the vogue and making them count more. In the 1956 Games, where many Japanese and American swimmers were taking fifty strokes to the lap, the Australians averaged forty-one. Murray Rose was swimming about thirty-seven. After they saw this, the Japanese coaches went back home and completely changed young Yamanaka, who had their technique down to perfection. When he made his records this past year, Yamanaka was swimming thirty-five strokes a lap with a wonderful Australian style.

The man who popularized hard work for swimmers, for runners, for everyone was Landy, the miler. Fate could have been kinder to John Landy. The glory of being the first man to break the four-minute barrier in the mile fell not to him but to Roger Bannister. Two weeks after Bannister ran his historic 3:59.4 at Oxford, Landy cracked this mark with 3:58 at Turku in Finland. In the Mile of the Century at Vancouver between Bannister and Landy in 1954, the honors again went to Bannister who overtook the Australian as they burst around the final turn. Nor did Landy fare too well in the Melbourne Olympics. Hobbled by inflamed tendons, he finished third on nerve alone after barely qualifying for the final. It is heart-warming to report that in his own country John Landy is not remembered as a man who was never quite first. He is admired perhaps more than any other athlete and, what is more, for the right reasons: for his unblinking sportsmanship at the bitterest moments, the modesty and honesty that characterized his conduct, and the fact that he was one of the finest runners in history. The Australian fans clearly understand—and they might have missed this point since there is a side of the national character that is impatient with subtleties—that if Landy was perhaps a too mechanical runner and lacked Bannister's racing instinct, this was the unfortunate consequence of the absence of any countrymen who could give him any race at all during his formative years and his subsequent reliance on the stop watch as his opponent. They understand also that his poor showing in the Olympics may have stemmed indirectly from putting his country above his own interests. After major pressure had been put on him, John consented to publicize the upcoming Melbourne games by going to the United States in the spring of 1956. Here he ran two sub-four-minute miles within a week, and they proved to be his last great performances.

Until Landy appeared, Australia had never had a middle-distance runner of note. As a matter of fact, the one sports facility lacking in Australia was cinder tracks. Until 1956 there was only one, and they didn't quite finish building that one. Landy has never believed that this absence of modern tracks was a serious handicap. "If the grass is too wet," he has said, "that's a disadvantage, but a good grass track will take a world's record." One day in December, 1952, Landy, an almost complete unknown, ran a mile on a grass track in 4:02.1. Australia hardly took any notice of it. We did in America, though. Our track experts pointed out that this now brought the four-minute mile within reach. Then, after this foreign acclaim, Australia took cognizance of Landy. As Ken Archer, a Sydney sports journalist, has phrased it, "Our national interest in track and field started when we realized what Landy had done. He gave the idea to us."

Everyone in Australia wanted to know how this young Landy fellow had made himself into such a runner. The answer came out by bits and pieces, all adding up to punishing, unglamorous hard work. At Geelong Grammar School the tall, stringy boy with the mop of curly hair and the intense dark eyes had run the 100-yard dash and given it up because he felt he didn't have sufficient natural speed. He had turned to the mile because he believed that over that distance what a person lacked in native talent he could make up for by pure, grinding stick-to-itiveness. The Finns and other European runners (Bannister certainly included) had

long realized the necessary part that hard work played in
the development of middle-distance runners, but no one
ever invited ordeal more openly than Landy as he prepared
to change himself into "a running animal" by running,
running, running. "A man who sets out to become an artist
at the mile," Paul O'Neil, the veteran track writer, has said
in one of his most brilliant bursts, "is something like a man
who sets out to discover the most graceful method of being
hanged. No matter how logical his plans, he cannot carry
them out without physical suffering. In his early years Landy
performed chilling feats of toil simply to convert his body
into the instrument he needed to satisfy his ambitions. In
four short months in 1951 he cut thirty seconds off his time,
brought it from 4:45 to 4:15 by literally running himself
into a state of absolute exhaustion daily." After Landy saw
Zatopek in the 1952 Olympics, he began to place more
emphasis on style but never relinquished his original prem-
ise that pushing yourself past reasonably strenuous limits does
not bring on staleness—staleness is all mental, anyhow, and if
you stick with a schedule over a long period, the body will
respond. He concentrated on interval running, undertook
enormous amounts of it. In an average workout he would
run ten, twelve, fourteen very fast quarter miles in an afternoon, running a quarter, reknitting himself by walking a
quarter of a mile, blazing off into another rapid quarter,
and so on and on. John Landy trained like this for two years.
He got so—this is what Australian students of training
noted—that he felt he could almost always count on himself
to break four minutes in the mile. Indeed, he had succeeded
in transforming himself into a running animal. Tests dis-
closed that his heart and pulse rates were forty-two—the
average is about sixty or seventy—and that where the ordinary man can breathe 120 quarts of air a minute and hold
four and a half quarts of air, Landy's lungs could take in 300
quarts and hold seven quarts. The point is this: If young

Australian girls of twelve are nowadays swimming twelve miles a day, as the daughter of a Sydneyside friend of mine is doing, it all goes back to Landy, for although the heavy-training advocates in the other sports were arriving at these same conclusions independently, it was the great miler who dramatized for his countrymen the nature and extent of its value.

It only remains to be added, briefly, that the substantial recognition an exceptional athlete receives in Australia has something to do with there being so many. Jack Kramer's candid comment as to why he likes to visit there comes to mind: "You're important in Australia in a way you like to be." When Kramer walks down the street in an Australian city, he is spotted by many passers-by and approached for a friendly chat by more than a few. In New York, when he emerges from his hotel, there is no such activity or interest unless, perchance, Sal Mineo should come sweeping out of the revolving door right behind him. As far as amateur athletes go—the Australian definitions of amateurism vary with each sport—only the tennis players are accorded liberal financial treatment. In professional sports, only the top tennis pros and cricketers do well by our standards of payment and, interestingly enough, unless a golf pro is a Thomson or a Nagle or a Crampton, he actually makes less than a plumber. But above and beyond this, it pays in many indirect ways to be an athlete in Australia. If you make a name for yourself in sport, you enjoy an agreeable place in society, a pleasant life, and you will generally prosper commercially if you are normally industrious. Take the case of Frank Sedgman, one of the country's most popular tennis stars, and deservedly so. In 1952, when Frank was teetering on the brink of turning professional, Australians contributed over $13,000 to a wedding-gift fund that would enable Sedgman to remain an amateur for another season and so be eligible to defend the Davis Cup. Frank used the money principally to purchase a gas station. This proved to be a good thing until the accelerated auto age resulted in a plethora of gas stations. He then sold this property. For a while Frank manufactured flavored straws (called Sedgies) but now the bulk of his investment is in a gymnasium with squash courts in Melbourne. He is doing very nicely.

Whither Australia and Australian sports? I don't think punditry and pronouncements are called for. In one direction, as life becomes more autofied and Americanized, there are sure to be more and more Australians seeking their pleasures away from the arduous oval and court. And yet one knows that for a long time to come the national passion for sport will be at least what it is today. An ever-increasing number of youngsters will set their hearts on emulating their heroes. Sport is in Australia's blood, even deeper than it is in our own, deeper probably than it is in any other nation's. It is as simple as that.

In my mind, these months after my visit, there are a hundred and one small "set pieces," sights and sounds which remain vivid and clear. May I give you just three.

The first, in truth, is hardly that. Robert Gordon Menzies, the incumbent Prime Minister, spoke with memorable wit at the Canada Cup presentation ceremonies, but I prefer to present to you Menzies the writer, for you will not come across a more evocative delineation of an athlete than Mr. Menzies' cameo of Norman Brooks, the tennis player who was Australia's first great international champion: "As soon as he served," wrote Menzies, "Brooks moved in. Such was his control of service direction and length that he limited the scope of return, and even appeared as if by some magic to control its actual direction. In spite of this, powerful opponents would seek to check him by driving to his feet as he advanced to the normally fatal midcourt half-volleying position. They soon discovered that to Brooks the half-volley was a weapon of attack, not of defense. Time after time I have seen him sweeping half volleys first to one deep corner, then to the other, with his opponent sweating up and down in vain.

"What a player! His long trousers perfectly pressed, on his head a peaked tweed or cloth cap, on his face the inscrutable expression of a pale-faced Red Indian, no sign of sweat or bother, no temperamental outbursts, no word to say except an occasional 'well-played.' A slim and not very robust man, he combined an almost diabolical skill with a personal reserve, a dignity (yes, dignity) and a calm maturity of mind and judgment. I have sometimes suspected that a modern coach, given control, would have hammered out of him all the astonishing elements that made him in his day (and his day lasted for many years) the greatest player in the world."

The second "set piece":

John Landy, today a Technical Officer of the National Parks Authority, sits in the living room of his family's airy home in Melbourne, across the street from Central Park, where he ran as a boy and still runs. As intent of eye as ever and extremely trim, there is about him his familiar thoughtfulness as he contributes a sentence or two here, a sentence or two there, to a conversation on track.

"You were given legs to walk with and run with. You were given a good body and it's got to be kept fit . . ."

"Australian kids today are bigger and fuller. I don't know if they're as hardy . . ."

"The reason why we've got those kids running at the Mountain School at Timber Top is they have an incentive. They understand that running can get them fit for hiking, which they like. Realizing this, they don't mind running. There're some boys up there fourteen and fifteen who can now run twenty-two miles in two hours and forty-four minutes . . ."

"Coaching to my mind is the ability to make a second-class athlete reach his full potential. . . ."

The third:

Herb Elliott is riding into Melbourne University from his home in the suburb of Clayton on his blue Japanese motorcycle. He had an auto but couldn't afford to run it. As you watch him make his way through the hazardous highway traffic, his exposed legs hugging the motorcycle's metal frame, you feel that there is something wrong about the world's mile champion running such a risk. Elliott, however, appears oblivious to this, as honestly composed as he was at home earlier that morning when he spoke about the race in May, 1958, at Santry outside of Dublin, where he set the present mile record of 3:54.5.

"Santry was perfect for me," Elliott said. "The Empire Games were over, so when I came to Ireland the tension was off. I liked the country atmosphere at the track. Trees grew all around it. That helped me to feel easy. Then, too, the race was held at a time of day that makes you feel relaxed. It was in the still of the evening, twilight, when the day was going into night. The track was a little damp, which was fine, of course. Well, the race got off. I start a race flat out and I try to go flat out all the way, so I never really know if I am running well until I hear the times at the half-mile. You hear them say 1:58 or whatever it is. I think it was 1:58 that day. I felt very strong during the third quarter. I can remember Lincoln passed me and I passed him back, which I knew was good for the race. During the last quarter I had a lot of strength left in me. I just ran as fast as I could. I'll tell you what helped me there. That wild Irish crowd started to yell and they kept yelling. When it was over, I knew we had run a fast race but I was astonished when they told me the time. It was one of those rare occasions, you know, when everything went right."

. . . These were the words. They [the members of the
ROYAL SPORT NAUTIQUE] *were all employed over the frivolous
mercantile concerns of Belgium during the day; but in the
evening they found some hours for the serious concerns of
life. . . . They had still those clean perceptions of what is nice
and nasty, what is interesting and what is dull, which envious
old men refer to as illusions. The nightmare illusion of middle age, the bear's hug of custom gradually squeezing the life
out of a man's soul, had not yet begun for these happy-starred
young Belgians. They still knew that the interest they took in
their business was a trifling affair compared to their spontaneous, long-suffering affection for nautical sports. To know
what you prefer, instead of humbly saying Amen to what
the world tells you you ought to prefer, is to have kept your
soul alive. Such a man may be generous; he may be honest in
something more than the commercial sense; he may love his
friends with an elective, personal sympathy, and not accept
them as an adjunct of the station to which he has been called.
He may be a man, in short, acting on his own instincts, keeping in his own shape that God made him in; and not a mere
crank in the social engine-house, welded on principles that
he does not understand, and for purposes that he does not
care for . . .*

*. . . There should be nothing so much a man's business as
his amusements.*

—ROBERT LOUIS STEVENSON,
An Inland Voyage, 1878

II

SOME
OF THE
HEROES

PEE WEE REESE:
THE HEART
OF THE DODGERS

This article was written in 1950 when Reese was just past the mid-point of his long and glorious career with the Brooklyn Dodgers. All in all, he was with the team for twenty years, nineteen as a player and one as a coach. He then accepted an offer to broadcast "The Game of the Week," and, as everyone who knows him fully expected, he has handled that job with his inveterate competence, taste, and tact.

There is no question that the Brooklyn teams of Reese's time were not quite as redoubtable as the Yankees, to whom they lost six of the seven times they met in the World Series. However, I would like to introduce—more as an interesting thought than as a tenet I am ready to defend into the late hours—the proposition that the difference between the two teams was the difference between the pitching staffs. For me, the finest fielding team that ever trotted out onto a major-league field was the Dodger team that had Campanella catching, Hodges, Robinson, Reese, and Cox in the infield, Pafko, Snider, and Furillo in the outfield. They were, with the possible exception of Cox, reliable hitters and they were fast, a grand collection of ball players. In my time there has been only one other infield I have enjoyed watching as much —the old Cub cordon of the mid-1930s that had Cavaretta at first, Bill Herman at second, Jurges at short, and Hack at third.

Thanks to the dedication of the splendid group of baseball writers who covered the Dodgers, Reese's attributes as a person as well as a player became well known to the sports public. (I was just thinking that people are probably disposed to like anyone with the nickname of Pee Wee, to begin with. Harry Crosby, similarly, I am sure, would have made the grade without the fetching handle of Bing, but that opened you to him, I think.) In any event, Pee Wee Reese was that unusual sports hero: a man with an intelligent understanding of the public and of public relations, yet above all a man with a genuine, uncomplicated feeling for human relations. Some people are simply born straight and grow straight.

Branch Rickey's decision to break the color line in baseball undoubtedly would have succeeded without Reese, for both Mr. Rickey and Jackie Robinson were the right men for the job. Reese, however, as the respected captain of the team, was providentially around to handle many tough situations with astonishing adroitness. In the article that follows, one such incident is told and I would like to relate two others briefly at this point. Reese did not bring them up. They were told to me by Robinson.

Near the end of the 1949 pennant race, one of the many cranks around baseball sent a letter to each of the white members of the Dodgers stating, in short, that all the credit for the team's victorious season was being given to Robinson, Campanella, and Newcombe and asking the other players if they were just going to sit back and do nothing about this. A day or so later, on the way to the ball park in the team bus on a road trip, Reese and Robinson happened to be seated next to each other. As Jackie tells the story, "Pee Wee reached into his pocket and brought out a letter he'd received. 'I don't think you got one of these,' he said, handing me the letter. 'You might want to read it.'

"I read it through. Compared to some of the abusive letters we used to get, it was pretty mild. But here was the important thing. No one on the team had mentioned the letter before, but when the other players saw me reading it and talking about it with Reese, they all began to speak up—you know, 'I got one of those, too,' and 'What do you get, Robby, that we don't get?' and things like that. With this little gesture of his, Pee Wee had brought the whole business out into the open and it was treated as a joke and forgotten. On the other hand, if Campy, Newk, and I hadn't heard about the letter until weeks after the boys had received it, I think it could have been damaging. We would have felt as if we weren't real members of the team and that a gulf existed."

The second incident took place a year or two earlier when the team was heading north from spring training and stopping off for exhibition games en route. Before a game in Macon, Georgia, Robinson received a serious threatening letter: the writer warned him that if he stepped out on the diamond that afternoon he would be shot. Robinson decided to play anyhow. When he came onto the field to warm up before the game, he walked over to join a group that happened to include Reese. "Hey, get away from me, Jackie," Reese said with a kidding but communicative smile. "I don't want to be any place near you if that guy takes a shot at you." It was an inspired way to break the heavy tension that Robinson felt.

Because a Negro ball player was involved, these stories have a dramatic dimension, but the true point is that Reese acted in these situations the way he acted all the time, never calling attention to himself as an appointed leader, quietly doing what he thought was right to do because that is the kind of man he is. As I say, the sports public, the Brooklyn fans especially, came to appreciate and honor his rare qualities. I wonder if any other evening in baseball history had the same intimate warmth and glow of that night at Ebbets Field late in Pee Wee's career when he was given a birthday party and, as the cake was brought in, the darkened ball park was lighted by the thousands of matches struck by the fans filling the stands. It is beside the point but on Reese's first trip to the plate when the game got under way, he lined a double off the left center-field wall. It was rather characteristic.

HAROLD HENRY "PEE WEE" REESE, thirty-one years old this season, is the ranking veteran on the Brooklyn Dodgers, the oldest regular both in age and length of service. Appreciating his unflamboyant virtues daily, Reese's teammates,

postwar tyros by and large, find it impossible to believe that
the rock of the Dodgers was once a rookie—moreover, one of
the most jittery youngsters who ever hit the big time, so subject to streaks of nervousness when he broke in in 1940 that
Manager Durocher had to bench him during several important series and take over at shortstop himself, and still so
erratic in 1941 (when the Dodgers won their first pennant
in twenty-one years) that he not only led the National
League shortstops in put-outs (346) but in errors (47).

"That was an awful year for me," Pee Wee was recalling
recently. "Every boot I made seemed to be the difference between winning a game and losing it. I remember one tight
game which Fred Fitzsimmons was pitching for us, against
the Cards. I kicked one in the seventh that let in a couple of
runs and put us behind, something like 2-1. When we came
to bat, Durocher had to yank Fitz for a pinch hitter. Fitz was
burning up—you know how he used to put his heart and
soul in every game. As he stomped to the dressing room, he
took a terrific crack with his fist at the infield-change bell
that was nailed to the wall of the dugout. He hit that bell so
hard he knocked it clean off the wall. I didn't appreciate that.
I was playing my heart out, too." When Fitzsimmons cooled
down, the old campaigner made it a point to tell the newspapermen that he considered Reese a very able shortstop
and, more than that, a young man who would keep on improving and become the best shortstop in the National
League. As a coach for the Giants, Fitz has been in an excellent position to appreciate the accuracy of his prediction.

Eight years can make a world of difference in a young man,
providing he has the stuff and is brought along right. In the
second game of the last World Series, for example, Preacher
Roe was moving along in fine fashion until a couple of Yanks
got on base and the ever dangerous Tommy Henrich stepped
into the batter's box. Reese walked over to the mound. "Let's
you and I have a talk," he said to the lean left-hander from

Arkansas. "O.K.," Roe responded. "What'll we talk about, Pee Wee?" "Oh, I don't care, Preach. Hunting or fishing," Reese said, and they both began to laugh a bit. Twenty seconds later Pee Wee handed the ball back to a much more relaxed Roe. Roe got Henrich and got out of the inning.

Whenever a Dodger pitcher isn't sure how to pitch to a hitter, he calls on Reese. "Pee Wee knows them all, their strengths and their weaknesses," Ralph Branca told a friend a short while ago. "In a game against the Cards last summer, I got into a spot and didn't know what to give Ron Northey, who was coming up. 'Throw him a fast one,' Pee Wee told me. 'Throw it right by him.' Pee Wee trotted back to short and I looked up for Campanella's signal. Campy called for a change-up. I shook him off. Then he called for a curve. I shook that off, too. Then Campy gave me the signal for the change-up again and I said to myself, 'O.K., I'll throw the change-up.' Northey powdered that pitch off the right-field wall and two runs scored. Pee Wee was really peeved. 'That's right, Ralph,' he said when he came over to the mound. 'Throw him one of those big lollipops so that he can pull it a mile. Nice going.' "

Baseball has its terms for players like Reese. They're called "an old pro" or "a ballplayer's ballplayer." The latest switch on these clichés is "glue man." This expression hasn't been kicked around enough yet to become trite, but it will be only a matter of time before someone like Eddie Stanky is christened "Mister Mucilage" and someone like Eddie Joost "Old Adhesive" and a fairly useful term will be ready for the bone yard (or glue factory).

The glue man, to be sure, is the player who holds the team together. He doesn't have to be a heavy hitter. He usually doesn't bat .300. He doesn't have to be a classy fielder, but he usually is. Generally he is an infielder, too, and most often a second baseman or shortstop. Solid teams are still built on that straight line between home plate and center field—

catcher, pitcher, the second-base combination, and center fielder. The especial attributes of the glue man are a lot more subtle than those of the slugging outfielder, for instance, or the fast-ball pitcher. You begin to appreciate just what a glue man does for a team only when injury forces him out of the line-up. Something happens and the team stops winning. The batting and fielding and pitching averages haven't changed, but something's gone wrong. The play that gets the team out of the dangerous inning isn't made, the key sacrifice isn't laid down, the correct anticipation of the play coming up has disappeared. Then the glue man returns to the line-up, does nothing spectacular, but the team begins to win.

The chief trait of the glue man, whether instinctive or acquired, is that he is in the ball game every minute, genuinely and untheatrically determined to win that game if it can possibly be won. He is fired by a sense of baseball as well as by a love of baseball, and he is able to communicate his concentration to his teammates. Pee Wee is all this. "Outside of being the best damn shortstop in the league, Pee Wee was the boy who held us together," Roy Campanella said in an appraisal that is typical of the regard in which Reese is held by his teammates. "There aren't many inspirational fellows in baseball, but Pee Wee is. You know, you'd be dressing for a game and you'd see Pee Wee stretched out on the trainer's table being all taped up, and you'd shake your head and say to yourself, 'I guess old Pee Wee won't make it today.' Well, he made it every day except one time in Cincinnati. I remember once when he was sick to his stomach just before game time and threw up at the edge of the dugout. But he was out there, right in the ball game, right on his toes every minute. I don't have to tell you what a fellow like Reese does for a ball club. You say to yourself, 'If Pee Wee can keep going like that, I can keep going, too.' "

Branch Rickey, the best friend a statistic ever had, employs a full-time team statistician, Alan Roth, who can give

you, for example, some positively incredible facts about
Reese's propensities as a base-stealer. In 1948 Pee Wee tried
to steal twenty-seven times. He was successful twenty-five
times. The catchers who threw him out were Del Rice of the
Cards and Dewey Williams of the Reds, oddly enough on
successive attempts. In 1949 Pee Wee slowed down a trifle,
stealing successfully on twenty-six out of thirty tries. The
Braves nabbed him on his one dash for home. Phil Masi
(then with the Pirates) nailed him at third on the front end
of a double-steal, but Reese was safe the three other times he
tried for third. In twenty-five attempts to steal second, he
failed only twice. Walker Cooper threw him out once when
he was with the Giants and got him the second time when
he was with the Reds, proving, among other things, that
though Walker has become about as catlike behind the plate
as Shanty Hogan, he still has one of the best arms in the
league. Reese's percentage of successful steals during the last
two seasons—fifty-one out of fifty-seven—is a feat no other
modern player has approached, and you have to go back to
old Max Carey of the Pirates before you strike a thief of
comparable slickness. "Reese really steals a base, in the sense
that a pickpocket steals," Branch Rickey likes to point out.
"He has a genius for timing his lead and the pitcher's motion,
and he's ready to take instantaneous advantage when he sees
an opening. Reese is fast but he's not the fastest man on the
team on the straightaway. But he's our finest base-runner,
and there's no question in my mind that he could steal many
more bases if he were thinking only of adding to his total. Pee
Wee doesn't squander outs. He doesn't go down unless having that man in scoring position is important."

In that obsolescent but essential art of advancing a runner
via a sacrifice bunt, Pee Wee is peerless. In 1948 he was
called on to sacrifice fourteen times, and fourteen times he
successfully advanced the runner or runners. Five of those
times he also beat out the bunt and was credited with a hit,

not a sacrifice. This past season he again was ordered to sacrifice fourteen times, delivered thirteen times and beat out seven of those bunts. He failed once; he was thrown out at first by half a step on a squeeze play attempted with two men out. As far as bunting expressly to get on went, Reese beat out five bunts in six tries in 1948, ten out of twenty-one in 1949. Here again his remarkable percentage depends as much on mental alertness as physical skill. He is always watching the third baseman out of the corner of his eye. He knows which pitchers are slow getting off the hill. Paul Derringer and Fritz Ostermeuller were two you could catch off balance. Herman Wehmeier and Howie Fox and Johnny Vander Meer, possibly because of their proximity to Bucky Walters, are three whom Reese respects as fielders.

A few final statistics before we leave Mr. Roth and his ledger domain. In 1949 Reese led the league in runs scored with 132. His 116 walks placed him second to Ralph Kiner (117). In the Brooklyn organization a great deal of importance is placed on the walk. In arriving at what Mr. Rickey alludes to as a player's On-Base Average, walks (intentional walks excepted) are figured as hits. Whereas Pee Wee's orthodox batting average for 1949 was a medium-weight .279, his On-Base Average of .391 topped all the Dodger regulars except Hermanski and Robinson. In another one of the Rickey-Roth frappés called a Clutch Average, an involved logarithm that essays to determine a batter's effectiveness with men on base, Pee Wee hit .309. The National League, a rather retarded outfit statistically and one that refuses to traffic in On-Base and Clutch figures, did announce, however, that the best fielding average for shortstops in 1949 was Reese's .977—eighteen errors in 788 total chances.

It is a well-known fact that statistics, unlike women, can be made to do nearly anything you want to do with them. Consequently, it comes as a relief to realize that while Mr. Reese plays good ball on paper, many aspects of his value as a team player can be appreciated only in the warmer climate of human relations. In sports there is an unwritten law, rarely bypassed, whereby writers say nothing rather than report critically about the stars. The average sports fan grows up believing that the athletic world is peopled almost exclusively by first-rate human beings, a distortion exceeded only by the willful myopia of movie fans. The chief trouble with not calling a spade a spade in sports is that only the relative handful on the inside know who are the true heroes and who are the undeveloped children who happen to have exceptional athletic talent. Reese is that rarity, a newspaper hero who is an authentic hero. He is a top-notch person when 40,000 are watching him, and when no one is looking.

One of Pee Wee's hunting trips last winter took him forty miles from his home in Louisville to Ekron, Kentucky, a backwoods settlement, lying between two hills, composed of a general store and eleven houses. Ekron is one of those villages that never changes. It was exactly the same in 1919 when Carl and Emma Allen Reese had their fifth child and second son, Harold Henry. Reeses and Allens are strewn in great numbers over Meade County, Daniel Boone's county, and have been for well over a century. "We've never traced the families all the way back," Pee Wee was saying a short time ago, "but every ancestor we've ever heard of was born in Meade County. They've been here so long they must have come with Daniel Boone."

Pee Wee was four when his father, a tobacco and corn farmer, moved the family to another farm in Brandenburg, seven miles from Ekron. Two years later Mr. Reese moved the family again, this time to the Portland section of Louisville. The move to Louisville followed his finding employment as a detective with the Louisville and Nashville Railroad, a job that did not pay too well but enabled him to bring money home regularly for his wife and six children—Pauline,

Willie Lee, Elizabeth, Carl, Jr., Harold, and Mary Helen. Harold was called Boy or Babe. "I don't know how that nickname of Babe began," Pee Wee recollected with amusement last winter, "but I know it didn't have anything to do with Babe Ruth. I imagine I must have been called Harold, too, but, thank goodness, I don't remember much about that." Pee Wee has been Pee Wee to his family and his friends since 1932 when, at the age of thirteen, he made the newspapers for the first time by winning the marble championship of the Falls City area (Jeffersonville, New Albany, and Louisville) and reaching the semifinals of the state tournament. The marbles used were called pee wees, and this is the genesis of Reese's sobriquet, not his diminutive stature as a boy.

The Reeses were vastly relieved when, five years after settling in Louisville, they were able to move the family out of the rough Portland section to a house directly across the street from the playground on Central Park. During his hours away from the railroad, Mr. Reese liked to throw a baseball around with Pee Wee and Carl, Jr., three years Pee Wee's senior. Mr. Reese had a reputation for being quite a ballplayer. When he had been courting his wife, whose parents had disapproved of playing ball on Sunday, he had surprised himself by the resourceful measures he contrived for sneaking her out of the house so that she could watch him play. For her part, Pee Wee's mother has been a baseball fan all her life and makes at least one trip each season to Brooklyn to watch her son's team in action. As a boy, Carl was a far better ballplayer than Pee Wee. He batted in the cleanup squad in the pickup games, and his kid brother led off, the natural slot for a youngster who was very small for his age. Pee Wee is now five feet ten and weighs 170 pounds. He never thought that he would come any place close to that size. When he was graduated from high school, he was the smallest boy in his class.

From the time they were old enough to sell newspapers, Carl and Pee Wee pitched in to help their dad in his struggle to support the large family. Pee Wee lined up an afternoon paper route and also sold papers on a corner in downtown Louisville. Before going to school in the morning, the Reese boys sold box lunches at the Louisville and Nashville plants. "Carl and I would get up at five in the morning," Pee Wee reminisced last winter, "and fill two suitcases with about fifty lunches. Then we'd haul them down to the L & N shops, and between six and seven sell them to the men as they reported to work. Boy, you'd freeze yourself to death some of those winter mornings." When the racing fans of America poured into Churchill Downs on Derby Days, Pee Wee picked up some extra money by circulating in the closely packed, thirsty crowd and vending, at a quarter a bottle, discarded soda bottles filled with tap water. Apart from the bicycle he bought to speed up his newspaper route, he put all of his earnings into the family kitty. The youngster's small size undoubtedly was the result of not getting all the rest a growing boy needed. Somehow he also found the time and assembled the energy to do his homework and become a good B student, and for five straight years he never missed a day of Sunday school.

When Carl started to play baseball for the New Covenant Presbyterian Church team, his kid brother followed him to the games and acted as bat boy. When the team was one player short, Pee Wee was stuck in right field, where he could do the least amount of damage. No one ever thought that the shy, sandy-haired boy had the makings of even a good sand lotter and he quite agreed with them. However, he did develop into an adept enough basketball player so that his friend Junie Andres tried to interest him in going to Indiana University on a basketball scholarship.

Pee Wee never thought of going out for the baseball team at Manual Training High School until his senior year.

Even then, the boy was so shy that Ray Baer, a supervisor at Central Park with whom Pee Wee played tennis in the mornings, had to lead him by the hand to the high-school coach. Reese did not start the season as a regular, but once he broke into the line-up he held down second base until he split his right hand between the second and third fingers handling the shortstop's overthrown double-play toss. (The injury mended fairly well but the hand has since split open three other times—once in spring training in 1940 when Pee Wee barehanded a hot shot off Barney McCoskey's bat; again in a pepper game with Durocher; and the third time when he slapped at a basketball during a Navy game in the South Pacific.) Reese was awarded his letter and sweater, a big red M on a white background. "Winning it was without a doubt the greatest thrill of my boyhood," Pee Wee has said. "It symbolized for me the highest honor I thought I would ever win in athletics. You know, I had no idea right up to the time I was signed by Louisville the year after I got out of high school that I'd be good enough to play pro ball."

As a boy who loved baseball, Pee Wee watched the Louisville Colonels of the American Association whenever he could. He twice paid his way into the bleachers at Parkway Field, and the other times he arrived at the same vantage point by climbing up and over the screen and the barbed wire which decorated the brick wall surrounding the field. The Cardinals, now the Dodgers' perennial thorn, were his favorite big league team. Paul Dean and Dizzy Dean and Durocher and Pepper Martin were a few of the heroes whose likenesses, found in Wheaties boxes, he tacked up on the wall in his bedroom. "I was really sold on Dizzy Dean," Pee Wee gets a kick out of remembering. "Dizzy'd stick his neck way out, and then he'd go out and back it up. When I see Diz in St. Louis and tell him that he was my boyhood hero, he acts like a big kid about it. 'Oh, Pee Wee,' Diz will say, 'you're just pulling my leg. You never *really* idolized me, did you?' "

The years 1936 and 1937 were crucial in deciding the pattern of Reese's life. After graduation from high school he went to work for the Mengel Box Company, earning twenty-five cents an hour for wrapping chairs, which he caught off the conveyor belt. The manager of the company's baseball team, called the Embeco Club, arranged for Pee Wee's transfer to the parcel post division where there was less chance of the shortstop's pulling a muscle in his back. Working indoors, however, did not appeal to Reese. Two brothers-in-law, employed by the telephone company, were able to line up a job for him as a splicer in the cable department. The pay was no better but the physical activity of climbing up and down the poles all day long proved to be exactly what Pee Wee needed. His shoulders and arms began to take on heft and sinew. He grew taller and stronger, and it showed in his baseball. Playing shortstop for his old club, the New Covenant Presbyterian Church team, he began to make plays that no other infielder in the city could come close to. He began to hit the ball out to the outfielders and, now and then, past them. For example, after he had led the team to the pennant in the Church League, Pee Wee opened the All-Louisville semipro play-off against National Distillers by slamming a double off the left-field wall at Parkway Field 350 feet from home plate. As the prize for winning the Church League, Reese and his teammates were given a free trip to New York for the last three games of the World Series between the Giants and the Yankees.

The Church League that Reese had suddenly set on fire had long been respected as an incubator for good baseball prospects. In 1935 Branch Rickey had given seven members of the winning club, the Messick Miniatures, tryouts with the Cardinals. Reese's play had caught the attention of a scout for the Baltimore Orioles and of Cap Neal, the manager of

the Louisville Colonels, and after Pee Wee returned from his
trip to the World Series he investigated their offers. They
were not overpoweringly flattering. Baltimore was not interested in going higher than a flat $200 for look-see privi-
leges. Neal, representing Louisville, offered Reese a contract
of $100 a month. Pee Wee and his dad and Keith Sparks, the
New Covenant coach, were excited and didn't dissemble
their feelings. Through some stroke of clear thinking, Mr.
Reese and Mr. Sparks requested that a clause be written into
the contract stating that, in the event of his sale to a major
league team, Reese would receive 5 per cent of the purchase
price. The wisdom of that reservation was materially apparent two seasons later when Pee Wee was sold to Brooklyn
for $35,000 plus four players valued at $40,000. When that
great day arrived in 1939 there was only one thing wrong.
Mr. Reese had died the previous December. "He thought the
sun went up and down with me," Pee Wee has said of his
father. "How often I've wished that he could have lived
long enough to see me make the majors."

Mr. Reese did live long enough, however, to watch his
son during the first of his two seasons with the Louisville
Colonels. He would drop into the park for two or three
innings whenever his job on the railroad permitted. He saw a
pretty good ballplayer out there at shortstop for Louisville.
In 1938, his first season in organized baseball, Pee Wee
batted .277, but he hit for extra bases (twenty-one doubles
and eight triples) and delivered with men on base. In his
second year with the Colonels he continued to improve. He
belted twenty-two doubles, and his eighteen triples topped
the American Association. He blossomed out as a base-runner; in thirty-six attempted steals, he was cut down just
once. But it was the things Reese did in the field, the way
his sense of anticipation and fine legs and fast hands made
the hard chances look routine, that drew the big league scouts

to Louisville early in the 1939 season. Ted McGrew and Andy High were looking him over for the Dodgers, Clarence "Pants" Rowland for the Cubs, ready to move if the Red Sox, who controlled Louisville, should decide to sell Reese to another club. "I was on the train, returning from the American Association's All-Star game," Reese was relating this March, "when a newspaper man pounded me on the back and told me I had just been sold to Brooklyn. I had pretty mixed feelings about that news. Every ballplayer dreams of making the majors, of course, but Brooklyn wasn't the club I wanted to go up with. I didn't know a soul on the Dodgers and I wanted to go to spring training where I'd have some friends. On the Red Sox I knew Charlie Wagner and Stan Spence, and I'd played against Ted Williams when he was with Minneapolis and I knew him a little—and I'd been thinking all along I'd be going with the Sox." Pee Wee smiled and then continued. "Those first reactions seem pretty funny now. I've enjoyed every minute I've spent with the Brooklyn team." Some Boston writers, on the other hand, have never forgiven the Sox for letting Reese get away.

Pee Wee weighed 145 pounds when he reported at the Dodgers training camp in Clearwater, Florida, in 1940. "I don't know how Durocher felt when he saw me," Pee Wee has said. "He probably thought, 'This can't be the guy who's going to take my place!'" Durocher, on the contrary, was immediately impressed with the rookie both as a person and a shortstop. He lost no time in placing Reese in the first infield with Camilli, Coscarart, and Lavagetto, and he personally tutored his successor in the niceties of double-play timing, fielding and throwing the ball in the same motion, and the different cutoff plays. Being Durocher, there were days when the Dodger manager would slow down a Reese booster, such as Ted McGrew, by declaiming with disdain that "Reese couldn't have carried my glove when I was at my peak." And there were days when the volatile Durocher, watching Reese move so naturally around the infield, would exclaim in admiration, "That kid's great, great! He's another Durocher!" John Lardner tells the superb story of how Leo took Pee Wee aside and instructed the youngster never to be bashful about asking him anything he wanted to know about playing shortstop. Pee Wee said he wouldn't. Days went by and then weeks, and while Durocher was always ready to lay wide open his vast storehouse of baseball knowledge, Reese never had any questions to ask. The rookie finally approached Leo one afternoon. "Mr. Durocher," he said respectfully, "I want to ask your advice about something." "Great, Pee Wee." Leo beamed. "I'm glad you finally figured I could tell you something. What do you want to know?" "Say," Pee Wee asked, "where do you get your clothes?"

Pee Wee always liked to play ball for Durocher. "Anything Leo did—bridge, dominoes, dancing, dressing, talking—he liked to do well," Pee Wee has said of Durocher. "On the ball field, he'd do anything to win a game. He didn't want his men to feel too friendly toward the players on the other teams. If you were passing the time of day chatting with the second baseman, you might miss a signal. Leo wasn't afraid to gamble. He'd take suggestions. He expected the players on the bench to inform him when they thought they detected anything they thought could be vital—the center fielder was playing too far over or the pitcher was losing his stuff. He believed that pepper never hurt a club. Being an old shortstop, he watched every move I made like a hawk, and that was rough on me. He bawled me out a lot in front of the other players, which isn't the most tactful way to get criticism across. But Leo played baseball the way I like to play baseball, and off the field he was like a father to me. I've enjoyed playing for Burt Shotton very much, but I am also a Durocher man."

Reese got off to a fast start in 1940 and rapidly established himself as an infielder of unquestioned major league ability.

While the twenty-year-old rookie showed all the baseball savvy his manager could ask for, Leo was disappointed with Pee Wee's disinclination to talk it up and take charge. When Leo had joined the Yankees, instead of being awed by the presence of Ruth and Gehrig and the other members of that magnificent team, he had taken it upon himself to straighten those boys out. He had let no opposing ballplayer push him around, and his audacity had flustered even Ty Cobb who was not used to having callow youths give it right back to him.

Leo's strong point has never been understanding persons of temperaments different from his. Reese's temperament is distinctly different. If Leo was probably the freshest busher who ever broke into the big leagues, Pee Wee was perhaps the most respectful. There was a good deal of the hero-worshiper in the boy. Whenever Dolf Camilli or Cookie Lavagetto or any of the other established stars asked him to come along with them to the movies, it was a great event in his life. He felt the same relationship to them on the ball field—the junior partner. Camilli was Reese's especial hero.

Two severe injuries marred Reese's otherwise successful freshman year in which he batted .272 in eighty-four games, made only eighteen errors, and won four games with clutch home runs. In July, batting against Jake Mooty of the Cubs at Wrigley Field (a park batters abhor because the white-shirted background of the fans in center field makes the ball hard to follow) Pee Wee lost a pitch and was struck on the side of the head. "I saw the ball when it left Mooty's hand; then I was looking for the ball—I never did see it," Pee Wee has said of his beaning. He was out for three weeks in all. On his return to the line-up he began wearing a plastic protective helmet inside his cap when batting. (He has worn one ever since.) He showed no signs of being plate-shy. He doubled hard to left-center on his first time at bat. The next time he faced Mooty, he looked at a couple of balls and then lined a single to left.

Pee Wee had been back in the line-up less than a month when he chipped a bone in his left ankle sliding into second in a game against the Phillies. Dixie Walker hit a ball that Reese thought was going through the infield. The shortstop, however, made a good play on the ball and tossed it to second to get the force on Reese. Pee Wee hit the dirt too close to the sack, caught his spikes on the bottom of the bag, and the ankle twisted and snapped. He was in a cast for five weeks and out for the remainder of the season.

One baseball superstition that continues to thrive is the "sophomore jinx." Gene Bearden and Richie Ashburn, the prize rookies of 1948, had distressing years in 1949. Reese, who had looked so precise and at times so elegant in 1940, went through a nightmare of a season in 1941. His batting average fell to .229. His failure to hit did not seriously affect a team which had an array of sturdy batters like Camilli, Medwick, Vaughan, Walker, Billy Herman (acquired in June), and the redoubtable Pete Reiser, up from Elmira for his first full year in the big time. A team like that could afford to carry a light-hitting shortstop. What did hurt the Dodgers, engaged in a hectic battle for the pennant, was Reese's erratic play in the field. No one was more acutely aware of this than Reese himself. He felt he was letting the team down, and in his determination to make up for his lapses he fell into that cruel vicious circle: overdetermination made him overtense; overtension led to errors in crucial junctures; his resultant despondency bred an overdetermination to atone; and so on and on. The pressure of the tight ones told on the kid who was trying too hard.

Reese's ordeal in 1941 might have been much harder on him had he not had in Pete Reiser a close, dependable, enjoyable friend. The two kids had started rooming together when Reiser came up with the Dodgers late in '40. After that, they were inseparable. (Their friendship has survived the deep grievances which Reiser came to hold against the Brooklyn management following his tragic succession of accidents. It has stayed very much alive in the face of inaccurate publicity and the emotional strains which have beleaguered Reiser during the past few seasons. Whenever the Braves play the Dodgers, Reiser practically dresses in the Brooklyn locker room, talking things over with Reese.) The mutual affection and regard of Reiser and Reese when they were the two youngest regulars on the prewar Dodgers was the closest thing to Damon and Pythias that grizzled big leaguers had ever seen. "Pete and I never had an argument," Pee Wee told a friend not long ago. "Usually when you room with a fellow, one of the two wants the lights on when the other wants them off. Little irritations like that come up. Somehow they didn't with Pete and myself. If Pete said he wanted to go to a movie, we went to a movie. If I felt like taking it easy, we took it easy. The first suggestion either of us made, that was what we did, and we got a helluva lot of pleasure being together." As a ballplayer, Reese thinks Reiser is "the nearest thing to Musial I've ever seen—he can do everything."

Reese's sporadic shakiness did not prevent the Dodgers from winning the pennant in 1941. They clinched it on September 25, when Whit Wyatt shut out the Braves. Pee Wee felt a massive release. On the special Pullman and diner that carried the team back from Boston, he let himself go completely. With Lavagetto and Reiser, he walked up and down the aisle pouring champagne and Worcestershire Sauce over his teammates' heads. As the celebration continued, Reiser found a scissors and snipped off Pee Wee's tie just below the knot. Grabbing the scissors, Pee Wee leaned over and clipped off Pete's tie. Then the two kids began to howl. Pee Wee had forgotten that Pete was wearing one of *his* ties.

In the first game of the World Series against the Yanks, Reese collected three hits, half of the total number the Dodgers got off Charley Ruffing. It looked as if he might be off on an explosive Series that would make up for his disappointing regular season. That was not the case. In the last four games—the Yanks took the series in five—Reese connected for only one safe hit in fifteen times at bat. He kicked three in the field. Remembering 1941 gives Reese about as much pleasure as Churchill derives from long thoughts on the Gallipoli campaign. On the other hand, there being no substitute for personal experience, absorbing the tribulations of 1941 accounts in a large measure for Reese's unusual sensitivity in understanding the problems that weigh heavily on the minds of the young players he captains.

In 1942, Reese's last campaign before entering the Navy, he gradually regained his confidence. You would call it a so-so season, a passable season. He batted a soft .255 but led the league shortstops in put-outs, assists, and double plays. Pee Wee remembers 1942 as the Honeymoon Year. He was Pete Reiser's best man when his buddy was married at Daytona Beach on March 28. The boys switched positions the following day when Reese married Dorothy Walton, culminating a romance that had begun over a back-yard fence in Louisville some three years earlier. "Pee Wee's sister lived next door to us," Mrs. Reese related this spring to an admirer of her husband who had requested a blow-by-blow account of their first meetings. "I was out in our back yard drying my hair one afternoon when I saw this boy in the yard next door. He came and leaned over the fence and we talked a little. The next afternoon I was inside our house when I saw him walking around the back yard next door. Since I couldn't very well wash my hair again so I could go out and dry it, I explained to my mother that I needed some excuse for seeing that very nice fellow I had met. I asked her if there wasn't some garbage I could empty. Well, we were all out of garbage at the moment, but my mother threw some together for me. Pee Wee and I talked a little more that day. My family moved into another house shortly after this, though, and I was afraid that he would lose track of me. One day, though, as I was getting off the school bus I saw Pee Wee waiting for me in his car. He started coming over to our house every night after that, ostensibly to play ping-pong with my brother. Then one night, about a week later, he asked me to the movies. After that—I don't know how Pee Wee felt—but I never had the least interest in anyone else. One of the amusing things about Pee Wee and me was that I had no idea he was a ballplayer until the first night he came over to play ping-pong. He had never mentioned it. But when I introduced him to my family, my brother became very excited. 'Sis, don't you know who this fellow is?' he began shouting. 'He's the shortstop for the Louisville Colonels. Wow!' "

In addition to being that rare thing, an unaffected woman, Dorothy Reese is a charming person, warm and extremely attractive. The Reeses have been very happy. They have one child, Barbara Lee, now six. Barbara was born in January, 1944, fifteen days before her father was transferred by the Navy from Norfolk to Hawaii.

Pee Wee and his wife and daughter live during the winter in Louisville. Their new home on South Western Parkway is a modest one—six rooms. Across the street is Shawnee Park with its eighteen baseball diamonds; to play there was one of the biggest treats of Pee Wee's boyhood. During the off-season he is connected with a storm-window and screen company which he organized with Max Macon, the old Brooklyn pitcher who was more effective in the batter's box than on the mound. Pee Wee's chief recreation is golf. His swing is sound and he plays consistently around 73 or 74. Having to give up golf was for Reese the most

difficult part of his convalescence this winter after he was
operated on for a hernia.

Pee Wee entered the service in January, 1943, and was dis-
charged on Armistice Day, 1945. The Navy assigned him, as
it did most athletes of his caliber, to its extensive physical
training and morale program. After his boot training, Reese
put in eleven months at Norfolk and eleven at Pearl Harbor
and spent the remainder of his time in the service as a Chief
Petty Officer, touring the installations in the South and
Central Pacific with ball teams. Hugh Casey, who was in
the same indoctrination class and the same overseas detach-
ment, thought he noticed a marked improvement in Pee
Wee's play at Norfolk. "Pee Wee played short on our team,
representing the Naval Air Station," Hugh was saying recently, "and Phil Rizzuto was at short for the Naval Operations Base team. We played each other something like forty-
six or forty-eight times. Rizzuto was at that time a completely
polished ballplayer, and I think Pee Wee came on a lot in
the friendly rivalry the two waged. They used to love to steal
base hits away from each other. Rizzuto's a pull hitter, and
Reese would play him deep in the hole and come up with
all sorts of circus stops. When we were in Hawaii in 1944,
Reese, as I saw it, had become a polished player. You could
notice the difference watching him go after a ball. Before,
you'd see his hands get a little nervous. Now he was sure of
himself, moved swiftly in front of that ball and got rid of it
underhand, overhand, or sidearm, as smooth as Durocher.
In the games we played at Hawaii against the Army, Bill
Dickey, who was in charge of our team, played Pee Wee at
short and Rizzuto at third. You couldn't buy a hit through
the left side of that infield."

Since his return to Ebbets Field in 1946, Pee Wee has replaced Marty Marion as the ranking shortstop in the National League, and there are many experts who assess his all-
around value a notch above the American League standouts,

Rizzuto and Boudreau. Aided by the shorter fences introduced into postwar baseball and abetted by his increased brawn, Reese became a far more consistent long-ball hitter. In 1947 he clouted twelve home runs and last year upped his production to a new high, sixteen. (He's a high-ball hitter, always has been.) He has batted in over seventy runs in each of the last three seasons, a notable mark for a lead-off man. In the World Series of '47 and '49, the near-goat of the '41 Series batted over .300 and was one of the few Dodgers who stood firm against the Yankee avalanche.

No longer surrounded by the old pros of the MacPhail Export-Import Company but by the young graduates of the several schools which comprise Rickey Tech, the postwar Reese exhibited a shade more assertiveness in 1946 and 1947. During those two seasons, however, Eddie Stanky appointed himself to take charge of taking charge (and, incidentally, did a bang-up job). When Stanky was shipped to Boston after the 1947 season, Dodger rooters were up in arms. They agreed with Rickey that Jackie Robinson might be a better second baseman than Stanky, but, with Stanky gone, who did the team have who could fill his shoes as a driving leader? They were definitely confounded when Rickey rebutted that he was confident Reese would handle those duties very capably. The complexion of the Dodgers in 1948 was mottled by the discharge of Durocher in midseason, and it was impossible to tell if the self-effacing and gentlemanly Reese possessed the qualities of leadership Rickey had claimed for him.

At a lunch at the Kentucky Hotel before the 1949 season began, Rickey appointed Reese captain of the Dodgers. He did it deliberately, recognizing that a person who detested every form of showboating as virulently as Reese would take command only if he were officially directed to assume that responsibility. Rickey made it completely clear what he expected of his captain. "Up to now, son," he said to

Reese, "you've been Pee Wee and you've been a kid and a youngster, and you've assumed that relationship with your teammates. However, all of the veterans are gone now. The day has come when you are the veteran. You're the Walker, the Wyatt, the Camilli—you're *it*. Be assertive. Don't be stagnant. Don't inhibit your impulses." From time to time Rickey discussed with his captain the methods of the great leaders, and he supplemented these talks by sending Reese a copy of *Crusade in Europe* by Dwight D. Eisenhower, a man who knew how to handle men.

Some persons swell up with authority, some digest it and grow larger. From the first day he took over as captain, it was evident to all observers that a tremendous untapped potential of Reese's was finally getting room to move in. Daily, in the early stages of the season, you saw quiet demonstrations of his perceptiveness in that fractious area where baseball relations meet human relations. Under the strain of the pennant race he continued to grow and grow naturally. Pee Wee on one leg, as Shotton expressed it, was more valuable than other players on two. The fullness with which he took hold surprised even Rickey. At the end of the season, the Branch who seldom goes out on a limb admitted that he considered Reese an excellent prospect as a future manager of the Dodgers.

Of course, when you thought back on it, Reese's growth should not have been the stunning thing that it seemed. He had always exhibited a constructive instinct and uncommon intelligence, and no one was in a better position to remark these qualities than Rickey himself. The brilliant success of Rickey's noble experiment, breaking down the color line in organized baseball, would not have been possible if his own team had been unwilling to accept a Negro. Many of the Dodgers were opposed to the idea. Shortly after the signing of Jackie Robinson was announced, Rickey was over-

whelmed by indignant protests. Southern outfielders asked
to be traded, and Northern infielders wanted to be traded
just as vehemently. These players backed up their personal
disaffection by quoting their teammates, as if to say, "We all
think the same." "But somehow," Mr. Rickey recently remarked, "no one could quote Reese. What did Pee Wee
think? No one knew. He hadn't said anything, just gone
about his business. For all that the players could tell you, you
would have thought that Reese was simply not around."

Reese comes from Kentucky. Not because of this or in
spite of this, but because he is a big-league person, Reese had
accepted the situation and was prepared to accept Robinson
just like any other ballplayer who could help the team. From
the beginning he communicated his position to Robinson
without words or posturing. "You always felt that Pee Wee
knew what was on your mind," Jack was saying a few weeks
ago. "I remember the first time I played alongside Pee Wee
at second. We were playing in Boston. While we were throwing the ball around the infield just before the game, a lot of
hollering and talk came out of the Boston dugout, directed
not at me but at Pee Wee. You know the kind of talk. I was
feeling pretty uncomfortable. Well, what happened was
this. Pee Wee left his position and came over and chatted
with me around second base. I actually don't remember a
word he said. All I know is that I got the feeling that Pee
Wee was saying that as long as I was helping the ball club and
was a good fellow, he was with me 100 per cent and so was
the team. You know, when we trotted back to our positions,
there was no noise coming from the Boston dugout."

Pee Wee is always studying his teammates. Whenever he
thinks he has spotted a detail that will help them, he passes
that tip on graciously. "Don't be afraid to keep throwing
that ball hard," he told Campanella who was blazing the ball
to the bases during 1949 spring practice. "Mickey Owen used
to throw a very heavy ball, but yours comes in light. It's easy

to handle, so keep throwing it hard." When Campy's pegs
began to get a dip in them later in the season, Reese straightened that out by suggesting that the catcher come more overhand on his throwing motion. Pee Wee helped Gil Hodges
out of a deep batting slump by diagnosing that Gil was upsetting his timing by striding too far, not waiting for the ball.
He keeps after Hermanski on Gene's throws to the infield,
works with Carl Furillo on his keeping his bullet throws to
third down low enough so they can be cut off. He assumes
that his teammates share his attitude that there is nothing
you can't learn to do better. "I always thought I was a natural
slider until I went to Vero Beach in '48," Pee Wee told a
group of friends with whom he was discussing base-running
technique. "One day I was in the group assigned to report to
the sliding pit. Branch Rickey, Jr., was teaching sliding that
day, and he asked me to try one. I thought I made a helluva
slide. 'How'd you like that?' I said, looking up at Branch.
'Not so hot, Pee Wee,' he answered. That surprised me, but
Branch was right. He pointed out that I was bending my left
knee before I hit the bag. That slows you down—hit the bag
and then bend that leg."

As far as Reese is concerned, the Rickeys are much fairer
men to talk contracts with than Larry MacPhail, who somehow got away with a reputation for largesse. Reese received
$6,500 during his rookie year in 1940. MacPhail was so appre-
ciative of the youngster's fine performance that he "raised"
him to $6,500 for 1941. The Dodgers won the pennant that
season and, carried away with generous emotions, MacPhail
tore up Pee Wee's old contract and wrote out a new one for
$6,500. "I was just a kid," Pee Wee has said of his dealings
with Lavish Larry. "I thought I was worth more than I was
being paid, but I didn't know how to talk finances. 'Mr. Mac-
Phail, I'm going to leave this up to you,' I would say. 'Son,'
he would answer, 'I have a job to do and so do you. You're
on one side of the fence and I'm on the other.' You know

who won that one." On Pee Wee's return from the service he did business for the first time with Branch Rickey, the notorious skinflint. Reese was boosted to $10,000. "El Cheapo" raised Reese to $15,000 in '47, $17,500 in '48, and $25,000 in '49. This year the Dodger captain will receive in the neighborhood of $35,000 for his services. Something's wrong with the Rickey legend.

A sounder approach to Rickey, the man with whom Reese's future may well be yoked, is to think of him as an exceedingly shrewd businessman, all right, but also as the most intelligent man in baseball today—or, to fall back on that choice Brooklynese description, "a man of many faucets, all of them running." You feel that you are talking (or listening) to a substantial, thorough person when you visit the president and general manager of the Dodgers in his office on Montague Street. A vigorous sixty-eight, Rickey sits behind a double-executive desk, rocking himself elaborately in his swivel chair, spitting out fragments of the cigar he smokes and gestures with.

What does Mr. Rickey think of Reese's eventually becoming the Dodgers' manager? The face is mobile, even the heavy eyebrows, and the voice is pliant with use. "Pee Wee, he's a lovable boy. Fine mother. Did you ever meet her? Yes, sir, she's top-notch. They're fine folks, that's all. . . . I ask myself, what has Reese shown me that I should consider him for a job as ramified, as difficult as managing a major league baseball team. Reese has displayed ability, poise, self-control. I think he has enough temper, too. That's under control, but there must be temper, response, reaction to situations."

A tilt of the swivel chair, a bite on the straggling end of a cigar leaf. "However, before I would be certain that Reese possessed the full capabilities of a manager, there are qualities to be examined, many sectors in an untested area to be investigated, observed. One." (Up goes the finger and the cigar.)

"How does he handle men? Does he handle this fellow this way, that fellow that way? You have to. I would have to know more about Reese's ability in that *most* important area. I think the boy probably has it.

"Two. Can he discern baseball ability? Can he tell a sheep from a goat, and know it early? I believe Reese has all of the native abilities in this line.

"Point three. Can your manager handle differences between players, the rhubarbs on the field, the clashes of personalities under the pressure of competition? He is the first solvent. There are some managers like McKechnie who will go upstairs immediately and dump every problem in the laps of the administration. Others, like our man Shotton—he settles the problems below. I won't even know about them. You can't let a club get out of hand, and keeping harmony among twenty-five players of various dispositions and divergent emotions calls for high talent. The *personal influence*, that's it."

The Great Enumerator attacked his cigar, tilted east, then south. "Point four. I would have to know better than I do presently if Reese can run a team in a ball game. He hasn't had the *final* decision to make yet in the field of tactics. Should we play back in this situation? Is this the situation for the team to go on the offense? Is this one of the first signs of weakening in this pitcher? Durocher was a good tactician. When the battle was being waged, he was alive, resourceful. But he was not a good strategist at all. He might not have contrived to have had the battle fought at the place and time most advantageous to him.

"Five. A manager's job in essence is to mold a winning team. He must have *acute* discernment. He must know when he has a team that can win, one that is expressive of a unit. Conversely, he must be able to isolate and correct the causes for a team's disunity. A team is like a great painting that is in competition. On the painter's canvas is a lovely girl, but there is something wrong with one eye that mars her loveliness and imperils the success of the painting. Can your manager correct that deficiency with a touch of his brush and thereby win the competition?

"And six, the last point." (Cigar up, finger up.) "Discipline. Good managers don't have many rules. Sometimes a manager has to impose discipline. Discipline can also be elicited, which is preferable. As far as Reese goes, his standard of discipline has only to comport with his own conduct. Reese is a good analyzer of character. I know that. He can take the ball club in civilian clothes and tell you who the captains are. Pee Wee knows a sheep from a goat."

And that's the way it stands at the moment in Mr. Rickey's very able mind.

MAURICE RICHARD:
FIRE ON THE ICE

This article was written in the fall of 1954 when Maurice Richard was beginning his thirteenth season in the National Hockey League. At that time, as he appreciated more clearly than anyone else, Maurice, at thirty-two, was past the peak of his powers and starting down the long slope on the far side.

As soon as they discover that their reflexes are slowing down, their speed is diminishing, and their bones are growing brittle, most hockey players retire. A few reach this decision voluntarily but most have retirement thrust upon them, quickly. Hockey is no game for the aging. One of the most amazing things about Richard was his ability to play exciting and sound hockey throughout his lengthy career. He never simply hung on. There was too much pride in the man for him to have accepted the role of the old seigneur who was just a shadow of his former self. In his last active years, after he was named captain of Les Canadiens, Richard muffled his temper as he had never been able to do before. It was strange to see the old firebrand out on the ice acting as a preserver of the peace, but this he was, departing from his restraint only when he thought his kid brother, Henri, needed some assistance. Henri usually didn't, but Maurice, nevertheless, watched over him with the fierce protectiveness of a chieftain of some primitive tribe.

In his last three seasons Richard met with severe injuries. In 1957–1958, in the fourteenth game of the season, his Achilles tendon was severed in a skate accident. He was out forty-two games but, typically, scored two goals when he returned. The following winter he broke the lower extremity of the left tibia just after mid-season and was not able to get back into action until the play-offs, and then only for token appearances. He was back, though, for the 1959–60 campaign and playing awfully well when, in the twenty-first game, he suffered a depressed fracture of the left side of the facial bone and missed the next nineteen games. The older you get, of course, the more subject you are to injury and the longer it takes to mend. Maurice always contended, however, that no one would have to tell him when to quit, he would know better than anyone else. That day at length arrived in September 1960. Once again he had gone to training camp to play himself into condition. At the conclusion of a routine practice session, with no particular fanfare, he announced that he had gone as far as he could go, and that was that. Without him, the Canadiens have not been what they were. It is not only what Maurice personally contributed that they miss but also the prodding inspiration of the mere presence on the bench of the grim old lion. As a player he was endowed with such magnetism that, as Al Laney has remarked, you could never take your eyes off him for a moment when he was on the ice. Perhaps this is why, when you go to a game today in which Les Canadiens are playing, something at the back of your mind keeps nagging at you: you are wondering where Maurice is.

Although he was not the all-round hockey virtuoso that Gordon Howe is, Maurice Richard undoubtedly was the greatest offensive player of all time, and no one has ever come close to doing the astounding things he could do when his fire was burning brightest. The multiple scoring marks he has left behind him will undoubtedly be broken some day, if not by Howe and Geoffrion, then by later stars. This past winter, for example, the two Richard records that looked to be the safest were equaled when Geoffrion scored in nine consecutive games and collected fifty goals during the season. (Geoffrion accomplished this over a schedule of seventy games, Maurice in fifty.)

In any event, here, for your study and admiration, is a year-by-year breakdown of Maurice Richard's lifetime scoring record for his eighteen seasons in the National Hockey League in which he scored 544 goals in regular season play, added 82 goals in the Stanley Cup play-offs, and, all in all, accounted for 101 game-winning goals.

YEAR	GAMES	GOALS	ASSISTS	POINTS
1942–43	16	5	6	11
1943–44	46	32	22	54
1944–45	50	50	23	73
1945–46	50	27	21	48
1946–47	60	45	26	71
1947–48	53	28	25	53
1948–49	59	20	18	38
1949–50	70	43	22	65
1950–51	65	42	24	66
1951–52	48	27	17	44
1952–53	70	28	33	61
1953–54	70	37	30	67
1954–55	67	38	36	74
1955–56	70	38	33	71
1956–57	63	33	29	62
1957–58	28	15	19	34
1958–59	42	17	21	38
1959–60	51	19	16	35
Totals	978	544	421	965
Play-offs	133	82	44	126
Grand Totals	1,111	626	461	1,091

FOR ALL that has been said and written about the heights of fanatic devotion achieved by the fans of the Brooklyn Dodgers, the Notre Dame football teams, and the Australian Davis Cup defenders, it is doubtful if there is any group of sports addicts anywhere which year in and year out supports its team with quite the supercharged emotion and lavish pride expended so prodigally by the citizens of bilingual Montreal on their hockey team, Les Canadiens—the Canadians. In June each year, four months before the next season begins, every seat in the Montreal Forum, save 800 or so that the management holds for sale on the day of the game, has been sold out for the entire seventy-game schedule. On play-off nights it is not uncommon for crowds seeking standing room to run into several thousands and to swarm over Ste. Catherine's Street and beyond onto Atwater Park.

Hockey is deep in the Montrealer's blood. After a fine play by a member of the home team or, for that matter, of the visiting team, the Forum reverberates from the rinkside to the rafters with sharp, enthusiastic applause. But many volts above this in feeling and many decibels above in volume is the singular and sudden pandemonium that shatters the Forum, like thunder and lightning, whenever the incomparable star of Les Canadiens, Maurice (The Rocket) Richard, fights his way through the enemy defense and blasts the puck past the goalie. There is no sound quite like it in the whole world of sport.

A powerfully built athlete of thirty-three who stands five ten and now weighs 180, having put on about a pound a year since breaking in with Les Canadiens in 1942, Joseph Henri Maurice (pronounced Mohr-riz, with the accent about equally divided) Richard (Ree-shar'), Gallicly handsome and eternally intense, is generally regarded by most aficionados, be they Montrealers or étrangers, as the greatest player in the history of hockey. Whether he is or not, of course, is one of those sports arguments that boils down in the final analysis to a matter of personal opinion. However, as Richard's supporters invariably point out, hockey is in essence a game of scoring, and here there can be no argument: the Rocket stands in a class by himself, the outstanding scorer of all time. Flip through the pages of the record book: Most

Goals—384, set by Maurice Richard in twelve seasons (with the next man, Nels Stewart, a full sixty goals away); Most Goals in One Season—fifty, set by Maurice Richard in a fifty-game schedule in 1944–45; Most Goals in a Play-off Series—twelve, Maurice Richard; Most Goals in a Play-off Game—five, Maurice Richard; Longest Consecutive Scoring Streak—at least one goal in nine consecutive games, Maurice Richard; and so on and on. The record book supplies no entry for Most Winning Goals, but several Montreal fans who lovingly compile all Richardiana can document that by the beginning of the season their man had scored the goal that won no less than fifty-nine regular-season games and eight play-off games.

It is not the multiplicity of Richard's goals or their timeliness but, rather, the chronically spectacular manner in which he scores them that has made the fiery right-winger the acknowledged Babe Ruth of hockey. "There are goals and there are Richard goals," Dick Irvin, the old "Silver Fox" who has coached the Canadiens the length of Richard's career, remarked not long ago. "He doesn't get lucky goals. Let's see, he's scored over 390 now. Of these, 370 have had a flair. He can get to a puck and do things to it quicker than any man I've ever seen, even if he has to lug two defense men with him, and he frequently has to. And his shots! They go in with such velocity that the net and all bulges."

One of the popular indoor pastimes year-round in Montreal is talking over old Richard goals—which one you thought was the most neatly set up, which one stirred you the most, etc.—much in the way Americans used to hot-stove about Ruth's home runs and do today about Willie Mays' various catches. In Irvin's opinion—and Hector (Toe) Blake and Elmer Lach, Richard's teammates on the famous Punch Line, also feel this way—the Rocket's most sensational goal was "the Seibert goal" in the 1945–46 season. Earl Seibert, a strapping 225-pound defenseman who was playing for Detroit that season, hurled himself at Richard as he swept on a solo into the Detroit zone. Richard occasionally will bend his head and neck very low when he is trying to outmaneuver a defense man. He did on this play. The two collided with a thud, and, as they straightened up, there was Richard, still on his feet, still controlling the puck, and, sitting on top of his shoulders, the burly Seibert. Richard not only carried Seibert with him on the way to the net, a tour de force in itself, but, with that tremendous extra effort of which he is capable, faked the goalie out of position and with his one free hand somehow managed to hoist the puck into the far corner of the cage.

There are two interesting epilogues to this story. The first concerns Seibert and serves well to illustrate the enormous respect in which Richard is held by opposing players. When Seibert clambered into the dressing room after the game, Jack Adams, the voluble Detroit coach, eyed him scornfully. "Why, you dumb Dutchman," he began, "you go let that Richard—" "Listen, Mr. Adams," Seibert cut in, interrupting Adams for the first time in his career, "any guy who can carry me sixty feet and then put the puck into the net—well, more power to him!" And that ended that. The second rider to the story is that Richard is perhaps the only hockey player who, to increase his ability to operate with a burden, has frequently spent an extra half hour after the regular practice sessions careening full steam around the rink with his young son, Maurice, Jr., "The Petit Rocket," perched on his shoulders.

There is no question that Richard's most heroic winning goal was "the Boston goal"—the one he scored against the Bruins three years ago to lift Montreal into the finals of the Stanley Cup play-offs. It came late in the third period of a 1–1 game in which the Canadiens were playing badly, Richard in particular. Early in that period Maurice received a

deep gash over his left eye. He was taken to the clinic inside
the Forum, and the cut was hastily patched up. Blood was
still trickling down from the dressing over his cheek when he
returned to the bench and took his next turn on the ice. "I
can see that goal now," Frank Selke, Jr., the son of the Canadiens' managing director, reminisced recently. "Hundreds
of us can. Richard sets off a chain reaction whenever he gets
the puck, even if it is just a routine pass. It's strange and wonderful the way he communicates with the crowd. Now, this
time he got the puck at our own blue line and you knew—
everybody knew—that the game was over right then. Here's
what he did. He slipped around Woody Dumart, who was
his check, and set sail down the right-hand boards. Quackenbush and Armstrong, the Boston defensemen, were ready for
him. He swung around Armstrong with a burst of speed,
using his right hand to carry the puck and fending off Armstrong with his left, but Quackenbush pinned him into the
boards in the corner. And then, somehow, he broke away
from Quackenbush, skated across in front of the net, pulled
Jim Henry out of the goal, and drove it home."

For ten years now, because of his courage, his skill, and that
magical uncultivatable quality, true magnetism, Maurice
Richard has reigned in Montreal and throughout the province of Quebec as a hero whose hold on the public has no
parallel in sport today unless it be the country-wide adoration
that the people of Spain have from time to time heaped on
their rare master matadors. The fact that 75 per cent of the
citizens of Montreal and a similar percentage of the Forum
regulars are warm-blooded, excitable French Canadians—
and, what is more, a hero-hungry people who think of themselves not as the majority group in their province but as the
minority group in Canada—goes quite a distance in explaining their idolatry of Richard. "If Maurice were an English
Canadian or a Scottish Canadian or a kid from the West, he
would be lionized but not as much as he is now," an English-

Canadian Richard-follower declared last month. "I go to all the games with a French-Canadian friend of mine, a fellow named Roger Oulette. I know exactly what Roger thinks. He accepts that the English are as good as anyone. But he would hate to see the French population lose their language and their heritage generally. He doesn't like the fact that the government's pension checks are printed only in English. He feels that they should be printed in both English and French since the constitution of the Dominion provides for a two-language country. For Roger, Maurice Richard personifies French Canada and all that is great about it. Maybe you have to have French blood, really, to worship Richard but, you know, you only have to be a lover of hockey to admire him."

As befits the Babe Ruth of hockey, Richard is the highest-paid player in the history of the game. While Les Canadiens' front office prefers not to divulge his exact salary, it amounts to a very healthy chunk of his estimated annual income of $50,000, which is filled out by his commissions for endorsing such products as a hair tonic and the Maurice Richard model windbreaker, his cut from the sale of *Le Rocket du Hockey* and other publications about him, and his occasional appearances during the off-season as a wrestling referee. "Maurice could earn much more than he does but he has been careful not to connect himself with anything cheap," Camil Des Roches, the Canadiens' publicity director, says. "If he wanted to, he could referee a wrestling bout every night of next summer. His appearance is enough to insure the success of any affair in the province, from wrestling to a church outing." A few years ago, Richard and his teammate Kenny Reardon dropped in for lunch at the Canadian Club, a restaurant in Montreal. "When the other diners spotted Rocket," Reardon relates, "they began to pass the hat for him. It was a spontaneous gesture of appreciation. They collected $50, just like that. People can't do enough for him." Richard, in consequence, is the perfect companion to travel with should you journey anywhere in the province of Quebec. No one will let him pay for a meal, for lodgings, for transportation, for anything.

And what about le Rocket? How does he react to this fantastic adulation? Perhaps the surest key is the way he conducts himself after he scores one of his roof-raising goals. Down on the ice, below the tumult of tribute, Richard, while the referee is waiting for the clamor to subside before dropping the puck for the next face-off, cruises solemnly in slow circles, somewhat embarrassed by the strength of the ovation, his normally expressive dark eyes fixed expressionless on the ice. In his actions there is never the suspicion of the idol recognizing the plaudits of his fans. The slow circles which Richard transcribes after he has scored serve a distinct purpose for him. They add up to a brief moment of uncoiling, one of the few he is able to allow himself during the six-months-long season. "Maurice," Toe Blake once remarked, "lives to score goals." It is not that Richard puts himself above his team or the game. Quite the contrary, in fact. But here—and he has never been any other way—is a terribly intense man who, like so many of the champions who have endured as champions, is forever driving himself to come up to the almost impossibly high standard of performance he sets, whose pride in himself will not let him relax until he has delivered decisively, and who, additionally, regards the veneration that has come his way as nothing less than a public trust that he must never let down. The immortal Morenz, though you would never have guessed it since he hid his emotions so well, also poured himself into hockey heart and soul. After a game in which he had played poorly and contributed to a Canadiens defeat, Morenz would warn all his friends to stay away from him and he would pace the streets of Montreal, sometimes until four or five in the morning, until he had quieted himself down and felt fit to live with people again. When Richard or Les Canadiens lose or when he is in the throes of a prolonged scoring slump, the Rocket does not pace the streets, but he will brood silently, sometimes for days at a time, limiting his conversations with his wife to "Pass the butter" or "More water." Success affects Richard no less deeply. After his monumental play-off goal against the Bruins he broke down in tears in the dressing room. His father came in and they talked together for a while, and then Maurice was all right. Even today, when victory and frustration are old stories for him, he remains so highly charged that he has a great deal of trouble sleeping the night before a game when the team is on the road. "Maurice can relax," Elmer Lach has said, "but not during the hockey season. After the last game, Maurice is a different fellow."

Richard's teammates remember the tail end of the 1952–53 season as the time of his most alarming mood. This was the year that Gordie Howe (playing a seventy-game schedule) was on the verge of breaking Richard's record for goals in one season, the fifty he had scored in 1944–45 when the league was playing a fifty-game schedule. With one game to go, Howe stood at forty-nine. The remaining game was in Detroit against the Canadiens. "The night of that game, that was the only time I ever was afraid to put a hockey player on the ice," Coach Irvin said not long ago. "I remember watching Rocket's eyes as we were going across the city in the cab. 'I can't play him tonight,' I said to myself. 'He'll kill somebody.' I played him, but I made sure he wasn't going to be on the ice any time Howe was. In spite of my precautions, one time they were for a few seconds—I think Rocket was coming out of the penalty box. He skated straight across the ice and charged right at Howe. Then he turned around and skated back to the penalty box. Rocket was proud of his record, but it was more than that. He would have felt humiliated if Howe had beaten or tied it playing against him or his team. Anyway, Howe didn't score. After the game Richard was in the dressing room breathing hard and little Gerry McNeil, our goalie, went over to him. 'Well, Rocket,' Gerry told him with a big smile, 'Howe will have to start all over again with number one.' "

Because of his own scoring proclivities, Richard has for a dozen years been subjected to far more physical punishment than any other player since the National Hockey League was organized back in 1917. To beat Montreal, you must stop the Rocket, and to stop him opposing teams assign one man and sometimes two to do nothing but stay with Richard "right into the dressing room" if necessary. Some of the men assigned to Richard play him cleanly but, more often than not, opposing "defensive specialists" resort to holding him, grabbing his jersey, hooking him, and, whenever they get any kind of a shot at him, belting him with their Sunday body check. One of the best ways to stop Richard, of course, is to get him off the ice. With this in mind, some of the rival teams have made it a practice to use a left wing against him with instructions to ignite deliberately the Rocket's red glare. Then, if Richard retaliates and the referee calls a double penalty, Montreal loses Richard and the other team a far less valuable man. Considering the abuse, both physical and verbal, he has taken from lesser men, Richard, all in all, has done a very good job of keeping his trigger temper under control, in recent years particularly. However, if he always ranks near the top in goals, he also does in penalty time, and not all of his penalties, by any manner of means, are the result of self-protection. The Rocket probably holds the league record for misconduct penalties, ten-minute "rests" that are awarded for telling the referees off in overly pungent language. The Rocket is always up among the leaders, for that matter, in major penalties, five-minute cool-off sessions for fighting. He has lost some fights but only when he has been ganged up on. In man-to-man combat he acquits himself extremely well. When Bill Juzda of the Leafs challenged him one night, Maurice stripped off his gloves and flattened Juzda with one blow. In 1945 he knocked down Bob (Killer) Dill of the Rangers twice on the ice, and when Dill decided to start things again in the penalty box, Richard knocked him out.

The ambition of most Canadian boys is to play hockey well enough to make the National Hockey League with their favorite team—Les Canadiens, if the boy is of French descent. Maurice Richard was never confused by any other ambition. He was born on August 4, 1921, in Bordeaux, a typical parish on the reaches of Montreal, the oldest child of Onésime and Alice Laramee Richard. After Maurice came Georgette, Rene, Rollande, Jacques, Margaret, Henri and Claude. Henri, now eighteen, plays for the Montreal Royals, the Canadiens' farm team in the Quebec Hockey League. Not too hefty, Henri has a great deal of his older brother's dash and scoring flair and has been dubbed "The Pocket Rocket." Claude is just seventeen and also has the makings, in Maurice's opinion, of a pretty fair hockey player.

With a family soon on his hands, Richard père was forced to give up any ideas he had about making a career in baseball. An accomplished center fielder although he stood not much over five feet tall, he continued to play semipro baseball until he was forty-five, but he earned his living, as he still does, as a workman in the machine shops of the Canadian-Pacific Railroad. Maurice began to skate when he was about four. In those days Canadian winters were much more severe than they are today. From October through April snow covered the outlying parishes such as Bordeaux, and deliveries of milk and bread were made by sleigh. When the snow in the streets had been packed down into a hard crust, the children would skate to school on top of it. After school was out at four o'clock, Richard remembers, he would play hockey till five-thirty when it was time to go home for supper. "Many days I kept my skates on while I ate," he says. "Then I would go out and play some more hockey until ten o'clock." When rink ice was hard to find, Maurice used to skate on the treacherous Rivière des Prairies, or the Back River, as it was called, since it is the branch of the Ottawa River that flows to the north or the back of the island of Montreal. Skating on the Back River was forbidden by law, but young Richard discovered that the ice within fifteen feet of the banks could be counted on to be reliable.

After finishing the ninth grade of elementary school, Maurice spent two years in the École Technique in downtown Montreal studying the machinist's trade. He played for the school team and for about four others simultaneously, a strong, rugged forward but not a player for whom you would have been instantly able to predict a glowing future. (One of the teams which Richard played represented the Garage Paquette and had been organized by a pal of his, Georges Norchet. The only significant upshot of this liaison was that Maurice met Georges' sister, Lucille, whom he later married. A sturdy, hockey-loving woman, Mme. Richard attends every Montreal home game. So does Richard's father. His mother misses a few now and then, but not many.)

Late in 1940, Richard was given an opportunity to join the Verdun Maple Leafs, the bottom club in Les Canadiens' farm system. He played with the Senior Canadiens in the Quebec Senior Amateur League the following two seasons, but it was impossible to get much of a line on him, for he was laid up with injuries the better part of both seasons, first with a fractured left ankle, then with a fractured left wrist. He was invited to the Canadiens' training camp in September the next year but simply because the team had been floundering at the bottom of the league and was grasping for any straw. He was kept on the squad only because Dick Irvin had never in his life seen a youngster so imbued with the desire to make good. The unknown quantity started off well with Les Canadiens. He piled up five goals and six assists in the first fifteen games. In the next game he fractured his right ankle in a collision with Jack Crawford. He was out for almost the entire season again, returning only for the final game.

A recurrent mystery in sports is how a player who has never shown any signs of greatness will suddenly and inexplicably "arrive" as a full-fledged star. When Richard reported to the Canadiens' training camp in Verdun prior to the 1943–44 campaign, everyone recognized that he was an altogether different and better hockey player. On the strength of his showing in these practice sessions, Coach Irvin, looking for someone to take Joe Benoit's place, gave Richard a crack at right wing on the first line with Elmer Lach, the superb center, and the veteran Toe Blake, "The Old Lamp Lighter," at left wing. Due to the scoring punch the new line supplied, Les Canadiens, who had finished a mediocre fourth the year before, won the league championship and went on to capture the team's first Stanley Cup play-off victory in a full twelve years. Richard eclipsed all play-off records by scoring twelve goals in nine games, and in one game against Toronto he went completely berserk and scored all five of the Canadiens' goals.

The Punch Line, as Blake, Lach, and Richard came to be called, played together through the 1946–47 season, a stretch in which they led the Canadiens to three more league championships and one other Stanley Cup victory. They were a marvelous line to watch. Fast-skating, spirited, and quick to take advantage of all opportunities offered them, they mapped out no set plays, but each of them, knowing his line-mates' style perfectly and sharing an instinctive understanding of how a play should be developed (and the necessary alternative moves, depending on how the defense reacted), always seemed to know, without looking, where the others would be. Together they could set up good shots on goal like few lines in the history of hockey. Blake's retirement in 1947, after he had suffered a fractured leg, broke up the Punch

Line. Lach and Richard, working with a variety of left-wingers, continued to team up until this season when Lach retired.

If there was anything unorthodox about the Punch Line, it was that Richard, a left-handed shot, played right wing. "I know he'd played some right wing as an amateur," Dick Irvin has said in explaining this move, "and there have always been a few left-wingers who do well on right wing. It doesn't work the other way so often. Most hockey players, you see, skate counterclockwise. Right wing was good for Rocket because it gave him a bit more leverage on his shot and a bit more of the net to shoot at. Besides, his backhand shot was as powerful as his forehand." Another aspect of Richard's sudden maturity was, oddly enough, the fact that he had fractured his right ankle the year before joining the Punch Line. After he had fractured his left ankle two years earlier, he had been inclined to overuse his right leg. After his right ankle was fractured he could no longer do this, and he began to skate with a far better distribution of leg drive. A long strider with amazingly quick acceleration, he rocks from side to side when he skates, a style that would be awkward in anyone else and, if anything, has added to his deceptiveness. As for Richard himself, he considers that the great break of his entire career was that he was able to come back after three fractures in three consecutive years.

The first time he saw Richard play, Conn Smythe, the head man of the Toronto Maple Leafs, offered Les Canadiens the (for hockey) fabulous sum of $50,000 for him. In making this offer to the Hon. Donat Raymond, the owner of Les Canadiens, Smythe declared in a characteristic Smythian comment that he was willing to go this high even though Richard was a "one-way man"—a player not remarkably conspicuous on defense. Raymond was not at all interested in selling his new star but suggested to Smythe that if they made Richard a two-way man, it would be only proper for him to double his figure. (Only a short time ago, Smythe was offer-ing $135,000 for Richard.) Jack Adams, the Detroit boss, after seeing Richard set a new league scoring record for a single game of five goals and three assists on the evening of December 28, 1944, declared him to be "the greatest hockey player I've seen in twenty years." This eight-point spree astonished Richard more than anyone. Before the game he had stretched out limply on a rubbing table in the dressing room. "I'm all tired oud," he had yawned wearily to team-mates. "Dis afternoon I move my 'partment 'bout tree block and can't get no truck. My brudder and me, we move every-t'ing. Tonight, don't depen' too much on me." After he had tallied his eighth point, to be sure, Richard's vitality perked up noticeably. (Richard, by the way, spoke no English at the time he joined Les Canadiens. He resented the fact that op-ponents made his broken English a target for wisecracks, and it is typical of the pride he takes in everything he does, the way he dresses, the way he handles his hobbies, that today he speaks just about perfect English.)

Richard's eight-point night was the high point of his sec-ond complete season, 1944-45, in which he set the league record of fifty goals. By this time he was the toast of the famous Millionaires Club, a group of exuberant Montreal rooters who attended the games wearing bright wool toques and Les Canadiens jerseys. The Millionaires Club was dis-banded after the war—it was a financial necessity for the management, since the members were paying only $1.25 or $1.50 for $2.00 seats—but Richard has not lost his standing in the affection of their heirs and all Montreal fans as the team's premier hero. New stars have come up, stalwarts like Bill Durnan (the six-time winner of the Vezina trophy for goalies), Emile (Butch) Bouchard (the four-time All-Star defenseman), Boom Boom Geoffrion (the colorful, carefree youngster with the big shot who is married to Howie Morenz' daughter), Jean Beliveau (Le Gros Bill) who made so much

money as the star of Quebec's amateur team that it was a
financial hardship for him to turn professional. There is room
for them all in the Canadiens fan's heart, but *Le Rocket*—he
has always been something special and apart. He is their
oriflamme. They urge him on with a hundred different cries,
but in a tight spot the Forum seems to rise up with one shout
in particular, *"Envoye, Maurice!"* This is a Canadian slang
form of the imperative of the verb *envoyer*, to send or to
expedite. *"Envoye, Maurice!"*—"Let's expedite this game,
Maurice!" *"Envoye, Maurice!"*—"Let's go, Maurice!" *"Envoye, Maurice!"*

Maurice has never let his fans down but there have been
moments when he has worried them sick. Largely because of
his tempestuous temperament, he is what you might describe
as incident-prone. A few years back, for instance, during a
Red Wings-Canadiens game in Montreal in which referee
Hugh McLean was officiating, the Rocket swooped in from
his wing to follow up a rebound and, in the resulting melee
before the Detroit goal, was sent sprawling to the ice by the
Detroit center who practically used a headlock. There was no
whistle for a penalty. Boiling with indignation, Richard
skated up to McLean and demanded to know what the referee was going to do about it. McLean did something about
it. He handed Richard a misconduct penalty for abusive language. Burned up by what he considered a vast miscarriage of
justice, the Rocket tossed all night in his berth as the Canadiens traveled by train to New York for a game with the
Rangers. The next day, still smoldering, he was sitting in the
lobby of the Piccadilly Hotel when he spotted McLean. He
rushed over and grabbed the official by his coat collar, but
before he had time to continue his protest, Camil DesRoches
and some teammates jumped on him and managed to pull
him away. It was very fortunate they did. For his assault on
McLean, Richard was fined $500 by President Clarence

Campbell of the N.H.L., the highest fine ever levied by the league, but he had been restrained in the nick of time. A real assault and Richard would have been suspended.

Last year this almost happened. In a game in New York, Ron Murphy of the Rangers swung at Geoffrion with his stick. He missed. Geoffrion, retaliating, caught Murphy on the head. The blow fractured Murphy's skull and he was out for the season. Geoffrion was suspended for all the remaining games against the Rangers that season. As Richard saw it, Geoffrion had been punished all out of proportion for a fight he had not started. Richard was then "writing" via a ghost a column for the *Samedi Dimanche*, a French-language weekly. "If Mr. Campbell wants to throw me out of the league for daring to criticize him," Richard stated in his column, "let him do it. Geoffrion is no longer the same since his affair with Murphy. . . . He is demoralized and humiliated for having dared to defend himself against a sneaky and deliberate attack by a third-class player. We know that on numerous occasions, he [President Campbell] has rendered decisions against Canadiens players. . . . Let Mr. Campbell not try to gain publicity for himself by taking to task a good boy like Boom Boom Geoffrion simply because he is a French-Canadian. . . . If this brings me reprisals, I will step out of hockey, and I know that any other players on the Canadiens will do the same."

Well, here was something—a direct challenge to the authority of the president of the league. Richard was clearly miles out of line. The affair could have been disastrous, not only for Richard but for organized hockey, had it not been handled with consummate intelligence by Frank Selke, the managing director of Les Canadiens, who has been a part of hockey since 1906. At the heart of the crisis Les Canadiens returned to Montreal after a road trip. Selke was at the station to meet them. He collected Richard, Geoffrion, Ken Mosdell, and their wives and took them to dinner at the

Windsor Hotel. He never once mentioned what was on his mind and everyone's. The dinner over, Richard and Selke found themselves seated alone together in the hotel lobby for a moment.

"I'm surprised, Mr. Selke," Richard said. "I thought you were going to be very angry with me."

"Maurice," Selke said quietly, "I've never known you to do a rotten thing in your life before. You're accusing President Campbell of things that aren't true. That isn't like Maurice Richard. I don't believe you wrote that column."

"No, I didn't, but I authorized it," Richard replied. "I take full responsibility."

"I want you to act like a big leaguer," Selke went on. "President Campbell's office is just across the street. I know he works nights. I want you to come over with me and see him."

Richard sat silently for a moment. Then the two got up and called on Campbell. Richard spoke up immediately. "Mr. Campbell, I want to apologize to you," he said, his deep voice almost an octave lower than usual. "I apologize not because anyone has told me to do so. I want to apologize because it is the decent thing to do. I have been wrong to say the things I said. It will not happen again."

During the weeks that followed Richard's apology, which ended the affair, many of the French papers accused him of selling out. He never batted an eye. "Maurice Richard never disappoints you," Mr. Selke said recently. "We have had a lot of dealings. When a mistake is pointed out to him and he sees it is a mistake, he has the character to recognize it and to make genuine rectification. He has great class as a person."

The Richards live in a modest, trim home in Cartierville, which adjoins Bordeaux. During the hockey season Maurice spends the bulk of his free hours at home playing with his kids—Huguette, eleven, a pretty girl who is a natural figure skater; Maurice, Jr., nine, whom the family calls "Rocket" as matter-of-factly as if it were a prosaic nickname like Bud; Normand, four; and André, an infant of six months. Richard is not just a devoted father—he is crazy about his kids. During the summer, at least once a week, Richard and his wife bundle the family into the car and head for the country for a day together in the open air. It is his truest pleasure.

Richard puts in some time in the summer as a sales representative for the Petrofina Company, a Belgian concern which operates gas stations in Canada, but a large part of every day goes to keeping himself in shape. It is his custom to take off on several three-day fishing trips when each hockey season is over. This is pure relaxation. After that he plays his sports with an eye to preparing himself gradually for the coming hockey campaign. In June and July he plays some softball, but principally he golfs. A ten-handicap man, he responds so well to competition that for the last two seasons he and Elmer Lach have won the tournament for major league hockey players that takes place before the big Canadian golf tournament, the Labatt's Open. Halfway through July he switches to tennis and handball. "I think they are very good sports for sharpening the eye and strengthening the legs," he told a friend not long ago. "When it is time to go to training camp, I find it not too hard to get into condition."

Richard has mellowed discernibly in recent years. In a relaxed mood he can be wonderful company, intelligent in conversation and very responsive to old friends. His shyness with strangers has lessened somewhat and he meets people far more gracefully. He has even displayed the edges of a dry sense of humor. Not long ago the exchange for Richard's telephone number was changed to RIverside. "Just dial RI," he said with a straight face to a rural photographer who had forgotten the exchange. "RI . . . for Richard." An old friend who stood by couldn't believe his ears.

Most of these relaxed moments, it goes without saying, take place from April to September. Then another hockey season is on, and while Richard today may be a shade less volcanic than formerly as he moves steadily toward his four hundredth goal, he still burns with a fierce sense of purpose. During a team slump or a personal scoring drought, he is still a good man to avoid. Silent and seething, he builds up intensity to such a pitch that, eventually, it must explode. Sometimes the Rocket explodes all over the place, in fights, in arguments with referees, in overly aggressive if fruitless hockey. Sooner or later, though, he will explode with a splurge of dramatic goals. On these evenings, it is an experience to be in Montreal, for it is then that the Forum roars like one huge happy lion, the most jubilant hullabaloo you can hear in the sports world. It is not an extravagant tribute. After all, of all the great athletes of our time, none has played his game with more skill, more color, more competitive fire, and more heart than Maurice Richard.

BOB COUSY: BASKETBALL'S CREATIVE GENIUS

The bulk of the material for this two-part article was gathered in the autumn of 1955, and the pieces were run early the next year. It was an extremely pleasant story to do, for basketball players are not so eternally beleaguered by their fandom or by the press, radio, and television as are baseball and golf stars, for example, and Cousy was able to give me large, uninterrupted portions of his time. We also got together at the right season, in the weeks before the start of the 1955–56 campaign when the Celtics were playing themselves into shape via a barnstorming tour of New England with the Royals, who were then out of Rochester. Bob and I made a few of those long drives from one town to the next by auto, and I recommend this as an excellent way, when you have a willing and resourceful subject, to go into all the details at a civilized pace.

Six seasons have gone by since that time. Each season basketball observers have expected to note the beginning of a mild decline in Cousy's play, since he is getting along in years, but this has not shown itself. His shooting, which was never his strongest point, is now a little less accurate, and there are nights when his man contains him very well. But there are nights, too, when Bob seems faster than he ever was as he leads the fast break and invents fresh and dazzling pass maneuvers. It is an especial treat to

watch him work with Bill Russell who handles the ball so beautifully off the boards. The last two seasons Bob has been able to
pace himself effectively and to rest up during sections of most
games, for the Celtics now have the Jones Boys, Sam and K.C.,
to spell him handsomely in the back court. I would suggest that
the best time to go to watch Cousy is when the Celtics are either
playing against the Royals or Lakers or are scheduled on the same
double-header bill with one of these two clubs. For all his many-
sided capabilities as a person, Bob is an artist essentially, and
whenever Elgin Baylor or Oscar Robertson is also performing,
this seems to give his pride in his own handiwork an extra goad
and usually lifts him into one of his most breath-taking displays.

The most skillful exhibition of basketball I have ever seen was
the Celtics' performance in the second period of the first play-off
game against St. Louis in 1960, when Cousy made something
like six lightning assists in a row that were out of this world. The
best single play I have ever seen him make—the best single play
I have ever seen *anybody* make—occurred in a regular league
game a season or two earlier. With time running out, the Celtics
seemed hopelessly out of it, but Cousy, that never-say-die finisher,
got them rolling and they closed the large gap swiftly. As I remember it, they were trailing by only one point with five seconds
left in the game when, after they had called for a time-out, play
was ready to be resumed at mid-court. It was the Celtics' ball, of
course, and Cousy took it out. The team obviously had set up
some play designed to give them that one vital shot. Cousy would
probably be passing in to Sharman, the Celtics' best shot, or
maybe the play had been set up for Ramsay, a great clutch-man.
As the referee handed the ball off side to Cousy and prepared to
blow the whistle that would signalize the start of those gaunt
final five seconds, one repondered the Celtics' possible strategy,
eyed the players on the floor as they began to maneuver skittishly
for position, and watched Cousy. He had no expression at all on
his face. He seemed, if anything, a trifle abstracted. The whistle
blew, and then, like a shot out of a cannon, it had happened
almost before you had realized it. Cradling the ball with his right
hand and wrist, Cousy had brought it back and flung it half sidearm, half overarm, something like the way a jai-lai player swings

his cesta, and had somehow snapped that ball like a pebble through the forest of bodies and arms on a line toward the basket, right into the raised hands of Tommy Heinsohn who had cut away from his man in a little semi-circle. Heinsohn jumped and dropped it in, and the game that was lost was won.

I

WITH THE SCORE tied 57–57 and about ten seconds to go in the Holy Cross-Loyola of Chicago game in 1949, Bob Cousy of Holy Cross was fed the ball and drove hard for the basket, hoping to get a half step ahead of his man and get off a fairly close shot, preferably a lay-up, with his right hand. He never got that half step ahead. The man guarding him, Ralph Klaerich, had held Cousy scoreless from the floor during the entire second half and was right with him again this time. If anything, Klaerich was a fraction of a step in front of Cousy, overplaying him to his right side as he had been doing with remarkable success, ready to block any shot Cousy might try to make as he finished his dribble.

This time, however, Cousy finished his dribble somewhat differently than Klaerich—or, for that matter, Cousy—was expecting. Realizing that the only way he could get free for a shot was somehow to get to Klaerich's right (his left), Cousy, hearkening to some distant drum, reached behind his back with his right hand and slapped the ball to the floor, found the ball with his left hand as it came up on the bounce to his left side, and then, without a break in his stride or dribble, drove to the left (yards away from the flabbergasted Klaerich), leaped into the air and sank a florid left-hander that won the game. "There was some talk at the time that I had been practicing that behind-the-back dribble and had only been waiting for the proper occasion to use it," Cousy recently recalled. "The fact of the matter is that I had never even thought of such a maneuver until the moment the situation forced me into it. It was purely and simply one of those cases when necessity is the mother of invention. I was absolutely amazed myself at what I had done. It was only much later that I began to practice it so that I could make it a reliable part of my repertoire."

A person of abundant imagination, Cousy over the years has enlarged and refined his ball-handling techniques to the point where today no old-timer remembers his equal and no contemporary player can touch him. To begin with, he is unanimously regarded as the game's most accomplished dribbler. The one man who might be compared with him, the old Globetrotter alumnus, Marques Haynes, honestly cannot be, since Cousy works against—and confounds—bona fide opposition in the National Basketball Association while Haynes operates on an exhibition tour with a well-drilled "opponent" helping him to display his remarkable wares. Much the same difference applies to any comparison of Cousy and Goose Tatum, whose humor and ball handling made the Globetrotters one of the most gratifying vaudeville acts since Singer's Midgets and Fink's Mules. Performed at the breakneck speed with which the pro game is played, Cousy's thesaurus now includes (along with his behind-the-back dribble, the pass off the dribble, the reverse dribble, and other plain and fancy locomotion) such exclusive Cousyisms as the behind-the-back transfer (in which he shifts the ball from his right hand to his left and then lays up a left-hander, all this while afloat in the air), the twice-around pass (in which he swings the ball around his back once and then passes it off to a teammate as he takes it around a second time, all this, of course, while in the air), and several variations on these themes which he resorts to when the situation calls for them. This virtuosity has won for Cousy such sobriquets as "The Mobile Magician" and "The

Houdini of the Hardwood" as well as the highest salary of any player in the NBA. He receives about $20,000 a year from the Boston Celtics, and in a world where few basketball players as yet get a slurp of the subsidiary gravy, he has been able to augment his income considerably by running clinics and by endorsing a chewing gum, a breakfast food, a tooth paste, a seamless basketball, and a Canadian sneaker. Far from resenting Cousy's fiscal eminence, his teammates and rivals are extremely happy about it, for there is absolute agreement that, since the retirement of George Mikan, Cousy, as pro basketball's greatest attraction, has almost singlehandedly been carrying the league to a prosperity it could never otherwise enjoy.

It is always a little misleading to talk about the astonishing things Bob Cousy can do with a basketball because it tends to distort a true appreciation of his genius for the game. Though you are apt to forget it some nights when a poorly played contest seems to consist almost entirely of tall men shooting from outside and taller men battling lugubriously under the basket, basketball, good basketball, is a game of movement. As in hockey, Rugby, soccer, polo, lacrosse, and other kindred games where two opposing teams try to gain possession of the ball and advance it toward the enemy's goal for a scoring shot, the really gifted players are not necessarily the high-scoring specialists but, rather, the men with an instinctive sense of how to build a play—the man without the ball who knows how to cut free from the opponent covering him, and, even more important, the man with the ball who can "feel" how an offensive maneuver can develop, who can instantly spot a man who breaks free, and who can zip the ball over to him at the right split second. Without this latter breed—the playmakers—basketball, or any other goal-to-goal game, can degenerate into a rather ragged race up and down the playing field.

Cousy's greatness lies in the fact that he is fundamentally

a playmaker and that his legerdemain, far from being empty
showboating, is functional, solid basketball. Equipped with
a fine sense of pattern and superb reflexes, he also has peripheral vision which enables him to see not only the men in
front of him but a full 180-degree angle of the action. Thus,
like nobody else in the game—unless it be Dick McGuire of
the Knicks on one of his outlandish hot nights—Cousy can
open up a seemingly clogged court by appearing to focus in
one direction, simultaneously spotting a seemingly unreach-
able teammate in another area, and quickly turning him into
a scoring threat with a whiplash pass. There is implicit
deception in Cousy's straight basketball, which is the secret
of any great player's success, and it is only in those exceptional circumstances when extra measures pay off soundly
that he resorts to his really fancy stuff.

Well aware that his feats of manipulation draw the crowds
and help to keep the league healthy, Cousy will flash a few of
his special effects near the end of a game in which the outcome is already surely decided, if he previously has not had
a chance to use them. Aside from this, he is all function.
There has been only one occasion, for example, when he has
deliberately trotted out a little of the old razzle-dazzle to
show up an opposing player.

This occurred a few years back in one of those high-pitched
battles between the Celtics and the Knicks. Sweetwater
Clifton of the Knicks, who can handle the ball with his
enormous hands as if it were the size of a grapefruit, had
been, as Cousy saw it, indulging himself far too prodigally in
exhibiting his artistry and appeared much more concerned
with making the Celtics look foolish than with playing
basketball. This aroused Cousy's French. The next time he
got the ball, he dribbled straight up to Clifton. Looking
Sweets right in the eye, he wound up as if he were going to
boom a big overhand pass directly at him. As he brought the
ball over his shoulder, however, Cousy let it roll down his

back, where he caught it with his left hand, and, completing that big windmill thrust with his empty right hand, stuck it out toward Sweets in the gesture of "shake hands." It brought down the house.

"It was an old Globetrotter trick I'd seen them use and had practiced for my own benefit a couple of times," Cousy explained not long ago. "I shouldn't have done it, but I was awfully sore at the time. Naturally the newspapers played it up that there was a feud between me and Clifton. The next time we played New York I looked Clifton up and told him I was sorry about the incident, for I was. Clifton isn't a wise guy. He's a helluva nice guy. I should have taken that into account at the time."

Even when he was a collegian, Robert Joseph Cousy's ability was so conspicuous that Adolph Rupp, the unquiet coach of Kentucky, acclaimed him "the greatest offensive player in the country." This is a tribute indeed when you consider that Rupp views it as only a little short of treason to find anything or anybody worthy of his praise except Happy Chandler, bourbon whisky, his own basketball teams, and other strictly Bluegrass products.

Today, twenty-seven years old, a discernibly improved player in his sixth season as a pro, Cousy is regarded by most experts as nothing less than the greatest all-round player in the sixty-four-year history of basketball. "I've seen many great ones since I began fooling around with a ball in 1912," Joe Lapchick, a stalwart on the famous old New York Celtics and presently the coach of the Knickerbockers, reflected recently. "I've seen Johnny Beckman, Nat Holman, that wonderful player Hank Luisetti, Bob Davies, George Mikan, the best of the big men—to name just a few. Bob Cousy, though, is the best I've ever seen. He does so many things. It's so hard to say that Cousy can think in the air or that Cousy does this or that. Cousy does everything. He's regularly one of the league's top five scorers. When a guy's a scorer, you usually don't expect him to be a leader in the other departments. One talent generally suffers from another. Bob, however, has been a top leader in assists for the last five seasons. He's become a very capable defensive player, a tremendous pass stealer."

Lapchick paused to find words to sum up his panegyric. "I was just thinking of the games we've played against Cousy," he resumed with a bittersweet look in his eyes. "He always shows you something new, something you've never seen before. Any mistake against him and you pay the full price. One step and he's past the defense. He's quick, he's smart, he's tireless, he has spirit, and he is probably the best finisher in sports today."

One Celtic-Knick scrap that Lapchick may have been musing on was their meeting on December 10, 1953. The Knicks were leading 93–90 with thirty seconds to go. Since they had possession of the ball, Boston having just scored, and there was no twenty-four-second rule to contend with in those days, the game to all intents and purposes was as good as over. The Knicks knew exactly how they would handle the play coming up to keep Cousy from getting his hands on the ball again. Carl Braun, taking the ball out of bounds, would wait until Dick McGuire cut toward him, carrying Cousy, his man, along with him. Braun would then toss the ball to Harry Gallatin, well behind the spot where Cousy would then be. Braun took the ball, McGuire came tearing along with Cousy, Braun threw the ball to Gallatin—and Cousy intercepted it with a pantherlike whirl. He drove in unimpeded for a basket that cut the Knicks' lead to one point. A moment later, up front on an all-court press, he intercepted a bounce pass. Boston (Cousy) immediately called time out. When play was resumed, Cousy hooked a pass to his teammate, Ed Macauley. Macauley was fouled before he could get a shot off. He made the foul. The final buzzer sounded: 93 all. In the overtime, in what many critics adjudge the finest exhibition of dribbling they have ever seen, Cousy controlled the ball for just about four of the five minutes of play, killing the clock once Boston was ahead and drawing foul after foul when as many as three Knicks at a time tried desperately to get the ball away from him. Final score: Boston, 113—New York, 108.

Like any athlete, Cousy has his big nights and his bad nights, though it should be added that most players would gladly settle for a straight diet of his bad ones. As to his greatest game, there is, to be sure, a sizable difference of opinion, the fan's choice depending in the last analysis on which games he has personally seen. A good many, for example, incline to think the high point was his performance in the 1954 East-West All-Star Game, where Cousy turned the overtime into a one-man show while scoring ten of the East's fourteen points. (The basketball writers, who had voted Jim Pollard the game's most valuable player at the end of the regulation four quarters, had no other course but to open the polls again and vote the award to Cousy.) Most of Cousy's New England following, however, who idolize him with a clamorous devotion which recalls the great love affair between Les Canadiens' rooters and Maurice Richard, are certain that no basketball player ever turned in a more magnificent job than Cousy did in a first-round play-off against the Syracuse Nationals two winters ago this coming March. Briefly, the tide of battle went something like this: at the end of the regulation four twelve-minute periods, the teams were tied 77–77. At the end of the first five-minute overtime, they were still tied, 86 all. At the end of the second overtime, still tied up, 90 all. Syracuse dominated the third overtime and, with time rapidly running out, was out in front by five points. With thirteen seconds to go, Cousy got loose for a pretty one-hander; he was fouled on the play and added the foul shot. With five seconds to go, he got the ball at mid-court and let go a long one-handed push shot.

Swish—99–99. In the fourth overtime Syracuse once again raced off to a five-point lead. Once again Cousy tied it up. Syracuse began to fade then and, with Cousy adding four more foul shots, Boston pulled away to win 111–105. Cousy's scoring total for the marathon was fifty points—ten field goals and *thirty free throws in thirty-two attempts*, still an NBA play-off record. Up to that evening Boston, seven years in the pro league, had been a rather shaky basketball town. Since that game, Boston has been a rabid basketball town—Cousy's performance was as conclusive at that.

In the Brobdingnagian world in which he operates, where a man six feet five has to look up to a good many of his team-mates, Cousy, who stands six feet one and one-half, is one of the few surviving Lilliputians. On the floor, as he darts in and out of the forest of young oaks populating the court, spectators unconsciously begin to think of him as a much smaller man, a mere whippet of say five feet eight or nine. It is a shock to them, when they meet him off the court, to find that by conventional or nonbasketball standards their hero is a big fellow who towers over most hockey players and who must slide the front seat of an auto way back to gain sufficient leg room. (In this connection—how environment changes a fellow's height—Cousy's running mate, Bill Sharman, offers a very amusing case. During the winter, those who watch him tend to peg him in their minds as "Little Bill" Sharman. Comes spring, Sharman switches to baseball—last year he batted .292 with St. Paul in the American Association—and instantly undergoes a metamorphosis. For the next six months he is "Big Bill" Sharman, at six feet two, one of the largest third basemen in organized ball.)

Cousy's weight is as deceptive as his height. Taking in his unobtrusive chest, his sloping shoulders, and his long, lean neck, most people guess him at 160 or 165 pounds. He weighs 185. Most of it is in his heavy, powerful thighs and legs, which, as Cousy sees it, are the key to a natural endurance that makes it possible for him to drive up and down a court long after other players in the pink of condition have retreated to the bench for a breather. However, his most valuable physical assets are his hands, with their very large palms and extraordinarily long fingers, both far out of proportion to the rest of his body. Besides permitting Bob to manipulate a basketball more facilely than most giants can, his hands, when added to his average-length arm for a six-footer—he takes a thirty-five sleeve—give him a reach some two inches longer than most men his size and enable him, among other things, to perform that old back magic. One look at Cousy's hand and enthusiasts of other professions, from pianists to golfers, while not arguing that he was wrong to choose a career in basketball, invariably try to persuade him that he could have achieved as much in theirs. Baseball men are particularly saddened when they learn that Cousy played their game until he was fourteen and then gave it up to concentrate on basketball. They see in him, when they add his speed, his eye, and his catlike reflexes to these enormous mitts, a great shortstop who got away.

When Cousy occasionally succumbs to blandishments that his hands and timing give him the ideal equipment for this or that other sport, the results often exceed the expectation. Two years ago he took up tennis as an off-season conditioner and now plays it so well that he can provide suitable rallying if not playing opposition for Jack Kramer. When he decided to learn how to fish last May, he needed only two hours of practice before he was shooting thirty yards of D-weight line the full ninety feet with the ease of a master caster.

While enjoying his ever-enlarging sphere of proficiencies, Cousy has no regrets whatsoever that the hospitality of circumstances in St. Albans, Long Island, where he grew up, led him to a life of basketball. He loves the game and thinks of it as a great game, well worth anyone's dedication. "To me," he once confided to a friend, "practice was never work. It was and is time spent at the thing I love the best. It gives me a chance to improvise, to create. Maybe I shouldn't put it on such a high plane," Cousy interrupted himself with a grin. "Anyhow, it does give you a chance to dream up new things and to polish them, and that is one of the reasons why the game has always had such a tremendous appeal for me."

Cousy pours so much of himself into basketball that when he is playing a game his absorption in the business at hand temporarily suffuses the rest of his personality. In the dressing room before a game, his normally expressive dark-brown eyes begin to lose their animation and a sort of glaze settles over and begins to tighten his mobile face. He becomes quiet and solemn and, in fact, somewhat drowsy. Part of this is natural—he has an indecent capacity to relax at hard moments. Part of it is calculated. He wants to play each game up to the hilt and he knows that he is expected to cut loose with some sensational stuff, and a spot of pregame torpor helps him to collect his energy and to shape his concentration. Once on the floor, he changes considerably. A tremendous, burning will to win comes over him. His eyes become narrowed with dourness and his Gallic features take on a Velazquezian gauntness. Except for those moments when he is arguing a point with the referee, Cousy's set poker face never alters for a moment, whether the Celtics are winning or losing, whether he is "hot" or "off," regardless of the score and the period. Coupled with the assurance and the audacity of his style of play, this facial immobility is often misread by anti-Celtic fans as hauteur, and they watch his moves with the grudging admiration that Ben Hogan, with his ice-cold, unshatterable poise, used to extract from the followers of Snead, Nelson, and other golfers.

Once a game is over, no matter how high the victory or how galling the defeat, Cousy usually manages to relapse almost instantly into an honest-to-goodness calm, much to the mystification of his teammates, who generally require a much longer period to settle down. It takes Cousy a half hour, nonetheless, before he has the game completely digested. A liveliness then comes back to his eyes, the contours of his face become rounder, and there is a merriment in his remarks and a ready enjoyment of other people.

The more you see Cousy, the more you come to realize that he is a person of honest individuality, as easy to admire off the court as on. He has packed a lot of maturity under his belt for a man of twenty-seven. He has a mind of his own, a good one, and an uncommon understanding of the responsibility his position carries along with its privileges. Perhaps the best way to delineate the mosaic of his substantial personality is to describe a piece here, a piece there.

For example, there is Cousy, the citizen of Worcester, his adopted home town and the site of his college, Holy Cross, quietly calling up basketball friends like Carl Braun last summer and organizing a charity game, the proceeds to go to the widows of two Worcester firemen who had lost their lives in a fire. Both had left four children and no insurance. The game raised $4,000.

There is Cousy—you do not learn this from him—deciding to accompany his teammate Chuck Cooper back to New York on the sleeper, after a hotel in Raleigh, N.C., had refused accommodations for Cooper, a Negro from Duquesne. Cousy and Cooper shared an apartment in Boston for three months when Cousy was waiting to move his family into a new house.

There is Cousy, so keyed for really lazy relaxation or all-out action that sports in which the tempo is not continuous are curiously difficult for him to take. At college he fell asleep while watching the first three football games he attended and never went to a game again. Last summer he walked out of a fairly crucial Yankees-Red Sox battle in the sixth inning.

"All they did was change pitchers," he explains. "Anyway, that was longer than I generally last. Three innings is about my quota."

There is Cousy, aware that there will come a time when his basketball days will be over, realistically planning for the future. Four years ago he became one of the three co-owners of Camp Graylag, a summer camp near Concord, New Hampshire. After the camping season, he now conducts an annual clinic there, attended by boys who come from all over the country. Tuition: $100 for the ten-day course. One of his associates in his noncamp ventures is Jack Richards, a Harvard graduate turned song writer. (The current hit song "He" is one of his numbers.) Cousy and Richards met two winters ago when Bob gave a clinic at a settlement house in a tough Cambridge district where Richards spent a lot of his time. "The next summer Jack sent ten of those boys up to my ten-day clinic at his own expense," Cousy relates. "That impressed me. You don't find many fellows who actually act."

There is Cousy, the head of the Players' Association, which he helped form in 1954 and which now has its headquarters in Worcester. It is a very necessary organization, for the NBA, still a young league, numbers among the owners of its teams quite a few promoters who have yet to graduate from the dance-hall era of early pro basketball and who continue to think in terms of the quick buck instead of the big league. While the players' salaries are now pitched at a proper level, the league president, Maurice Podoloff, has much of the time acted as though he were solely responsible to the club owners and not equally responsible for safeguarding the legitimate interests of the players. With the NBA now a prosperous circuit, most veteran basketball hands consider the Players' Association to be more than justified in its efforts to obtain a reasonable limit to the fatiguing preseason barnstorming tours, small payment fees (like other pro athletes receive) for players who publicize the league through personal and television appearances, concrete steps by the league to improve the quality and uniformity of the still capricious officiating, and other such improvements. As the game's young statesman as well as its outstanding player, Cousy was the logical choice to represent pro basketball at the White House luncheon last July when leaders from all sports met with President Eisenhower to discuss what sports can contribute in the nation's over-all campaign against juvenile delinquency.

Putting these several pieces together, it becomes clear that basketball is fortunate indeed in having a man like Cousy as its current personification, for in an odd way, but a definite one, the game, despite its popularity in many sections of the country, still has to combat in other sections a marked prejudice. In those latter quarters it is extremely fashionable to dislike basketball, whether or not you know what it is all about, and retail as your reasons that it is a game dominated not by attractive stars but by unco-ordinated skyscraping goons, a game without patterns and riddled furthermore by senseless rules, a game that has had its fix scandals and is thick with tramp athletes, a game which principally attracts the poolroom set in between wrestling and fight nights—in short, a poor, sweaty, unsavory relation trying to edge itself into the proud tradition of major American sports.

There is an element of truth in all this, of course, but also as great an element of distortion as there would be in glibly characterizing hockey as a game without patterns and furthermore riddled by senseless rules, football as a game for behemoths only in which the ball is hidden from the spectator as well as the opposing team, or golf as a game of rigged Calcuttas, baseball as the game of the Black Sox scandal, and so on and so forth. The most intelligent rebuttal to the charges of an antibasketball man (besides taking him to watch Cousy) would be to shanghai him to a high-school game in some midwestern town where the whole population turns out to watch and forms a modern Currier and Ives scene. One evening in such a locale and your man will understand why basketball, the youngest of all major sports, today is participated in by uncountable millions throughout the world and annually attracts the largest number of spectators of any major American sport, some 95,000,000.

No sport ever had a more dramatic genesis or a finer father. He was Dr. James Naismith, a Canadian who grew up in a country town in northern Ontario. Orphaned at eight, Naismith early gave a memorable indication of his native inventiveness: too proud to ask his uncle to buy him a pair of skates like the other boys had, he hied himself to his uncle's machine shop and made himself a pair by setting two old files firmly into strips of hickory. In the autumn of 1883 he enrolled at McGill University to study for the ministry. Although contact sports were then frowned on as a wayward pursuit for a theology student, Naismith played center on the college Rugby team for seven years. "Much to my amusement," he later wrote, "I learned that some of my comrades gathered in one of the rooms one evening to pray for my soul." The rough-and-tumble life on the Rugby field, requiring self-control as well as ardor and developing many valuable traits among any team of players, was one of the main influences that led Naismith to decide, after much reflection, that "there might be other ways of doing good besides preaching." He dropped the ministry in favor of spreading the gospel of health through sports and entered the YMCA's International Training School in Springfield, Massachusetts. It was at Springfield in 1891 that James Naismith invented basketball.

How he did it is a marvelous chronicle for, under the stress of circumstances, Naismith deliberately set out to make up a new game. It all started with the realization by the faculty at Springfield that American boys, attuned to flexible, competitive sports like baseball and football, were bored and impatient with the gymnasium classes that conventionally filled in the hiatus between the close of the football season and the first game of scrub when the snow was gone. Late in 1891, after several other young instructors had tried unsuccessfully to devise some indoor recreation that would please the discontented members of the young men's class, the head of the athletic department, Dr. Luther Gulick, asked Naismith to take a crack at it for a couple of weeks. Knowing that what was needed was a new game, Naismith first tried modifying Rugby, eliminating the tackling. The class thought it was awful. He next tried an indoor variation of soccer. Even the few men who could still walk in their sneakers after the melee were enthusiastically against it. He got the same reaction when he tried to modify lacrosse for the small sixty-five-foot-by-forty-five-foot gym. "The day before my two weeks ended I met the class," Naismith recalled years afterwards. "I will always remember that meeting. I had nothing new to try and no idea of what I was going to do . . . With weary footsteps I mounted the flight of narrow steps that led to my office directly over the locker room. I slumped down in my chair, my head in my hands and my elbows on the desk. I was a thoroughly disheartened and discouraged young instructor. Below me, I could hear the boys in the locker room having a good time; they were giving expression to the very spirit I had tried so hard to evoke."

As he sat there at his desk, Naismith decided to take a new tack. Previously he had been trying to adapt old games, and that had failed. Now he began to ponder the nature of games in general from the philosophical side. Well, first, nearly all games used a ball. Some also used sticks, but they demanded more proficiency and lots of space. As he mulled over the kind of game that was needed, he concluded that a soccer ball would probably be the best ball. It was sufficiently large so that it couldn't be hidden from sight by a player. Moreover, it was easier to handle than an oval football. All right, then, say you wanted your game to have some of the same patterns as American football without the tackling and other strenuous contact: how then would the players advance the ball? As he visualized the action in his mind, Naismith hit on the first of his original devices: the player in possession of the ball could not run with it after getting it but would be required to stop or pass the ball immediately. How about the goals then? If you took a lacrosse goal and—no, that wouldn't work out; a group of defending players could block off any scoring simply by massing in front of it. Why not place them off the ground above the heads of the players? Then it would be useless for players to mass in front of a goal to block scoring throws. Additionally, vaguely like a good shot in the back-yard game of duck-on-the-rock, the shot that would put the ball into such an overhead goal would call much more for accuracy than for sheer power. That was certainly a step in the right direction.

The next morning as he was walking down the hall near the gym, about an hour and a half before the class was due to meet, Naismith met the building superintendent and asked him if he had two boxes eighteen inches square. The superintendent said he hadn't but he had two old peach baskets in the storeroom. He brought them up and Naismith nailed a basket to the lower rail of the balcony at both ends of the gym. He went back to his office, quickly wrote out thirteen rules for the game, and had them typed. "The game was a success from the time the first ball was tossed up," Dr. Naismith later wrote. "When the first game had ended, I felt that I could now go to Dr. Gulick and tell him that I had accomplished the two seemingly impossible tasks he had set for me: namely, to interest the class in physical exercise and to invent a new game."

No sport in history caught on like Dr. Naismith's baby. Within a month of the historic first game, girls were playing basketball. (Naismith, by the way, married a member of the first girls' team.) By 1892 the game was being played at the University of Iowa, a year later at Stanford. By the turn of the century, with YMCA men carrying the ball wherever they went, there were hundreds of hoops in South America, China, Japan—all over the world. As it grew, the game changed. Players with a gift for it came up with all kinds of new maneuvers. For example, the dribble, first conceived as a defensive aid to help a man stuck with the ball to keep free until he could get off a pass, swiftly was turned by talented dribblers into an element of the attack. As the game changed, rules had to be added and changed—a rule to make official some unarguable improvement the players had hit on, such as the rule that the team which did not touch the ball last before it went out of bounds throws it back into play; a rule to curb certain unanticipated excesses which were hurting the game, like the one limiting the number of fouls a player could commit before being disqualified for the rest of the game. Today, sixty-four years old, basketball is still in the process of evolution, a game that has not yet found its best expression. It has changed tremendously just over the past twenty years, when the abolition of the center jump and the ten-second backcourt rule and the advent of the fast break so greatly speeded up the game.

But it hasn't all been progress in a neat straight line. Bad trends have been recognized and rules instituted to prevent them, and as often as not the new rules have fostered greater ills than the ones they proposed to cure. There have been periods, many of them, in fact, when the game got itself so fouled up that the elements which had made for its appeal had all but disappeared and what had arisen in their place wasn't basketball at all. A good deal of the trouble, to be sure, has resulted from the unavoidable proposition that in a game where the goals are set ten feet above the ground, a big man will always have a valuable advantage, and you cannot legislate against height in basketball any more honestly than you can restrict the bulk of the linemen in football. You must deal with it within the spirit of the game.

Up to now, whenever basketball has found itself all snarled up in a jungle of unforeseen developments and unnatural rules, someone has always appeared to lead the game out of the wilderness. Sometimes it has been a wonderful team like the Original Celtics, sometimes a rules committee cleaving to the heart of the matter, and sometimes a single player. In recent years, when the game was coming very close to developing into a race-horse shooting match between men who had developed unstoppable shots and who could do very little else, Bob Cousy, above and beyond anyone else, has blazed the trail back to good basketball. Cousy has, in truth, gone much further: he has opened the road to better basketball. Perhaps no player or coach in the game's history has understood the true breath of basketball as well as he. He has shown, in what has amounted to an enlightened revolution, that basketball offers a hundred and one possibilities of maneuver no one ever dreamed of before. Reversing your dribble or passing behind your back and so on—those stunts had been done for years, but if you combine those moves with a sense of basketball, then you are going someplace. Increase your repertoire of moves, and the man playing you, by guarding against one, gives you the opening you need to move into another. It is not unlike learning to speak a new language. The larger your vocabulary, the better you will speak it, as long as you are building on a sound foundation.

Bob Cousy has been called a once-in-a-lifetime player. He may prove to be. But from now on the new stars that arise will play like Cousy. You can see his influence in the back yards throughout the country. Where all the kids used to be practicing special shots, you now find them trying to do

something with the ball in the style of the master and sub-
mitting rather stoically, when the maneuver fails, to that
inevitable come-uppance: "Who do you think you are anyway—Cousy?"

II

In a game this winter in which the league-leading Philadelphia Warriors defeated the Boston Celtics 109–108, Bob
Cousy of the Celtics enjoyed what was, even by the standards an expectant public imposes on the finest all-round
player in basketball today and perhaps the finest ever, a very
good night. During his forty minutes on the court Cousy
scored twenty-nine points on nine field goals and eleven foul
shots. Not that this was all he did by a long shot—as usual he
built the plays that set up 80 per cent of his team's baskets,
pulled off such exclusive Cousyisms as his twice-around-the-
back pass, and his unquenchable will to win fired the Celtics
to a furious last-quarter rally that all but overcame the
Warriors' twelve-point lead. But a brief recapitulation of the
various ways Bob scored from the floor that evening affords as
handy an avenue as any to appreciating why Cousy is held to
be, in knowledgeable quarters, the essence of imaginative,
exciting basketball.

Cousy scored first on a right-hand hook shot after a combination play with Bill Sharman and Ed Macauley. He scored
next on a running lay-up with his left hand, slipping in from
the left and collecting a perfect pass from Macauley, who
had faked a jump shot from ten feet in front of the basket.
His third score was a long left-hand hook (off the backboard)
from the left corner after dribbling to the center of the
court from the left side, finding no one to pass to and no
place to go, and then reversing his course and firing as he
spun around. Next came on a soft one-hand push shot from
just beyond the foul line. Next, a full-tilt lay-up after he

had broken up a Warrior play at mid-court and stolen the ball. Next—a real beauty—a semi-underhand shot with his right hand which he somehow shoveled under the arm of one of the two men who apparently had him completely tied up with his back to the basket to the right of the foul line. He followed this with a comparatively unpretty basket, a little two-handed jump shot from about ten feet out after a set play from out of bounds had gone sour and the rebound from a hurried shot had been kicked around. Finally, as he directed Boston's last-ditch rally, Cousy scored twice more from the floor in addition to five times from the foul line. The first was an orthodox straight-on lay-up, after he had dribbled the length of the court and effected his opening through the defense by faking his patented behind-the-back pass as he hit the foul line, stuttering that split second, and then driving in hard. His last one came after he had caught one of those desperation "forward passes" and, with only one defensive man to beat, feigned a drive to the left and simply dribbled around the man in a quick semicircle to the right. Heavier scorers you will see, but a virtuosity comparable to Cousy's, no.

Whenever a sports fan watches an ultra-athlete like Cousy, that old speculation always crosses his mind: how much derives from sheer natural ability, how much from plain hard work? The answer in Cousy's case is fifty-fifty. Nature endowed him with about the full complement of physical assets for basketball—peripheral vision, huge hands and long fingers, a reach two inches longer than the average man his height, sufficient height, very sturdy legs, and, as one Madison Avenue type has couched it, "the equilibrium of an antelope, on the rocks, of course." On the other hand, few athletes have surrendered the hours and attention to their sport that Cousy has. At fourteen he gave up baseball, since, as he now explains, "I realized that if I played two sports, I wouldn't be able to give basketball the time it needed." In

St. Albans, Long Island, a town on the eastern rim of the borough of Queens where he grew up, Bob practiced and played basketball straight through the four seasons and practically every moonlit night, a diurnal inhabitant of either the O'Connell playground or the schoolyard of P.S. 36. He has always been and continues to be that rarity in sports, the tireless but intelligent practicer. Three winters ago, for instance, Ed Scannell, the sports editor of the *Worcester Gazette*— Cousy has made his home in Worcester since graduating from Holy Cross in 1950—happened to drop into a local high-school gym on one of Cousy's days off between Celtic games. There was Cousy, alone in the gym, ripping up and down the court, leaping each time he hit the foul line and tossing up a one-hander. The teams in the NBA, he explained to Scannell afterward, were playing him to pass when he reached the foul line, and he was working on his jump shot, the better to keep them guessing.

This winter the maestro has been practicing a two-hand set, a shot he hasn't used since his sophomore year in college. "You can get the one-hander off quicker," he was recently explaining to a high-school inquisitor, "but you can't count on being too accurate with it from more than twenty-two or twenty-three feet out. Now that the teams are using the 'sagging defense,' I think a player will need to have a shot in his repertoire that he can rely on from thirty feet out. That means the old two-handed set."

St. Albans, where Bob Cousy first caught the basketball bug, was a hard place to escape it. The local high school, Andrew Jackson, had built up a reputation for winning teams, and it became the ambition of every boy in the district to make the team. Basketball was *the* game in St. Albans, no question about it. Bob's parents, Joseph and Juliette Cousy, had moved to that community from Manhattan when their son, their only child, was about eleven years old. They are extremely interesting and appealing people, the Cousys. Joseph Cousy—a short man of about five feet six inches, by the way—was born in Belfort near the eastern border of France, the son of a farmer who raised cherries, apples, pigs, and some cattle. None of the earlier Cousys had possessed any extraordinary gifts, athletic or otherwise, aside from the family's traditional ability for running one of the most prosperous farms in Alsace-Lorraine. Joseph Cousy's only fling at athletics, if it can be called that, was a short career in automobile racing before World War I, when he competed in a local event, Le Ballon d'Alsace, a road race to the top of one of the highest peaks (3,000 feet) in Les Vosges. He fought in the war, was captured, and returned after the armistice to see how the old Cousy farm had fared. Like all border property, it had been trampled into nothing. He looked at it, and the feeling went through him that no efforts could ever restore it, and he turned away from it forever. He went into the auto repair business, and when he had saved up enough to buy an auto, he rented his car and his services out to rich families who wanted to tour Europe that way. In 1927 he married Juliette Corlet, the daughter of a maître d'hôtel, who had been born in the United States while M. Corlet was with the Touraine Hotel in Boston. When she was five she had gone back with her father to his home town, Dijon, and had in time become a teacher of languages, tutoring the children of well-to-do families. A very French woman, animated, intense, and excitable, Mrs. Cousy, a fairly tall woman, was, as she recalls with pleasure when questioned by people seeking clues to her son's exceptional co-ordination, not a bad tennis player.

The Cousys emigrated to New York, and their son Robert Joseph was born about a month after their arrival. The best job Mr. Cousy could find in the city was driving a taxi. The best home he could afford was a couple of rooms on Eighty-third Street in Manhattan's roughneck Yorkville section.

("The games there were stickball and breaking windows,"
Bob recalls.) Mr. Cousy stood it until he could stand no
longer to see his son growing up on the streets. Then, mort-
gaging himself up to his ears, he bought himself a small house
in St. Albans, a neighborhood in those days of trees, spaces,
some air, and some quiet. Mr. and Mrs. Cousy—he presently
works at Idlewild Airport as an administrator in Pan American's maintenance department—still live in that same house
in St. Albans, along with a small aviary of twenty-five canaries
and parakeets which Mrs. Cousy keeps. They are basketball
fans, and you can see them at most games when the Celtics
come to New York to play the Knickerbockers—a small,
neat, bespectacled, self-contained gentleman and a tallish,
slim, quite handsome, and emotional lady, both of them still
a little dazed that their son now derives an income of well
over $30,000 a year through his proficiency at a game which
they long viewed with alarm as a passion that might prejudice his chances for learning a profession or a trade and
finding a secure living.

The ideal temperament for a competitive athlete to have
inherited from such a set of parents would have been a fusion
of his mother's exuberant spirit and his father's rational self-
control. Cousy did. During a game he gets so overcome by
his desire to win that, beneath his sheath of coolness, he is
Gallicly aboil. The moment a game is over, however, that
solid base of placid practicality, present all the time if not
conspicuous, takes over in force. It stills his emotion instantly, almost with a thud, and he begins to speak with his
customary slowness, which is almost a drawl. These days
Cousy rarely speaks French except when he is visiting his
parents, but his bilinguality has on occasion proved an oddly
serviceable asset. This last summer, for illustration, Cousy
and coaches Red Auerbach of the Celtics and Adolph Rupp
of Kentucky were invited by General Garland of SHAPE to
conduct a basketball clinic in Landsberg, Germany, which

was attended by representatives from American military units stationed in Europe and also by delegates from seven basketball-playing European countries. Cousy found that things worked out best for this complex audience when he conducted the lecture portion of his classes in English and the question-and-answer part in both English and French.

It may come as a source of encouragement to aspiring young athletes to learn that Cousy, Beau Basketball himself, did not make his high-school squad during his freshman and sophomore years. Lack of height had nothing to do with it; he stood five feet ten inches as a sophomore—tall enough. It was simply that Lew Grummond, the coach of Andrew Jackson High, had such a wealth of material that many fine prospects like Cousy could hardly expect to win a suit unless they happened to have the exact qualifications Grummond was looking for. After he was cut in his sophomore year, Cousy went back to playing for a team in the local CYO league sponsored by the *Long Island Press*. It was at one of these league games which Grummond attended that Bob first caught the coach's eye. "I didn't know it at the time," Bob was relating not long ago, "but Grummond had a spot open on the team for a left-hander. I'm a natural righty, but almost as soon as I started playing basketball, when I was twelve, I started practicing with my left hand, too. Anyhow, Grummond thought I was a left-hander when he saw me play. He talked to me after the game and told me he wanted me on the squad, whether I was a natural lefty or not."

Bob played a season of jayvee ball for Andrew Jackson, the last half of his sophomore year and the first half of his junior year. He was then promoted to the varsity and came on fast enough to be named in his senior year to the All-New York City public high school team. A number of New York colleges were interested in his future plans, but Bob, his mind set on going to a school outside of the city where there was some vestige of college life, turned them all down and decided on Holy Cross after also mulling over Dartmouth and Boston College. He spent the summer between high school and college working at Tamarack Lodge in the Borsch Belt, waiting on tables and playing for his alpine alma mater in its classic clashes with its ivied rival, the Nevele Country Club. During his vacations from Holy Cross the next three summers, Cousy returned to Tamarack Lodge. "The mountains were crowded with first-class players," he says, "and the competition was a wonderful thing for all of us. That is how I have always learned—observing some player who could do things I couldn't and seeing if I could get up to his level." Cousy's first and enduring idol, by the way, was Dick McGuire, the superb playmaker of the New York Knickerbockers. "Dick's a couple of years older than I am," Cousy said recently, "so I never got to play against him when we were kids, although we grew up pretty close to each other. I always admired the way he did things, and I still do. One of the events I look forward to each year now is making the All-East team, particularly because of the chance it gives me to team up with Dick against the West in the All-Star game. Working with Dick you can experiment with moves you wouldn't dare to try during a regular league game. You're so loose they usually work. For me, the finest pleasure in basketball has always come from making some unorthodox pass that results in a basket."

At Holy Cross, Cousy had his first opportunity to improvise freely. The coach was Doggie Julian who had no staid or set ideas on how he wanted his team to play and encouraged his players to be inventive. Holy Cross was loaded with talent, perhaps the most competent squad ever assembled at any college in New England—men like Joe Mullaney, Bob Curran, George Kaftan, Dermie O'Connell, and Ken Haggerty. There were, in fact, ten men who could play first team. Doggie made the most of his embarrassment of riches by two-platooning his squad. One five would play the first ten minutes; the second five (including Cousy who, under the postwar rules, was eligible to play for the varsity as a freshman) would come in for the second quarter. The first five would return for the third quarter and then the second five would finish up the game. Occasionally but not often, Julian broke up his alignment, but there was little provocation for big measures since the team was far and away the class in its section. As such, it received an invitation to the NCAA tourney and won it by defeating Navy, CCNY, and Oklahoma. The next season, 1947–48, the team won twenty-six and lost four, was again invited to the NCAA, but this time, after beating Michigan, lost to that celebrated Kentucky outfit by eight points.

During Cousy's last two seasons at the Cross, top-notch players like Bob McMullan, Frank Oftring, and Andy Laska came along to replace the stars who had been graduated. Buster Sheary, who had succeeded Julian as coach—Doggie had gone into the pro ranks to coach the Celtics—dispensed with the two-platoon business, but for the most part went happily along with the fluid style of offense featuring the swift and tricky ball handling for which the Holy Cross teams had become known. Sheary's first club failed to make the NCAA when it was beaten by Yale (led by Tony Lavelli, probably the most graceful of all the hook-shot artists and probably also the least skillful basketball player in all other departments of all the scoring specialists who caught the public's fancy). In Cousy's senior year, Holy Cross ripped off twenty-six straight victories before falling into an unaccountable tail spin and dropping four of its last five, including its two games in the NCAA. Cousy was a unanimous All-America choice that year. "Those things are all a matter of publicity," he once remarked in the hardheaded way he reacts to all hoopla. "Winning those twenty-six straight put the spotlight on our team, and I benefited from that. I think I may have actually played a shade better my junior year."

During his four collegiate seasons, Cousy compiled a new record point total for a Holy Cross player, 1,775 points in 117 games for an average of 15.1 points a game. He won a lot of games with eleventh-hour heroics—for example, he sent one game against Bowling Green (which Holy Cross eventually won) into overtime with a Merriwell heave from fifty feet out which actually entered the basket after the final gun but counted nonetheless since it was in the air when the gun went off. What made him a back-yard name throughout New England, though, was his finesse as a floorman. "We never had the big man, so we developed a hundred and one variations on the give-and-go," Cousy says of the Holy Cross teams he played on. "They claim we sold basketball to New England, but we may have also retarded it. We possibly oriented the people in the wrong direction by emphasizing the spectacular. Nowadays if a Worcester crowd sees a legitimate offense based on a tall man in the pivot, they think it's dull stuff, kid stuff. They want that old behind-the-back passing, that old open bucket."

College was all Cousy hoped it would be, and then some. He made close friends and they, as much as his aversion to the impersonality of a big city like New York, were responsible for his later decision to make his home in Worcester. He got over the shyness he had in meeting people and became much more at home when called on for a few words at banquets. (He has a slight speech defect that turns his r's into l's.) A conscientious student, he was regularly on the dean's list, majoring in business administration but taking more and more courses in sociology. He wrote his senior thesis on "The Persecution of Minority Groups."

At the time of his graduation from college, Cousy had devised just about all of the ball handling abracadabra that is now synonymous with "The Cooz," though, to be sure, he has refined and polished his moves as a pro, trebled his variations on them, and learned how to integrate them far better into his own play and the play of his teammates. As he looks back today, Cousy has some very lucid ideas on what he happened to do right at an early age in hitting on a fundamental concept of basketball that enabled him to develop a greater diversity of maneuver than any player before him. Briefly, these are his thoughts on the essentials of good basketball:

The primary skill a young player must try to acquire is to master his weak hand, his left hand if he is a righty. Learning to shoot with it amounts to only a small advance. To be a true threat, a man must be able to move equally well both to his left and right, and this includes being able to dribble, pass, and shoot while going in both directions. The whole art of dribbling, for instance, depends on keeping your body between the ball and the man guarding you. Against a capable opponent, you cannot drive forward from right to left, say, unless you can dribble with your left hand. Otherwise the ball is unprotected.

Unless he also possesses an accurate shot, an agile dribbler can operate only at 50 per cent of his effectiveness. If he is no threat shooting from the outside, his man can afford to give him room and let him shoot, gambling that he will make a poor percentage of his shots. By giving him this room, the defensive man acquires a margin for error which allows him to stay between his man and the basket even if he has been slightly faked or has anticipated a move incorrectly.

The key to offensive play for a maturing player is enlarging his number of moves, his variety of shots. Just as a good pitcher in baseball throws every pitch with the same motion, a good basketball player begins all of his moves from the same position, the better to confuse the defense.

While there are certainly situations in which personal virtuosity gets him someplace, in the final analysis a player is about as good as his teammates. If your passes increase their effectiveness, that effectiveness in return increases yours. (Cousy works especially well with Bill Sharman, a solid all-round player and as fine a shot as there is in the league, and with that other member of the Celtics' perennial Big Three, Easy Ed Macauley, who, as Cousy sees it, has the greatest variety of moves of any big man.)

These are the classic fundamentals, practiced intuitively by the top-notch players since the game, along with just about every other American sport, entered its "modern" phase as part of the great coming of age of athletics in this country at the close of World War I. The team that made America basketball-conscious was the New York Celtics. In the early and middle '20s the original Celtics and the later editions— featuring stars like Johnny Beckman, Nat Holman, Pete Barry, Davey Banks, Dutch Dehnert, Chris Leonard, Horse Haggerty, and Joe Lapchick—ranged up and down the eastern half of the country playing one-night stands against the best local opposition in gyms, dance halls, or any available enclosure large enough to accommodate a court and some spectators.

The Celtics did not run up overwhelming scores—forty points was a staggering total in those days—but what made them worth driving miles to see was the fashion in which the entire team handled the ball, whistling it around with a speed, a crispness, and a command of pattern that no other team could come close to. The ball moved so fast sometimes that opposing teams literally lost sight of it. The Celtics sold basketball wherever they went and to their considerable satisfaction, for they approached their arduous touring with the passion of missionaries. It was this dedication to presenting the game on the highest possible level that, one evening in 1926 in Chattanooga, accidentally resulted in the invention of the pivot play, from that night on a standard pattern of offense. During the first quarter that night the Celtics had been unable to work the ball around with their characteristic precision. "One big fellow had planted himself at the foul line, and he was making it rough for us," Joe Lapchick, at six feet five inches by far the tallest man on the Celtics, was remembering this winter. "To block that man out so that we could get our passing game started again, Dutch Dehnert got the idea of taking up a position right in front of that guy with his back turned to the basket. We started feeding the ball into Dutch, and he whipped it back as fast as it went in. This must have looked awfully good, for the fans started screaming with delight. A little later on in the game one of our players shot the ball into Dutch from the right, and another player cut by from the left. As he did so, Dutch fed the ball to him, and there he was right in for a perfect lay-up. At another time the man playing Dutch tried to intercept a pass before it reached the pivot. Dutch got the ball and then simply pivoted around and faced the basket. He had an easy unguarded lay-up. Then we began to get excited. It had become clear to us that we had hit on a brilliant new style of attack that was not only good to look at but a very functional style that released a tremendous variety of optional plays."

In addition to their barnstorming, the Celtics also played forty-four games a year in the old American League. They were the perennial champions, and in time, with the fans turning out only to watch the Celtics, the league was not prospering as it hoped to. The cry went up to "break up the Celtics." In the late '20s they did.

Soon after the partition of the Celtics, pro basketball, with an assist from hard times, dwindled into a shadow of its former self. It took the next tremendous upsurge of sports in general, following World War II, to bring about a renaissance of the pro game. During the twenty-five-year interval, basketball went through a transformation that might be compared to the usual result produced when a naturally pretty if somewhat unfinished country girl is taken in hand by a Hollywood studio: many of the changes wrought are indeed for the better and make her more attractive, and everything would be fine except that at least an equal number of the other changes invariably rob her of her natural charm and make her almost unrecognizable. Anyhow, basketball changed. The center jump went out, which speeded up the game and produced higher and higher scores which people claimed that "people" liked. The ten-second backcourt rule came in, an undeniable boon. From out of the West in the middle-late '30s came a real Lochinvar, Hank Luisetti of Stanford, a breath-taking player years ahead of his time who could do everything (including dribble behind his back) and who, among his other accomplishments, was the man who popularized the one-hand push shot. As developed by Luisetti, the one-hand push was thrown much softer and with much less spin than the customary two-handed set. As a result, if the shot was slightly off the mark, the ball had a much greater chance of bouncing off the rim and in. At least as important was the fact that a player could shoot a one-hander much more quickly than it took him to get set for a two-hander. Consequently, the one-hander became much more than a vogue; it became a standard. The advent of the one-hand set, incidentally, was not hampered by the gradual decrease in the size of the basketball. A decade earlier it was probably an inch and a half larger in diameter, and it took a Horse Haggerty to palm one upside down.

From out of the West also came the fast break. There were many fans who didn't think this style was real basketball, but they were forced to admit that it was an effective means of scoring when a team had an agile big man breaking up the court and other agile big men to pick the rebound off if the lead man missed his shot. With this one fast movement, a team had arrived at the same position where it would have taken many moves in orthodox "possession" basketball. As a result, coaches everywhere tried to corral as many big men as they could find, and the era of the ungainly big man began. The next natural step was the development by these tall players of unstoppable shots which they could get off even if they were closely guarded and completely out of position to shoot. As the offensive specialist—meaning a player who had no idea of how to play defense—became the order of the day, the skillful floorman became scarcer and scarcer and a superb all-round player like Bob Davies of Seton Hall was a valid rarity.

This, then, was the shape basketball was in, a hodgepodge of advanced skills and rank defacements, when two new pro leagues (later merged into the NBA) hopefully began distributing franchises in 1946. A fan naturally expects the pro version of a sport to be markedly superior in technique to the collegiate version, and since pro basketball wasn't, it got off to a rather shaky start. It began to catch on when Joe Fulks began to score. A strong, heavily muscled man who stood six feet five inches and who could get way off the floor and stay there for hours, Fulks was the master of the two-hand jump shot. He could start his jump with his back to the basket and wheel around in the air, and he could throw this shot from all angles. Fulks' high scoring brought out the crowds who had read in the papers about his scoring thirty points here and forty points there and who wanted to see in person how any one man could ring up that phenomenal total. Jumping Joe reached his peak one day in 1949 when he threw in twenty-seven field goals and nine foul shots and amassed sixty-three points all by himself—a total that would have exceeded the two-game totals of a good team in the '20s and early '30s. (Paul Arizin's later modification of Fulks' specialty into a one-hand jump has been the last big step in shooting techniques.) When Joe began to fade, George Mikan, six feet ten inches tall but a bona fide athlete, stepped

in and carried the load for the league. And then along came
Cousy.

It took Cousy about a season and a half to find himself in
pro ball. In his first year with the Celtics, 1950–51, he finished ninth in the league in scoring and was chosen rookie of
the year, but, in truth, his over-all play was not really impressive. Too often when he tried his fancy stuff he fooled his
teammates as badly as the rival team. When an unexpected
pass from Cousy ripped by a teammate completely unprepared to receive it, it would have been inaccurate to have
attributed the mix-up to the fact that Cousy was just too fast
for his colleagues. Like many freshmen in the pro ranks, he
was prone to force openings where none existed, and his defensive play was shown to be extremely spotty. Midway
through his sophomore year, he suddenly blossomed into a
different ballplayer, a commanding figure in every game he
played. The major credit for this quick maturity belongs, to
be sure, to Cousy himself, but a sizable share should go to
Arnold (Red) Auerbach, the brown-haired coach of the
Celtics. Though he has often succeeded in disguising his
ability as a coach by carrying on as if theatrical referee-baiting
was his first love, Auerbach knows the game. His big move in
helping Cousy to release his bottled-up potential was to develop an offense based on the fast break, with Cousy as lead
man. Auerbach also diagnosed that a key reason why Cousy
had been getting himself tied up by the defense had been his
predilection for trying to work the ball in too close to the
basket. The foul line, he pointed out acutely, was the point
where, in the large majority of situations, Cousy should make
his decisions.

Then it all began to come. Familiarization with the styles
of his teammates did the rest. "Bob is a wonderful team man,
let me make that as clear as a crystal in case you might have
picked up some erroneous ideas to the contrary," Auerbach

said this winter. "The only kick I have with Cousy is that he makes practice sessions hard on a coach. All the others players just want to stand still and watch him."

In spite of what Cousy has done for basketball by his personal magnificence and his influence on other players, the game, as both its harshest critics and stanchest supporters agree, has quite a distance to go, in certain areas which even a Cousy cannot affect, if it hopes to develop into a better and not a worse game.

The difficulties which beset basketball as it tries to deal with its now chronic problem—how to keep from becoming a game dominated by taller and taller men with room for only occasional superlative "small men"—is epitomized by the changing attitudes of Forrest (Phog) Allen, the very vocal coach of Kansas. For years Phog was the loudest exponent of controlling the tall man's advantages by raising the basket higher off the ground. Now that Kansas has acquired Wilt "the Stilt" Chamberlain and his seven feet two inches of ability, Phog sees no reason in the world for raising the baskets. Ten feet is perfect for Chamberlain and for Allen. In the opinion of not a few veteran observers, one possible solution of the tall-man peril would be to enlarge the court both in width and in length. Their feeling is that this larger court, by placing a greater premium on speed, quickness, maneuverability, stamina, and basic basketball sense, might restore the stature of athletes of average height and make it essential for the giants to be truly first-rate athletes like Mel Hutchins and Maurice Stokes. It might also serve to bring back that almost lost art: skillful defensive play. In this connection, the other principal area in which many of the outstanding coaches and players think that basketball has gone astray from its best expression has been the evolution of a type of game in which the action is stopped far too frequently by the calling of fouls. It would appear that piecemeal revisions have no effect in the long run and that a whole new study of what is permissible body contact and what is a foul is needed. Too many referees today seem to forget that a man effecting a clean block of a lay-up, to cite one example, will necessarily establish some body contact with the shooter; while this body contact really hasn't interfered with the shooter's chances of scoring, today the calling of a foul approaches the automatic. One thing is certain: when you have seen a game in which more foul shots are made than field goals—frequently the case these days—you have not seen enjoyable or genuine basketball.

The hardest part of the life of a pro athlete is learning how to adjust to the fact that he will never quite adjust to the plexus of eternal travel and topsy-turvy hours. Cousy is luckier than most of his brethren inasmuch as he can fall asleep in ten minutes on any reasonably soft horizontal surface. Furthermore, as every outstanding athlete must, he has acquired the hardy mental stamina that enables him to play his usual game after snagging only a couple of hours' sleep or when he is burdened by physical miseries that would render the average person hors de combat for pinochle. On the other hand, some aspects of the nomadic life are harder on Cousy than on some others. As anyone would be who was brought up on pot-au-feu, he has discriminating taste buds, and this makes things a little tough on him when a game finishes at eleven and the only eating places still open specialize in fishburgers and papaya juice. Moreover, his active mind requires something more stimulating than that favorite time-killing pastime of traveling athletes: sitting in a hotel lobby hours on end, watching everything and nothing. If it happens that he has caught up on his sleep and extra hours are still hanging awkwardly around, Bob usually takes in a movie with his roommate Sharman and some of the other players. "I've seen as many as four in one day," he remarked ruefully this winter. "I probably see more movies in a year than Louella Parsons." For all these reasons—plus the pleasure he takes in his home, his wife Missie, and their children, Marie Colette, four, and Mary Pat, three—Cousy's spirits always rise when a road trip is ending.

The pro season is a long, enervating grind. Practice starts around the first of October and the play-offs linger on into April some years. During the off-season Cousy is able to lead a relatively normal life, but the only period in which he is able to get away from basketball completely is the two months between the end of a season and mid-June. Then he goes up to New Hampshire to ready Camp Graylag, of which he is one of the three co-owners, for the influx of the campers. Graylag offers a wide range of activities but, as you might expect, its heart is a large central area paved with concrete, lined for two basketball courts, encircled with other baskets set at heights suitable for younger players, and equipped with floodlighting. The ball is bouncing practically all of the time. After the camp season comes the clinic season and sometimes, if there is room, a little missionary work. (Cousy has a standing offer to visit Finland, a country in which basketball is now giving middle-distance running a run for its money.)

"I suppose it's a good thing I love my work," he said the afternoon before a game this winter when he was lolling about his living room with some friends, listening to some Nat Cole records and watching his very cute daughters turning handsprings over the furniture and unconsciously exhibiting a co-ordination and balance that would bring a gleam to the eye of a scout for a high-wire aerial act. "Maybe we'll let them play tennis," Cousy said with a wink as he looked away from his daughters. "Thank goodness they look like their mother," he added wryly. "The poor kids, they've got my feet and my hands."

BEN HOGAN
AND SAM SNEAD:
ON THE EVE
OF TWO OPENS

1. BEN: THE 1955 OPEN
AT OLYMPIC

During the period when I was writing a great deal of golf for *Sports Illustrated*, it was our practice to present early each June a preview of the upcoming National Open. Sometimes the preview concentrated on the course the players would be tackling, other times on a particular group of players or on one commanding figure, such as Hogan or Snead. We devoted the preview to Hogan in 1955 because, were Ben to fail to win that year at the Olympic Club, it would be the first time since 1948 that he had gone two years without taking a major title and would signalize the end, perhaps, of The Age of Hogan. Our reason for selecting Snead the following June was that the 1956 Open at Oak Hill marked the end of a full score of years since Sam's debut in the national championship.

As it turned out, Sam was never in the running in the 1956 Open, but Ben in 1955 appeared to have won his fifth championship until Jack Fleck came ghosting home in the twilight to tie him with a brilliant birdie on the last hole and on the next day defeated Ben in a dramatic play-off. Both Hogan and Snead, extraordinary athletes, remain entirely capable of winning the Open today even though they are approaching fifty. Snead, who might have captured many Opens if his putting had been up to the standard of the rest of his game, has lately developed into a really first-class putter. Sam's personality in recent years has grown a shade more baroque, though, and that has not helped him in his quest of the one major title that has evaded him. Ben, on the other hand, at his peak always very steady on the greens and a wonderful holer of the critical six-footers and four-footers, has been afflicted with all kinds of putting woes the past few seasons. Were he able to putt with his old confidence and effectiveness, this exceptional man would still be winning major championships. From tee to green he remains unapproached for his confounding, continuous accuracy. On the double-round on Saturday in the 1960 Open, for example, Hogan hit the first thirty-four greens in par before finding the hazard before the 17th in his bold attempt for a birdie that might have won for him.

THE WINNER of the 1955 National Open Championship this weekend could very possibly be Ben Hogan. It is almost a simple matter of presence. Over the past eight years, regardless of how muddy other affairs have turned out to be, it has become remarkably clear that if Ben Hogan is entered in a tournament, there is an extremely strong likelihood that the winner will be Ben Hogan.

In the opinion of golf's most thoughtful observers, however, the chances of another Hogan victory loom somewhat less overwhelming than they have in the past on the eve of the Open. On one hand, his opposition should be tougher. There is considerable ground for believing that the players comprising the Young Guard and the Middle Guard have gained sufficient confidence not to rush headlong away from the responsibility of being crowned champion should they play themselves into a position where that heavy burden presents itself. In recent months, on the other hand, there have been a few fairly definite indications that Hogan, a human being despite the colossal evidence to the contrary that he has exhibited in his mastery of one tournament after another, is at length, and at forty-two, slowing down just a trifle. He now misses the fairway off the tee occasionally, like other fine golfers. He now pops an occasional approach a few yards short of the green, like other fine golfers. He even occasionally fails to hole a five-foot putt. Ben, as we should know by now, is so consummate a strategist, shotmaker, and competitor that when he is fifty he could still "take it all," but in the event he does not carry off the Open this week it will be of more than passing significance. It will be the first time since the war that he will have gone two consecutive years without winning at least one major championship—the Open, the British Open, the Masters, and the PGA—and this will mark the end of a historic period in golf, the Age of Hogan.

Celebrated as Ben's reign has been both by the golfing and the nongolfing public throughout the world—for after his comeback from his near-fatal accident Ben became a human-interest story and a powerfully popular figure for thousands who "never swung a tee"—we are probably still too close to his separate triumphs, still too bedazzled by his commanding, combative, concentric personality, to appreciate how phenomenal he has been over a period of years purely and simply as a golfer. In years to come, I am sure, the sports public, looking back at his record, will be struck by awe and disbelief that any one man could have played so well so regularly. The boosters of that age will resort to explaining that Hogan could only have cut the swath he did in a period when he had no competition and so on and so forth, just as they do today when trying to comprehend the consistent dominance of earlier superchampions like John L. Sullivan, Ty Cobb, Bobby Jones, Bill Tilden, Jim Thorpe, Howie Morenz, Walter Johnson, and Paavo Nurmi. Ben Hogan, the outstanding sports personality of the postwar decade, has, to be sure, secured a place among the very great athletes of all time.

Perhaps as good a way as any, particularly on the eve of a National Open, to begin to understand Hogan's genius as a tournament golfer is to set down without flourish his record over the past fifteen years in this most important of all tournaments:

1940—tied for fifth	*1949—injured*
1941—tied for third	*1950—first*
1942–'45—no Open	*1951—first*
1946—tied for fourth	*1952—third*
1947—tied for sixth	*1953—first*
1948—first	*1954—tied for sixth*

Two other men have records in the Open which compare with Hogan's. Willie Anderson, a dour Scottish pro transplanted to Apawamis, took the event in 1901, 1903, 1904, and 1905. The second man, of course, was Bobby Jones, and since his is the only other modern record in the same class with Hogan's, we might do well to set it down year by year again.

1920—tied for eighth	*1926—first*
1921—tied for fifth	*1927—tied for eleventh*
1922—tied for second	*1928—second*
1923—first	*1929—first*
1924—second	*1930—first*
1925—second	

As documents of sustained brilliance over a period of years, Hogan's and Jones' records speak for themselves. But just as the two men are quite different personalities, their careers were shaped differently, as one or two brief elaborations on the tables above incisively demonstrate. When Jones first cracked through in 1923, for example, he was a young man of twenty-one playing in his fourth Open. Bob had been a helluva golfer back in 1916 when, at fourteen, he had gone to the quarter-finals of the Amateur. The period between 1916 and 1923 struck him as "the seven lean years," for he was so good so early, a bona fide child prodigy who never lost his stuff. When he retired in 1930 after his Grand Slam, Bob was only twenty-eight. Hogan, in contrast, was thirty-five (almost thirty-six) when he captured his first Open. Twelve years before, in 1936 at Baltusrol, he had qualified for the championship but had failed to "make the cut"—that is, he did not finish among the top seventy-six scorers for the first two rounds and so was not eligible to play the last thirty-six holes. In 1939 he finished the Open in a tie for sixty-second place. He was almost twenty-seven at this time, an age when a golfer must expect some success or get out of the profession, and it would not have been beyond reason for the name Ben Hogan never to have become better known to the sports public than the names George Slingerland and Frank Gelhot, the only two men who played the final thirty-six holes in that Open and did not bring in lower totals than Hogan's. The point is not a new one, that Hogan was anything but a born wonder, but it is worth the re-making. No athlete ever worked harder, or waited longer, to become a champion. It explains an awful lot about the man.

By 1940 Hogan was an accomplished enough golfer to have won the Open. He was ripping through everything else but "the big ones" and led the money winners for three consecutive seasons before entering the service in 1942. When he returned to civilian life and combat golf, he quickly reaffirmed his position of standing with Snead and Nelson as the country's best. At length in 1946, years behind schedule, he won his first prestige championship, the PGA. I doubt if ever in the long line of fierce and fiery spirits who set out to win at "games" anyone matched the smoldering intensity of the Hogan of this period, a volcano always on the brink of eruption, so white-hot in his overdetermination that you were charred by propinquity, and yet so controlled, so inflexible, and so terribly purposeful that it gave you a chill to watch him at his work.

Hogan's opponent in the final of that PGA was Ed Oliver. At lunch Oliver stood three up, but in the afternoon Hogan rushed out in thirty strokes and by the thirty-first tee stood five up. The two drives on the thirty-first finished about equidistant from the green, and the referee resorted to tossing a coin. Hogan won the toss and elected to play first. He put his approach three feet from the hole—finis, six and four. He played like a killer that afternoon, and many afternoons afterward, for earlier that year—and you can imagine the depth of the anguish and self-recrimination a person like Ben underwent—he had taken three putts on the seventy-second green in both the Open and the Masters when two putts would have enabled him to have tied for the top and opened up the chance of victory via a play-off. After these crucial disappointments he seemed always to be goading himself to relax not for an instant, to make every shot count, to show the other fellow (and himself) no mercy.

The Hogan of this period, just prior to his initial victory in the 1948 National Open at Riviera with his record score of 276, was something to behold. When people talk of a man drilling an iron or rifling an approach shot, nearly always that is "golf language" loosely used. But Hogan did drill those irons and his shots did buzz like bullets. My, how they traveled—low, hard, even viciously. In the third round of one Masters, I think it was, I remember Hogan coming to the thirteenth in the thick of the battle, not far behind the leader. Attempting to cut the corner as closely as possible and set himself up for getting home in two for his birdie, he hooked the ball slightly and it rolled into Rae's Creek. Well, it cost him a valuable stroke to lift, and there he was, standing with his hands on his hips and his cigarette wedged truculently between his lips, collecting himself before he played his third. He pulled out what looked like a one-iron, and no one who watched that shot will ever forget it. He hit it with everything. Scarcely had he finished his follow-through, it seemed, when the ball was already on the green, lying quietly twelve feet from the cup—it had gotten there that fast! Hogan was playing a different kind of golf, both in thought and in execution, when he won his first Open and, subsequently, his three other Opens, his second PGA, his two Masters, and his British Open. He had become a better golfer, as his success in itself made clear. However, for the pure excitement of watching a man attack a golf ball, no one in our time has generated the clubhead speed and unleashed a shot like Hogan did just before he learned how to win.

Depending on how you look at it, everybody knows or nobody knows the change Hogan mastered in his method of striking a golf ball the season he won his first Open. If one means the exact key to his method of imparting a controlled fade to his shots—the exact key being what is referred to as Hogan's Secret, since he has no desire to reveal it to the rest of the trade—then no one knows. If one means more generally doing everything to retain his power and yet everything to guard against a hook, then everyone knows what Hogan does. The swing he compounded and learned so well that he could execute it flawlessly under fire has varied somewhat in its details from season to season, but it had, and has, as its features (bypassing Hogan's true fundamentals of perfect balance and his wide "forward" arc) such anti-hook staples as the left thumb down the shaft and the right hand riding high, the slightly opened stance, the club taken back a shade outside, the outward thrust of the right forearm at the beginning of the downswing that produces what the pros call the triangulation action, and the maintenance of an anything-but-shut clubface as he biffs through the ball.

Hogan lost some roll as the result of "the slight fade" but what he gained was ten times as valuable. His approaches became a softer kind of shot. They coasted over the flag and dropped gently onto the green. More important, when he failed to meet his drives just right, the ball did not hook into trouble; it merely veered a few yards to the right in a far safer and "slower" parabola than a hook describes. Before effecting this change, when Ben had played an unbroken competitive stretch, he had been prone to tire near the end of a tournament. When he was tired, he hooked. When he hooked, he incurred rough lies and sometimes penalty strokes. When he incurred these extra strokes, it defeated him. His revised swing gave him margin for unpenalized error and proved to be the difference between Ben's becoming a great champion and not remaining just a great golfer.

Contrasted with a swing like Snead's, which is natural and (because of Sam's exceptional leverage) naturally powerful, the swing Hogan built was not a picture-post-card lyric. It was constructed, as its critics pointed out, too much like a stairway of compensations. When these broke down—and they did to some degree in the Masters in 1952 and 1954 and in the last two rounds of the '52 Open—Hogan had his problems. But Hogan's swing, when he had the time to tune it up properly and the physical reserve to maintain it as he wanted it, was so functional and assertive that it had a smooth, efficient beauty of its own.

Hand in hand with Hogan's altered swing went an altered program of participation. In 1948 and in the seasons following his accident, he eschewed his previous habit of playing the tournament circuit almost without a break in favor of picking his spots. He conserved his energy and concentration for the significant events, resting and practicing in between. It helped to make the difference and Ben realized this perfectly. "The most important factor in playing a championship is to be fully prepared," he said in his acceptance speech at Oakmont after his fourth triumph in the Open, picking his words as carefully as he picks his clubs. "I look forward to playing in the Open as long as I am able to prepare my game and myself properly."

Hogan's most unusual effort in preparation was part and parcel of his dramatic invasion of Scotland to play in the 1953 British Open. His subsequent victory was so utterly triumphant that it has today the aura of a romantic novel about it. For a man who had never before played a competitive stroke in Britain, Ben made a phenomenal adaptation to the foreign conditions. Discovering, for instance, that he hurt his wrists when he played his irons off Carnoustie's hard turf with his usual swing, he modified his hitting action. "He ended," Sir Guy Campbell has said, "taking the ball almost exactly like the great Scottish golfers had done years and years before." To get to know the deceptive course, on the evenings preceding the start of the tournament he walked the holes backward until he had memorized the natural features and the concomitant problems in tactics. He won with 73-71-70-68. "And if he had needed a 64 on his final round," Bernard Darwin has remarked, "you were quite certain he could have played a 64. Hogan gave you the distinct impression that he was capable of getting whatever score was needed to win."

Since his accession in 1948, Ben has provided such a cornucopia of skill and courage that to choose his finest shots, his finest rounds, and his finest tournaments would be mighty difficult and would, eventually anyhow, resolve itself into personal choices. We will take Ben's selections, then, in those cases where he has indicated them.

His top tournament: the 1953 Masters which, as he has expressed it, represented the best golf he ever played over a seventy-two-hole stretch. Ben was 70-69-66-69—274—and the game's most erudite camp followers cannot remember four consecutive rounds of comparable errorless character. On a testing course, Hogan was literally on the pin with just about every shot. (It was after this exhibition that everyone began clamoring what a crime it would be for such a golfer not to take a shot at the British Open; when Hogan was assured of the accommodations he would need at Carnoustie to "prepare himself fully," he went, as we know.)

His best round? He has intimated that it was the final 67 that won him his third Open at Oakland Hills in 1951. Late that afternoon, Clayton Heafner got around in 69, the one other player in a superb field who succeeded in breaking 70 over the four rounds on perhaps the severest layout on which the Open has been played. The chief incubus to the scoring was controlling the tee-shot. Robert Trent Jones, who had remodeled the old Oakland Hills specifically for the 1951 Open, had filled in the obsolete traps 220 to 240 yards from the tee and had constructed in their stead new traps which flanked the wasp-waisted fairways 240 to 260 yards from the tee, far enough out so that the long-hitting pros could not carry them. This tight arrangement panicked just about the entire field with the exception of Paul Runyan, who would have had a hard time reaching the obsolete traps. Hoping to avoid error, many of the pros switched to brassies, spoons, and irons off the tees, leaving themselves a succession of arduous second shots and, all in all, letting the course play them instead of playing the course. Hogan started with an erratic 76. Round by round he improved his figures—a 73, a 71, a 67.

Hogan's performance proved to most observers that the course had been a fair test of championship golf. Hogan did not see it that way, even in victory. "I am glad," he stated grimly at the presentation ceremonies, "I brought this course, this monster, to its knees." It came as somewhat of a shock to hear this, for after his recuperation from his accident there had been some indications of "a new Ben," "a mellower Hogan." It served as a reminder that, as long as he remains a competitive golfer, Ben will probably never be so new or so mellow that the chip on his shoulder will entirely disappear.

He seems to like it that way, or maybe it is more accurate to say that he continually translates any opposition, animal, vegetable, or mineral, into a personal challenge and derives immense satisfaction from responding to that challenge with all the sense and sinew at his command.

Totally absorbed with producing his best game and a game calculated to win, Hogan necessarily has precious little to say to his opponent or caddie. When he and his old rival, Byron Nelson, played a friendly round the first day of the 1954 Masters, Nelson acting as host for the Augusta National, Ben as defending champion, Byron would drive and Ben would say, "Beauty," Bcn would drive and Byron would say, "Beauty," and this was about the extent of their conversation. In this same connection, there is the classic description by the more gregarious Snead on what it is like to play with Hogan: "The only time Ben speaks to you is to tcll you, 'You're away, Sam,'" This trenchant silence is one of the elements which make up the memorable picture of "a man at work" that no one who has watched Hogan is ever likely to forget. There he is, moving up to his approach shot, walking with that little waggle, his eyes fixed straight ahead down the fairway, like a man heading for a spot in the woods where he has marked his ball. He wears the straight-visored, white cap over his tanned countenance. It is a countenance—the mouth set, as ever, in that locked grin which should never be mistaken for Ben's enjoying either the morning air, the devotion of his worshipful gallery, or the shot he has just played, however fine it was. The mind is moving ahead, thinking out the next step in the big picture, filing through this check point and that check point to make certain the next step is the wise step. He stands beside the ball, hands on hips. He examines the lie, studies the type of grass, the wind. He discusses inwardly the best position on the green to place that approach in order to set up the most holeable putt, the type of shot he will play, the club he will play it with. He takes his time, walking ahead sometimes as much as twenty yards as he ponders this decision. Other players go through the same motions but they seldom give you the impression Hogan does—that he is genuinely thinking about what he is doing. Then, the mind made up, there is that light practice swing, the meticulous settling into his stance, the always decisive stroke. If it has been a good shot, there is no expression on Hogan's part to show he acknowledges it as such. However, after he has played a poor shot at a stage of a tournament where it may be costly, there is a change of expression. The grin becomes ironic and his cold gray eyes widen and widen until they seem to be a full inch in height, and when you look at this man, so furious with himself, he is, as his colleagues refer to him, "The Hawk."

No one, I suppose, ever set himself so high a standard of performance. What trying to achieve this standard would take out of the average tournament golfer, no one knows, but one can guess that few others would have the stamina to find it tolerable for long. Ben has talked of championship golf being the result of "20 per cent ability and 80 per cent management," and so it is, but for this formula to function in one major tournament after another, a tremendous giving of one's self is required. It has functioned for Hogan for, without any question of a doubt, no other golfer has ever dedicated himself so unanimously to golf.

2. SAM: THE 1956 OPEN
AT OAK HILL

Every June, as another United States Open Golf Championship comes into view, two ancient enigmas are annually pondered by golfers throughout the world. Will Sam Snead win the Open this year? Will Sam ever win the Open? It hardly seems possible, but when Sam tees off at Oak Hill on the fourteenth of June, it will mark twenty full seasons since his first start in that most important of all golf competitions. Over those two decades, he has won one British Open (1946), three PGA's (1942, 1949, 1951), and three Masters (1949, 1952, 1954). He has garnered more points in the international Ryder Cup matches than any other golfer, British or American. He has four years won the Vardon Trophy for the lowest strokes-per-round average in PGA-endorsed competitions, and, though the arithmetic gets complicated, he may well possess the lowest career-length strokes-per-round average of any golfer. He has won more tournaments than any golfer who ever lived. He has won more prize money than any golfer who ever lived. However, as everyone knows only too well, Sam has never been able to win "the big one," the U.S. or National Open. Snead is forty-four now, and, though his wonderfully supple frame and co-ordination have endowed him with a remarkable athletic longevity, Sam had better hurry up and win that Open or he may never do it. If he never does, it will be, historically, as tragic an injustice as if Rogers Hornsby had never captured a National League batting crown or Paavo Nurmi an Olympic title. If he ever does—and each June every contestant in the Open field hopes that if he himself doesn't win it, Sam will—it will be, without overstatement, one of the most popular triumphs ever recorded in the complete annals of sport.

The times Sam has come close to winning golf's most important championship constitute perhaps the game's epic tragedy. In his first attempt in 1937 at Oakland Hills, un-harried then as he was to be later by any complex about the Open, Sam was second. He finished comparatively early in the afternoon with a 71 for a four-round total of 283, the low score up to that point. It stood up until late in the day when Ralph Guldahl, on the wings of a seventy-yard chip that rolled into the cup for an eagle on the eighth, shuffled around in sixty-nine strokes for a total of 281, incidentally a new record for the event. (If Sam had managed to win that first time out, many observers were to conclude years later when his problem had become patently acute, he would have probably gone on to take a slew of Opens.) Then there was 1939, the cruelest year of all. He stood on the tee of the seventy-second hole of the Spring Mill course of the Phila-delphia Country Club needing only a 5 on a routine par-5 hole, 558 yards long, to lead the field. He proceeded to take that awful 8—one, in the rough to the left; two, a ducking wood into the side of a fairway trap; three, still in that trap; four, out but not well out; five, barely onto the green with a wobbly chip; and then, to cap the whole sad sequence, three putts. (He should have played safely for his 5 and would have, but he was not informed about what score was needed to win.) In 1940 at Canterbury, Sam was up front with 18 to

go. A 72 would have seen him through by a stroke. In a col-
lapse that brought back shuddering memories of old Mac
Smith foundering in the 1925 British Open at Prestwick,
Sam took an 81.

And so it continued to go. In 1947—the first of the two
climaxes is generally forgotten—the hard-luck man went
briefly out of character when he holed a fifteen-footer on the
seventy-second green of the St. Louis Country Club to tie
Lew Worsham for first. In the play-off, though, he tossed
away a one-stroke advantage down the stretch and ultimately
lost out when he failed to get down a thirty-and-one-half-inch
putt on the last green. In 1948 he led at the halfway mark
with 69–69–138, a new record for the first 36 of the championship. Then he began to miss those crucial four-footers
and seven-footers, and Hogan pulled away to the first of his
four great victories in the Open. Next came 1949, another
"almost but" year. With the 71st and 72nd to go, the first a
reasonably stock par 3 and the second a stock par 4, Sam
needed only two pars to tie for the top, and a par and a birdie
would have won for him. He got his par on the 72nd all
right, but it was of no matter since he had previously taken
three to get down from off the fringe on the 71st. (Broadcasting Snead's finish, Bill Stern, in one of his finest moments of misidentification, mistook Bobby Cruickshank,
playing from the 71st tee in the group just ahead of Sam's,
for Sam; before the appalling letdown set in, golf fans
thought it was Sam and not Bobby who had placed his tee
shot ten feet from the pin and had that all-important birdie
right in his hands.)

At Oakmont in 1953 Sam lay one stroke off Hogan's pace
after 54 holes, still one stroke behind after 63. On the long
66th, where he had his best chance to catch the true-tempered Texan, Sam mis-hit his second and finally three-putted
for a 6—not that a birdie would have, in the final analysis,
made much difference, the way Ben finished that round. In

1955 at the Olympic Club in San Francisco, off with a miserable 79, practically out of the tournament before it began, Sam buckled down hard to business and midway in the final round was miraculously in a position to win. He couldn't hole—he couldn't even come close to holing—five or six eminently holeable birdie putts, and at length he faded out of contention on the 70th. All in all, in this long chronicle of frustration, Sam has had to be discontent with four red ribbons and the blues.

The tremendous hold Samuel Jackson Snead has on the affections of the sports public rests on many other things besides the indubitable fact that he is the greatest golfer who has never won the Open. To begin with, he is abrim with natural color both as a person and a player, more so perhaps than any golfer since Walter Hagen. His appeal extends to every type of golf fan. Wherever he plays, he is followed not only by the most sedate pillars of the host club but also by "da poolroom crowd" which adopts him as its guy and roots as pugnaciously for him as if it were spurring on a hard-pressed Marciano. As a result, the salvos of applause that arise from Snead's gallery carry, as you hear them erupting in other sectors of the course, a barrel-house belligerence that is different from the sound sent up by any other worshipful gallery. In the Greensboro Open Sam is almost unbeatable because he invariably plays excellent golf there, but he is so *sympathique*—to use that old North Carolina expression—to the loco gentry that they have had to be restrained from improving his lies and lousing up his closest competitors.

What does Sam's fabulous appeal consist of? A large part of it, naturally, is that his whole personality projects like a ton of bricks. There he is, wherever he is, the likable, handsome, impressionable mountain boy from the Appalachian town of Hot Springs. Over the years Sam has acquired a formidable poise (which, among other things, has transformed the erstwhile inarticulate young man into one of the country's most engaging and accomplished after-dinner speakers), but a spectator can still feel what Sam is going through every minute of a tournament, his emotions and his thoughts are that readable. At the heart of the man, there is on most if not on all occasions a kindness of spirit and an innate sportsmanship surpassing that of many athletes celebrated for their sportsmanship—and these qualities somehow come through. Besides this, of course, it is just plain exciting to watch Sam Snead hit a golf ball. The first driver in the game's long history who was both very long and very straight, Sam possesses a swing of such beauty that a person who knows nothing about golf can recognize at once that he is watching something as functionally and artistically "right" as the motions of an Astaire or a Toscanini. Like no other, Snead's renowned swing integrates strength and ease—"flowing power," as Bill Campbell once termed it. Hogan's magnificent swing conjures up the image of a dynamic machine approaching metallic perfection, but Snead ripples into his shots with a lazy, controlled, lyrical grace that explodes into a tremendous burst of boff as his body uncoils and his hands unleash their pent-up power when he enters the hitting area. (The terrific unleash Sam gets has been explained as deriving from his being double-jointed; he is but only to the extent that he can bend his wrists back a bit farther than most people can.)

Some knowledgeable old golf hands contend that there never was and never will be a "natural golf swing," their argument being that the movements involved come naturally to no one and must be mastered. Be that as it may, if anyone was born to hit a golf ball, it was Sam. Propelling a ball with a stick is hardly less native to his talents than walking. In 1945, playing with one hand—his left—he toured the Homestead course at Hot Springs in consecutive rounds of 83–82–81. (This included holing a three-iron for a hole-in-one.)

Last year, for the curiosity of it, he played the Old White course at White Sulphur left-handed. He had an 86 which, with practice, he felt he could have improved on considerably. Sam can apparently play any which way and with any equipment.

Two years ago, in mind of his boyhood when he had banged at rocks with sticks of hickory and dogwood he had cut from the woods, he decided to see if he had lost that skill or enhanced it over the years. He found, growing near a creek, a piece of swamp maple which had a knobby bulge, shaped something like the head of a golf club, curving out of the "shaft." He trimmed down the shaft (which was about forty-eight inches long), got the head balanced, added a leather grip, and was ready to go. Using only this club and a wedge, he got around Old White in seventy-six shots. Other golfers couldn't get the ball off the ground with the homemade wood, but Sam could smack it great distances and once carried on his second shot into the trap before the green on the 17th, a fairly long par 5.

As this last feat of timing suggests, Sam has an extraordinary sensitivity for the "feel" of a shaft as it relates to the head of a club. As is generally known, he still uses the same driver he had back in 1937 when he shot into the spotlight. "You can put that driver," he claims, "into a room with twenty or thirty other drivers and then blindfold me and Ah'll go in and tell you which one it is." He has broken the club three times but has always gone back to it, for none of the duplicates made to replace it has struck him as having exactly the same nice balance or quite the same look as the head sits to the ball. The original shaft of that beautifully battered relic is still patched to the original head. For fifteen years now the head has been cracked and the crack kept packed with wood filler. The seasons have worn all the markings off the sole plate and the plate is as thin as a razor blade. The lead weight insert in the head, jockeyed about by impact, is all beat up. The insert in the face has been replaced three times. The complete antique has been refinished five times. Sam carries no brassie, going with the driver whenever he gets that rare blessing, a perfect brassie lie, and he plays his one-iron instead the rest of the time.

Over the years his swing has remained remarkably constant. "Ah've tried to keep it as simple as possible," he explains, "but Ah git those periods when mah backswing gits out o' whack. When that happens, Ah'll come too much over the ball and have to block the shot out with mah left hand. To correct things, Ah try not to change mah swing one eeny bit. Ah've changed mah turn a li'l bit sometimes or reset the feet a trifle, but mostly Ah work to git mah timing back where Ah want it." Sam is almost unique among his colleagues in the deep pleasure he receives from picking up a club, when he is hanging around a course on a nontournament day, and swinging it back and forth lazily and sensing that his rhythm is right. "When Ah play mah best," he once stated, "Ah feel Ah'm playin' with mah legs and mah feet."

Behind the natural golfer lies the natural athlete. During his boyhood in Hot Springs—his father worked as an engineer at the town power plant—Sam played all the sports in season. A halfback on the high-school football team, he handled all the kicking and had a punting average of over forty yards. He was one of a neighborhood bunch of five boys who began playing basketball together in the sixth grade and who went on to form the high school's starting five from their freshman through their senior years. Not a really tall man—he is only five feet eleven, although he gives the impression of being much larger—Sam's co-ordination made him, as you would expect, an unusually good rebounder. In the spring he pitched for the school team and also for the town team, the redoubtable Independents. He sandwiched in some track since he could run the hundred in ten flat.

(Sam can still run like a youngster.) Since Hot Springs was a resort town, he also came into contact with tennis, although most of his traffic with that sport was confined to beating a spoiled young star and receiving fifty cents every time he did so from the prima donna's appreciative father. "Ah had a good chop and not much else, that kind o' game," Sam has said of his tennis. He gravitated to golf quite by accident. In his senior year of high school, he broke his left hand playing football and took to swinging a club since he had the idea it would help the hand to knit flexibly and well. (Like Walter Hagen, who was also a gifted all-round athlete, Sam had, even as a boy, a great love of clothes. He spent many of his odd hours at his mother's sewing machine taking in or letting out the seats of trousers, making French cuffs, turning collars, lengthening jackets, and generally bringing his inexpensive clothes more in line with those worn by the fashionable vacationers at the Springs. His mother thought he would probably become a tailor.)

Above all, Sam was at home in the woods and the mountains: behind the natural athlete lies the natural backwoodsman, the "ridge-runner" of the Appalachians. He began hunting when he was nine. As a fisherman, he became adept enough to catch trout with his bare hands. "When you know the spots in the pools where they gather," he once described this recondite art, "why, you jes' reach in with your hand and rub them along the belly, workin' up towards the hid. You work up softly like and then, pingo!—you pinch that trout right back o' the gills." In wintertime he trapped—fox, coon, possum, rabbit, wildcat, and weasel, also skunk and mountain hawk, since you got a dollar for a skunk's hide and a fifty-cent bounty for every hawk. In Sam's neck of the woods the man who could bring in a wildcat alive was highly esteemed. Sam brought in three. "Man, Ah really knew those hills," he was recalling recently. "Ah knew the name of everythin' that moved and every li'l bush and shrub."

Two decades in the somewhat more civilized frontier belt of professional golf have dulled the instincts of the natural ridge-runner hardly at all. For example, if all the touring pros were to walk behind a fence which covered them from view from the knees up, Sam could identify each of them simply from the way he walked. He still gives full play, as the woodsman does, to all his instincts and senses. "You know, you can be in the woods," he has said, "and you know there's somethin' close to you, though you cain't see it or smell it or hear it. Some extra sense tells you it's there, and if you wait, you learn it always is. Ah always make it a point to heed that intuition." This brings up an interesting theory about Sam. Many veteran golf observers are of the opinion that this sensitivity to everything that may be stirring, wondrous as it is for the hunter, can be quite injurious to the tournament golfer. To say it straighter, they think that one of Sam's major handicaps has been that he heeds too much on the golf course. On the other hand, they point out, there is Ben Hogan, the complete opposite extreme, who has trained himself to notice only what is beneficial to his golf and who, walled off in his isolation booth of concentration, has no memory after a tough round of exchanging a hello with an old friend, who cannot even remember having seen the friend on the course. In any event, Sam is inveterately less relaxed in a stroke-play tourney, when he has the always phantom field to worry about, than he is in match play when he knows he has to heed only what he sees happening.

While the vagaries of temperament may account to a fair degree for Sam's inability to work all the wonders of which he is capable, there are, naturally, other more terrestrial contributing factors. To begin with, there are days and weeks, as there must be, in which, superlative shotmaker that he is, other great contemporary stars simply play better golf than he does. Then, too, there are times when the wisdom of his over-all strategy or his immediate tactics is questionable. When Snead is in a bellwether mood, he sometimes will drill for every pin. On a tricky, punitive course, this can be costly. (Gene Sarazen, one of Sam's strongest admirers, has long thought that if Sam had spent more time caddying, he would have breathed in right through the pores a shrewder sense of when to gamble, when not to.) On other occasions, when he has made up his mind to take the conservative, steady route and walk hand in hand with par, Sam, that extremely human being, tends to inhibit his flair for scoring. On those days a gifted observer, such as Al Laney of the *New York Herald Tribune*, can tell after watching Sam play only a hole or two that he is not in a "winning mood" or likely to be.

Apart from all of this, to be sure, there is Sam's putting. For many summers it has been so infuriating a cliché to point out that erratic putting has been Sam's Achilles' heel that, for an almost equally long time, it has been hardly less bromidic to assert that this is not precisely so, that Sam has a nice rhythmic stroke, is one of the best approach putters in the business, and is a darn good holer from around twelve to fifteen feet. While this is substantially supportable, nevertheless it *is* incontestable that Sam's work on the greens can be so profligate that it breaks your heart.

Many mornings of anguish come to mind. For example— it is still as clear as if it happened yesterday and not in the 1952 Masters—there is Sam, on his third round, I think, playing the fifth. The green on that hole is a treacherous, terraced affair. A severe dip separates the upper level at the back from the lower front level which, roughly, divides itself into a depression at the left and a similar depression to the right. Sam's approach that morning finished on the lower level to the left, fifteen feet or so before the crest of the dip; the pin was set some twenty feet farther up the slanting

upper terrace, over to the right. In such cases it is a tempta-
tion to rap the ball an ounce harder than you know is required in order to be sure and be up. This is undoubtedly a
wiser error than to underhit the ball and wind up many
yards short. Well, there we were, all of us wondering if
Sam would show us a new and more assured Snead on the
greens, for he had been putting splendidly up to that point.
What he did was strike that approach putt so feebly that it
had exhausted what little juice it had by the time it had
breasted the dip. The ball began to slip off to the right as it
died, and, gathering just enough speed to keep trickling, it
rolled back down the dip and into the depression at the right.
Now he was five feet farther away from the cup than he had
been before his first putt! And then what did he do? He
stepped up and holed that impossible forty-footer. After
that, we walked to the tee of the short sixth murmuring
sagely, we thought, that only a "new Sam" could have held
his poise like that. Watch him go now. Sure enough, he
wafted a lovely six-iron nine feet past the pin. His try for
the birdie slid two feet beyond the cup. He missed the two-
footer. Same old Sam. He couldn't have felt much worse
about it than we did.

In Sam's greatest victory to date, his conquest of the 1946
British Open, the foreknowledge that no man was going to
putt his way to victory on St. Andrews' huge greens was of
incalculable help to him. "Ah knew Ah could win if Ah
could outplay the other fellers from tee to green," he has
said. "Besides, Ah was rested. Ah knew Ah wouldn't git that
salt-water taste you git in your mouth when you're over-
golfed." After fifty-four holes, Sam was tied for the lead with
Dai Rees, Bobby Locke, and Johnny Bulla. He was the last
of the contenders to go out in the violent wind that was
rampaging over the course. After the first four holes, he was

three over par, two three-putt greens playing their share in this. "Now that fifth, that's a long hole, over 500 yards," he has recounted. "Mah drive was way over to the left, way over in Hell Bunker on the next fairway. Ah hit a three-iron out and Ah really tagged it, but that wind jes' flipped it around like it was a kite. That ball sailed right acrost two fairways and lands up in the rough in that prickly pear sort o' bush them Scotchmen call whins. Ah'm lucky, though. Mah ball is lyin' in them whins jes' where there's a li'l ole rabbit path, jes' wide enough for me to swing mah club through. Ah really whooshed that ball out but Ah'm in more trouble. Ah'm in that deep bunker to the left o' the green. Ah've got to git up close. Ah'm three over par. Ah'm hurtin' alriddy. So Ah give that bunker shot that li'l extra whip and Ah catch it real good but it gets snuffed out in the grass at the top o' that bunker and barely skids onto that green. Ah still got a long, long putt but Ah stroke it up close and Ah hole that pesky li'l short one. Ah'm tellin' you, that was the greatest six Ah ever made in mah life."

Sam went to the turn in forty. He learned then that none of the other front runners had been able to do any better. He ripped home in thirty-five and won, going away, by four shots.

When Sam is as tenaciously disposed as he was at St. Andrews, the magnetic, volatile picture-player can win any tournament, even the National Open. The right attitude, arriving with it and maintaining it—that, of course, is the big trick. It necessarily becomes a bigger trick every year, for his multiple disappointments have inexorably bred overdetermination and overmulling, not to mention overadvice from friends who have counseled him to do everything from "get sore and serious sooner" to "make believe you're just loafing through a practice round in the West Virginia Open." If Sam wins the Open it will be an enormous victory of spirit as well as of skill. The rejoicing will be something to remem-

ber. And if he doesn't—why, we will all patiently wait till
next year and resume hoping just as hard. It is the least you
can do when a fellow has played the game so beautifully and
so well for so long.

YOGI BERRA:
UP FROM THE HILL

Yogi Berra was on the verge of beginning his thirteenth year with the Yankees at the time this article appeared in 1959. Since then, at this writing, he has put in two more good full seasons, participated in his eleventh World Series, moved into a more stately mansion, and continued to demonstrate his sturdy sense of values by endowing (with the contributions he was showered with on a Yogi Berra Day at the Stadium) a scholarship at Columbia.

In the 1960 World Series against the Pirates, Yogi in the seventh game pumped out his eleventh Series home run, placing him in a tie for third with Duke Snider, behind Ruth and Mantle. That blow was his twenty-first extra-base hit in Series play, one fewer than Ruth collected. In addition to this, after extending his previous marks, Berra now holds eight World Series records and is tied for the leadership in a ninth department:

> Most Series: 11
> Most Games: 68
> Most Times at Bat: 245
> Most Runs: 39
> Most Hits: 68
> Most One-Base Hits: 47

> Most Two-Base Hits: 10 (tied with Frisch)
> Most Total Bases: 111
> Most Runs Batted In: 36

In an effort to prolong to the maximum Yogi's longevity as a player, the Yankees are now using him more in the outfield than behind the plate—he looks as if he will be able to hit forever—and so there is a fairly good chance we may yet see Mister Berra in another Series before his monumental career is concluded.

ONE FINE DAY last autumn Yogi Berra, the affluent Yankee, had a relatively free stretch to enjoy himself. That is, there was no bottling convention to attend on behalf of the Yoo-Hoo chocolate drink company (in which he has a considerable investment), no business to transact with Mr. George Weiss, no television or banquet appearances, no household chores of any particular urgency. Accordingly, he and Phil Rizzuto, his old friend and guide, had been able to make their two visits (one to a hospital and the other to an orphange) quite early in the morning. A little before noon, Berra returned to his hillside home on the wooded outskirts of Tenafly, New Jersey, and, finding it bare of Mrs. Berra (who was out shopping) and the two oldest of his three sons (who were at school), he played for a few minutes with Dale (his youngest), who is two years old, helped the maid to locate the old baseball-type golf cap he was looking for, and headed for the White Beeches golf course in Haworth. Yogi drives a gray Pontiac with the license plate YB 8, eight being the number on his Yankee uniform. Unlike most Americans, for whom lack of sufficient recognition is a besetting problem, Berra's problem is to avoid too much recognition, and the identifying license plate is one of the few luxuries in the other direction that he allows himself.

White Beeches is a relaxed and friendly club, just right for a budding squire who has his feet firmly on the ground.

After his round—an 86 that was better than the figures indicated, since a strong November wind was out—Yogi sat around for about an hour in the grill with his foursome. One of them, a skiing buff, wanted to know if Yogi would be interested in going up to Tremblant with him on his next trip there. Before Yogi had time to reply, a third party piped up, "Casey would love that, huh? The news you were trying out the ski slopes." Berra, who makes it a point to avoid discussing Yankee business and personalities whenever possible, let that serve as his answer. The conversation shortly after this got around to the colossal amount of time wives and children spend on the telephone nowadays. One member of the group, a soldier of progress who spoke with a tone of endorsement, informed the others that you could now get a special phone installed for the teen-agers in your family who wanted to talk with their teen-age friends.

"Your boys will be needing one soon," he suggested to Berra.

"Well, they won't be getting one," Yogi said. "I want to do all I can for my kids," he added softly, "but, golly, that isn't one of them."

Yogi had dinner at home with his wife Carmen and their two oldest, Larry, who is nine, and Timmy, seven, and then was off for Clifton, another New Jersey town, about twenty miles away, in which the Berra-Rizzuto Alleys, a gleaming forty-lane emporium, is located. The alleys were officially opened last spring, but each time Yogi enters the building he feels the same intense glow of pride he did on opening night. This particular evening he was set to bowl for the team representing the Glendale Display and Advertising Company, and in his office he changed into his bowling shoes and the green-and-black Glendale bowling shirt. He bowls on Wednesdays for that team and on Mondays for a team of Yankees whose star is Bill Skowron (who has about a 160 average) and whose roster includes Phil Rizzuto, Elston

Howard, Johnny Kucks, Ralph Houk, and Gil McDougald. Since he had about twenty minutes in hand before the evening match was scheduled to begin, Berra moseyed down to the Dugout Restaurant for a cup of coffee and then made a quick tour of the rest of the premises. In the Stadium Lounge, where the bar is built in the shape of Yankee Stadium, he chatted about business with his brother Johnny, who is in charge there, and cast an approving eye at the large blowup photograph of the décolleté songstress who was to appear there that weekend. As he returned to the promenade behind the alleys, a middle-aged man, attired in the purple-and-white bowling shirt of a local bank, came up to him and told him how wonderful the alleys looked. "The whole place," he said, "is so spotless you would think you fellows opened it yesterday." Berra lights up like a child at certain compliments and did so then. "You know who works for the company that polishes our alleys, Tommy?" he said with exuberance. "McDougald, Gil." This was the first of a slew of chats, long and short, in which Yogi was enmeshed the rest of the evening. A very homey atmosphere obtains at the alleys. Berra seemed to know everyone who approached him—most of them by name—and each of the patrons wanted to know how business was and seemed personally pleased at Yogi's report that things were going pretty good and Phil now thought the main problem was getting enough business during the daylight hours. At nine o'clock the match between Seabert's Delicatessen and Glendale Display got under way. Yogi had a very good evening for him, rolling an even 200 on his first string, his high for the year, and finishing with a respectable three-string total of 504.

Just before he entered the office to change out of his bowling togs, a superbouncy woman of vaguely thirty who appeared to know Yogi well—and everyone else at the alleys for that matter—handed Yogi a small package tied in a bright ribbon. "It's a gift from me to you," she instructed

him. "You should make sure you open it in private." He did,
so to speak, in the office, where Freddy Rizzuto, Phil's
brother, who is the alleys' assistant manager, was on duty.
The contents turned out to be a carton of the cigarettes Yogi
endorses and a selection of six comic books. Mixed emotions,
including one that indicated they'll-do-it-every-time, came
over Yogi's face. "Well, Freddy," he said at length in an
administrative tone, "I can always give the books to my
kids."

Yogi left for home shortly after eleven. In the main lobby
there is a large glass case in which four magnificent American
League MVP plaques, the one which Rizzuto won and the
three Yogi won, are on display. Yogi slowed down his stride
and looked at the case for just a moment. Then he half
walked and half trotted out into the night.

It is pleasant to contemplate the good fortune which has
come the way of Lawrence Peter Berra. If it is coming to any
athlete, he has it coming to him. Aside from being a person
of unusual decency and natural charm, he has, from a fairly
inauspicious beginning in the big leagues, achieved over the
last dozen years a place among the memorable players in the
long history of the game—one of that extremely small number of players who have performed in the years following
World War II who is a certainty to be elected to the Hall of
Fame. Over and above this, Berra is a personality of such
original force and magnetism that sometimes it has even
obliterated his real stature as a player. He is, as Joe Trimble
has called him, the Kid Ring Lardner Missed, and possibly
more—the last of the glorious line of baseball's great characters.

In this age where ballplayers have kept growing taller and
more statuesque until the breed is now in appearance a
combination of the stroke on the college crew and the
juvenile lead in summer stock, Berra adheres to the classic

blocky dimensions of the old-time catcher. He stands five
feet eight and weighs about 192 and looks even chunkier
(especially in a baseball uniform) than these figures would
augur, for he has the broad and wide-set shoulders of a much
taller man, a barrel chest, and enormous arms. Unlike most
men of similar musculature, Berra is very lithe, very loose—
in fact, there is such friskiness in his movements (except
when he is catching the second game of a double-header)
that, as he approaches thirty-four, he still conjures up the
picture of a beknickered boy of thirteen or fourteen. Berra's
build is quite deceptive in other ways, or at least it has led
a number of observers into glib deductions that are strikingly
wayward. For example, nearly everyone decided years ago
that a man with his nonmissile dimensions would *ipso facto*
have to be a slow runner. Only in recent years has it been generally appreciated that Yogi has always been extremely fast,
one of the Yankees' best base runners, in fact. Even stranger
is that ivied slice of myopia which depicts Berra as all awk-
wardness at bat, sort of a slightly more skillful Pat Seerey who
slams the ball out of the park by sheer brute strength. This
is simply not correct. While there is assuredly little aesthetic
splendor about the way Yogi bunches himself at the plate, he
handles the bat beautifully, with a delicacy and finesse which
few place hitters approach and which is rarer still, of course,
for a power hitter. He has magnificent timing, releasing his
wrist action at the last split second. This explains why when
Berra is hitting, he can hit anybody or anything, including
more bad balls than anyone since Joe Medwick. In the 1955
World Series—not the 1956 Series, in which he hit three
home runs and batted in ten runs, but the 1955 Series, in
which he made ten hits and batted .417—Yogi put on one of
the finest demonstrations of straightaway hitting in modern
times, meeting the ball right between the seams again and
again and lining it like a shot over the infield, very much in
the fashion of Paul Waner and Nap Lajoie. "There's no one

more natural or more graceful than Yogi when he's watching the pitch and taking his cut," Phil Rizzuto said not long ago. "He's all rhythm up there, like Ted Williams."

Williams and Berra are alike in one other respect: they are talkative men. Splendidly endowed as Williams is in this department, he is simply not in Berra's class. In truth, no player in the annals of baseball has been, and those who potentially might have challenged his pre-eminence made the mistake of playing the wrong position. Stationed behind the plate, Berra has a steady flow of new faces to ask how things are going, and during lulls between batters there is always the umpire. Early this year Casey Stengel, a fairly articulate man himself, had a few words to say about Berra's verbosity. Asked if he considered Berra to be the best late-inning hitter in the game, a claim many have made for him, Casey replied that he didn't know about that. "I'd have to look into it," he said. "He could be the best late-inning hitter in baseball because he's got to hit sometime during a game, and he is a very bad early-inning hitter. Sometimes Mr. Berra allows himself to grow careless. He forgets to start the game with the first inning. He's out there behind the plate saying hello to everybody in sight. Oh, Mr. Berra is a very sociable fellow. He acts like home plate is his room."

In all of Yogi's actions on the ball field, as these vignettes may suggest, there is a beguiling spontaneity and a total lack of affectation. Beyond this, a tide of friendliness comes pouring through, and it communicates itself in a wondrous way not only to the people within earshot of his gravelly banter but also to the outlanders perched in the deep recesses of the stadium. It is difficult to think of another performer in sports who possesses Berra's particular quality of empathy. You just sense you like that guy. Viewed at intimate range—and it is a pleasure to report this, since it is all too seldom true of national figures who are irresistible in their public roles—Berra turns out to be the same guy he appears to be: friendly, full

of unposy vitality, marvelously good-natured. There are times
when Berra's exceptional energy gets worn down and responding to his fans becomes a nervous strain, but he has absorbed the niceties of applied public relations and employs
them well at these moments. What is remarkable, though, is
the genuine consideration which Berra, on most occasions,
shows the countless strangers who yell to him wherever he
may be or who come over to talk with him—he treats them as
if they were neighbors he has known all his life. In this connection, the story of Yogi at Ruggeri's (first told by Bob
Burnes of the *St. Louis Globe-Democrat*) comes to mind.
One winter, not long after he had made his mark in the
majors, Yogi took on the off-season job as head waiter at
Ruggeri's restaurant on The Hill in St. Louis, his home
town. One evening when he was catching up with two young
couples who were walking toward their table, Yogi overheard
one of the two men, awed by the high style of the restaurant,
nervously confide to the other, "Gosh, I feel out of place."
"Relax," Yogi interjected. "After you've been here ten
minutes you'll think it ain't any different than a hamburger
joint."

There is, however, a lot more complication in Berra than
meets the casual eye. When Sal Maglie joined the Yankees, a
friend asked him what if anything was different about the
players from what he had expected. "Yogi," Sal replied.
"Yogi worries a great deal." These periods do not last too
long, but when Yogi is troubled, it goes all through him; he is
not only grave, he is gloomy. He is also quite a sensitive person, which many people miss, though they shouldn't. Moreover, there is considerable shyness in him. At social gather-
ings away from the park, he will on some occasions hang
mutely on the edge of a group engaged in conversation, keeping his distance momentarily, but when he joins in, he arrives
in force. All of this makes Yogi not one whit different from
you or me—except that most of us lack his buoyant good na-

ture and the grit and instinctive soundness which knit him together—but it is rather important to mention these things in Berra's case since he has been so invariably portrayed as a happy-go-lucky child of nature.

This distortion, to a considerable degree, stems from the incomparable Berraisms which he has produced since he first came up. They are the Sneadisms and Goldwynisms of baseball. The only qualifying point that need be made about Yogi's *authentic* Berraisms is that they are not the product of stupidity but rather of the pleasure he gets in participating on all fronts and expressing himself. He is anything but facile at translating his thoughts into words but, far from being a slow man on the bases upstairs, Berra has an essentially good mind and a very active one. If there is a fund of good will in Yogi, there is also a native shrewdness. He has, for instance, invested his money very soundly. He now represents himself capably in his salary symposiums with George Weiss, having matured tremendously over the years in his sense of values, his own included.

Berra's remarks can be incisive as well as comic; for example, after sitting in on a strategy conference before an All-Star Game in which a long time was spent debating the best methods for pitching to Musial: "The trouble with you guys is you're trying to figure out in fifteen minutes something no one has figured out in fifteen years." He also has the gift of good taste which he has demonstrated most markedly, perhaps, in his choice of Mrs. Berra (Carmen Short, also from Missouri), a fine-looking girl with a very crisp, perky personality. Thanks to Carmen and to his great friend Rizzuto, Yogi has long since abandoned his celebrated allegiance to comic books. It was slightly exaggerated anyhow. He never was able to rise higher than vice-president in the Ghoul Club, an organization made up of Yankees—Don Larsen, president —who feasted on horror comics until the books were banned as injurious to minors. Yogi made his debut as a hard-cover man with Robert Ruark's *Something of Value*, a suitable bridge. Halfway through the book, he lost it, suffered agonies at the thought of the money he would have to shell out for another copy, but eventually did. That was the turning point. He now reads a fair amount and enjoys it, his favorites being realistic novels like *The World of Suzie Wong*.

As far as baseball goes, Yogi, despite the camouflage of his mannerisms, thinks well and swiftly and has become a master of the hard art of talking shop and thinking baseball. While he is gabbing away with batters, another part of his mind is setting up a pitching pattern for instant use as well as filing away for future reference pertinent dope on each hitter. "On a number of occasions," Casey Stengel has opined, "I am aware I have held a meeting in the clubhouse before a game when there was some doubts among the coaches and myself on how we should pitch to particular hitters. If we don't agree on a decision, we have asked Berra what he thinks about it, and we have generally gone along with what he has suggested. He is a good studier of hitters." Stengel, who has been known to refer to Berra as "my assistant manager" because of his veteran catcher's ever-readiness to contribute his knowledge to the common cause, not long ago meandered into an oblique shaft of revelation which recalled his famed soliloquy on the short-fingered Japanese during his appearance before the United States Senate. "Berra," said Casey, "is alert because he's got very good hearing. He has better ears than any other catcher in the game. He hears everything that's said on the field and not only there but away from the field. He knows all the scandal. If Topping wasn't there, he'd run the business for him, or George Weiss, his business, or me, he'd take over my job."

Stengel has also long been struck by Berra's knowledge of sports in general. So is everyone who knows him. Yogi's old friend Joe Garagiola, the former Cardinal catcher who currently is a highly successful baseball broadcaster and after-dinner speaker, frequently tells his audience on the banquet trail that "funny as it will sound to many of you, Yogi could have been an A student in college." Joe then elaborates on this by stating that Yogi has an exceptionally good memory for anything he wants to remember, such as sports.

This is a very significant part of Berra—his abiding love of sports—and it explains the man directly. In a sports-oriented nation like ours there are literally hundreds of thousands of boys and grownups who are attached to sport before any other consideration, but it is really extraordinary to find an experienced professional athlete for whom agents have not withered nor customers staled his first youthful affection for his game and others. Here Berra is plainly exceptional. After all these bruising seasons he has somehow managed to retain a boy's fullhearted enthusiasm for the game of baseball. This has always been so obvious that it used to be said that he would probably be delighted to play for the Yankees even if they paid him nothing. Well, Yogi has seen to it for quite some time now that he is well rewarded for his services but, once he enters the dressing room, that spirit of the young boy, all eagerness for the game, clutches him wholly. He loves to play ball the way other men like to make money or work in the garden. And this is what makes Berra the ballplayer he is.

Moreover, as Stengel's and Garagiola's remarks adduce, Yogi is infatuated not only with baseball but with all sports. For him they are practically the staff of life. They have always been.

The outline of Yogi's early years and his road to the top are fairly well known to sports fans, and to summarize them elliptically is probably enough for our purposes. He was born in St. Louis on May 12, 1925, the son of Paulina and Pietro Berra. Mr. Berra worked in the kilns in one of the local brick factories. The Berras lived at 5447 Elizabeth Avenue, the Garagiolas at 5446, on "Dago Hill." (At banquets Garagiola is at his drollest when he tells his audiences, with the air of someone explaining something quite abstruse, "A lot of Italian families live on that hill, you see, and that is the reason it is called Dago Hill.") Yogi left school at fourteen after completing the seventh grade. After this he had a long series of small jobs in various plants. He lost one after another because sports came first; whenever it was a question of whether to play in a big game or pass it by and stay on the job, he chose the former. Deep within him he clung to the obscure hope that somehow or other he might be able to make a career in sports. As he has always been the first to admit, he owes the chance he had to pursue this hope to his older brothers, Tony, Mike, and Johnny. All three were fine athletes, and two showed such talent for baseball that they were approached by big league clubs to join teams in their farm system. (Tony, the oldest brother, Yogi has always claimed, was the best ballplayer in the family.) The pressure to bring money into the hard-pressed family forced the older boys to forsake their ambitions in baseball and to knuckle down to wage-earning in local plants. However, when Yogi began to blossom out in American Legion junior baseball, his brothers insisted that he be given the chance they had never had, and they were so adamant about this that they eventually broke down the opposition of their parents. In 1942, when he was seventeen, Yogi was signed by John Schulte, a scout for the Yankees organization, for $500. This was the amount which Joe Garagiola, eight months younger than Yogi, had received from the St. Louis Cardinals after he and Yogi, both of them left-hand-hitting catchers, had been given a tryout the year before. The Cards had also wanted to sign Berra but had not offered him a bonus for signing. Though it almost killed him to do so, Yogi had turned down their contract, not because of envy of his pal—there is no envy in Berra—but because he felt he was worth $500, too. In 1943 the Yankees assigned him to Norfolk, their affiliate in the Class B Piedmont League.

The fact that two members of their gang had been signed by big league clubs was a towering feather in the hats of the kids on The Hill. Mulling over Yogi's chances of making good, they were positive he would, for they had known him as a superlative all-round athlete, a mainstay for their team, the Stags, in their organized league games as well as in their sand-lot games and street games. For instance, when as young kids they had played football on Elizabeth Avenue, Yogi not only always did the kicking for his side but on fourth down he was switched to the opposing side to kick for them. He was the only one in the bunch who could be counted on to control the ball so that it came down in the street and not through somebody's window. One autumn day when Yogi (then about fifteen) was watching a Southwest High practice scrimmage, an episode with all the hallmarks of one of those Hollywood "discovery scenes" took place: the kicker for the high-school team got off a short wobbly punt which twisted over the side line near where Yogi was standing. Picking the ball up, Yogi, wearing sneakers, casually boomed the ball back half the length of the field. Over to the side line rushed the coach to find out who was the unknown star who could kick like that. On learning that Yogi had quit school and was working, the coach pleaded with him to "join" the high school, assuring him that he could arrange things so that he would have the lightest study load imaginable, but Yogi, ruining the perfect scenario, would have none of it.

Yogi was an average if clamorous basketball player, pretty fair at roller hockey, and truly outstanding at soccer, a game that has long been big in St. Louis. He played halfback and was so fond of the sport that he went on playing it even after he had definitely arrived in professional baseball, and he probably would have continued to play it had not the Yankees, fearful of injury, ordered him to retire. It was typical

of him that he became an ardent pro football fan at a time
when most St. Louisans were either uninformed or apathetic
about the NFL, and was so rabid a devotee of ice hockey, a
game he had never played, that on the nights when the St.
Louis Flyers' home games were scheduled he would take a
two-hour nap late in the afternoon so that he would have the
pep to stay awake. "The main thing about Yogi that impressed us as kids," Garagiola was remembering recently,
"was how fast he picked up any sport. One time the Italian-
American Club wanted some kid to represent them in the
city boxing matches. They got Yogi. If you wanted something
done, you always got Yogi. He'd never boxed before, but he
turned out to be darned good at it. I think he had five fights
and won them all, two by knockouts, before his folks made
him quit. Another time I remember we went up to the
YMCA and found a ping-pong tournament going on. Yogi
had never played the game before but he entered. In his first
match he was just trying to return the ball across the net, but
he got the hang of it quick and went all the way to the final."
Garagiola paused a long moment. "Just talking about those
old days," he resumed, "brings back to your mind what a
wonderful guy Yogi was even as a kid. He was never one to
come forward and try to stand out, but he was the fellow who
got the other fellows together. He was a peacemaker kind of
kid. More than that, he had a lot of strength and cheer in
him. When you were troubled about something, there was
no one like him. Why, just to see him come bouncing around
the corner half solved your problem. 'Here comes Yogi,'
you'd say to yourself. 'It isn't as bad as it looked.' "

As far as baseball went (and its close relatives, softball and
corkball, an offshoot particular to St. Louis), Yogi as a youngster did some of the pitching for the Stags and played every
position except first base. He did little or no catching until
he was fourteen. "I got the job because no one else wanted
it," he remembers. "You took quite a beating back there.

You didn't have any shin guards or belly protector." He did the catching, when he was sixteen and seventeen, for the Fred W. Stockton Post American Legion team, and he was one of the chief reasons why the team in 1941 and 1942 was the class of its section and reached the final round of the national championship finals. Up with Norfolk in '43, Yogi blew hot and cold, batting a mild .253 for the season, but in 1946, following his wartime tour of duty with the Navy, he hit .314 with Newark, the Yankees' farm club in the AAA International League, and was considered ready to go up with the big club. In the Navy, incidentally, he had seen action of the roughest kind in the landings in Normandy and later in southern France. He was a rocketman on a Coast Guard boat, one of a group of thirty-six-foot LCSSs (Landing Craft Support Small) which on D-day were disgorged from a larger vessel some 300 yards off Omaha Beach to help open the beach for the first wave.

During his first full year with the Yankees, 1947, Berra, a very young twenty-two, was nervous and conspicuously unpolished behind the plate. Although he drove in fifty-four runs in eighty-three games that year and a thumping ninety-eight runs in 125 games in 1948, he made many costly errors in judgment behind the plate as well as physical errors. Work as he did to correct them, he continued to make them and was frequently played in right field, where he could do far less damage. These were days of anguish for him, because on top of these concerns he was the target of some of the most brutal personal riding any newcomer to the majors has ever been subjected to. In the final analysis, it was his own hardy character that saw him through, but he was extremely fortunate in the men he was associated with. He was fortunate, for instance, that his idol, Joe DiMaggio, was around to support him in many critical moments. One typical example of DiMaggio's help occurred during one of those stretches when Yogi had been exiled to right field. Way down in the dumps after popping up his previous time at bat, Yogi shuffled dejectedly out to right at the beginning of the next inning. DiMaggio noticed this. An inning later, as Yogi was gallumping out to his position, Joe, instead of sprinting out to center as was his hustling habit, followed out after Yogi and yelled to him to get moving. "Always run out to your position, Yogi," Joe continued as they ran out together. "It doesn't look good when you walk. The other team may have gotten you down, but don't let them know it."

Yogi has also been fortunate in playing under managers like Bucky Harris, a kindly man, and Casey Stengel, who has directed the Yankees since 1949. When Casey first took over, he set about building up Berra's confidence in himself as a catcher, and here his most valuable contribution was his decision to turn Yogi over to Coach Bill Dickey, that most accomplished technician, for a full course of instruction. "There was a lot he had to be taught which he'd never been," Casey has said. "He squatted too far away from the hitter and was off balance and a poor target. Another thing, he didn't know how to block a bad pitch with his body. Dickey showed him how to drop down on his knees. Then, he didn't throw well because nobody had ever taught him how to take that step. He has a strong arm and he became a very accurate thrower. He'd throw runners out for us when you couldn't have blamed him if he didn't, for he was working with a poor pitching staff in that respect. Many of the pitchers we've had, I don't know if you know, have been no good at keeping the runners close to the base." Dickey not only instructed Berra in every facet of the mechanics of catching but also taught him how to call a game. "Yogi before Dickey and Yogi after Dickey—the difference was like night and day," Rizzuto has commented. "Before, he was never thinking ahead like a catcher must. He hesitated all through a game calling the pitches. He didn't know how to set a batter up for the curve with the fast ball, and so on. He was really shaky and the result was that the pitchers didn't have any confidence in him. After his schooling with Dickey, he started to think ahead automatically, he set up very good patterns and he began to study the hitters intelligently. Our pitchers began to lean on his judgment very quickly after this. Only Reynolds and Raschi ever shook him off, and they didn't do it very often."

Above all, Yogi was fortunate in having Phil Rizzuto as his roommate on the road trips and as a staunch friend at all times. Yogi was (and is) stoical by nature. Never one to moan or alibi, he prefers to keep his troubles to himself. During his first seasons in the majors he simply had too many troubles to absorb and sometimes they accumulated into a ponderous burden, and you cannot overestimate the good it did the young man, so distrustful of his ability to get across what he felt in words, to find himself understood when he opened himself to Rizzuto. Rizzuto showed Berra all the ropes, additionally, but he was beautifully unpaternalistic—he never forced his advice on Yogi, merely gave his opinion when asked, and let Yogi make his own decisions, which were invariably quite logical. "Yogi is an iron man and it really works against him," Phil reflected recently. "All the fellows on the team know he's caught innumerable double-headers after only five hours of sleep. They know that over the last dozen years he's caught many more games than any other catcher—many more. He's gotten out there and done the job despite a staggering number of painful injuries, jammed thumbs and split fingers and the rest. That's why Yogi never gets any sympathy. No one thinks he needs it."

When Yogi is learning something new, he customarily gives the impression that his mind is wandering and that he isn't following his instructor. For instance, he never gives back a paraphrase of what the other person has been saying, which is the most common method by which students indicate that they understand a new thing. For all the ambiguity of his reactions, Yogi has a first-rate aptitude for learning. It is, in fact, hard to think of a man who has done as much for himself. Today he leads a rounded and enviably full life at the core of which is his home in Tenafly. There is a lot of pep and sense in the Berra household. "Once in a while after we've lost a tough one or if I've played a lousy game," Yogi was saying not long ago, "I get angry and I'm still angry when I get home. My wife doesn't let me get very far with it. Carm will tell me, 'Don't get angry with me. You played badly. I didn't.'" The spirited Mrs. Berra has a lively interest in baseball, but her major pastime is antiques. She has acquired for the house some handsome pieces, both American and European, among them an old table of Italian walnut at which the Berras eat breakfast and their snack meals. All smiles at the shoe being on the other foot for a change, Yogi loves to tell about the morning Bill Skowron walked into the breakfast room, studied the table for a moment, and then declared, "With all your money, Yogi, you can certainly afford to buy a new table."

While Yogi has indeed come a long way from St. Louis, the wonderful thing about him is that in many essential areas he has not changed a bit from the kid on The Hill. For him— and this is just one phase of that appealing immutability— anybody who can play sports a major part of his hours is still the most privileged of people. His zest for reading sports and watching sports and talking sports when he is not playing sports has diminished not at all. During the autumn, when many baseball players are tapering off from the season's grind by hunting, Berra gets his mind off baseball by traveling to some spot like Pinehurst for a therapeutic week of golf and then indulges his passion for football by going not only to the New York Giants' games but to those of local high school teams. As the colder weather comes on, Berra becomes almost as regular in his attendance at the basketball and hockey games at Madison Square Garden as Gladys Gooding, the well-tempered organist. Mrs. Berra has now cut down on the number of events she attends but still goes to a few with him. On other occasions Yogi takes his two oldest boys or goes with friends from the Yankees or friends in his neighborhood with whom he also plays golf. And sometimes Yogi just drives in alone, sure in the foreknowledge that at courtside or rinkside he will run into some fellows he knows.

At the half-time interval of the first game of a recent pro basketball double-header which he went to with a neighbor from Tenafly, Yogi, after getting in a few hands of klob in the Knickerbocker office with some newspapermen, returned to his seat just in time to be slapped on the back by a tall, athletic-looking fellow. "Hey, you character, where you been keeping yourself?" the tall man, who turned out to be Joe Black, the old Dodger pitcher, asked with obvious affection. Yogi's eyes lighted up with pleasure. "This guy's a no-good catcher," Black explained to the friend he was with. "Trouble with him is he can't hit." Yogi and Joe gabbed about old times and new jobs until the second half got under way. In the break before the start of the second game another tall, husky fellow, circulating in the courtside section, spotted Yogi and came over for a similar reunion. "That was Doby," Yogi later explained to his friend from New Jersey, exhibiting more than a little of the same pride an average fan would take at being on speaking terms with a real big-leaguer.

This high regard applies to all athletes Berra admires, not just to baseball players. They are "his people." A flavorful illustration of the kick he gets from knowing them took place last December when Berra was invited by Herb Goren, the Rangers' public-relations director, to watch a game against the Montreal Canadiens from the press box. While the teams were whirling through their pregame warm-up drills, Berra was seized with the urge to say hello to Boom Boom Geoffrion, the Montreal star, whom he had got to know last April when the Stanley Cup play-offs and the baseball season over-lapped. Berra shouted down to Boom Boom a couple of times but was unable to get his attention, not that this was too surprising considering that the press box hangs high above the ice and Berra's foghorn voice has neither the penetration nor carrying power of, say, Maria Callas' or Leo Durocher's. Goren happened to pass at this moment and, when Berra made known his problem, Goren said he would telephone down to the Canadiens' bench and have them point out to Geoffrion where Berra was seated.

Berra sat with his eyes riveted on Geoffrion during the next five minutes. Nothing happened. He was still waiting watchfully when Goren returned. "I changed my mind, Yogi," he said dourly. "This is an important game for us. If Boom Boom knows you're watching him, he'll play harder than he might otherwise."

"All I want to do is wave hello," Yogi protested, a little downcast.

"I'm sorry, Yogi, but that is a thing not good for the Rangers," Goren said, slipping into an inexplicable Hemingway-type speech pattern. "We must forget it. Boom Boom would get full of courage if he knows you are here."

As a loyal Ranger fan, Berra agreed that Goren's psychology might be right. However, it was a full ten minutes before he could shake off the glum mood that overtook him in his disappointment, and twice during the game, when the path of play brought Geoffrion to that part of the rink nearest Yogi's position in the press box, he suddenly stood up and yelled "Boom Boom" to Boom Boom, without success, however.

During the off-season, when Berra must endure the hardship of having no assured supply of conversational fodder presented to him in the shape of enemy batsmen, his encounters with old friends at athletic events help to provide his gregarious soul with the communication it constantly craves. On the other hand, unlike the modern sports pundit who views each event as a springboard for his trenchant, altogether Toynbeen comments, Berra is a quiet, intent, and excitable spectator with what nowadays amounts to an old-fashioned point of view: he focuses not primarily on the stars but on the team play and the winning and losing of a game. He roots for the New York teams but makes an exception when the Knickerbockers play the St. Louis Hawks. "I can't go back on my real home town, can I?" he explains in his most serious voice. "And Ed Macauley, he was a big hero of mine when he was playing college ball. I've got to be loyal to him."

Berra stays in shape during the off-season by cutting down on his eating—he frequently skips lunch—and by fairly regular exercise. One of those men who are bored by calisthenics and point-to-point walks and for whom a workout has to be the unconscious by-product of playing a game, he fools around with a basketball on the back-yard court he has set up (for the kids, of course), bowls, and golfs. When Yogi warily took up golf some ten years ago, he merely used an adaptation of his baseball swing. Hitting from the left side, he was a very wild and woolly golfer, and the few powerhouse blows he got off generally journeyed in the wrong direction. Three autumns ago when he was playing a round (and an anguishingly bad one) at White Beeches with Tommy DeSanto, one of the club's best players, DeSanto suggested on the eleventh hole that Berra borrow one of his right-handed clubs and see how he made out. Berra proceeded to hit his best shot of the day. He played in the rest of the way with DeSanto's clubs and has played right-handed ever since, though, interestingly enough, he continues to play his wedge shots and to putt left-handed. Since switching over, Yogi's golf has shown steady improvement, and his club members now consider his 14 handicap about two shots too high. He has had an 88 on the awesome Pinehurst No. 2, an 81 at White Beeches, and a 38 for nine at Miami Springs. Berra's long hitting is not the strong point of his golf. His approach to the game is. He understands its fine fabric as only the natural games player does. He is an intuitive appraiser of the strategy of holes and the demands of individual shots. He has a proper seriousness about trying to play each shot as well as possible and a proper humor about his failings—"Whatta touch!" he continually berates himself whenever his putting stroke lets him down. He is interested in the games of the people he plays with, he chirps good conversation and at the right times, he competes just hard enough and without gamesmanship, and, all in all, he is almost the perfect golf companion.

There are few people who can match the bonhomie which emanates from Berra when he is in an expansive mood, which he was one day last November after he had finished a particularly satisfying round at White Beeches. He had played with two friends from New York who wanted to round out their safari into the hinterland by visiting the Berra-Rizzuto Alleys which lie a complicated half-hour drive away from the course. It was arranged that Berra would lead the way in his car and they would follow in theirs. "There are two tolls," Berra informed them. "You'll need a quarter for the first and a dime for the second. You got it?" They had, and the abbreviated caravan rolled off.

Some minutes later Berra swung his Pontiac into an entrance to the Garden State Parkway. He paid his toll and gabbed a moment with the toll attendant. His friends then drove up to the attendant, and the driver held his hand out with a quarter in it. The attendant waved it away. "Mr. Berra," he said, "has already taken care of it."

III

PERSONS
AND
PLACES

A DISQUIETING ROUND AT THE ROYAL CALCUTTA GOLF CLUB

Written at an earlier date than any other in this collection, this article appeared in the January 1945 issue of *Town and Country*. I have chosen to include it because, being a wartime report, it serves to call back to mind, however tangentially, something of the mood of the times at the beginning of the period with which we are dealing, 1945–1960.

In 1957, coming back from Japan, I broke up my return trip in order to go into Calcutta, which I had known fairly well during the war, to see how it had fared in the dozen years since I had been there last. For some reason or other, I expected to find it a sunnier, more orderly city than the one I had known. After all, India had gained its independence and the war was long past. I found instead that Calcutta had grown vastly more depressing and that it weighed heavier on the human spirit than any other place I have ever been. It was a bad hour. Refugees were streaming back from East Pakistan into the already overcrowded city; the new government had obviously not solved the terrible problems of hunger and poverty; Communist agitators were daily busy in the Maidan, and Chowringhee Street was filled with pickpockets. The thick yellow sky over Calcutta always seems to hang very low, just above the treetops, and on this trip it seemed to press down lower than I ever felt it before. I paid no return visit to the Royal Calcutta Golf Club.

THE ROYAL CALCUTTA GOLF CLUB lies in a shabby suburb
called Tollygunge. You can reach it in half an hour by street-
car, but American soldiers coming in from their rude camps
prefer to lounge in the lemon-colored, open Overland taxis
driven almost exclusively by bearded Sikhs. By taxi the ride
to the club takes about ten minutes—and a very interesting
trip it is, since during the first nine minutes and fifty seconds
there is no break in the customary suburban scenery. The
mangled stalls, hovels, and paths continue even as the car
moves down an undernourished lane called Golf Club Road,
and the anxious golfer steels himself to finding that the Royal
Calcutta Golf Club will be just another bright euphemism,
like the British "rest camps" where a sizable portion of the
American troops are quartered. During the last few seconds,
however, the placid Sikh maneuvers his Overland through a
gate in a high stone wall and into a courtyard that is so clean
it is almost prophylactic. Indian bearers in white uniforms are
moving swiftly in, out, and around a clubhouse that has all
the vertical phlegm of Stoke Poges or Walton Heath. British-
ers in shorts and pith helmets sit on the large verandas looking blankly at the fairways. At first the American cannot
reconcile the worlds within and outside the stone wall, but
then he wonders why he was in the least surprised, remembering the considerate habit the British have for laying out
courses the moment they have hoisted the flag and inspected
the water supply.

It is with the feeling that the British are darn good lads,
then, that the golfer borrows an archaic set of clubs and two
cut balls, changes into shorts and helmet, and walks to the
first tee with his Indian caddie. It would be very helpful if
more Americans played golf here, for it would lead to better
understanding. Anglophiles were never numerous west of
the Appalachians, but south of the Himalayas it is difficult to
find the American soldier who loves the British with the

warmth recommended by the OWI. You hear dozens of reasons for this antipathy. Some GI's dislike the British an hour after their first meal on British rations, and this dislike increases with the amount of bully beef and hardtack they consume. Soldiers who had never been out of the States before and expected India to be a Ramon Novarro picture now believe that there are probably more tiled rooms in New England alone than in all the Eastern hemisphere. Indian squalor is the product of British neglect, they infer. And, of course, it will be a long time before they will accept the old guidebook explanation that the Tommies' reserve is merely acute shyness.

However, a golfer stepping up on the first tee of the Calcutta eighteen is definitely in favor of inverted chevrons, tea, kippers, and plus fours, and is not too hard on Sir John Simon and Sir Samuel Hoare. Five minutes later his Indian caddie has erased all reflections on the state of the British Empire and made him buckle down to the game at hand. This is easily explained. Just before you hit your approach— or shall we say your first approach—to the first green, a good many of the caddies explain that they are registered playing-caddies and would find it no bother at all to play round with you. Most Americans generally accept the suggestion, figuring that nothing could look more democratic and that no barefoot boy in a sash is going to beat them, no matter how long they have been away from the game.

The only thing occidental about Hakim, my caddie, was a ragged green sleeveless sweater, and as he teed his ball very low on the second tee I was wondering what mystic novelties he would introduce in his swing. Hakim spread his brown feet and then went into the stylish pivot and loose follow-through usually conceded to be the private property of the American caddie. He was down the middle and past the 200-yard marker. He muttered something about a slight fade on the shot and then made good his chagrin by playing the rest of the first nine in one over par.

Before we reached the ninth tee, Hakim's golf and easy talkativeness had about convinced me that the Indian problem was greatly overrated, that a couple of fair statesmen with about the same handicap could settle in one weekend on the links the problems that had vexed England and India since the days of the East India Company. I admired the way Hakim let me use the putter on the heavy greens and himself putted—very nicely, too—with the midiron so as not to slow up the game. I was fascinated to learn that his brother was a golf pro and that he himself had spent the last fifteen years— he was twenty-nine—as a professional caddie. The club discouraged players from paying a caddie American or English fees, but Hakim had a few British officers for whom he acted as regular playing-caddie, so his family of four always had enough rice, even during the severe Bengal famines. I liked the way he didn't try to cure my hook.

Yet, as we hit the in-nine, much as I disliked having to change my pleasantly glib impression that young India, personified by Hakim, was easy to understand and easier to like, our increasing intimacy brought out some of Hakim's points of view that forced me to admit that nobody is kidding himself when he talks of the complex subtleties of India and Indians. For example, on the twelfth tee Hakim asked if I wanted to use one of his personal golf balls, a not too lacerated Dunlop–65 that was practically just out of the wrapper when compared to the two wounded balls the caddie master had allotted me. This was puzzling since I had asked Hakim on the first tee if he happened to have any good balls and he had described the relic he produced as his only one. Our relationship became more involved when I offered to buy the Dunlop–65 for the six rupees he said the prize was worth. This was an out-and-out blunder. Hakim was all for keeping the ball and for my giving him the six rupees as a gift.

On the twelfth green, just after he had chipped dead to the pin out of a water ditch, Hakim went into his begging routine which, one soon learns, is almost a natural reflex when the natives of this impoverished land encounter a foreigner. GI coaches have given the ordinary approach of "Bakshish, sahib—no father, no mother, no sister, no brother" an additional twist by teaching many youngsters to add, "No allotment, no per diem." This is not because Americans grow callous to poverty. Not at all. One feels and one gives, but indiscriminate charity just doesn't work out. Give an anna to one boy and you will be followed for blocks by twenty others. Then the patent, by-the-numbers approach of the Indian beggar makes you wonder if you are not simply the gull for a suave little racket—this despite your knowledge that poor people in India are among the poorest in the world.

Hakim, as I say, could pitch like a Vardon and a moment later turn into an entirely different person, the Indian beggar. Rice was up, considerably. "You rajah." His wife and three children, increasingly hard to feed. "You maharajah." His wife's family, his parents, relying wholly on him. "You rich senator." His wife, expecting a child, and, a premonition told him, probably getting twins. At this point it was my turn to putt out, and I grabbed the number-two iron he had been using on the greens. Hell, it was a much better way of playing the bumps than with the putter.

A few holes later, however, after Hakim had extracted a thorn from his foot, the strain between us had disappeared. Like everyone else, he wanted to know something about New York, for, like everyone else, he thought he might go there when the war was over. How soon would it be over, he asked. I gave him a conservative answer: summer, 1946, if we fought a good fight. Hakim was not only dismayed but seemed to make the slightly incorrect inference that Americans looked forward with immense relish to the long months ahead. "Why not peace?" he asked with a smile. Our conversation from this point on was one Hindu cliché against one American cliché, I suppose, and it is worth while only to note that no one sold anyone a bill of goods. I reflected that the soldier guides are probably right after all in advising you against talking politics. Hakim, that odd blend of the East and the West, confused me all the more by fading a sweetheart of a mashie to the eighteenth green.

There is a sign outside the caddie shop which states that a player should inquire after his round as to the caddie fee, as caddies had been fleecing the customers left and right. Hakim had taken good care of me during the two hours and a half we had played and talked, and I certainly intended to take good care of him, yet a steer from the management might prevent my rewarding him out of proportion. It is customary to pay ricksha boys a rupee (thirty cents or so) a mile, which they cover in about fifteen minutes, and so, I reasoned, three rupees for Hakim wouldn't cause inflation. The caddie master, a gray-haired Indian who spoke splendid English, laughed when I suggested three rupees. One rupee would serve the caddie handsomely, and if I insisted on a tip, two or three annas should be the limit. The caddies had never had it so good.

The two rupees I gave Hakim brought neither a howl nor a handclasp. I changed back into uniform and made a call on the caddie master. He had looked after me well and could no doubt use a rupee for his family, his godfather's family, and the quintuplets his half sister was no doubt expecting. He refused the rupee. "Thank you very much," he said gravely, "but I am paid by the club." I continued to hold the rupee out. He took it and bowed.

In the courtyard the lemon Overlands were lined up. I picked the Sikh with the purple turban, and in a moment we were through the gate and down the road.

ST. ANDREWS:
THE CRADLE
OF GOLF

This piece was written in 1950 and was published in *Holiday* the following spring. Since that date some changes have taken place even in that secluded, time-resisting corner of Scotland. Commander Carson has been succeeded as the secretary of the Royal and Ancient by Brigadier Eric Brickman, a crisp and tidy administrator who makes what may be the hardest job in golf look easy. Like the Commander, the Brigadier, it is a pleasure to report, has a penchant for tweed knickers and wears them well. A change of a quite unanticipated nature took place at the R & A in 1955 on the occasion of the Commonwealth Cup matches when, for the first time in history, ladies were invited into the clubhouse. Aside from a few grumbles from the invariable rear guard, most of the members found that cocktail party not only surprisingly painless but actually a good sort of thing, you know, and another such mixed affair was held with equal success on the eve of the first World Amateur Team Championship in 1958. This championship brought back to the old gray town the golfer it loves the most, Bobby Jones, who had returned to captain the American team. Jones was made an honorary freeman of St. Andrews and was presented with the freedom of the borough by his old and adoring friends in a ceremony so full of deep-felt emotion, on both sides, and so moving that many who attended were unable to voice their thoughts for many minutes afterward. I shall always remember what Billy Joe Patton, from North Carolina, said about Jones when he finally spoke up on the way home, his voice charged with feeling and sectional chauvinism: "He's the greatest Southerner who ever lived."

There is one other change that might be mentioned. The official record for the Old Course has now been lowered to 66. This occurred in the 1960 British Open in which Arnold Palmer, a most popular visitor, made his gallant and driving bid to add the British Open to his previous victories that year in our Open and the Masters, and ultimately failed by only one shot.

THE HOLD THAT St. Andrews has over the world's 10,000,000 golfers has not yet reached that point where, at five regular intervals each day, the game's devotees abruptly drop the cares of the hour, kneel, and face the old gray town on the North Sea where the game was nurtured. There is, however, little to choose between St. Andrews and Mecca in the frenetic fidelity they extract from their followers. Every pious golfer dreams of making a pilgrimage to St. Andrews, and a considerable number realize this ambition. Since the war an average of 8,000 visitors has journeyed to St. Andrews each year. For a few of them, the attraction is a tourist's sight of the house on South Street where Mary Queen of Scots slept, uneasily; the Church of the Holy Trinity, where a local boy, John Knox, cut loose with one of his most inflammatory sermons; and the noble buildings of St. Andrews University, Scotland's oldest, which dates back to 1413. But, by and large, the thousands who make their way annually to St. Andrews come to worship at the Old Course, the most famous links in the world.

Considering that it is only thirty-three miles northeast of Edinburgh, St. Andrews is not an easy place to get to. The sacred town lies on the eastern tip of Fifeshire, a peninsula which noses into the North Sea between the Firth of Tay on the north and the Firth of Forth to the south. The train ride from Edinburgh, on the main line north to Aberdeen, offers a fairly spectacular crossing of the Firth of Forth via the high, gaunt railroad bridge on which Robert Donat performed his acrobatics in *The Thirty-Nine Steps*, but passengers for St. Andrews must descend at Leuchars, five miles distant, and there change to a spur line which operates on a capricious schedule. Most golfers choose to close in on the old town by auto. The road from Edinburgh, once the ferry across the Forth has been negotiated, plods through somber coastal towns, each with its links and its "golf hotel." The approach from Glasgow, on the West Coast, a drive of three hours, is far more rural and relaxing and would be altogether preferable were it not that *leaving* Glasgow necessarily presupposes *being in* Glasgow. Whatever road he travels, the pilgrim, because of the ambivalence of the route markers at all key intersections, will lose his way on the average of once every twenty miles, and he will learn from asking directions that the proper Scottish pronunciation of his goal is *Sintandrooz*.

St. Andrews makes a stirring first impression. Perched on a rocky plateau fifty feet above the Firth of Tay, not a smokestack in view, its medieval towers gleaming gray-white in the sun, it looms solemnly before the pilgrim, completely unrelated to the countryside through which he has passed. St. Andrews was named for the patron saint of Scotland, and while it is legend and not history that the relics of St. Andrew were carried there in 735 by St. Regulus, the town is old enough to have run through several full careers: Pictish stronghold, headquarters of the Roman Catholic Church in Scotland, storm center of the Reformation, prosperous trading port, plague-struck and all but deserted village—all this before the spread of golf throughout the world, beginning

just about a century ago, gave the old town something new
to live for.

In this town the only native who hurries to snatch the
minute is the golfer. His small canvas bag over his shoulder,
he strides briskly past the golf hotels lining the seaside strip
called the Scores, quickening his pace as he nears the Old
Course at the foot of the town in order not to be late for
his assigned starting time on the first tee. The rest of the
9,000 regular inhabitants operate less by the watch than by
the more luxurious chronometer of chimes and church bells.
The milkman chugs his truck from house to house, resting
at the wheel while his wife makes the deliveries. In the cafés
the university students talk easily over coffee between classes,
the girls wearing their bright-red college gowns, as they do on
many occasions when they are not required, because the
gown "does more" for them than any other number in their
wardrobes. The slow pace and good air of St. Andrews have
made it a favorite retreat of superannuated military and naval
officers. It is also a fine place for thinking as well as retiring.
Carlyle, Froude, Thomas Hughes, Trollope, Mrs. Oliphant,
Kingsley, Millais, and Landseer are just a few of the prominent artists and writers who found they flourished in St.
Andrews in summer.

It is a salutary circumstance that the town of St. Andrews
is charming beyond expectation for, at first meeting, the Old
Course—the shrine itself—is a majestic letdown. To an
American accustomed to mounting a raised tee and squinting
down a tree-lined fairway, the Old Course, a billowing sea
of grass-covered dunes, doesn't even look like a golf course.
Bobby Jones, who ended up thinking the Old Course the
finest he had ever played, was sure it was the worst after his
first round. A decade later, Gene Sarazen, on his first visit,
walked off the eighteenth green indignantly demanding to
know how a pasture which had traps smack in the middle of

its fairways could presume to be considered a peerless test of golf. Sam Snead flew to St. Andrews expressly for the 1946 British Open, took one look at the course, asked if he were in the right town, and, finding that he was, wanted to fly right back again. Sam stayed on and proceeded to win that championship, aided in no small way by the conviction, acquired after he and the Old Course had got better acquainted, that if he honestly played better golf shots than anyone else in the field, the course would see to it that no one beat him.

It is familiarity which breeds respect and love for the Old Course. It is like no other. In the United States, for example, our courses are constructed—fairways blasted through hillsides, streams diverted to fit the strategy of the approach shot, greens built to order by bulldozers. The Old Course wasn't made. It was always there. Today the word links is used indiscriminately by most golfers as if it were simply a synonym for course. Actually a links, or linksland, is a stretch of sandy soil deposited by the receding ocean. Linksland fringes the eastern coast of Scotland, and it was the logical place for playing golf, a game which may have been imported in germ from Holland but which was developed by the Scots into its present sublimely contagious form.

In a strange and wonderful way, the inhabitants of St. Andrews from the earliest days sensed that nature had blessed them with the best of all links for golf. Nature alone has been permitted to alter the topography. The incredible result is that the links, in general contour, probably looks much the same today as it did in 1100, the round year that historians have fixed on as the date when the natives of St. Andrews first began to put their links to its historic use.

Until late in the nineteenth century, the Old Course, hemmed in by the Firth of Tay and the estuary of the Eden River, was the only course on the thumb-shaped spit of linksland below the town. Two other eighteen-hole courses, the New and Jubilee, laid out in 1894 and 1946 respectively,

now occupy the reclaimed land between the northern bound-
ary of the Old Course and the Firth; a fourth eighteen holes,
called the Eden, was wedged in between the southern bound-
ary of the Old Course and the Eden estuary in 1914. The
ocean has receded about one hundred feet during the last
seventy-five years, and assuming that this has been its customary pace of retreat over the centuries, its waters must
have at one time washed up to the very edges of the Old
Course and determined its singular snakelike design. It is
as narrow as a course can be. The first seven holes march in
an almost straight line away from the town; the eighth,
ninth, tenth, and eleventh perform a small clockwise loop
around the tip of the promontory; then holes twelve through
eighteen march straight back to town alongside the first
seven. The adjoining fairways are not separated by rough,
and there is always ample room to the left, except on the
loop holes. They are tightly flanked on the right by out-of-
bounds or by heavy rough composed of gorselike whins and
heather, presenting the slicer with far less latitude for error
than the hooker. Not only are the parallel fairways fused into
one wide fairway but, save on the first, ninth, seventeenth,
and eighteenth, an outgoing hole and an incoming hole
share the same green, the second with the sixteenth, the
third with the fifteenth, and so on. The cups for the two
holes are at opposite ends of the huge double greens. The
largest of these, servicing the fifth and thirteenth holes, is
over an acre; putts 140 feet long are often a nerve-racking
reality.

The contours of the greens are treacherous, their surface
is slippery, and the earth itself so hard and resilient that a
player cannot stroke his approach for the pin and hope to
have the ball sit down abruptly, as it does on our soft, watered
greens. Instead, he must resort to a pitch-and-run approach,
landing his shot a calculated distance from his target so that
the ball, after its bound and roll, will stop in the neighbor-

hood of the pin. An equal accuracy is demanded on the tee-shots to avoid the mélange of fairway bunkers, those celebrated pits which were burrowed, long before the invention of golf, by sheep nestling behind the dunes to keep out of the bitter wind. On the direct line from tee to green on the fourteenth or Long Hole, for example, the golfer is first menaced by a formidable group of bunkers, the Beardies, lying in wait for him at the 200-yard mark. A hundred yards farther down the fairway stands Benty Bunker, backed up by Kitchen, and at the 400-yard mark he must deal with Hell, most feared of all the bunkers on the Old Course. To attempt the straight-line route to the green is folly on the fourteenth, and, for that matter, on nearly every hole of the eighteen. A golfer must tack back and forth among the hazards like a sailor. He must study the immediate mood of each hole each time he mounts the tee, for the slightest change in the wind requires a new strategy. It takes brains as well as technical skill to meet the challenge of St. Andrews, and therein lies its enduring greatness.

The Old Course is moderately long, measuring 6,572 yards from the regular tees, 6,883 yards from the back or "Tiger" tees, created in 1946. From both sets of tees, par is 73, and the record for the extended course, held by Dai Rees, the Welsh professional, is 67. No man has ever played a round without taking at least one 5, though Bobby Jones once got as far as the seventeenth with nothing above a 4 on his card and missed his 4 there only because he muffed a two-foot putt. This seventeenth—called the Road Hole because of the road which runs directly behind the green—is, along with the fourteenth and the eleventh (the Eden), the best known and most frequently copied of the individual holes. About 466 yards long, a most difficult par four, the seventeenth is an easy hole to collapse on. The ideal drive involves a risky carry over the roofs of Auchterlonie's drying sheds, and the knowledge that the road lurks behind the green inflicts overcautiousness on even the seasoned golfer as he plays the long second shot. The eleventh, one of the two par 3's on the course, can be reached some days with an easy seven-iron; on other days a full spoon is not too much club, so drastically does the direction and force of the wind influence the playing character of its 164 yards. The slanting green is protected by deep, high-walled bunkers, and two finalists in one amateur championship, after frolicking in these pits, halved the hole in eighteen.

Men who have golfed on the Old Course all their lives are startled to find that they keep on uncovering new and hidden ways to play the holes. The most notable case is that of Ted Blackwell, the game's longest driver at the turn of the century, who swore up and down for thirty-five years that the sixteenth hole didn't belong on the same course with the other seventeen. No matter where you hit your drive, the contours around the green were such that you couldn't get your approach shot to sit down within birdie distance of the pin. In his thirty-sixth year of playing the Old Course, Blackwell stumbled upon the secret to the sixteenth. Left of the bunker called the Principal's Nose, Blackwell reported, there was an all but imperceptible hollow in the fairway. If you placed your drive in that hollow instead of swatting it for distance, when you looked toward the green, you saw a perfect channel down the fairway and over the apron to the pin. After this discovery, Blackwell actually was able to birdie the sixteenth on an average of once every three rounds.

The natives of St. Andrews have been reared from the cradle to regard golf as a part of living only a little less basic than eating. Seventy-five per cent of the population plays the game, and the nongolfers know the Old Course intimately from their Sunday walks when golfing is prohibited (except on the Eden) and the links becomes the village green. In the evenings there is usually a group of townfolk gathered behind the eighteenth green, smoking pipes and chatting as they watch a pilgrim struggle home, chuckling among themselves as he lines up his putt, since they know he will fail to notice that the green slopes, almost invisibly, down from the back right-hand corner.

St. Andrews astonishes itself, and those who know it, with the wanton way it loses its characteristic dignity and turns into a Glendale of bobby-soxers when a famous pilgrim, such as General Eisenhower or General Bradley, shows up for a round of golf. The town's most fantastic performance in recent years came on Monday, May 22, 1950, when the first round of the British Amateur got under way. This was the first time since the war that St. Andrews was the scene of that tournament, and the lure of the Old Course attracted a record number of entries (324) which included a record invasion of Americans (35) which in turn included Bing Crosby. For the Scots, Crosby stands forth as the consummate American personality. When the word was released that Bing had mailed in his entry for the Amateur, St. Andrews began to seethe with an excitement it had not known since John Knox inflamed his parishioners to sack the cathedral. Crosby teed off at nine fifty-five that memorable Monday morning against his first-round opponent, a local carpenter and hillbilly singer named Wilson. A cold wind was snarling off the sea and a disagreeably wet rain was falling, but over 7,000 spectators, many of them transported by special bus from other corners of Fifeshire, were happily squashed along the roped-off perimeter of the course straining for a glimpse of the glamorous pilgrim. Bing came through magnificently. He drew spontaneous applause from his vast gallery by scoring two beautiful birdies on the first three holes. Though he ultimately lost the match, 3 and 2, he demonstrated that he was a bona fide golfer. On top of this, he did not play *too* well. He didn't avoid the Old Course's pitfalls. That would have been sacrilegious. Bing left town almost immediately after his match, and St. Andrews gradually regained its composure.

St. Andrews is extremely susceptible to love affairs with certain types of Americans and never forgets the deeds of its heroes. It is twenty-four years since Bobby Jones won the British Open on the Old Course and twenty-one years since he won the British Amateur there, but Bobby's miracles are as fresh in the minds and hearts of St. Andrews as if they were accomplished yesterday. It is impossible for a caddie who is toting for an American to walk down the fourth fairway without pointing out Cottage Bunker from which Bobby holed a full spade-mashie shot. Whenever Jones played, all of St. Andrews streamed down to the links to admire its adopted son. On the afternoon that Bobby opposed Cyril Tolley in the 1930 British Amateur, the town was completely deserted, a fact that did not escape the attention of Gerald Fairlie, a novelist. In plotting his next mystery, Fairlie selected that afternoon as the time when the villain committed murder in downtown St. Andrews and, though covered with the stains of his crime, was able to make his escape undetected in broad daylight down the empty streets.

Any visitor can play the Old Course by paying a green fee of three shillings and sixpence (about fifty cents). The Old Course is a public course, owned by the "ratepayers" of St. Andrews and regulated by the Town Council. Until 1946, when a Provisional Order was passed permitting the Council to charge ratepayers thirty shillings a year for their golf privileges, a green fee had never been levied on legitimate St. Andresans. It was their links and they could prove it in writing, going back to the parchment covenant of January 25, 1552, when the provost and bailies of the town, in granting to Archbishop Hamilton permission to raise rabbits on the north part of the links, made certain that he clearly recognized the townsfolks' right to use the links for drying their fishing nets and bleaching their linen and for enjoying their "golf, futball, schuting, at all gamis, with all uther maner of pastime."

One of his successors, Archbishop Gladstanes, went a step further and issued a charter in 1614 which stated that title to the links was vested in the town. Towards the end of the eighteenth century, however, St. Andrews, to rescue itself from debt, sold the links to Mr. Erskine of Cambo. No one stopped playing golf, but titularly the town had lost possession of the links. In 1894, when the Royal and Ancient Golf Club of St. Andrews was attempting to buy the land back from the Cheapes of Strathyrum, into whose hands it had passcd, the town was roused to action. If anyone had a right to purchase the links, the Town Council argued, it was the citizens of St. Andrews and not a private club. The issue was debated in Parliament, and two months later, in June, 1894, St. Andrews formally regained its links by paying the Cheape family 5,000 pounds.

Most of the ratepayers of St. Andrews live so close to the links that a locker room is a superfluity, but for the golfer who likes to play his extra holes in sympathetic company, there are three clubs he can join. The New Club, founded in 1902, is the one to which businessmen and professional men belong. It has close to 800 members who pay annual dues of thirty shillings if they live within the town limits or twenty-one shillings if they live in the country. The New Club's modest clubhouse fronts on Links Road beside the eighteenth fairway. Close by stands the St. Andrews Club, the tradesman's and the artisan's club, established in 1843. Since its members, who presently number about 900, must cough up all of fifteen shillings (or $2.10) a year, it is easy to understand the sudden paralysis that overtakes Scottish emigrants after they have innocently asked the cost of joining an American club. The Royal and Ancient, the third club, is an entirely different type of organization and a story in itself.

The Royal and Ancient is the most important institution in the world of golf, an eminence which its members have come to accept with equanimity. The R & A is not the world's oldest golf club—it is just about everything else— for the Honorable Company of Edinburgh Golfers had banded together a few years before the "twenty-two noble-men and gentlemen" of St. Andrews formed their club in May, 1754. At this first meeting, certain articles and laws, thirteen in number, were drafted to govern the members' play—the oldest surviving code in golf. A century later, when the R & A issued a revised codification of twenty-two rules, the club's prestige as a legislative authority had reached the point where all the other golf clubs in Britain willingly ac-cepted the R & A's codification. (The most significant in-novation was that eighteen holes constituted one round of golf.) Today, golf clubs throughout the world, with the ex-ception of those in the United States and its outlying posses-sions, adhere to the rules promulgated by the R & A.

The prestige of membership in the club is enormous. The dues are not. Local members are charged ten guineas annu-ally; English members, eight guineas; and foreign or "super-numerary" members, one guinea. The entrance fee for all is twenty guineas, and the total number of members is limited to 1,000, a figure that has seldom been approached. Earl Mountbatten, Field Marshal Montgomery, General Eisen-hower, and the Aga Khan are a few of the front-line person-alities who presently belong to the R & A. Winston Churchill was invited to become an honorary member but begged off on the grounds that he had no interest in golf. The super-numerary list includes about sixty Americans, headed by Bobby Jones and Francis Ouimet.

The R & A and the United States Golf Association, the official governing body for American golf, see eye to eye on most important issues, but there are a few interesting deviations. The official British and American golf balls, for example, weigh the same ("not more than 1.62 ounces avoirdupois"), but whereas the American ball must not be less than 1.68 inches in diameter, the R & A specifies a minimum of 1.62 inches. That six-hundredths of an inch makes a surprisingly great difference, especially on gusty days when the "heavier" British ball bores through winds which blow the American ball right back into the golfer's face. The American ball putts a little better. The R & A regulation which our golfers criticize most frequently is the one barring the Schenectady putter. This ruling, which was apparently conceived in a petulance uncharacteristic of the R & A, went on the books a few years after Walter J. Travis, a choleric but skillful American golfer, had putted his way with his Schenectady model to the British Amateur title in 1904, delivering a terrific blow to British pride, since no foreigner had ever before captured that championship. In this country we define a Schenectady as a putter in which the shaft is joined to the center of the blade. In the British interpretation, however, any putter in which the minutest fraction of the heel extends beyond the intersection of the shaft and the blade is outlawed.

The home of the Royal and Ancient is a stately sandstone clubhouse, approximately a century old and suitably weather-stained, poised directly behind the first tee of the Old Course. Through its corridors of Canadian yellow pine have passed a succession of members whose main object in life was the advancement of their club, but it is doubtful if any single individual contributed as much as Maj. Murray Belshes of Buttergash. Up to 1834, when Major Belshes swung into action, the club was called the Society of St. Andrews Golfers. In Major Belshes' mind, that wasn't good enough. Nothing short of royal endorsement would do. In a letter to Sir Herbert Taylor, the private secretary of King

William IV, Major Belshes retailed his club's glorious history and requested that the king honor the club by becoming its patron. Sir Herbert replied that he was sorry, but consent was out of the question. If the king agreed to be the patron of one golf club, every other golf club in the realm would kick up a fuss. This flat refusal did not perturb Major Murray Belshes. Perhaps he hadn't made things clear, the major wrote; St. Andrews merited a privileged rating and he couldn't see how granting it would be at all indiscreet, especially since the king happened to be Duke of St. Andrews. In 1836, King William agreed to become the club's patron and to permit the club to style itself the Royal and Ancient. In addition, the king sent along a gold medal which became the first prize at the annual autumn tournament.

Most men would have rested on their laurels, but not Maj. Murray Belshes. He next went after Queen Adelaide. She should really become the club's patroness, he argued nicely. After all, *she* was the *Duchess* of St. Andrews. Queen Adelaide gave in. In 1838 the new patroness presented the R & A with a silver medal which, since that date, has been worn by the club captain on all public appearances.

The captaincy of the R & A is held to be the highest honor a British golfer can receive. Originally, the member who turned in the lowest score at the autumn tournament automatically acceded to the captaincy, but this formula was scrapped in 1806 and a rotation set up whereby the captain for one year would be a Scot who was a prominent golfer, to be followed the next year by a distinguished member of Scottish life, to be followed in turn by a local laird, a commoner who held office—then back to a prominent Scottish golfer to start a new three-year cycle. Toward the close of the nineteenth century, after a tremendous fervor for golf had swept over England, this rotation was amended so that the captain every fourth year should be an outstanding English golfer. From time to time the sequence has been interrupted

and members of the royal family have been invited to head
the club that King William IV made royal as well as ancient.
Edward VII accepted the captaincy in 1863, when he was
Prince of Wales, and the line has been continued by Prince
Leopold in 1876, the Duke of Windsor (then Prince of
Wales) in 1922, King George VI (then Duke of York) in
1930, and the late Duke of Kent in 1937. The next member
of the royal family slated for the captaincy is the Duke of
Edinburgh. The incoming captain inherits, among other
things, the locker used by Allan Robertson, the greatest
golfer of the first half of the nineteenth century and the
R & A's first noteworthy custodian.

One of the many traditional ceremonies which the R & A
nourishes calls for the incoming captain to "drive himself
into office." On the third Wednesday in September, during
the autumn meeting, he steps onto the first tee, the Queen
Adelaide medal around his neck. Spread down the fairway
before him stand the caddies. Since the caddie who retrieves
the captain's ball receives a gold sovereign, each caddie takes
up the position where he thinks he has the best chance of
fielding the drive. This can make for a delicate situation.
When the Duke of Windsor drove himself into office, some
of the caddies, in the words of Sir Guy Campbell, "stood
disloyally close to the tee." Gold sovereigns are all but extinct nowadays, but rather than default on any part of this
ceremony, the R & A has used its influence with the Bank
of England to have a small supply of these coins struck
specifically for the club. As for the captain's golf ball, it is
traditional to cast a facsimile in silver (or in gold when the
captain is a member of the royal house) and to fasten it to a
silver golf club. All space on the original Silver Golf Club
was filled before the nineteenth century had been long under
way, and a replacement was then procured by subscription.

At the annual autumn dinner, the silver golf clubs, each
dripping heavily with silver golf balls, are displayed in front

of the head table where sit the former captains in their pink coats. After the toasts and speeches have been concluded and the new captain installed, the members file past and kiss the silver clubs and golf balls. These visible symbols of the club's continuity are draped in blue and white, the club's colors, and carried in front of the R & A contingent on national occasions such as the abdication of King Edward VIII and the proclamation of the present king) when the club participates in the procession through the streets of the town. The balls and clubs are draped in black for R & A funerals, the most exotic of the club's continuing rituals. To qualify for an R & A funeral, a member must be buried within the city boundaries, for the clubs and balls cannot be taken beyond those limits.

There is at the Royal and Ancient, as in every august British club, a small but articulate coterie of members who have acquired the deep grain of stuffiness invariably produced by life in a leather chair. This ultraconservative element regards the R & A as its private preserve and is daily on the prowl to discover some new grounds for outrage. An inexhaustible subject of discussion among this set is the financial beating the club has been subjected to as a reward for developing the golf links. This point of view is shared by the other members. The R & A, up to 1894, voluntarily supplied the funds for keeping up the Old Course in the style it thought the old girl deserved. Then under the provisions of the Links Act and subsequent governmental ordinances, the R & A, almost as if it were being penalized for some wrongdoing, was directed to assume the cost of maintaining the Old Course, ordered to build the New and the Eden and the Jubilee courses and to underwrite the maintenance of the New Course. The expense of keeping the Old and the New in top-notch condition now comes to a pretty farthing, £5,800 in 1949, for example. The Town Council, which is required by law only to chip in what it considers a fair amount, has seldom contributed more than £500 in any one year.

During the two centuries it has been operating the Old Course without owning it, the R & A has made many astute moves, but none quite as brilliant as the appointment in 1865 of Old Tom Morris as custodian, a combination of greenkeeper and professional. More than any one other person, Old Tom was responsible for investing golf in St. Andrews with its unique and remarkable charm. As a golfer Old Tom was not quite as proficient as his son, Young Tom, the finest golfer of that century, or Allan Robertson, who was never beaten in a stake match played on level terms. However, it was the man himself and not the golfer who came to be enshrined a good many years before his death as the game's authentic Grand Old Man. His chief traits were an unsticky kindness and courtesy and a love of his fellow golfer that warmed the home-town crony or the eager pilgrim who came within a putt's length of his shop beside the eighteenth green.

Old Tom Morris died in 1908. He was buried in the cathedral yard, alongside Young Tom and Allan Robertson, and the eighteenth hole was named in his honor. The custodianship then devolved on one Andrew Kirkaldy, almost the antithesis of Old Tom, a rough and ready customer who couldn't open his mouth without swearing—or saying something witty. Andra made so many wonderful cracks that countless others he may not have made were attributed to him. He is credited, for instance, with being the first person who, asked how the world was treating him, spat in reply, "Vera seldom, sir, vera seldom." A typical Andraism concerns the time he was playing with a golfer who was unfortunate enough to be trapped in Hell Bunker. Beginning with his mashie and changing to a more lofted club after each failure, the golfer tried vainly to extricate his ball.

"What should I do now, Andra?" he hollered up from the depths after his desperate sequence had taken him through every club in his bag and his ball still remained in the bunker. "If I were ye," Andra answered brusquely "I'd tak' the nine-forty train."

The current professional, or custodian, is Willie Auchterlonie, a man cut from the same fine fabric as Old Tom. Willie, who is seventy-eight, is paid fifty pounds a year by the R & A. His functions are honorary ones. In conversation Willie spins the same subtle spell as Old Tom. The ideal place for the pilgrim to catch him is the sitting room of his home above the Auchterlonie golf shop, now run by his son Laurie.

The spirit of St. Andrews has seldom failed to evoke relief and affection in the visiting golfer: he feels honestly at home at the home of golf. The Royal and Ancient, on the other hand, has rarely given the unintroduced pilgrim a similar sense of belonging. The pilgrim doesn't expect members of the R & A to turn cartwheels when they see him enter the front hall, but don't the members realize that golfers on every continent have a print of the R & A clubhouse hanging on the wall and have come to think of it as their club, too?

Since the war an agreeable trend has been shaping within the R & A. The reactionary clique remains as condescending as ever, but the vast majority of the members has come to realize that the club has certain responsibilities to all golfers. In 1946, professional golfers were allowed the use of the clubhouse for the first time. Participants in the 1950 British Amateur were given free run of the club and were warmed with sincere hospitality and an occasional Whisky Mac-Donald (whisky and ginger wine). Later in 1950 the R & A delighted British golfers by voting honorary life memberships to Willie Auchterlonie and those other two magnificent old champions, James Braid and J. H. Taylor.

A leading factor in this gradual humanizing of the R & A has been the club's secretary, Commander J. A. S. "Sandy" Carson, a rotund, congenial and progressive forty-three-year-old ex-civil servant and naval officer. Carson is a newcomer by St. Andrews standards. He was serving in the Far East in 1946, where he had been Commander of Supply on the aircraft carrier *Unicorn*, when his wife, knowing that he had talked of going into golf-club administration after the war, took the liberty of answering an advertisement for a secretary which the R & A had placed in the *Glasgow Herald*. Carson was selected and immediately plunged into the toughest job in golf. As secretary of the R & A, he acts as secretary for its eleven committees. (The General, the Rules of Golf, and the Championship committees are the most important.) Since the Championship Committee is in charge of running the British Open, Amateur, and Boys' Championships, plus the Walker Cup matches, a good portion of Carson's time is spent in the field.

Between tournaments Carson superintends the work of three R & A staffs. The staff of Golf Court, a manageress and eight maids, operates that guest house provided for out-of-town members. The Green Staff is composed of a crew of ten and the head greenkeeper, currently Andrew Corstorphine. Then there is the Club Staff: the head porter, the head steward, the cook, and eleven waiters and waitresses. Cameron, the head steward, came to the R & A twelve years ago along with Mrs. Cameron, who does the cooking. Tea is served daily, but since the war luncheon is provided on Saturdays only. Cameron handles the potables department, and in the opinion of veteran drinkers who have outlasted several stewards, he is credited with mixing a pretty fair Stymie. This is an exclusive R & A bolt of sunshine compounded of Italian vermouth, French vermouth, gin, and a secret ingredient.

Beneath Commander Carson's Harris tweed jackets there

beats a nautical heart. He runs the club like a ship and is
fortunate in having aboard Archibald Lamb Davidson Eunson, the head porter, a first mate of finicky efficiency. Eunson,
who hops about like a bespectacled Disney chipmunk, was
recruited from a fishing hotel in Banchory. That was in
1928, and he has been a fixture ever since. Just before three
o'clock each day, Eunson drops whatever detail he is caress-
ing and delivers the members' "ballots" to the Ballot House
behind the eighteenth green. A ballot is a card on which a
player writes his name, address, and the starting time he
desires for the next day; starting times are staggered at five-
minute intervals. Balloting for the next day's times closes
promptly at three, when a man from the Town Chamberlain's office arrives at the Ballot House and collects the cards
filled out not only by R & A members but by all golfers who
intend to play the Old Course. In the Chamberlain's office
the ballots are placed in a box, stirred with a handle, and the
draw accomplished with great scrupulousness.

The head porter's desk is fed by a three-way telephone line
to the starter on the New Course and the caddie master,
Willie Radley, and by a separate line to the starter on the
Old Course, Jimmy Alexander. A one-armed veteran of the
Battle of the Somme, Jimmy took over the starter's box in
1919 on a one-month's trial and is still waiting to be told if
the job is his. No one tees up on the Old Course until Jimmy,
having checked his list and his clock and the traffic on the
first fairway, calls the players by name. No one tees off until
Jimmy has uttered his "Play away, gentlemen." On the first
tee Jimmy is king, and his natural geniality is instantly
replaced by high dudgeon if his prerogative is ignored. Udo
Reinach, a broker from New York entered in last year's
British Amateur, made the mistake of accepting an invitation
from some friends on the first tee to fill out their foursome
for a practice round, this without first clearing through the
starter's box. In the course of the thorough dressing down

he received from Jimmy, Mr. Reinach was admonished that on future occasions when he had no definite starting time he should report this fact to the starter and the starter would then deal with his problem.

One of the best times for a golfer to make his pilgrimage to St. Andrews is in the late spring. The winters are cold and damp and it requires a native hardiness to enjoy a round without a portable fireplace. The spring is no tranquil pushover for that matter, the wind seldom somnolescent, rain not infrequent. However, it is somehow wrong to play St. Andrews when the wind is not stirring the heather and when there is no threat that a golfer may have to climb into his rainproof trousers and jacket. An excellent fortnight is the first two weeks in June, when the weather is just warm enough, just brisk enough. There are over thirty hotels in St. Andrews for the pilgrim to choose from. On his walk from his hotel to the Old Course to fill out his ballot for the next day, the pilgrim finds himself surrounded on all sides by golf. On the vast municipal putting greens by the sands, children and their mothers, having paid the fees of tuppence and thrippence, are playing the afternoon, away. The full flavor of St. Andrews cannot be savored, to be sure, until the pilgrim is actually on the Old Course, taking that wonderful examination with only his caddie to help him. The caddie fee is six shillings and a penny, but few golfers give their caddie less than a ten-shilling note.

The golfer who does not take a caddie at St. Andrews denies himself the wine of the country. They are a race apart, survivors of another age. McLaren Brown, the dean of the forty-five regulars, is seventy-eight now and not caddying too regularly. Lawrence Buddo Gourley, right behind him at seventy-seven, is almost through caddying too. Back in the nineteenth century, gentle old Gourley taught King Edward VII and the Grand Duke Michael of Russia how to play the

game at Cannes. He enjoyed an Indian summer of distinction in the '20s when he became the Prince of Wales's
special caddie. The most loquacious member of the old
guard is Bill Hutchison, a brother of the famous Jock. Bill
Hutchison may or may not have been teaching golf to the
British officers in Egypt when the Boer War broke out. He
may or may not have been a boy prodigy who would bet
anyone he could hole twenty-five consecutive stymies for a
penny. He may or may not be the seventy-three he claims
but hardly looks. You have to take Bill Hutchison with a
whiff of salt air. During the busy season, starting in May, this
corps of regulars is supplemented by young men in their
twenties and thirties. They caddie until the slack season sets
in in October, then go up to the Labor Exchange and find
odd jobs. In the old days many of these young men would
have made caddying their career, but under the Labour
Government it is an expensive way of earning a living.
Caddies are classified as self-employed individuals and, as
such, must purchase a weekly National Health and Unemployment stamp, which comes to six shillings and four pence.
In another twenty years the old St. Andrews caddie will be as
extinct as the mammoth.

The old St. Andrews caddies do not know every blade of
grass on the course but they do know every inch of the colossal greens, each bump in the billowy fairways, the temper
of each hazard on any particular morning. They also know
golf. They can gauge the game of a stranger on the basis of
three or four shots and his reaction to them. From the second
hole on, they can tell precisely where each shot will end up
simply by watching the player strike the ball—they know
how each yard of the Old Course will behave and their bones
fill them in on the weather. They take such intense pride in
their work that to challenge their "call" on a club is, in their
eyes, an attack on their personal integrity. The old regular
who caddied for Johnny Bulla in the 1939 Open laid down

the bag and walked off the course when Bulla persisted in thinking his next shot was a five-iron after the caddie had counseled a four.

The old St. Andrews caddie doesn't "butter up" his man, but no one can be more genuinely understanding of the full gamut of a golfer's feelings. When he is working with an "honest golfer," whether the player is an expert or a duffer, there is no limit to his resourcefulness in "reading the course" for his man. In the 1950 Amateur there was an unusually dramatic illustration of this quiet partnership between player and caddie which undoubtedly is the essence of St. Andrews. In one of his early matches, Willie Turnesa, the former American and British Amateur champion, hooked his tee-shot far off line on a long par four. His ball ended up at the base of an abrupt rise which shut off all view of the fairway and the green beyond. Willie's caddie studied the situation for a brief moment. He then handed Willie his five-iron and, pointing an old finger at the sky, said dryly, "Just hit that cloud." Willie hit that cloud and found his ball six feet from the cup.

GAM INC.:
GUSSIE MORAN

This short piece was written early in 1951 when Gussie Moran was about to embark on her professional career. As I reread it, it strikes me as being a shade more detached and unsympathetic than it might well have been. As a matter of fact, though I had thought the contrary would be true, I remember meeting few sports personalities as honest about themselves as Gussie Moran and as genuinely friendly. It has been a source of pleasure to all her well-wishers that, with tennis now behind her, she has built a very nice career in broadcasting as a member of a team of "experts" on a New York radio station who daily dissertate on all phases of sport. In running through the day's baseball results, Gussie is good for at least one slight technical error or a mispronunciation of some multisyllabic name that would give us all pause, and she is the first to see the humor in it. In the postwar era, what she brought to tennis made her a new sort of sports phenomenon, a harbinger of a more commercial day, and, oddly enough—or not so oddly—she will be remembered long after better tennis players are forgotten.

THERE IS one unarguable fact about Gertrude Augusta Moran, California's latest, most supple, and most controversial gift to tennis: Gussie has gotten almost as much mileage out of a pair of lace panties as Lady Godiva got from her white horse. As the most publicized attraction in Bobby Riggs' professional tennis troupe, Gussie is guaranteed a basic $75,000. From her tie-in with a Beverly Hills clothing house masterminded by Dan Grayson, the man who put the youth of America into Hopalong Cassidy outfits, Gussie will be bolstering her income by designing a line of sports clothes, with and without lace, aimed at the working girl between eighteen and twenty-seven. She has a standing offer from London's Wembley Stadium and other European sports promoters to let them know whenever the feeling to do some overseas barnstorming strikes her. This is not bad going at all, considering that Gussie has never ranked closer to the top than fourth among American women tennis stars and was seventh-ranking last September when she was offered a far more lucrative contract than Suzanne Lenglen or any later woman champion received for turning professional. It would seem to prove that nowadays some people like tennis pure and simple but that more people like their tennis in just proportions.

Gussie's climb to the top of the entertainment world began in June, 1949, at the conservative All-England Club in Wimbledon, the historic capital of international tennis. Gussie had gone over to compete in the All-England Championships—which amount to the world championships—and there was nothing pretentious about this. The previous summer, coached by Bill Tilden and Dick Skeen, she had worked industriously on her tennis and had vaulted to fourth in the national rankings, right behind Margaret Osborne duPont, Louise Brough, and Doris Hart, the perennial Big Three of postwar women's tennis. Furthermore, in the winter she had won the National Indoor Singles Championship, an accomplishment not to be cast lightly aside even if none of the big names had chosen to enter. The Gertrude Moran who traveled to Wimbledon was twenty-five, serious about her tennis, certainly not the stuff a champion is made of, but a girl you had to admire for transforming herself into a creditable singles player and a very useful partner in doubles. At home she had attracted audible but not explosive attention from the tournament crowd because of her fine West Coast figure, her feline grace on the court, and her penchant for pastel-colored outfits in that traditionally all-white world.

While practicing at Wimbledon, Gussie met Colonel Teddy Tinling, a fortyish, personable ex-war hero who acted as Wimbledon's major-domo—calling the players from their dressing rooms at match time, escorting them onto the court, generally serving as a friendly guide and dispeller of nervousness. Colonel Tinling was in the dress-designing business. He frequently made dresses for his friends in tennis, and after meeting Gussie and being favorably impressed, he asked if she would like to wear one of his creations at Wimbledon. Gussie said she would be delighted to, and added that she had one idiosyncrasy about tennis clothes: she liked to have the undergarment made of the same material as the dress or skirt. The idea of edging the undergarment with lace, which gave it the heady aura of the boudoir, was the colonel's own subsequent inspiration. During the matches, Gussie covered the court with at least her usual energy, and the full extent of the colonel's handiwork was frequently visible to the gallery of lingerie-hungry Englishmen who, it must be admitted, have long lived on austerity rations where female glamour is concerned. Their enthusiastic response to this unexpected pleasure found its way into the newspapers and transocean wire services, and by the time the tournament was over, Gertrude Moran had become Glamorous Gussie and a junior-grade international celebrity. As for Colonel Tinling, he was forced to resign his major-domoship because Wimbledon felt he was using the tournament for commercial publicity.

Since the spring of 1949 Gussie's tennis has not improved. This is not surprising inasmuch as Gussie recognized as clearly as anyone that the lace panties were the best thing that had ever happened to her and has concentrated since their emergence on being a first-ranking tennis celebrity rather than an also-ranking tennis player. In Cairo, last winter, she added to her growing reputation as a trail blazer in fashion by appearing for her semifinal match clad in black gabardine shorts. Next came the Balmain frock. Pierre Balmain, the renowned *couturier* who knows a good walking advertisement as well as the next *couturier*, called on Gussie at the Lancaster Hotel in Paris and asked if he could make her a tennis dress gratis. Sketches of the Balmain number, a low-necked filmy job, received a big play in the newspapers in France, England, and the United States. When Gussie decided not to wear the Balmain at Wimbledon in 1950, she could say, and with reason, that Pierre had no kick coming on the score of publicity. At Wimbledon, Gussie wore a Tinling creation which featured apple-pie panties. By this stage of the game, she had blossomed into an unprecedented phenomenon in the annals of sport: she was not a champion or even a near-champion, but she was the best draw in tennis and personally pulled many tournaments out of the red for the first time in years.

Gussie would have been shortsighted not to have turned pro and cashed in when her publicity was burning brightest, and she is not that kind of a girl. She knows the value of a bank account, never having had one and having lived among the well-heeled followers of tennis who do. She has astutely set herself up legally as a corporation (G A M Inc.—a title composed of her three initials) from which she draws $150 a week for her expenses. In her social relations she is extremely forthright, less sophisticated, and more erratic than most women. As she sees it, she has been close to marriage three times—twice with Pat Di Cicco, the former Hollywood agent, though she thinks their relationship is now turning into a friendship. (It was Di Cicco who counseled her in 1942, when she was at loose ends to know what to do for a career, to go back to tennis in which she had achieved mild success as a junior player; there was nothing else she knew how to do, he told her with a frankness Gussie appreciated.) The third time was with Tony Davenport, an English export-import man whom she met in India last winter. "It was Christmas and I was away from home," Gussie recently explained to a friend who had been mystified by the rapidity with which Gussie had announced her engagement to Davenport and the equal rapidity with which she had broken it. "India was a strange country and I was lonely. On top of that, I had fallen sick. I remember looking at a map of the world and saying to myself that if I lived in Bombay, it really wouldn't be so far away from Santa Monica. I could fly home in a couple of days. Then I began to think things over. It costs money to travel on airplanes."

Gussie's parents, Harry and Emma Moran, live in Santa Monica in what Gussie describes as "the oldest house in town, I think, one of those places that looks like a haunted house and gets painted once every fifteen years." She has an exceptional attachment for her father, who has worked at Universal-International studios for almost thirty years, first as an electrician, now as a sound technician. Gussie is seldom more animated than when describing the affectionate esteem in which her father is held by his co-workers. "Whenever a director finishes shooting a scene," she recently reminisced, "he'll turn to Dad as if he were running the show and ask him with a big smile, 'How was that, Harry? O.K.? Can we print it?'" Her taste for fashion—which was far superior before she turned pro and began emulating a circus performer—was acquired through her mother, who has always made most of Gussie's clothes.

Gussie doesn't think she slays the male portion of her galleries and resents the implication that she thinks she does.

"If a man is with his wife or girl friend, he thinks of me only as a pretty good-looking tennis player, not as a person. When you're on the court, you're an actress, and I can sense, for instance, that European men like me better than American men do." Amateur female psychologists, which means all women, take vast pleasure in analyzing Gussie for men. One popular view is that Gussie unconsciously courts notoriety —that is, she is one of those girls who has always thought of herself as less attractive than she would like to be, and, as a result, has a constant need for exhibition to prove to herself that she can command attention and admiration. A more charitable explanation casts Gussie in an "early Joan Crawford" role: the ambitious working girl who has realistically appraised her assets and has tried to use them, even as you and I, to get some of the nicer things in life. Both theories are probably right.

HARVARD
NEVER LOSES
AT HALF TIME

This article for the now defunct *Collier's* came out in November 1951, shortly before the Harvard–Yale game. The Harvard team played extremely well that gray afternoon against their favored opponents and were unlucky to be held to a tie. The Harvard band was in great form, the glockenspiel section in particular turning in far and away its finest performance of the year.

In the decade that has since elapsed, Harvard's football fortunes have risen appreciably over what they were in the late 1940s, though the teams in the last few years have had a curious disposition to dissolve into mediocrity just when they seem to be on the verge of sustained success. The band, as ever, has been a Gibraltar. Only one change must be noted, the untimely passing a few seasons back of the band's beloved director, Malcolm Holmes.

It might be mentioned that in recent autumns the college bands in the East—and, for all I know, in other parts of the country as well—have gone in for a new and regrettable approach to their half-time shows. Marching, visual formations, and rousing music are out. What is in is a sophomoric brand of public-address-system humor: a spokesman announces to the assembled that the band will offer several tableaux depicting, say, high points in

American history—and we get such witty stuff as a rendition of "I Don't Want to Set the World on Fire" to illustrate what Mrs. O'Leary said to her neighbors in Chicago. Terrif! While the Harvard band has also succumbed to this national epidemic wherein everyone apparently aspires to be Bob Hope, at least it has done it far more agreeably than its rivals. For example, the song dedicated to Oedipus in the half-time "Western Civilization" show at the 1960 Yale game turned out to be "I Want a Girl Just Like the Girl that Married Dear Old Dad." Maybe what is needed is a good stiff letter from some powerful alumnus, such as the nation's ranking touch-football star, the Attorney General, to get the band back to "Wintergreen," where it belongs.

ON THE MORNING of the game against Princeton's bruising team last November, the *Crimson*, Harvard's undergraduate daily paper, faced the impending debacle with courage and humor. "Two powerful elevens will take the field in Princeton's Palmer Stadium this afternoon," the *Crimson* declared. "In a few minutes they will be joined by Harvard's football players."

In its attitude of noble resignation to harsh reality (and the two-platoon system), the *Crimson* spoke for all Harvard undergraduates and alumni who have had the stamina to follow the college's consistently futile postwar football teams. Over the past two seasons, for example, Harvard managed to amass the poorest record of any major university, winning only two of its seventeen games. To make matters worse, in the last ten games against its traditional rivals, Yale and Princeton, Harvard has gone down to defeat no fewer than eight times. By reputation, Harvard men are supposed to behave with "studied indifference," and the chronic ineptness of their team has given them an excellent chance to exhibit this trait. During one recent Yale game, after Yale had racked up its third quick touchdown, a group of students in the deactivated Harvard cheering section held aloft a ban-

ner which proclaimed: WHO GIVES A DAMN! Oklahoma was
never like that.

Autumn Saturdays would have been—and would still be
—scarcely tolerable for Harvard rooters were it not for the
Harvard band. So far this season, the band has gone undefeated against all comers. This is no more than was expected.
During the past two decades, it has been unanimously acclaimed the best college band in the East, if not in the entire
country, and has steadily grown more formidable. As a result, a curious transfer of emotions has taken place among
Harvard men. Frustrated by their football teams, which give
them so few chances to cheer, Harvard rooters have come to
enshrine the band as their pride and joy, the symbol of their
superiority. It has now reached the point where Harvard
men, on being asked how the game came out, have been
known to reply exuberantly, "Came out fine. The band was
never better."

The transformation that comes over Harvard rooters at
half time when the band comes on the field has to be experienced to be believed. At the mere sight of the bandsmen filing to take up their marching block formation behind one of
the goal posts, the haggard haze of apology seems to lift from
the Harvard stands. They greet the visiting band—which
always parades first at Harvard Stadium—with the cordiality
that the man who holds the ace can afford to show the king.
And then, at the first roll of the drums of *their* band, the Harvard stands rise as one man, and the shout that goes up is not
"Harvard" at all. It is strictly Siwash, a frenzied Niagara of
affection and pride. "Oh, they were a magnificent contingent, too, when we were winning back in '41," an emotional
alumnus recently confessed, "but now—we almost worship
those boys. They allow a Harvard man to hold his head up
proudly. We'll never forget them. In our season of drought,
they came to our rescue like Horatius at the bridge." When

a Harvard man mixes his metaphors, it is proof that he is genuinely moved.

The Harvard band—150 strong this year—marches crisply, but it is not celebrated for its razzle-dazzle military maneuvers, the hallmark, for example, of the superb Michigan and Ohio State outfits. Rather, the band's reputation has been built on its unrivaled musicianship and the quality of its arrangements, plus the inventiveness of its visual formation and a knack for rising to the occasion that is absolutely uncanny. In 1949, for example, the Dartmouth band, first onto the field at half time, cut loose with an ambitious drill, forming a beer stein, the contents of which diminished to the strains of appropriate music. The Harvard band proceeded immediately to top that, as its partisans felt certain it would. The band began by forming a champagne bottle which tipped and filled a thin-stemmed glass. A bandsman dressed up to represent the Dartmouth Indian then drank from the glass, bubbles formed, exploded into thin air, and were instantly replaced by the word "hic"—this to the accompaniment of "How Dry I Am" and "Show Me the Way to Go Home." This drinking bout was purely coincidental, of course, but for its share in the liquid afternoon, the Harvard band received a letter of protest from the W.C.T.U. and a mild reprimand from the Associate Dean of Harvard College who felt that the Indian should not have reeled so emphatically. Ordinarily, the only appreciable protests against the band are lodged by the students who run the food concessions beneath the stadium stands. They regularly complain that they are losing their shirts since so few people leave their seats at half time to buy hot dogs and coffee.

In return for trampling over Harvard 49–0 last October, Army was treated to "Substitutions Unlimited," a brilliant parody by the band on the two-platoon system presently employed by Army and other powerhouses. While an announcer described the movements over the public address system, the band split up into two teams. One half, the A team, performed on the field. The B team remained silently behind on the bench. The Harvard "coach"—Malcolm H. "Mal" Holmes, the band's conductor—first sent in a few substitute clarinets and flutes, then relieved the tired trumpet section with fresh replacements who had been warming up on the side lines. Several measures later, the A team trotted off the field and the B, or defensive, team went in en masse, heavily muscled with tubas. The high point of the satire was reached when eight bandsmen raced onto the gridiron and, arranging themselves across the fifty-yard stripe, removed their white gloves with great aplomb. Like all big-time teams which had specialists who entered the game for one specific play only, the Harvard band, the announcer explained, had *its* specialists. "Not one of these men can play more than two notes and some of them can only play one, but these men are the best performers in the country on their particular notes." With each specialist sticking to his one note, the octette collaborated on a brief melody. The drill wound up with a "musical scrimmage." Half the band blasted out Army's "Slum and Gravy" while the other half blared Harvard's classic version of "Wintergreen for President," with the strains of "Wintergreen" finally emerging clear and unchallenged.

The basic idea for "Substitutions Unlimited" was germinated in the lively mind of Mal Holmes, a member of the class of '28 who has been the band's conductor since 1942. Suggestions for these half-time shows, both music and maneuver, are culled from all the members of the band, but more often than not the "working up" of the production the week before a particular game is handled by Holmes and the band's undergraduate officers. Many of these officers have regularly come from Massachusetts, a state of events in keeping with an unplanned but apparently inevitable band tradition. "If you're a band-conscious kid and you live close enough to Cambridge to catch the band at a Saturday game," Frank Hopkins, a slim trombonist from Springfield, Massachusetts, who is the band's current manager or ranking officer, was explaining this October, "you seem to be drawn to going to Harvard and playing in the band, just about the way local football players who catch the Harvard football team in action seem to gravitate to Notre Dame or Tennessee." On the other hand, the band is anything but a regional group. In this year's outfit, there are students from over twenty states.

Band officers are chosen because of their administrative, as distinct from musical, talents. The outstanding instrumentalist in the 1951 band is Charley Lemmond, a sawed-off youngster from Forty Fort, Pennsylvania, who leads the trumpet section. "He's been a tower of strength for four years," Conductor Holmes was sighing as he watched Lemmond expertly "tune up" the band at a recent Friday night rehearsal on the jayvee football field. "I know just how a football coach feels. I'll hate to see that boy graduate. My only consolation is that Charley has a younger brother, a wonderful trumpeter, too, who'll be up at Harvard in another year." Unlike many of the midwestern colleges which pride themselves on their large and excellent bands, Harvard does not recruit talent, and the university offers no musical scholarships to lure schoolboy stars into the fold. However, the board which passes on scholarships for boys interested in attending Harvard favors applicants who present outside activities along with their academic qualifications. It never hurts to play the sousaphone.

The Harvard band is not ready to tackle the J. J. Shubert stuff, like "Substitutions Unlimited," until the season has reached the halfway mark. At the opening game this autumn against Springfield, for example, the band contented itself with such elementary designs as "Glad You're Back" (directed at the visitors' cheering section), "Hello '55" (for the freshman class), and "Let's Win, Harvard" (for the aid and encouragement of the team). From a musical point of view as well, it takes the band about a month to sound like the Harvard band. "Our main trouble against Springfield, Holy Cross, and even the third week against Columbia was the erraticness of our drum roll," Conductor Holmes was remembering on the eve of the Army game. "Everything else was in relatively good shape. We had a veteran tuba section, and coupled with the largest number of baritone saxes the freshman class has ever fed us, this gave us the sturdiest 'bottom' since '47. Pretty fair 'top,' too—all the melody instrument sections more than adequate. But our drum roll was the shakiest we've had in years, and when you consider the unusual marching block formation we use, you can see why the whole band lacked the punch we like to have. In order to gain the tightest possible cohesiveness from 'top' to 'bottom,' our drums march in the middle ranks, cementing the bass instruments, which are placed up front, with the melody instruments to the rear. Well, after Columbia, we called a special section rehearsal for the drummers, drilling them to a metronome set at 135 beats a minute until the beat permeated right into their pores. I know the student body is counting on us to shoot the works tomorrow, and we won't let them down. We'll have a good, rich 'middle' and a lot of other things ready for Army."

The attachment Harvard men have for their band often leads them to claim that the organization is the perfect representative of Harvard wit, taste, and imagination. This may be true, but it is not the impression an outsider receives. The strength of the band, as one observer from Wisconsin put it, is that its members do not behave like Harvard men at all but carry on with a spirit closer to the campuses of the hinterland which are still untouched by the overcivilizing influences of Brooks Brothers, tea, the Groton accent, intellectual girl friends, and the Hasty Pudding Institute. In any event, the Harvard band is one of the few organizations in the Ivy League (Harvard, Yale, Princeton, Dartmouth, Cornell, Brown, Penn, and Columbia) whose members take an unashamed delight in being "collegiate" in the old-fashioned sense. Last fall, for example, en route by bus from Cambridge to New Jersey for the Princeton game, the band arrived in New Haven at twelve-thirty A.M. on Saturday morning. After directing the buses down dark and deserted High Street, the band assembled on the Old Campus and serenaded the sleeping Yale men with a short but noisy medley of Harvard songs until bags of water were dropped from the windows of adjacent dormitories and a menacing crowd gathered round. Some four hours later, around five in the morning, the buses rolled into Princeton and were parked near the stadium. Shrouded in a heavy mist, the band marched quietly to the center of the campus. Then the drums rolled off to split the stillness of the early morning, and the band at full blast paraded through the endless archways.

The cost of transporting the band to Yale or Princeton—one of these big games is played away from home each year—is assumed by the Harvard Athletic Association. This amounts to the sum and total of the financial aid the band receives from any university source. It is up to the band to raise through its own resources the remainder of the $20,000 it annually requires to underwrite its other expenses, principally traveling to other "away" games. Revenue from fifteen to twenty concerts brings in something over $2,000. Contributions from alumni bring in another $3,000. (The H.A.A. allows the band to enclose a crimson slip tastefully mentioning its existence in the football ticket applications mailed to graduate subscribers east of the Mississippi.) But the large bulk of the band's income, amounting roughly to $12,000 to $15,000 a year, is derived from the sales of its three albums of records, "Up the Street," "Half-Time," and "Ivy League Album." These recordings, as is understandable, have found their way into many of the better homes and gardens populated by Harvard grads. What is amazing, though, is the popularity the albums have achieved in remote necks of the country and abroad as well. This past summer the band's treasurer filled orders from Venezuela, Hawaii, Rome, and the Free University in the American sector of Berlin, and the secretary is presently engaged in a lengthy correspondence with a company in Amsterdam which is dickering for distribution rights in the Low Countries.

This financial independence is one of the many factors that has bred a terrific *esprit de corps*. Band members may graduate from Harvard but many refuse to graduate from the Harvard band. When the band is going through its pregame rehearsal on Saturday mornings, be it in Cambridge or on the road, six or seven band alumni are sure to show up all set to march and play. The drillmaster rapidly alters his formation designs to work in these additional starters. Dr. Masao Yatsuhashi, who joined the band as a freshman clarinetist in 1935, turned up for all home games during the next fourteen autumns, frequently arriving breathless and all in white, his band uniform under his arm, during his days as an interne. Dr. Yatsuhashi will probably be good for another fourteen years when he completes his present tour of duty with the Army Medical Corps. The band obviously meant *too* much to one undergraduate, a bagpiper from Texas. He had fallen behind in his studies and was ordered by the dean to give up all extracurricular activities or face immediate dismissal from the university. The Texan stayed away from the band for almost a week, but the sight of his colleagues marching to the game on Saturday was too much for him. He grabbed his pipes and joined them. Outside of Scotland a bagpiper is the last musician who can perform inconspicuously. It was the Texan's last weekend as a Harvard man.

The oldest member of the Harvard band, and its only "associate member" or ringer, is Paul Touchette, a forty-six-year-old fireman who plays solo trumpet. This is a story in itself, and a charming one. One of the stations of the Cambridge Fire Department is situated next door to the Gothic Alp called Memorial Hall, where the band holds its musical practices. One evening, as they were breaking up after a rehearsal, a group of bandsmen heard a few clangorous notes issuing from the firehouse. Upon investigation, they found the fire department band knee-deep in rehearsal. The boys joined the band, a number of their friends followed suit, and in no time at all the Cambridge Fire Department Band was composed chiefly of Harvard undergraduates. In return, Paul Touchette, who at one time played with the Boston Symphony Orchestra, joined the Harvard band. Touchette usually manages to arrange his duty schedule so that it allows him to make all of the home games and most of the trips.

As befits an organization whose only airs are musical, the band's headquarters are remarkable for their elegant lack of plushness. After operating from a basement room in Lowell House suitable for storing instruments, the band moved in 1947 to its present location, a larger basement room in Paine Hall. (According to university legend, in prohibition days this grotto served personnel in the science and maintenance departments as a distillery.) Fifty-odd photos of band formations now obscure one of the rough walls beneath the steampipes. Two other walls are lined by shelves, ten rows high, on which the band's 155 arrangements are stored. A Harvard Alumni Directory reposes in a prominent position amidst eight easy chairs, a not so easy couch, a supply of beer, battered tubas, a stout record file, and a collection of drums that includes a bass drum stolen by Dartmouth students and ultimately returned with "Dartmouth 14 Ahvud 13" inscribed in green paint. Over the doorway, in crimson paint, looms the band's famous motto: *Illigitimum Non Carborundum.* Freely translated, this is rendered "Don't Let Them Wear You Down." Several Latin variations and several brisker translations caught on with General Bradley's headquarters during the war, and the motto has since been taken up by many business concerns, a number of which claim to have originated it. In the opinion of scholars who have been provoked to research the motto's history, there is little doubt that credit for its origination belongs to the Harvard band. Yellowing copies of the band's correspondence disclose that members invariably included it in letters to each other back in the middle Twenties and had probably been using the motto informally from the band's earliest beginnings.

The founder of the Harvard band was Frederic L. Reynolds, a Boston lawyer who was a member of the class of 1920. Aware that many students, like himself, had been members of wartime regimental bands, Reynolds believed that they could form a musical aggregation that would lend far more flavor to the football games than the University Banjo and Mandolin Clubs which then entertained the spectators. The forty students who answered Reynolds' call for volunteers played their first game on October 2, 1919, when Harvard, then a football power, soundly defeated Boston College 17–0. They made the trip to Princeton. The week after that, supplemented by forty students who couldn't play instruments but held them handsomely, the band presented an impressive eighty-man delegation as it marched through Harvard Square and across the river to Soldiers Field for the Yale game.

During the first few years, the official uniform consisted of white duck trousers, white shirt, and white sailor hat. Harvard bandsmen go bareheaded today, and their uniform is not much more ornate than the original ones. Each musician provides his own black shoes and black socks, his white shirt, and his knitted crimson tie. The band supplies him with a pair of white ducks piped with a three-quarter-inch stripe of crimson and either sells or rents him a heavy wool, weatherproofed, unpadded, two-button crimson jacket. A lyre stitched in gold thread decorates the breast pocket. These jackets have the heft of a bath mat, a virtue on chill November afternoons, and will not crease when they have been slept in for two days. Even by the standards of the Ivy League, where the bands frown on dressing up like a Hollywood military school, this is a staid costume. The Princeton band, for example, gains a certain jauntiness by wearing straw hats. White shoes do the same for Yale bandsmen in their otherwise supercasual blue jackets and gray flannels. Members of the Harvard band have lobbied from time to time for snapping up their appearance by wearing derbies or fezzes, but these and other suggestions have been vetoed as out of character with the band's traditionally conservative attire.

In the early and middle Twenties the Harvard band was not only outdressed by its opponents but outplayed as well. Dartmouth had the best band in the East. Built around the stars of the famed Barbary Coast dance orchestra, Dartmouth's football band was, in effect, an augmented jazz band. The saxophones played lush figures, the trombonists waved hats over their horns, and in capturing in music the spirit of the raccoon-coat era of college life, Dartmouth was in a class by itself. Yale's band showed a distinct improvement in the late Twenties when a transfer from the University of Maine, one Hubert Prior Vallée, took over. Rudy was a sound organizer and occasionally had flashes of brilliance, like playing "Marching Through Georgia" when Yale played Georgia. The Harvard band might have remained just another band if a succession of talented leaders had not arrived on the scene.

The first of these stimulants was Harold Holland, a young man from Ohio. Before Holland went into action, showmanship, as the Harvard band understood it, began and ended with painfully forming an "H" and countermarching into the stands. Holland shook the band off its haunches by assuring them that high-school outfits in the Midwest could march circles around them. He worked out visual drills—like a plumed crusader for Holy Cross and a bear for Brown— and personally introduced the midwestern custom of having the drum major flip the baton over the goal post as the band headed down the field. Holland was followed by Guy Vernon Slade, a martinet with the working vocabulary of a Marine and a flair for visual, gag, and letter drills. Not only did Slade know what words to spell out, but his words were the most legible any college band had been able to achieve. He planned his letters with scientific exactness on three-by-five-inch cards, and to give them bolder definition for his audience of thousands, he had the bandsmen crouch close to the turf when he fired his blank pistol as a signal. Slade's passion was to present as many formations as possible during the seven minutes allotted the band for its half-time show. This led him to abandon the orthodox method, whereby a band marched and peeled off into its formation designs, in favor of the so-called "jump drill." Today, as in Slade's day, each bandsman, at the bark of the pistol, sprints to his new position in the next maneuver. Slade got his one hundred men to jump so rapidly that one afternoon he formed no less than seventy-three letters, a national intercollegiate record that probably still stands today.

During Slade's four years at the helm—he retained the leadership through his first two years in Harvard Law School —the Harvard band gained the slickness and the style which other eastern college bands used as their criteria and continue to copy today. The man who made the band a conspicuously able musical organization was Leroy Anderson. In the last few years, after two decades as a quiet Harvard hero, Anderson has suddenly acquired a national reputation, first as an arranger for the Boston Symphony "Pops" Orchestra, most recently as the composer of "Sleigh Ride," "The Syncopated Clock," "Blue Tango," and a number of other bright, well-bred instrumental novelties. The summer before his senior year, Anderson took it upon himself to fashion the first written arrangements of "Harvardiana," "Ten Thousand Men of Harvard," and "Soldiers Field." "We sounded somewhat smoother after that," a band contemporary of Anderson's was reminiscing this autumn. "Piccolo players weren't going off in all directions with their own inspired improvisations. Anderson picked up our tempo, too, from a stodgy 6/8 to a 2/4 that gave you a real lift. Then he made those wonderful college medleys and topped it off by giving us 'Wintergreen.' "

Though Harvard's alma mater song is "Fair Harvard," the lyric by the Rev. Samuel Gilman (class of 1811) set to the old Irish air which also serves Tom Moore's "Believe Me If All These Endearing Young Charms," and though it is sung with proper feeling at the conclusion of every football game, it stirs few Harvard men as does "Wintergreen for President," the band's trade-mark and the college's unofficial alma mater. "Wintergreen's" genesis was an interesting one. In the fall of '32, Anderson, then attending graduate school but continuing as the band's arranger and conductor, experimented by presenting a medley of Dartmouth songs at the Dartmouth game. Not knowing how Dartmouth would react, Anderson cautiously played it when the band was facing the Harvard stands. He was astonished when it evoked boisterous cheers from the Dartmouth side of the field. He was casting around in the back of his mind for another medley to follow it up with at the Army game, when a few evenings later he went to see "Of Thee I Sing," the Pulitzer Prize-winning musical comedy. The opening chorus of the show, a political satire, described an election rally. As the paraders moved across the darkened stage, holding their torches and

banners, they broke into their campaign song, "Wintergreen
for President," a kind of rhythmic chant into which were
interpolated snatches of "There'll Be a Hot Time in the Old
Town Tonight," "The Stars and Stripes Forever," and other
robust Americana. "The idea suddenly hit me," Anderson
was remembering recently. "Why not make an arrangement
of 'Wintergreen' substituting the songs of, say, Harvard,
Yale, and Princeton for the old campaign songs? Well, we
played it the next week. Just as we were finishing the number,
such a cheer went up that I turned around to see if the football team was coming on the field for the second half. The
team was no place in sight. The next Saturday, the minute
the band appeared, the Harvard stands began shouting for
'Wintergreen.' I guess they've been shouting for it ever since.
It's hard to explain just why it caught on the way it did. It
was one of those happy flukes where supply and demand
happened to interlock perfectly."

The combination that is playing "Wintergreen" this
autumn is composed, roughly, of thirty-six clarinets, thirty-
two trumpets, fifteen saxes, eleven French horns, five baritone saxes, eight flutes, seventeen trombones, three glockenspiels, nine tubas, fourteen drums and cymbals, and a bass
drum six feet in diameter that is reputed to be the largest in
the world. When the Associated Harvard Clubs held their
1928 convention in Philadelphia, they generously instructed
the band to buy itself a fine drum and to send them the bill.
The band took full advantage of this carte blanche. The
colossus it at length acquired from Ludwig & Ludwig, the
celebrated drum-making firm, cost $1,500, since it was en-
tirely handmade and each drumhead represented the seasoned skin of one whole cow. The drum is presently valued
at $9,000. It has become traditional for the partisans of
opposing teams to attempt to derail this mammoth before
it starts down the field mounted on four bicycle wheels, and
to prevent injury to the prize, the band takes the precaution

of having it chaperoned—successfully, most of the time—by
a small battalion of "jumpers," hefty undergraduates who are
known for their love of body contact.

In the Twenties the band's most notable brass instrument
was the baritone sax superintended by Johnny Green, who
later composed "Body and Soul," "Coquette," and other top
song hits. A finicky perfectionist who played alto sax, Green
believed there were too many altos in the band for correct
balance. He bought himself the baritone and lugged it
around uncomplainingly all season. The band now owns the
world's largest brass instrument, a bass tuba a good eight feet
high manufactured originally for John Philip Sousa by an
English locomotive company. Bill Reinhardt, who was
graduated in '47, mastered this super-tuba with the help of
two assistants, who held the horn up while he twisted himself into the mouthpiece.

Reinhardt also distinguished himself as the driving force
of The Hungry Five, one of the smaller outfits which have
from time to time been established by members of the band.
The Hungry Five is momentarily inactive but most of its
functions have been taken over by a twenty-five-piece band
subsidiary, the present edition of Schneider's Silver Cornet
Band—"available for parties, picnics, parades, weddings,
wakes, grape-crushings, and keg-tappings," as its business
card informs prospective clients. Schneider's was founded
near the beginning of the nineteenth century by Johann
Schneider, a Harvard professor whose need for a musical
outlet led him to organize a band which played Sunday concerts on Boston Common. The precise date Professor
Schneider formed his little combo is not known, but the
year 1807 has been fixed by the Harvard bandsmen who have
intermittently revived the band. This date of birth, by the
merest of coincidences, makes Schneider's exactly one year
the senior of the Pierian Sodality, a Harvard orchestral
group which was founded in 1808 and has always liked to

consider itself the oldest permanent American musical society. Schneider's specializes in old German-band versions of popular songs and will play at the drop of a beer can.

One September in the late Twenties when freshmen candidates were trying out, a veteran bandsman approached the leader in a somewhat agitated state. One of the flutists he was auditioning was a Chinese, he reported. He was wondering what to do, since he didn't know if the band took in Orientals. "Can he play?" the leader asked. He could and was in.

If the Harvard band has a policy, it is summed up in that fine, undeliberate phrase, "Can he play?" The band has always included a sizable percentage of graduates of the fashionable prep schools but the majority of bandsmen are boys who have entered college directly from high schools, which customarily place a larger store on proficiency with a band instrument. Freshmen candidates are tried out on (1) a march they are likely to have played before; (2) some Harvard song; (3) a march of reasonable difficulty they are not likely to have played before, to test their ability to sight-read; and (4) a concert number, to check their tone and intonation. This high level of musicianship is necessary because the Harvard band (unlike the bands at many midwestern colleges whose members practice a minimum of ten hours a week and receive academic credit) confines itself to a two-hour musical rehearsal on Wednesday evenings.

Practicing the drills is limited to another two hours. On Friday evenings the band assembles at one of the practice football fields adjacent to the stadium. After quickly describing each new formation, the drillmaster—let's say he is working on a "Wah Hoo Wah" for Dartmouth—calls out the number of bandsmen required for the "W" and the yard line he wants them to form on; next, the number of men needed for the "A" and their yard line; and so on down the word or design. On Saturdays, from twelve to two, the band rehearses at top speed, putting the music and maneuvers together. Usually there is time for only a quick smoke before heading into the stadium under a full head of "Our Director." The band marches at 135 steps to the minute, fifteen more steps to the minute than the standard infantry marching pace.

In the opinion of the incumbent manager, Frank Hopkins, the band's consistently high performance, despite this bare minimum of rehearsal, is due to its *esprit de corps.* "We make plenty of mistakes," Hopkins once told a beaming old grad. "If you were down at Princeton last year, you saw us smartly spell out '10,000 Mien of Harvard.' The wonder is we come off as well as we do. An hour before game time we're generally a complete hash. When the chips are down, though, something comes over the boys. The knowledge that we're the Harvard band—this is the only way I can explain it—seems to do for us what putting on a Yankee uniform does for a ballplayer. We've got a great reputation to live up to.

"In the pinch," Hopkins continued, "there's always Mal Holmes, our conductor. In '48, for example, we arrived at Cornell on Saturday morning after a bushing all-night bus trip. At the drill rehearsal we were dead on our feet. Nothing we did went right. Mal called for a break and pulled out a copy of that morning's *Cornell Sun* and read us a long, glowing article about the Cornell band—you know, how good they were and what wonders they were going to perform that afternoon. There was one line about us, the last line: 'The Harvard band is also expected to appear.' Mal read it with appropriate sarcasm and then dropped the paper to the ground sort of dramatically. We all let out a wild cheer of defiance. Our tiredness vanished immediately. We were damn good that afternoon."

Mal Holmes has been the Harvard band's resident Rockne for a dozen years now. Largely because of his light touch, rehearsals, which can easily degenerate into laborious sessions, are a constant pleasure. "This will have to come to a screeching halt," Holmes will remonstrate, for example, after squelching a particularly raucous passage. Presently the dean of the New England Conservatory of Music, Holmes was active in musical circles as an undergraduate but he did not join the band until he was in Harvard Business School, and then he was an emergency bass drummer. Accordingly, whenever the band is asked to describe Holmes, it is the custom to refer to him as "an inspiring American success story—a man who rose from second All-America drummer to leader of the Harvard band."

Holmes has, among other things, developed the semicircular "concert shell" from which the band plays its halftime specialties, and has instituted the practice of serenading the football team after every game, win, lose, or draw. However, his major contribution unquestionably has been in keeping the band intact at the close of the football season and continuing it as a full-fledged concert band able to handle Milhaud's "Suite Française" or Prokofiev's "Opus 99" as comfortably as "Boola Boola." Last season the band played seventeen concerts, ranging from a Commencement Eve appearance in the open-air Tercentenary Theatre in Harvard Yard to a command performance at the convention of the National Association of Manufacturers. Besides mailing along a check for $1,500, the N.A.M. transported the band to New York in four private pullman cars and put the boys up at the Waldorf-Astoria in exchange for a twenty-minute concert. Because of the unusual circumstances, the band decided to waive its traditional policy of not appearing with female talent and permitted five majorettes from Hempstead High to sling their batons in tempo with a rousing Harvard medley. This anti-feminist policy is purely professional. The bandsmen's dates sit with them at the games, march with them after the games, and some girls of rugged constitution travel with them on their bus trips to the away games.

On the occasion of the Harvard-Army game in 1949, Harvard bandsmen held the first college band reunion in history. A hundred band alumni poured into Cambridge. Fred Reynolds, who had founded the organization thirty autumns before, was back along with eight other charter members. A father and son combination returned: Karl Rohde, a dance orchestra leader who played trumpet in the 1919 band, and Karl, Jr., a trumpeter in the '46 edition. Leroy Anderson came up from New York to conduct "Wintergreen." Johnny Green was unable to arrange leave from his duties at M-G-M, but Bud Schur, an old cymbals star, flew in all the way from Los Angeles.

Mal Holmes led the combined undergraduate and alumni bands—250 pieces, including eleven glockenspiels, forty trumpets, thirty-two trombones, sixteen tubas, and twenty-two snare drums, four of them loaned by the band's trusty auxiliary, the Cambridge Fire Department. On the eve of the reunion, Holmes, assaying the wealth of brass at his disposal, had predicted, "It's a squad with depth. We should be able to employ both offensive and defensive glockenspiel. The show should be tremendous. In fact, it will probably sound like all the factories of the American Radiator Company in action at once." Harvard men thought it sounded perfect.

XCEED XPECTATIONS,
YELL YOURS,
ZIP ZIP:
THE STORY OF HAZEL
HOTCHKISS WIGHTMAN

This profile of Hazel Hotchkiss Wightman appeared in *The New Yorker* in the summer of 1952. Over the last decade Mrs. Wightman has grudgingly slowed down her pace a fraction, but hardly more than that. I had a letter from her this past winter in answer to one of mine asking what she had been up to lately, and I can think of nothing half as good to bring us up to date on Mrs. Wightman as to quote the central section of her letter.

"I did play in the National Senior Doubles last summer [1960] with Mrs. Mike Blanchard, who needed a partner at the eleventh hour. We won our first match and were easily defeated in the next. I had played very little for a month, but enjoyed it. I had only eight girls staying at my house during the week of the National Doubles, which was quite a change and very simple.

"I gave up my Saturday morning classes at Longwood this past winter and enjoy being not so tired these days. Two and three times a week youngsters come to my garage for instruction and sometimes eight or ten are there at a time. It is very pleasant and constructive, I find. I still captain the team on Monday mornings at the Red Cross canteen and the Friday morning Medical Center Lunch Shop team. Two other mornings I do a few hours a week of Red Cross sewing, and once a week I have an enjoyable ladies' doubles at tennis, where two of the players are considerably younger than my other friend and me. Now and then I get a few thirteen-year-olds on the court to run them around. I get a couple of bridge games in each week, too.

"I have a family reunion for a birthday or a visiting relative often. My life is not dull at all but not as active as it used to be since I am now seventy-four."

OF ALL THE TIGHT LITTLE WORLDS that have grown up around the popular sports of our age, the most civilized by far is the one inhabited by the people who play and follow lawn tennis. To the outsider's eye, this world appears to be an unruffled and exclusive Eden of green grass, multicolored umbrellas, crisp white duds, sunshine, good breeding, good manners, good bodies, fair enough minds, good English, and good credit at the bank. To its inhabitants, however, it can be a highly fractious and nerve-racking place, for the pressures brought on by competition, social or athletic, have made them extremely adept at the double-edged remark and the well-thrown tantrum. Cliques spring up like weeds, and it is the rare afternoon indeed when some new vendetta is not stirring uneasily on the terrace.

The comparative peace which has prevailed during the last quarter of a century in women's tennis, the Balkans of the tennis world, has been largely due to the good offices of Hazel Hotchkiss Wightman. A bouncy, warm, unpretentious accumulation of unnervous energy, Mrs. Wightman, who is now sixty-five, has reigned officially, if unregally and often invisibly, as the Queen Mother of American tennis since the inauguration in 1923 of the Wightman Cup matches between teams of women players representing the United States and England. As the friend, tutor, and housemother of two generations of girls who wanted desperately to play championship tennis, Mrs. Wightman has probably developed more players than any other dedicated amateur, given more lessons than most professionals, and, by way of example, won more national championships than any other player in the history of the sport. When she carried off her ninth Women's Veterans' Doubles Championship in 1950 in partnership with Mrs. Marjorie Gladman Buck, a slip of a girl of forty-one, it brought the number of Mrs. Wightman's national titles to forty-three. These include four United States Women's Singles Championships (1909, '10, '11, and '19), six Women's Doubles Championships (1909, '10, '11, '15, '24, and '28), six Mixed Doubles Championships (1909, '10, '11, '15, '18, and '20), two Indoor Women's Singles Championships (1919 and 1927), ten Indoor Women's Doubles Championships (1919, '21, '24, '27, '28, '29, '30, '31, '33, and '43), five Indoor Mixed Doubles Championships (1923, '24, '26, '27, and '28), and one Clay Court Mixed Doubles Championship in 1915. This is one of the few records of our times which seems to have a fair chance of surviving our national habit of record-breaking. "Hazel had brilliant footwork and the finest sense of anticipation I've ever seen on a court," R. Norris Williams, with whom Mrs. Wightman won the mixed doubles in 1924 Olympic Games, recently told a group discussing her astounding longevity. "To my way of thinking, though, her principal gift, the one that enabled her to win the indoor doubles with Pauline Betz in 1943—a full thirty-four years after she won her first national championship—is the way that woman can concentrate. We played our matches in the Olympics under the worst conditions imaginable. The French completed the courts at Colombes, outside of Paris, barely three days before the tournament began, so a fine spray of dust blew in our faces all week. The main stadium, where the track and field events were going on, directly adjoined the tennis courts, and there was no knowing when a pistol would suddenly go off or a national anthem blare forth or just some announcement bellowed and rebellowed in several languages. The officials running the tennis tournament allowed vendors to circulate all over the stadium and to hawk their oranges, bananas, and ice cream at the top of their lungs. On top of this, the officiating was really the poorest I have ever encountered. On several days only the umpire showed up and the line-judges had to be recruited from patrons in the stands. I was on edge the entire tournament, but nothing bothered Hazel, nothing at all. I don't think she even heard them selling those bananas."

Mrs. Wightman has lived in Boston since 1912 when she married George W. Wightman, a Bostonian who later became president of the United States Lawn Tennis Association. (They were divorced in 1940.) She has come to be regarded, along with Bunker Hill Monument and the Jordan Marsh Company, as one of the more durable features of the local landscape. A compact woman, she is just over five feet tall, and the stalwart contours of her chin, the dominant nose, the steady penetration of her gray-blue eyes, and the periphery of brisk white hair make her accommodatingly Bostonian in appearance. The qualities which have made her so able a Queen Mother, are, however, those of the nineteenth-century Californian. Mrs. Wightman, who was born of covered-wagon stock in the town of Healdsburg, sixty-five miles north of San Francisco, has the frontier woman's distaste for political and verbal maneuver, her sense of frustration in doing only one thing at a time, and her hopelessly grooved zeal for helping her neighbor. These cardinal attributes of the proper Healdsburgher, rare enough in the world at large, are almost the exact antithesis of those most often found in the microcosm of tennis. "She's been like a long, cool breath of fresh air in the hothouse," a former national women's champion said of Mrs. Wightman last spring. "She's not at all like the rest of us dames. You can't gossip about her. She's so completely old-fashioned that she thinks people can get along with each other. I don't know anybody

else who'd have dared to invite Helen Wills and Helen
Jacobs and their mothers to share the same roof at the same
time, but the four of them stayed with Mrs. Wightman
and they honestly enjoyed themselves."

The two sternest criticisms which are made of Mrs.
Wightman are comparatively fangless when the articulate-
ness of the tennis world is considered. Women who pride
themselves on their reputations as doubles players are seldom
reticent in insinuating that Mrs. Wightman's multiple triumphs in doubles depended to a large measure on the skill of
her partners. This is very true. Mrs. Wightman's partners
have included such players as Bill Tilden, Jean Borotra,
René Lacoste, R. Norris Williams, Helen Wills, Sarah
Palfrey, and Pauline Betz. The second criticism, which is
also not without grounds and which is usually hurled by
her exact contemporaries whose aspirations she fulfilled, is
that "Hazel has done entirely too much for tennis."

The divergence between the Queen Mother and the bulk
of the ladies and gentlemen of her court was never more
clearly illustrated than by the appearance in 1933 of Better
Tennis, a book which Mrs. Wightman wrote in short install-
ments in her auto while waiting to collect her five children
at their various schools. The usual autobiography of a tennis
champion is couched in a high-pitched tone of self-vindica-
tion, as if the writer felt obliged to answer charges that he
or she was entirely devoid of culture and had no connections
on a first-name basis with celebrities on every fashionable
continent. "After my fortunate victory at Wimbledon"—so
runs the S.O.P. for the tennis memoir—"much as I hated to
hurt Gus's feelings, I just had to tell Augustus John that the
portrait he wanted me to sit for would just have to wait until
I helicoptered back with the Aga Khan from St. Tropez.
There, after a small festival in good taste was thrown in my
honor, Aga and I played a moonlight match against our old
dauntless adversaries, Noel Coward and Haile Selassie. Noel

and Haile won the first set, 6–4, and then we changed courts, flying to Aga's private court in India for the second set." The autobiographical portion of *Better Tennis* is written in low-flying prose and drops only two names, John McCormack and Queen Victoria Eugenia of Spain. The section devoted to instruction is equally earth-bound. Mrs. Wightman does not advise the novice to hammer nails into a wall in order to develop the basic service stroke (as Mercer Beasley has advocated) or to tie a string to the center of the racket, hold the other end of the string firmly in the left hand, and then keep the string taut when sweeping through a forehand (Bunny Austen's sure-fire gimmick for shifting the weight correctly). Good old-fashioned practice, Mrs. Wightman repeats patiently, is the only method she has ever discovered for improving strokes, balance, and rhythm. The one corner of *Better Tennis* which possesses the traditional *personalismo* of tennis literature is an alphabet of alliterative maxims presented at the end of the book. Beginning with *Always Alert, Be Better,* and *Concentrate Constantly,* Mrs. Wightman barks out her tips, hurdling the difficult Q with *Quash Qualms,* subduing the treacherous U with *Umpire Usually,* and meeting the ultimate challenge with *Xceed Xpectations, Yell Yours,* and *Zip Zip.* On the court Mrs. Wightman is a chronic talk-it-upper, and the staccato delivery of these maxims forms a running obbligato during her practice sessions with her pupils. Mrs. Wightman is not slow with a compliment, but experience has strengthened her conviction that pampering explains the failure of so many young players to fulfill their promise, let alone *Xceed Xpectations.* At an early stage in the career of her protégée Sarah Palfrey, during a match in which Sarah was beginning to lose a comfortable lead, Sarah's mother turned to Mrs. Wightman and remarked worriedly that it was much too hot a day for her daughter to be playing tennis. "It's just as hot for the girl on the other side of the net," Mrs. Wightman answered.

"Sarah can win this match easily if she'll only *Quash Qualms.*"

During the last two decades, although no one else has noticed a diminuendo, Mrs. Wightman has been constantly fearful that she might be losing her old *Zip Zip.* One February weekend two winters ago when Wightman Cup business called her out of Boston, she entrusted her Saturday morning tennis class to Judy Atterbury, one of the best young players in New England, and was gigantically relieved to learn on her return that Miss Atterbury had become exhausted after the first half hour and had not been able to continue with the lesson. Mrs. Wightman has been conducting this winter-season Saturday class on the indoor linoleum courts of the Longwood Covered Courts Club in Chestnut Hill every winter since 1923. It is a fairly demanding workout. At seven forty-five the pupils begin arriving from Brookline, the sundry Newtons, and the less social suburbs of Boston. At eight o'clock, twenty to thirty girls of all degrees of co-ordination line up along the wall at the back of one of the courts. Mrs. Wightman takes up her position at the center of the base line across the net, and class commences. For three hours Mrs. Wightman sends over soft, arching lobs for her pupils to deal with with a forehand drive, a backhand drive, an overhead smash, a block volley, or whatever stroke is being emphasized at the moment, all the while keeping one eye on the ball and the other on each pupil's stroke and shouting a continuous chatter of individual and group instructions as she retrieves the scattered shots hit in her general direction and lobs the ball accurately back to the next girl in line. In the winter of 1949 Mrs. Wightman tore a ligament in her right upper arm in a fall from an icy step. Rather than cancel her class for three weeks, she decided to see if she could play well enough with her left hand to keep the class going and was elated when she discovered that she was adequately ambidextrous. Mrs. Wightman has placed one of her children's old playpens in the balcony overlooking the covered courts so that young mothers who can't afford sitters will not have to give up the game.

Mrs. Wightman's dedication to tennis makes it difficult to get her off a tennis court once she is on it. Two summers ago, Mrs. Edith Sullivan, a cohort of hers who was endeavoring to stir up interest in the game among a very untennisy set in Belmont, asked Mrs. Wightman to come out and give a strokes demonstration. Mrs. Wightman did this. She then played a set apiece with the two most advanced girls. Feeling that it would look unfair if she went away without at least rallying with the forty-odd other girls who had turned out, she gave each of them a brief individual lesson. "I don't know how she did it!" Mrs. Sullivan was exclaiming a short while ago. "It was a hot June day, a real broiler, and Mrs. Wightman stayed on the court for seven solid hours. She didn't even stop for lunch. Around two I handed her a tuna fish sandwich and she ate it out of one hand and kept right on playing with the other." Mrs. Wightman's obstinate refusal to slow down is a source not only of wonder but of mild irritation to the younger women who partner her in doubles competitions. In 1948 she invited Mrs. Marion Zinderstein Jessup, one of her first protégées, with whom she had won four National Indoor Doubles Championships between 1919 and 1927, to play with her in the National Veterans Doubles Championship. "It was really a thrilling experience," Mrs. Jessup has said of their reunion as a team and their subsequent victory. "Things didn't work out precisely the way I thought they would, though. In the old days Mrs. Wightman had carried the load, but almost a quarter of a century had gone by since we'd last played together, and I figured that though I wasn't any chicken, Mrs. Wightman still was twenty years older than I was. Naturally I thought that I'd be expected to serve first for us and play the backhand court—which is a little tougher than the forehand—

you know, generally shoulder the burden. When we walked
onto the court for our first match, Mrs. Wightman marched
right over to the backhand court. After we'd taken the first
game on our opponents' service, Mrs. Wightman waltzed to
the base line and waited for me to toss her the balls. Nothing
had changed. It was just as if we were back in 1919. I was
almost a spectator. A couple of times Mrs. Wightman did
run over to tell me how wonderful it was to be playing again
with someone who liked to storm the net, but outside of that
—1919."

To the outside or unsneakered world, Mrs. Wightman,
apart from her connection with the cup and the international matches that bear her name, is best known as the
teacher of champions. In the last thirty years there have been
few, if any, topflight American women players whose development has not been directly influenced by her. She met
Helen Wills in the summer of 1920 on one of the trips she
made biennially to California to visit her family and inspect
the tennis crop. Helen was fourteen when Mrs. Wightman,
cruising critically over the grounds of the Berkeley Tennis
Club, watched her belt a series of drives and went over and
introduced herself. During the remainder of her six-week
stay in Berkeley, Mrs. Wightman worked with Helen on her
two weakest points, her volley and her footwork, a regimen
they continued the following summer when Helen and her
mother came East as Mrs. Wightman's guests. Two years
later, in the summer of 1923, Helen won her first national
title, defeating Molla Bjurstedt Mallory, the sturdy Nor-
wegian with the Gallic temperament who had held the
championship almost without interruption since 1915. A
substantial measure of the credit for Helen's sure and rapid
rise belonged to "Pop" Fuller, the professional at the Berkeley Tennis Club, who had grounded her well, and the major
share, to be certain, belonged to Helen herself, a disciplined

if not an overdisciplined athlete. In Mrs. Mallory's excited opinion, however, Mrs. Wightman was wholly responsible for Helen's victory over her and had, in fact, been training Helen for that specific purpose. "There was no truth whatsoever in Molla's accusation," Mrs. Wightman once commented on this 1923 outburst of trouble in paradise. "I just tried to bring Helen along the way I try to help any player who wants my help. Helen would have become a champion without my coaching. I may have speeded up her development so that Helen's game reached a champion's pitch a year or so before she would have otherwise got there, but that was all."

Mrs. Wightman's close friendship with Helen Wills did not deter her from giving equal tutorial and personal attention to Helen Jacobs, another product of Berkeley, who became Helen Wills' bitter and abiding rival. Mrs. Wightman met the second Helen on her visit to California in 1923 and practiced with her three hours on Monday, Wednesday, and Friday mornings as long as she was there. "She was wonderful to work with, that girl," Mrs. Wightman has said of Helen Jacobs. "How that girl would listen to what you were trying to get across and how she'd concentrate on applying it! Helen Jacobs was the most responsive and, in a way, the most satisfying pupil I've ever taught." At one time, before it became apparent that the Wills-Jacobs feud was irreconcilable, Mrs. Wightman tried to get the two to play regular practice matches together, suggesting that these workouts would benefit both of their games. They tried it twice and then called it off to their mutual relief. Whenever the two Helens clashed in tournament play, Mrs. Wightman, despite her efforts to enter a temporary state of Buddhistic suspension of all feelings, found her sympathies torn between the two antagonists and invariably took a deep emotional beating.

Mrs. Wightman, who can detect a natural aptitude for

tennis as instantaneously as a Rodgers and Hammerstein
hero can spot his true love, discovered Sarah Palfrey in the
autumn of 1923 when Sarah was eleven. "Mr. Croker—he
was the professional at Longwood then—told me to be sure
and come down to the courts on Saturday," she recently told
a friend, "and he'd show me the finest young prospect I'd
even seen. He was really crowing. On the Saturday I went to
the club and watched Mr. Croker giving a lesson to a very
graceful young girl, about thirteen. After the lesson Mr.
Croker came over with a smile a mile wide on his face and
asked me what I thought of his prize. I said that she seemed
to have all the earmarks of a first-class player, and then I told
him, 'There's a better player here you've missed. Take a look
at that little thing on number three court. That's the one *I*
want.' Mr. Croker's pupil was Mianne Palfrey, one of Sarah's
four sisters, and I, of course, had Sarah."

Under Mrs. Wightman's tutelage Sarah became the number four player in the national rankings in 1929 when she was
seventeen, but she never succeeded in winning the championship until 1941 when her husband, Elwood Cooke, helped
her, as Sarah saw it, to correct a deficient backhand. "Her
backhand was always a good stroke, I thought," Mrs. Wightman told an old Longwood hand who had asked her analysis
of Sarah's long-overdue arrival at the top. "I don't think Elwood gave Sarah a new backhand. He gave her a confidence
she never had before in tight matches against the big guns.
That's all Sarah ever needed."

An unplanned but felicitous by-product of Mrs. Wightman's coaching activities is the abundant supply she has always had of splendid women's doubles partners. She and
Sarah took five National Indoor Doubles Championships.
The team of Wills and Wightman won two Wightman Cup
matches, two United States Championships, the Olympic
tournament of 1924, and one All-England Championship at
Wimbledon. They were never defeated. In reminiscing about

their campaigns, Helen customarily refers to herself as the assiduous young lieutenant and to Mrs. Wightman as the cool and equable general, a not inaccurate description of their relationship. Mrs. Wightman established the tactics for the team and punctuated their matches with commanding cries of "Yours," "Up now," and "Run, Helen." The last phrase cut so sharply and so repeatedly through the polite stillness of the air at Wimbledon that the English made it a part of their tennis folklore and it continues to be shouted today, if with less imperativeness, at innumerable Cynthias, Daphnes, and other slow freight of all nomenclature.

Mrs. Wightman is aware that earning a living is as important for professional tennis coaches as developing good players is for her personal equation, and she restrains herself accordingly from muscling in on their territory. She has done so, nevertheless, on several occasions when she has been convinced that an improper mental attitude, as opposed to any technical flaw, was the reason somebody else's pupil was unable to play up to her full potential. In the case of Alice Marble, the results justified the intervention. The next great Californian to follow the two Helens, Alice experienced little difficulty in winning our championships in the late Thirties but was prone to mystifying lapses of form, particularly at Wimbledon, and was regularly defeated by players she should have outclassed. Alice was the pupil of Eleanor "Teach" Tennant, an extremely talented coach from Los Angeles. Never averse to publicity, Miss Tennant did not discourage Alice from indulging in a set of court mannerisms associated usually with Tilden and other self-consciously theatrical stars. "There was no question that the galleries ate it up when they saw an attractive girl like Alice kick the ball after a bad shot or whack it into the backstop," Mrs. Wightman has said of the touches of golden California temperament Alice injected into her matches, "but that's exactly where Alice was going wrong. She was thinking too much of the impression those displays were making on the galleries, and it was hurting her tennis." Mrs. Wightman checked herself from offering her advice until Alice approached her in a very disconsolate mood after she had been ousted by Helen Jacobs, 6–4, 6–4, in the semifinal round of the 1938 Wimbledon championship. She asked Mrs. Wightman why she thought she had lost the match. "You lost it in the eighth game of the first set," Mrs. Wightman replied. "You lost it when you began dramatizing yourself all over the court after you netted that drive, Alice—you know the one I mean. You were playing just as well as Helen. Let's see, you were behind 3–4 in games and you had 40–30 on your service, one point from tieing it up. Then you netted that drive. You slipped on the shot and fell down, right? What did you do then? I'll tell you. You didn't brush off your shorts and get back into the match. No, you patted your fanny and you got a nice ripple of laughter from the gallery. So you continued to pat your fanny, and while you were amusing everyone, you netted two more simple shots and tossed Helen the set. Your mind wasn't on your tennis. It took you *two full games* before you got back to business, and after that you never caught up. Even a girl with your natural equipment can't win if she allows *anything* to break her concentration." ("She took it very well," Mrs. Wightman once remarked of her talk with Alice, "a lot better than 'Teach' did when she got word that I was tampering with her pupil. I don't think 'Teach' minded it, though, when Alice finally broke through at Wimbledon the next year.") Mrs. Wightman likes her girls to move with vigor, hit with force, and fight hard for victory, but to her way of thinking there is a definite line between feminine athletic prowess and theatrical manners. Her ideal personality, she told a tennis historian who had asked her to create a composite colossa, would have Helen Wills' concentration, Alice Marble's dash, Sarah Palfrey's grace, Louise Brough's determination, Margaret du Pont's innate sportsmanship, and Didi Vlasto's looks. "I think I'd throw in Suzanne Lenglen's shots," Mrs. Wightman added. "They might come in handy if she was having an off-day."

One of the more beneficent arrangements of Providence, in Mrs. Wightman's opinion, is that any person with adequate co-ordination can become a respectable tennis player. The knowledge that she possesses an exceptional gift for transmitting a sense of tennis and a love of tennis fills her with a feeling of massive responsibility, for she firmly believes that a competent tennis game not only insures its owner innumerable hours of pleasure but, especially in the case of young girls, can often mean the difference between a frustrated life and a full one. "Whenever I give a demonstration at a girls' school and the girls gather around," she remarked at an informal tennis luncheon last summer, "the first thing that catches my eye is the grace of this girl, the fresh good looks of that one, someone else's unforced charm. That's only natural, I suppose. The second thing I notice— you feel it as much as see it—is the large number of awkward girls and shy girls. 'Now if I can only get these girls interested in tennis,' I say to myself, 'I'll be giving them something.' I've seen it happen a thousand times. To start to get confidence in herself, a girl who isn't attractive, or who doesn't think she's attractive, has to do something well that other people admire. A good tennis game can do that. It gives her a chance to meet other young people, to associate with boys on an easy, friendly level. Then she begins to get around and acquire a little poise and, before you know it, she's beginning to express herself spontaneously. Tennis can open a whole new world for those girls."

Following up this reasoning, Mrs. Wightman spends an average of twelve hours a week visiting colleges, preparatory and high schools, clubs, camps, and churches that have invited her to talk about tennis or put on a demonstration. When she was in England in 1946 with the Wightman Cup team, the tennis reporter for the *London Daily Express* mentioned in one of his columns that Mrs. Wightman had never been known to turn down a reasonable request for a personal appearance. The next morning and each ensuing morning, her box at the Dorchester Hotel was crammed with letters from the principals of Putney High School, Beckenham County Grammar School, Queenswood, and other girls' schools asking if the story were true and, if it was, when she could come out and see their girls. Mrs. Wightman was unable to fill all these requests but rearranged her schedule so that each morning she could dash to a different school, present an abbreviated demonstration, and whistle back to Wimbledon in time to assume her duties as captain of the Wightman Cup team.

Mrs. Wightman's confidence in the transformation that tennis can work for ugly ducklings does not preclude her from personally giving the process a helping hand. At the Massachusetts State Girls Championships, which she administers at the Longwood Cricket Club every year, she is frequently jarred by a girl's apparent neglect of her appearance. "You ought to work on your posture," she will inform one girl. "And when you get home, you tell your mother to buy you a blouse like the one Barbara's got on." "The next time I see you," she will inform another, "I want to see your hair looking neater. You get yourself some bobby pins. You don't want to look like you've just been struck by a tornado." When the tournament is on, Mrs. Wightman sets up her table and chair at a shady vantage point from which she can watch the play on as many as fourteen courts and keep an eye on all the players. Her tips on the better appearance, delivered in a joshing tone devoid of the threads of maternal concern, are part of the elliptical conversations that take place at the table as the players report the results of their matches and Mrs. Wightman enters the scores on the tournament sheet, introduces opponents, forms doubles teams, doles out cookies, assigns courts, and tries to dispel the nervousness of contestants who are gingerly poking their toes in tournament water for the first time. Her method for dealing with players who have been defeated is to get them occupied before they have time to feel sorry for themselves. "That wasn't a bad showing at all, Janet," she will say to a loser who has just stammered the tragic result and is trying to disappear behind the handle of her racket. "You go into the consolation round now, don't you? Let me see who you play . . . you play Esther McGrath. She's that auburn-haired girl with the green sweater over there. Got it? You'll have a good match with her. Now as soon as number eleven is clear, you and Esther take that court." Winners need no comparable therapy, but whenever Mrs. Wightman uncovers a prospect who looks as if she will go a long way, she is careful to acquaint her, in small oblique doses, with the code of the champion. In Mrs. Wightman's books, a champion, since she serves as a model for thousands of impressionable girls, has many responsibilities above and beyond performing with excellence. Her conduct must be exemplary in all respects, and this includes not confusing the tennis court with the stage and making too striking an appearance. This past season a contingent of fifteen-year-olds asked Mrs. Wightman what she thought of the black shorts which Gussie Moran, the game's current glamour girl, had worn in a tournament in Cairo. "I don't think there was really any need for it," Mrs. Wightman replied. "Didn't Gussie say that she had to wear those black shorts in the semifinals because she had only one pair of whites and was saving them for the final? Well, there was no reason in the world why she couldn't have worn the whites in the semifinals, washed and ironed them after the match, and had them ready for the next day."

One champion who possibly took the code a little too seriously was Helen Wills, and Mrs. Wightman is among the few people who could get along with her comfortably. In the company of Mrs. Wightman, Helen shed her poker face and the monarchical measure of her words and gestures, and relaxed. On occasions she was hardly recognizable as the same girl whose life was so chained to the conservation of a pure schedule and the safeguarding of her physical resources that she had balked at visiting the battlefield at Waterloo one morning for fear that she would not be at her best for an unimportant exhibition in Brussels that afternoon. Mrs. Wightman's secret for bringing out Helen's lurking humanity was to treat her as an unqueenly and imperfect human being. "I think Helen took it from me," Mrs. Wightman was saying a few months ago, "because I had met her when she was just a young girl, before she began to cover up from the spotlight and developed that protective layer. Helen was really an unconfident and awkward girl—you have no idea how awkward. I remember one morning—it must have been in the summer of 1922, because we were at Bass Rocks and I had just had my daughter Dorothy—Helen came banging down the stairs violently enough to shake the whole house apart. I asked her to go upstairs and come down again, and this time to walk with rhythm and ease and lightness. It was almost as bad as the first time—not quite. 'You try that once more,' I told her, 'and this time, lay those nine-double-A's of yours down with just a suspicion of femininity.' She came down pretty well that time. You see, where I differed from most of the tennis crowd was that I thought of Helen as an honestly shy person who was bewildered by how difficult it was to please most people. For example, at Maidstone, I think it was, Helen was criticized for not attending the luncheons at the club like the other players. When this was brought to her attention, she explained that she wasn't trying to be snooty but that she always liked to eat promptly at twelve if she had a match at two and, furthermore, that she always ate the same lunch, a lamb chop, green peas, a baked potato, and a scoop of ice cream. So they arranged for Helen to have this menu at the luncheon, and then everyone criticized her for having to have special food of her own. I never found the slightest fault with Helen's behavior on the court. In tennis, after all, the idea is to win your matches as efficiently and as swiftly as you can, not to win a popularity contest. I wasn't at Forest Hills in 1933 when Helen walked off the court in the third set of her match with Helen Jacobs. How often I wish I had been! I listened to the broadcast of that match at home, and from the very beginning I had the weirdest sensation: I knew positively that something was wrong with Helen, that she was worried about her back injury and was afraid, deathly afraid, of falling and injuring herself permanently. I don't think that girl really knew what she was doing when she walked off that court or, for that matter, at any time during the match."

A fairly large number of the younger inhabitants of the tennis world, having listened to the veranda-bound old-timers at their club reviewing the innovations that Mrs. Wightman brought into play in '06 and '09, have picked up the idea that there was no tennis before Mrs. Wightman arrived on the scene. This is an understandable error but an error nonetheless. Hazel Hotchkiss Wightman was born in Healdsburg, California, in 1886, five years after the United States Lawn Tennis Association was founded, eleven years after the All-England Lawn Tennis and Croquet Club laid out its first court at Wimbledon, and thirteen years after Major Walter C. Wingfield, a retired British Army officer, worked out a primitive form of lawn tennis to serve the same Victorian garden-party functions as croquet and bequeathed to his baby the happily short-lived name of Phairistiké. Both sets of Mrs. Wightman's grandparents made the transcontinental journey to California, though their modes of travel differed. Benoni Hotchkiss, her paternal grandfather, was living in Campbellsville, Kentucky, when he decided on the spur of the moment, in the spring of 1850, to join a covered-wagon caravan that was passing through the village and looking for one more wagon to complete the train. William Grove, her mother's father and a native of Staunton, Virginia, transported his family West after the Civil War under slightly plusher conditions. The Groves journeyed by rail most of the way and carried all their belongings with them, including the old square piano. The Hotchkisses and the Groves settled on adjoining ranches along the Russian River in the Sonoma Valley, and in the best Harold Bell Wright tradition one of the Hotchkiss boys, William Joseph, conducted a successful open-air courtship of one of the Grove girls, Emma Lucretia. They purchased a 1,500-acre ranch and proceeded to raise a family in an orderly manner. Hazel, their one daughter, was six years younger than Miller, four younger than Homer, two younger than Marius, and two years older than Linville.

Mr. Hotchkiss was a large, amiable, casual man who got things done. Starting as a grower of grapes, apples, alfalfa, and spinach, he became, successively, a member of a combine of farmers who decided to can their own products, the inventor of the Hotchkiss Glass Jar Label—the first label to depict graphically and in color the fruits and vegetables within the tin—and, eventually, one of the founders of the Central California Canning Company which put out the Del Monte brand of canned goods. Mrs. Wightman's vigor and staying power stem from her mother's side of the family. When Mrs. Hotchkiss was in her sixties, she was the victim of a freak automobile accident. She had parked her electric auto on an incline and was walking away when the brake slipped and the heavy auto rolled over her left foot before she could get out of the way. Mrs. Hotchkiss stayed on her feet and managed to yank the door open and pull the brake on the runaway before she collapsed in great pain. A Christian Science reader read to her several hours that evening. The next morning she was up and bustling around the house as if nothing had happened.

The drive to compensate for some early physical disability, most acutely observable in the number of crack sprinters whose legs were injured in childhood accidents, would seem to account for a high percentage of our champion athletes. Hazel Hotchkiss, in any event, was an extremely frail child, so subject to headaches that she could not attend school regularly. On the advice of the family doctor, her parents encouraged her to spend as many hours as possible outdoors, and her brothers were instructed to include her in their games. Hazel developed into a fair pole vaulter and halfback and a stylish baseball player. In 1900, shortly after Mr. Hotchkiss had moved his business offices to San Francisco and his family to Berkeley, a commutable distance across San Francisco Bay, the two middle boys, Homer and Marius, took up tennis and captured a local tournament the first year they played the game. In an effort to interest their sister in tennis, a suitable sport for a young lady, her brothers took her to San Rafael in the summer of 1902 to watch the Pacific Coast Championships. Hazel fell in love with tennis at her first sight of good tennis. "The feature match was the final between two of the famous Sutton sisters, Ethel and May, and they were mighty impressive," Mrs. Wightman has said of that portentous day. "Both of them had fine forcing forehands, and May particularly could soak that ball. But what caught my fancy even more than the Suttons was the doubles match put on by the Hardy brothers, Sam and Sumner. They'd been in a class by themselves on the Pacific Coast for eight or nine years, and they were a skillful team. The way girls played singles in those days, there was no net game at all. They didn't budge from the base line. The ball passed over the net as many as fifty times in a single rally before someone made an error or finally won the point on a placement. Doubles like Sam and Sumner Hardy played it—now that appealed to me. They were awfully quick up at net, and even a greenhorn like myself could appreciate the precision with which they volleyed and smashed and their split-second maneuvers for drawing their opponents out of position and setting up their openings. I decided that afternoon that I'd go in for tennis and model my game on the Hardys'." As it turned out, the graveled back yard behind the Hotchkiss' home, where Hazel and her brothers did the bulk of their practicing since there was only one court in Berkeley, compelled them to play like the Hardys. The bounces off the gravel were so erratic that the ball had to be volleyed—that is, played before it struck the ground. It was all net play, and since the net was simply a rope strung between the house and a cluster of rosebushes, the players soon learned that if they wanted to avoid a fine patina of black-and-blue welts, they had to get their rackets in front of every ball hit at them. The brilliant anticipatory sense that later characterized Mrs. Wightman's game—and excited Wallis Myers, the English critic, to rank her alongside Suzanne Lenglen in that rare company of players whose racket seemed to attract the ball —was born in self-defense on the graveled back yard at 2985 Claremont Avenue.

Berkeley's one tennis court at the turn of the century was an asphalt one belonging to the University of California. The court was open to the public, but girls were not allowed to play on it after eight in the morning. In order to bypass this regulation, Hazel and her brothers rose daily at five. A friend of Homer's, who made the fourth for doubles, would awaken him by jerking a string that was wound around Homer's big toe and which ran out the window and down the side of the house. Homer would then rouse Marius and Hazel. They would grab an apple from the kitchen for breakfast and eat it as they trotted the mile to the court in the ocher light of dawn. These workouts came to an end at six-thirty when Hazel returned home to practice the piano for an hour before heading for classes at Berkeley High School. Whenever Hazel could find no one to rally with on the gravel, she worked on her strokes by banging a ball against the wall of the Hotchkiss house, evolving increasingly complex patterns during these drills—forehand-backhand, two forehands-two backhands, three forehands-one backhand, and so on. She has always contended that solo practice against a bangboard, no matter how rude, can be the making of a tennis player. When she visits the homes of her friends, she constantly baffles them by complimenting them on their garage and driveway. "I don't think you realize how lucky you are, Grace!" she will exclaim in a burst of exuberance that most women reserve for a spacious drawing room perfectly appointed down to the last nonpopular Dufy. "Look at the concrete on this driveway! Beautiful. And those lovely wide garage doors! I bet they give you a very true bounce. Grace, I envy you. You have the perfect place to practice." In 1947 Mrs. Wightman presented the Longwood Cricket Club with a new bangboard. The one stipulation she made was that the new board be positioned close by the clubhouse, since she believes that boys and girls are less reluctant to undertake the drabness of practice if they know their industry is being observed. The position of the new bangboard also works out nicely when Mrs. Wightman wants to play some tennis and simultaneously to see to it that her grandchildren and other beginners, lined up at the board, are getting an equal opportunity to use it. Even when she is engaged in a sharp match on a nearby court and apparently totally absorbed in it, she periodically hurls a cry of "Change" in the general direction of the bangboard. At this signal, the youngster who has been whaling away at the board instantly gives way to the next practicer.

In December, 1902, six months after she had taken up tennis, Hazel Hotchkiss entered her first tournament, the

Bay Counties Women's Doubles Championship, sponsored by the San Francisco Park Department. On the ferry across the bay, she ran into a girl named Mary Radcliffe and learned that she also was going to play in the tournament. Mary, like herself, was waiting to be assigned a doubles partner by the tournament committee. The two girls decided to team up, and although neither had previously seen the other play, they went on to win the championship without the loss of a set. It was an historic day in women's tennis because of the revolutionary tactics that Hazel Hotchkiss introduced. Standing a yard and a half from the net when her partner served, she intercepted the majority of their opponents' drives and volleyed them for winners. She rushed forward during rallies whenever a short return provided that opening, and she stayed poised at the net instead of retreating to backcourt. She followed in after her better serves, just like the Hardy brothers and her brothers did, to volley the return. These measures thoroughly demoralized her opponents, who had been brought up to think that woman's place was the base line. After Mrs. Wightman had showed the way, other women, notably Mary K. Browne, Eleonora Sears, and Elizabeth Ryan, learned to play net, and the emancipation of the woman from the backcourt was definitely under way.

Following this satisfactory debut, Hazel Hotchkiss quickly established herself as the girl to beat in the local tournaments. Her game continued to improve, largely because of the unrelenting criticism of her brothers. "The favorite adjective young people used in those days to express displeasure was 'rotten,' and, believe me, I heard it a lot," she recently told a friend. In doubles, Hazel was unapproachable; she could win with any partner. In singles she was a degree less formidable. Her service was well placed but not too hard to handle. Her ground strokes—when the ball is played after the bounce—were chopped and, as a result, not true attacking weapons. "If Hazel had stayed on the base line, she would have been absolutely overpowered by a player with first-class drives," Mrs. William MacKenzie Kalt, for many years the chairman of the Women's Ranking Committee of the U.S.L.T.A., has said. "Hazel, however, was smart enough to realize that she couldn't live on the base line. She had to get to net to win, and she knew it. She couldn't get up there behind a forcing service or drive, the way most players do it today, because she didn't have those shots. Here's how she got there. Two moves. First, after she had chopped a backhand or forehand deep into her opponent's court, she could get as far up as mid-court, about halfway between the base line and the net. That's no man's land for a tennis player. You're easily passed down the side lines, and most of the balls you get there land at your feet. You're lucky if you can play a strong defensive shot. Now what Hazel could do, and she *alone* among the women could do it because she could volley and half-volley like nobody's business, was to turn mid-court from a wretched defensive position into a very comfortable offensive position. Then, mind you, after she had made her volley or half-volley at mid-court, *then* she could get all the way to net and put the ball away with an angled smash."

To expose the deficiencies in Hazel Hotchkiss' singles game, a girl had to be a hard and accurate hitter, and there were no players of that caliber in the San Francisco area. When she continued to clean up all comers in tournament after tournament, the Northern Californian tennis fans began to speculate hopefully as to whether or not they had finally produced a player who could put Southern California, already its infamous rival, in its proper place by defeating all or one of the remarkable Sutton sisters.

There were five Sutton sisters in all, the daughters of an English naval captain who had transplanted his family from Plymouth to Pasadena after his retirement. Adele, the oldest, didn't care much for tennis, but Ethel, Violet, Florence, and

May, who followed in that order, spent their childhood on the family court. The Suttons began to emerge around 1900 and soon dominated the tournaments they elected to enter with such unchallenged finality that even people who didn't follow tennis kept abreast of their deeds and enjoyed invoking the popular slogan, "It takes a Sutton to beat a Sutton." By 1904 Hazel Hotchkiss had widened her tournament orbit so that it took in Del Monte, Colorado Springs, and other Californian oases where the Suttons competed. Hazel absorbed several good lacings before she defeated her first Sutton, Ethel, in the 1906 Pacific Coast Championships at San Rafael. Shortly after this, she overhauled Violet and Florence. May, the youngest Sutton, was a different proposition. A year younger than Hazel, stocky, square-shouldered, and with the uncomplicated belligerence of a bulldog, May was *the* Sutton. She had gone East in 1904 to see what the National Championships were like and had won without exerting herself. She never chose to appear in the Nationals again during her heyday. In 1905, however, she invaded England and became the first American girl to win at Wimbledon when she outlasted the top-ranking English star, Dorothea Douglass. Miss Douglass turned the tables on May in the Wimbledon final the next summer, but in 1907 May regained that championship, again defeating Miss Douglass. That satisfied May and she never went back. May's great stroke was her forehand drive. In the opinion of several tennis experts, the outstanding forehands of later periods— those of Molla Mallory, Helen Wills, Maureen Connolly, and May's own daughter, Dorothy Bundy—never touched May's. She used an extreme Western grip, the racket held so that the knuckles faced the ground. (In the Eastern grip, which Mrs. Wightman fell into naturally, the player more or less shakes hands with the racket.) May struck the ball low in its bounce, the racket face almost parallel with the ground, and imparted a terrific top spin to the ball. "She not only socked the ball with speed and pace but she could put it on a dime," Mrs. Wightman once commented. "I was standing near May one afternoon when a reporter asked her how she managed to put the ball in the corners time after time. She told him it was easy, that the lines on the court seemed to stand upright, like fences."

In her first matches against May Sutton, the base-liner, Hazel Hotchkiss, the volleyer, gave herself, her brothers, and Northern California little to cheer about. May polished her off with the average loss of five games in two sets, blasting away with her forehand with such severity that Hazel had few opportunities to move up to mid-court. Gradually, however, Hazel began to take more and more games, and in one of their meetings early in 1910, though she ultimately lost the third and deciding set, she did succeed in taking a set from May, something no American girl other than a Sutton had ever done. There were four principal reasons, as the duel progressed, why Hazel was able to keep closing the gap and to make it very warm for May. She learned to become less disturbed by May's unsettling swagger and her knack of inciting the galleries with her love of battle. She found she could cope somewhat better with May's forehand by watching the direction of May's racket head the instant before impact—undoubtedly the root of Mrs. Wightman's theory that anticipation is vision put to use. She perfected her smash during long practice sessions with Maurice McLaughlin, a fellow Northern Californian, who became the first men's national champion produced in the West and was renowned for the unprecedented velocity of his serve and overhead. (Their training routine was calculated to give them the confidence to smash for winners not only at net but from all positions on the court; the first hour McLaughlin would feed Hazel lob after lob to put away, the second hour she would feed him, and so on.) Above all, she kept hammering away at May's relatively negative backhand. There are some vet-

eran tennis fans who think that Mrs. Wightman's years of
furious concentration on breaking down May Sutton's backhand left such an indelible mark on her that ever after she
automatically played everyone's backhand and thirty years
later was indoctrinating her pupils to do the same even if
their opponent's backhand was as impregnable and her forehand as unsteady as Helen Jacobs'.

The Sutton-Hotchkiss rivalry, which had been gathering
steam as the matches became closer, erupted into a fiery,
full-fledged sectional feud in 1910, when Hazel was twenty-
three and May twenty-two. That spring Hazel finally made
it, beating May in the Ojai Valley tournament. The scores
were 2–6, 6–4, 6–0, and May offered no handshake at the
conclusion of the match. They faced each other six months
later in the final of the Pacific Coast Championship at Del
Monte. May took the first set 7–5 by running around her
backhand. Hazel fought back to take the second at 6–4 with
a mixture of drop shots and smashes. Feeling that she had
May on the run, she was waiting on the base line, eager to
get on with the crucial third set, when May sauntered off the
court without a word, announced regally to the umpire that
she felt like a cup of tea, deposited herself in a wicker chair,
and sat in silence until a waiter appeared from the hotel
carrying her tea on a tray. Twenty minutes later, May was
ready to resume play, and she pulled out the final set, 6–4.
After this controversial episode—the Southern Californians
considered it the resourcefulness of a true champion, the
Northern Californians shocking sportsmanship—there was
seldom an empty seat in the stands when the two rivals
clashed, and their partisans traveled hundreds of miles to
cheer them on. Over 2,000 fans, a whopping crowd for those
days, coaxed their Pope-Hartfords and Hupmobiles up the
scabrous incline that twisted to the top of Mt. Washington,
California, when their champions met in the final of the invitational tourney staged by the Mt. Washington Hotel.

The officials, who had expected to lead the two finalists onto the court with genial dignity, were unable to elbow a passage through the overflow crowd, and the Misses Hotchkiss and Sutton had to be guided to the rear of the grandstand and boosted through a hole hurriedly cut in the wire netting. This match, and the others they fought, began in an atmosphere vaguely resembling the tinkling teatime correctness Major Wingfield had in mind for lawn tennis, but after the first minutes the opposing camps would warm up and see which could outdo the other in continuous exhortation. "Come on, come on, you Berkeley girl" was the standard cry of the Northerners. The Southerners, always a shade more flamboyant, favored "Smash her, May." At Mt. Washington, May produced her most magnificent tennis and triumphed in straight sets without the benefit of tea.

In this strong and colorful rivalry, which continued without diminution of ardor until 1912, when Hazel Hotchkiss married and moved East, the real winner was California. Hitherto the state had exhibited a patchy and rather casual concern for tennis, but the dramatic overtones of the Hotchkiss-Sutton series created in both the upper and lower sectors of the state a profound tennis-consciousness that California has never lost.

In the fall of 1908, just before this synonymity of California and tennis was established, a delegation of crack Atlantic seaboard stars, including Irving Wright, Nat Niles, and Wallace Johnson, and shepherded by the veteran Boston sportsman, George Wright, toured the West Coast with the purpose of promoting interest in tennis, a coals-to-Newcastle mission of the first scuttle. Hazel Hotchkiss was then three-quarters of the way through her conquest of the Sutton sisters, but the news of her rise had not filtered back to the East, and the unbriefed visitors were doubly impressed by her revolutionary all-court style of play. After several talks with Mr. Hotchkiss, they persuaded him to bring his daughter East the following summer to play in the National Championships. In June, when Hazel had completed her sophomore year at the University of California, she and her father crossed the country to the Philadelphia Country Club where the women's singles, women's doubles, and mixed doubles championships were traditionally held. Hazel idled away the hours on the train by cross-stitching the design on six towels she was fashioning into Christmas presents.

It was a successful trip. Hazel won the mixed doubles with Johnson and the women's doubles with Edith Rotch of Boston. She completed her sweep of the three titles, the first player to do so, by defeating the titleholder, Mrs. Maud Barger-Wallach of Newport, in the singles. Until 1919 the defending champion did not have to play through the early rounds; she stood by as the aspirants to her title battled it out in an elimination tournament, called the All-Comers, to determine who would play the champ in the Challenge Round—roughly the same structure that obtains today in Davis Cup competition. Mrs. Barger-Wallach, a fragile artist in her thirties, had been in poor health, and she was not sure up to the last moment whether or not she would attempt to defend her title. She at length decided she would and, with her trained nurse seated in the grandstand in the event of emergency, took to the court dressed in a wide-brimmed garden hat and a flowing white gown that gave her the appearance of a displaced Renoir. It was no contest. Miss Hotchkiss ran through the first set in ten minutes with the loss of only seven points. Halfway through the second set, which was following the same pattern of an orderly rout, Hazel abruptly stopped playing Mrs. Barger-Wallach's nonexistent backhand. She also stopped coming to net. From that point on until the end of the set, which Hazel won 6–1, she fed Mrs. Barger-Wallach's forehand, and in the long and pleasant rallies which ensued, Mrs. Barger-Wallach, who had looked like no tennis player at all, played creditable forehand tennis. She walked off the court an unhumiliated ex-champion. The new champion boarded a train for San Francisco an hour after the presentation of the cups and cross-stitched six more towels on the long journey home. "I don't think that Hazel's courtesy towards Mrs. Barger-Wallach was lost on many of us who saw her on that first trip East," a venerable U.S.L.T.A. official was recollecting not long ago. "Of course, it was her overhead that we talked about the most. Remember, none of us had ever seen a girl who could wallop a smash like a man. Until Hazel came along, you know, mixed doubles had been quite an ordeal for the female half of the team. The men gallantly directed their fire at the female on the opposing team whenever they needed to clinch an important point. The men took all the putaway shots, and a number of them, notably Raymond Little and Bill Tilden's older brother, Herbert—they took everything. Hazel restored a balance to mixed doubles. It was very enjoyable, I must admit, watching this unassuming girl from California smash the ball plumb at the feet of our celebrated court-hogs."

Hazel Hotchkiss successfully defended her three titles in 1910 and again in 1911, a season in which everything went right for her and which is recognized as the high point of the "Hazel Era" of American tennis. Recurrent showers during the week of the championships threw the schedule out of kilter, and the three finals had to be squeezed into one afternoon. Hazel first took to the court at three o'clock for the singles final against Florence Sutton. With the sets at one all, Hazel was trailing 6–5 in games and 40–30 on Florence's service, one point from defeat, when she killed a deep lob, drew up to deuce, pulled the game out of the fire, and went on to win the set and the match, 8–10, 6–1, 9–7. The final of the mixed doubles followed immediately; Hazel and Wallace Johnson took this, 6–4, 6–4. A sudden squall

forced her to sit down and rest until the court dried out, but
at six o'clock she was back in action in the women's doubles
final, which she and Eleonora Sears, the original Boston
glamour girl, won by the scores of 6–4, 4–6, 6–2. Between
three o'clock and seven forty-two, the triple champion played
eighty-nine games, a feat the more remarkable when one
considers that the women players lugged around several
layers of undergarments beneath their starched linen shirts
and ankle-length white duck skirts. Hazel Hotchkiss was a
conventional dresser for the most part, but she did introduce
at Philadelphia the sleeveless blouse which was applauded
in avant-garde circles as a "common-sense outfit."

As her college graduation present, Mr. Hotchkiss allowed
Hazel to stay East for four months after the 1911 champion-
ships. She made the tour of the summer circuit, winning the
Western Pennsylvania Championship in Pittsburgh; the
Middle States Championship at Orange, New Jersey; the
Western at Chicago; the Metropolitan in New York; and the
tournaments at Niagara-On-The-Lake, Newport, and Long-
wood. On the turf courts of the Queen's Royal Hotel at
Niagara-On-The-Lake, Hazel and her old antagonist, May
Sutton, came up against each other again in the final, their
first meeting outside of California and their first on grass.
May marched through the first set, 6–0, as if Hazel were Mrs.
Barger-Wallach. She reeled off three more games in the
second set, dropped a game on her own errors, and then
picked up two more to lead 5–1. "I couldn't do anything
against her," Mrs. Wightman was calmly recalling this April.
"Nothing I tried worked, and May was playing beautiful
tennis. Then, all of a sudden, the thought struck me that I
wasn't making enough allowance, any allowance, for the
heaviness of the ball. It had been drizzling on and off, and
any dummy should have known that the balls would soak
up the moisture. I tried to reorganize my concentration once
again then and I kept telling myself not to give up, that 40–

love is no lead in a game and 5–1 is no lead in a set. I began smashing everything. My game started to pick up, and as I came on, May started to go off. Her drives began going out by inches and I couldn't miss a shot. Momentum gives you an immeasurable psychological advantage. I won six straight games to pull the second set out and I just kept rolling and ran off six more in a row for the third and the match. That was quite a day for me." This was the last match between the two great rivals during their athletic primes. As they grew older, each of them mellowed to the extent that she could regard the other with objective admiration, but there remained perhaps a certain absence of warmth in their relationship. When they met in an early round in the National Championship in 1928—Mrs. Wightman won 6–4, 11–9— both battled desperately to win, as if they were still fighting to see who was the best woman player in the country. May accepted an invitation to play on the Wightman Cup team in 1925. A decade later her daughter, Dorothy Bundy, for whom Mrs. Wightman has a tremendous affection, was on the team.

In her swing around the tournament circuit in the summer of 1911, Hazel Hotchkiss met George Wightman, a slim Bostonian who was entering his senior year at Harvard. Their engagement was announced during the visit he made to the Hotchkiss homestead in Berkeley the following winter, they were married in June, and they settled in a yellow frame house situated three flat forehands from the S. S. Pierce store at Coolidge Corner. While he was not the nationally known personality his wife was, Mr. Wightman was a sportsman of more than passing attainments. As a boy he had achieved a certain prominence in yachting circles by outsailing Charles Francis Adams in several races off the resort town of Hull, and for many years he was a contender for the national championship in court tennis, the intricate ancestor of lawn tennis. Mr. Wightman's skill as a lawn tennis player did

not match his love of watching good tennis and being in
the company of tennis players, but he was proficient enough
to team up with Mrs. Wightman and carry off the mixed
doubles in the 1913 Longwood Bowl tournament. After
serving the customary apprenticeship as a committee work-
horse, treasurer, secretary, and vice-president, Mr. Wightman became the president of the U. S. Lawn Tennis Association in 1924.

In the seven years after her marriage in 1912, Mrs. Wightman played only occasional tournament tennis, a semiretirement occasioned for the most part by the birth of three
children. In 1919 her urge to see if she could keep pace with
the new stars who had come to the fore prompted her to
return to tournament tennis. In the opinion of veteran
tennis critics, it is questionable if Mrs. Wightman could
then have stayed with the defending national champion,
Molla Bjurstedt (later Mrs. Mallory). Molla, however, did
not choose to defend her indoor championship, and in the
outdoor championship on grass she was eliminated in the
semifinal round by Mrs. Wightman's protégée, Marion
Zinderstein. Mrs. Wightman faced Marion in both of the
finals and captured them largely by giving Marion the shots
she knew she was weakest on. Whenever two of her pupils
meet in a match, it is Mrs. Wightman's policy to cheer for
neither but inwardly to root for whichever girl is playing the
better tennis. Quite similarly, whenever she has opposed her
pupils in a formal tournament, as she did Marion in 1919,
Mrs. Wightman has gone all out to win and has had to
quash no qualms about having been uncharitable if she has
outplayed her pupil. The only match that Mrs. Wightman
has ever thrown involved royalty. In 1924 the Tennis Club
of San Sebastian invited the members of the United States
Olympic team to be its weekend guests at the pleasant perch
on the Bay of Biscay where the Queen of Spain, a keen tennis
fan, maintained her summer palace. Mrs. Wightman, Vin-

cent Richards, and Julian S. Myrick, the manager of the team, accepted the invitation. They were informed on their arrival that the American ambassador, Alexander P. Moore, had arranged for them to play an exhibition for the royal family. "On Saturday morning Ambassador Moore presented us, informally, to King Alfonso and Queen Victoria Eugenia and their children," Mrs. Wightman says of her command performance. "Then we walked down through a very charming garden to the court—a nice red clay court shaded by tall oaks which we later found got in the way of lobs. On the walk down, the two youngest princes kept asking their mother why she wasn't playing and she kept shushing them and explaining to them in a low voice that she wasn't good enough to play with champions. We all declared that this wasn't so, and after a few minutes the Queen sent her daughter Beatrice back to the palace to fetch her sneakers. We played doubles, the Queen and Vinnie Richards against Mr. Myrick and me. They won in straight sets, something like 6–3, 6–4. The Queen played very well, I thought. I'd like to have had her for two weeks to work on her return of service, but, all in all, she had the foundation of a good game. After the match the King told us that he had enjoyed it very much but that he wasn't surprised that the Queen's side won. 'Whenever I play polo,' he added with a little smile, 'my side always wins and I am always the outstanding player on the field.' "

Mrs. Wightman's successful re-entry into the lists in 1919 brought her numerous messages of congratulation from her faithful followers in the "Hazel Era" and a gracious letter, which turned out to have considerable significance, from Suzanne Lenglen, the young French whiz who had won her first Wimbledon championship that spring. At this time Mrs. Wightman was practically the only bridge between East Coast and West Coast women's tennis. For a number

of years the sun-kissed prodigies sprouting in California had
shied away from making the cross-country journey to the big
tournaments, even if the necessary funds were available,
because they had no friends on that distant shore to show
them the ropes. Mrs. Wightman made it a point to meet
these girls during her visits to California and to invite them,
should they decide to take a crack at the eastern tournaments,
to make their headquarters at her home in Brookline. An
ever-increasing number accepted. In July and August, when
the young Californians moved in with their several rackets
and changes of bandeaux, the yellow frame house on Charles
Street seethed with the coloratura hum of a girls' dormitory
as their housemother gave them careful instructions on what
tournaments to enter, how to line up partners, where to stay
on the circuit stops, what clothes to wear, how much to tip
waiters, what evening invitations were preferable, and, last
but not least, how to improve their tennis. The letter from
Suzanne was the little shove Mrs. Wightman needed to ex-
pand her activities from a national to an international scale.
"I'd been thinking for a long while that the women tennis
players in different countries would like to get to know each
other," she said recently. "The men had had the Davis Cup
since 1900, and that had taken hold so well that, after the
first World War, over twenty countries were entering teams.
The standard of men's tennis throughout the world had been
improved by the Davis Cup—no question about that. And
the players had loved it. It gave them a chance to travel
and see foreign countries and make many good friends.
Hearing from Suzanne, whom I had never met, crystallized
my feeling that the time was ripe to do something about organizing an international team match for women along the
lines of the Davis Cup. I presented this idea to Mr. Myrick
of the Lawn Tennis Association and told him that if they
wanted a trophy for such an event, I'd be more than glad to
donate one. Mr. Myrick told me to go right ahead." The

next week Mrs. Wightman walked into N. G. Wood & Sons
on Park Street in Boston and purchased for $300 a tall silver
cup on which she had engraved *Challenge Cup—Ladies
Team Match.* "It wasn't exactly the type I had in mind,"
Mrs. Wightman has said of the trophy, which is always referred to as the Wightman Cup although her name does not
appear on it. "I wanted something more graceful—something more classical and flowing and urnlike. However, it
was the only thing that Wood had in the shop, and by nature
I'm a purchaser and not a shopper."

Upon receipt of the Wightman Cup, the U.S.L.T.A.
sounded out the tennis associations of the countries which
supported Davis Cup teams. Most of the replies were apathetic, pointing out that footing the bill for the Davis Cuppers made it impossible to send other players abroad. The
idea of an international women's team match was quietly
dropped and then forgotten. Mrs. Wightman was in California in 1923, four years after she had presented the trophy,
when the first Wightman Cup match was hastily cooked up.
Work on the new stadium at the West Side Tennis Club in
Forest Hills had been completed that summer and the
U.S.L.T.A. was pondering a distinguished opening event
when someone remembered that a group of England's best
women players was on its way across the Atlantic to play in
our tournaments and someone else remembered the Wightman Cup. In a ship-to-shore exchange of radiograms, an
international match, England versus the United States, was
arranged for Forest Hills to begin on August 10. (A day's
postponement later became necessary when the tenth was
set aside as a day of national mourning for President Harding,
who had been fatally stricken with food poisoning in
Alaska.) The first word Mrs. Wightman received of these
developments was a telegram informing her that she had
been selected to represent the United States in a Wightman
Cup match and requesting her to return to New York imme-

diately. When her train reached Albany, she bought the
New York Tribune and learned that she had been appointed
captain of an American team consisting of Helen Wills,
Molla Mallory, Eleanor Goss, and herself. The first Wightman Cup match—they are two-day affairs—was at length
unfurled at Forest Hills on August 11, 1923, in a blaze of
pomp and circumlocution. Four trumpeters, serried along
the top row of the west side of the stands, blew a fine series
of tantaras. A military band, massed on the turf in the
middle of the concrete horseshoe, solemnly rendered "God
Save the King" and "The Star-Spangled Banner." Flags
went up, speeches went off, and then the tennis got under
way. A close contest had been predicted, but on the opening
day the American side took the two singles and the one
doubles, and on the second day it swept the remaining three
singles and the second doubles to make the final score 7–0.
(The breakdown of a Wightman Cup match goes as follows:
the number one and number two singles players face both
the opposing number one and number two players; the number three singles player meets the opposing number three;
the number one doubles team meets its opposite number,
as does the number two doubles team. A victory in each of
the even contests is worth one point.) In the first Wightman
Cup meeting, Mrs. Wightman teamed with Eleanor Goss
in the number one doubles to defeat Kathleen McKane and
Mrs. Ethel Covell in a genuinely exciting duel, 10–8, 5–7,
6–4. In 1924, when the match was held on Wimbledon's
number one court—in the even-numbered years England
is host—Mrs. Wightman paired with Helen Wills to win
the number one doubles, the only point gained by the
American team in its first encounter with the English on
their home grass. In 1931 Mrs. Wightman made her last
appearance as the playing captain of the American team. She
served as nonplaying captain, off and on, until 1949 when,
believing she had been captain long enough, she asked to be

relieved of that assignment and nominated Mrs. Marjorie Gladman Buck to succeed her.

The Wightman Cup series was an extremely even rivalry through 1930. England won four of the first eight meetings. Then, as has been the inveterate trend in Anglo-American sports competitions, the American teams asserted a progressively marked superiority, due, among other things, to the greater number of players to choose from, a climate more congenial to year-round practice, and a far more serious and competitive environment for the incubation of star players. Though the English teams failed to win any of the meetings between 1930 and 1939, they dropped four of them by only a 4–3 score and were never shut out. However, since the revival of the series in 1946, following a six-year shutdown during the war, the English have provided little more than the trappings of opposition, eking out one scant point from a possible thirty-five in the first five postwar matches. After witnessing the first of these runaways in 1946 when the American side did not lose a set, Mrs. Wightman became worried over the steep decline of English tennis. She gave talks and demonstrations all over England and encouraged the members of the American squad to do the same. On her return to the States she shot motion pictures of Brough, du Pont, Hart, and the other American stars playing their soundest strokes and sent this film to England to be circulated among girls' schools and tennis clubs. "Those English girls need someone to wake them up," she told a friend. "None of their own players are stimulating them, and this film may help them to turn out some real good players. At least it's bound to interest a lot of girls to take up tennis and open the full life for them. They've got too many governesses over there anyhow."

During the twenty-six-year span in which she ran the American team, Mrs. Wightman sat at mid-court on one side of the umpire's perch, the English captain on the other side. "Mrs. Wightie never had very much to tell us when we came over to her chair between sets," Margaret Osborne du Pont, who has played on several Wightman Cup teams, was reminiscing this spring. "Just before you went on court, maybe she'd remind you, if she thought you looked a bit tense, not to hit out too hard the first game or two, to warm up gradually and get your timing going before you began to hit aggressively for placements. Once a match was on, she never pointed out what you were doing wrong or advised a change in tactics. She believed that that sort of master-minding from the side lines confused the player more often than not and broke your concentration. Mrs. Wightie tried to solve all our problems before we went out onto the court. For example, it drizzles a good deal at Wimbledon and you never can tell when you'll have to contend with a very slippery surface. When we arrived in London, Mrs. Wightie would pass out a couple of pairs of heavy men's woolen socks, about size ten or eleven, to each of us. If we had to play on wet grass, we'd pull these socks on right over our sneakers, and they really helped you keep your footing." Mrs. Wightman was criticized in some quarters, when the matches had become lopsided affairs, for not benching stars and substituting the secondary lights on the squad once the American team had secured four of the seven points and thus assured victory. "I would like to give all the players a chance, and I don't believe in running up the score for the sake of running up the score," she replied gravely to a tennis writer who had posed this criticism. "But an international *team* match is different from a personal tournament in which it's individual against individual. You're representing your country. A captain would be letting her country down if she didn't try to win every singles, every doubles that could be won and to use the players who could best win those matches." This feeling of national responsibility pervaded Mrs. Wightman's play at the VIIIth Olympiad in

Paris in 1924, the last time tennis was included in the Olympic program. "After each event the flag of the victorious country is hoisted to the top of the pole," she was relating recently, "and that country's national anthem is played. When I saw the American flag go up to the top twice and knew I had played a part in putting it there, it was far and away the most thrilling moment of my life."

Mrs. Wightman's activity annually comes to its busiest bubble during the third week of August when the United States Doubles Championships are held at Longwood, eight deep lobs from the rambling, brown-shingled house on Suffolk Road in Chestnut Hill, where Mrs. Wightman has lived since 1940. In order to devote her full energies to the bevy of beautiful backhands which descend on her home, Mrs. Wightman cancels for that week all outside lessons and demonstrations and gets down to the business of running a small hotel. Not counting a few itinerant competitors who knocked on the screen door late at night and were given improvised lodging for an evening, Mrs. Wightman's guests during National Doubles Week this year numbered fourteen: Doris Hart and Shirley Fry shared one upstairs bedroom; Margaret Osborne du Pont, Louise Brough, and Thelma Long (of Australia) shared another; Maureen Connolly and Anita Kanter roomed together in a third; Sachiko Kamo, the Japanese champion, and Joan and Andy Ross-Dilley, the English twins, were assigned cots on the closed-in porch; the ping-pong table was moved to one corner of the basement game room, and Kay Hubbell, Lois Felix, and Connie Bowan were moved in. Chestnut Hill, like every tennis-respecting community, is peopled with hostesses who would gladly turn over their snazziest bedroom and a private maid to any of these stars, but staying with Mrs. Wightman is tantamount to an invitation to quit the Wardman Park and move into Blair House.

During the tournament week, Mrs. Wightman rises at

six o'clock, a half hour earlier than usual. While her house-
keeper, Mollie Lennon, squeezes the orange juice for fourteen or more breakfasts, Mrs. Wightman, after raking the
leaves from her lawn and checking her garden, jumps in her
Studebaker and collects the day's provisions. On her return, she stations herself at the frying pan until the last
breakfasters, invariably Brough and du Pont, have been fed
and packed off to their matches. Lunch is staggered, the
girls returning to Suffolk Road whenever their schedules
allow. Dinner is communal and vocal. After it is over, Mrs.
Wightman, who plays in the veterans' division and runs
the women's part of the doubles, relaxes over a cool Bendix
washing machine in a basement alcove. She regards the
Bendix as a touchy instrument that needs an experienced
operator, and there is an unwritten law that while guests
may iron their clothes, nobody washes except Mrs. Wightman. Around eight o'clock Chestnut Hill neighbors, male
competitors, old Longwood hands, boy friends, and star-
struck pupils start to drop in, and for the next hour or so
the decibel rate (often helped along by Mrs. Wightman's
strenuous piano work on "The Maple Leaf Rag") and the
floor load of the house go up enormously. When the traffic
has returned to normal, Mrs. Wightman is ready for a nice
long tennis talk. To make certain that she doesn't loll
around unorganized at any time during the day, Mrs. Wightman scratches memos to herself on a blackboard in the
pantry and so is able to remember to drive to St. Joseph's
Cemetery and water the flowers on Mrs. Lennon's husband's
grave, to bake two batches of brownies and Toll House
cookies daily, and to write and dispatch a dozen or so post
cards, a supply of which she carries in her purse. This im-
passioned "carpeing" of the "diem" is accomplished in a
blaze of inconspicuousness, and it is the more astonishing
in that Mrs. Wightman's vitality apparently doubles in direct
proportion to its expenditure. At the conclusion of their

stay at Mrs. Wightman's during the tournament week in 1940, Pauline Betz and her mother made a brave attempt to commemorate in verse the indefatigable Zip Zip of their hostess. The Betzes tabulated her dawn-till-midnight schedule in nine frenetic stanzas, and then, still puffing a little, added as an earnest epilogue:

> No matter where our footsteps go,
> Wherever we may roam,
> For us there'll never be a place
> Like Mrs. Wightman's home.

THE BEST SINCE KLEM

This study of Al Barlick, the colorful National League umpire, was written for *The Saturday Evening Post* in 1952. A few years after that, illness forced Barlick into temporary retirement, but he is back in harness now as vigorous as before, the old larynx booming out the calls as loud as ever. Many of the men who were colleagues of Barlick's at the time this piece was written, such as Lee Ballanfant, have retired or drifted into other professions, but the young men who have replaced them have learned quickly under fire, and their standard of performance has generally been quite high. Major-league umpires miss a few, but they are, when all is said and done, the most expert field officials in all of sport.

EARLY LAST SEPTEMBER, when the 1951 National League race had narrowed down to the hot pursuit of the Dodgers by the Giants, the two rival clubs clashed in a five-game series. Fireworks were expected, and President Warren Giles of the National League decided to assign to the series four of his most experienced umpires—Lee Ballanfant, Bill Stewart, Jocko Conlan, and Al Barlick. It proved to be an astute move. Both teams were continually on edge, and what with the two managers, Dressen and Durocher, rubbing against each other like flint and steel, the games were always threatening to flare up all over the premises.

In the third inning of the third game, for example, with Sal Maglie pitching for the Giants and Preacher Roe for the Dodgers, Maglie sent Jackie Robinson sprawling into the dirt to get out of the way of a fast curve ball breaking into his back. When the inning was over, Al Barlick, umpiring behind the plate, strode out to the mound and summoned the other three umpires. He informed them that there was no question whatsoever in his mind that Maglie had deliberately "dusted off" Robinson. Furthermore, he told his colleagues, he had a hunch that Roe might dust off some Giant in retaliation. In the event that that happened, he suggested that the game be stopped then and there and both managers warned that any pitcher throwing another beanball would be ejected. The four umpires agreed on this procedure. In the next inning, Roe hit Monte Irvin with a pitch. Barlick abruptly stopped the game, the umpires made their intentions superbly clear to Dressen and Durocher, and the game was then resumed and finished without further incident.

This ability to anticipate rough situations and handle them decisively has made Al Barlick not only one of the outstanding umpires in the game today but also, in the opinion of many veteran observers and players, one of the best of all time. In a curious way, Barlick's proficiency has always been expected of him. When Al broke into the majors in 1940, the late Bill Klem, then in his thirty-sixth campaign as a National League umpire, went way out on the limb after watching the young man work a handful of games. "The boy is a natural," the Old Arbitrator enunciated. "If Barlick's grandmother and his worst enemy were out there on opposite sides of a ball game, he would call everything the way he sees it, favoring neither one nor the other. He's got all the other qualifications. He's going to be the best umpire in history."

Some of the more tempestuous National League managers cannot go as far as Klem in their appraisals of Barlick, but it is significant that they will go as far as they do. In Eddie Stanky's book, "Barlick has real skill for his work and is one of the best in the business." Leo Durocher, who would almost rather be caught slapping Charley Dressen on the back than complimenting an umpire, has intimated that Barlick controls a game fairly well. Dressen is less reserved. "I've had my run-ins with Al, but I respect him," he told a friend last fall. "He's a good umpire mechanically—probably the best on balls and strikes in the league—but what he's really got special is hustle. I'd be happy if all my players hustled like Barlick."

Albert Joseph "Al" Barlick, who will be thirty-eight this April, is an intense, ingenuous man with a ruddy complexion, wavy black hair, twenty-twenty eyes, and what might be described as an ideal physique for an umpire. Strong-shouldered and bull-necked, he stands just under six feet tall and, by scrupulously watching his diet, weighs no more than a burly 185 pounds. He is fast afoot and he has endurance. During his ten full seasons in the National League, he has never missed an inning because of bad health. This record was threatened in 1946 when Barlick, scheduled to work a night game behind the plate, was running a temperature of 103 degrees. "I decided to try it anyhow and go as far as I could," Barlick recalls. "Funny thing, I got stronger as the game went on. I felt perfect the next day. I guess all that sweating knocked the fever right out of me."

Barlick's most striking physical asset, however, is his voice. It has always been his trade-mark—the growling, booming basso in which he roars out his calls. A "Barlick game" is invariably charged with a sense of high drama and high spirits from the first pitch, which is either a "stee-ruck-huh" or a "bah-wole," both expelled like a volcanic eruption. The fans lean forward and the dugouts immediately come to life. "Speak up, ump, speak up," the dugout riders yell. Or they call, "Anybody hear a seal?" On a good day, when the air is dry, Barlick can maintain this vocal voltage for an entire game. As one of his admirers has put it, Al may or may not be the finest umpire in the game today but he is without a doubt the loudest umpire in the annals of organized baseball.

Umpiring is to Barlick, as it was to Klem, something more than a job. It is a solemn trust, almost a religion. His duty, as he sees it, is to get each decision right. If this means correcting a mistake, he is prepared to do so. Barlick is probably the only umpire on record who wittingly admitted that he had "pulled a rock" to 43,403 fans—the size of the crowd gathered at Wrigley Field on a July afternoon a few years back. George Shuba of the Dodgers was at bat and the count was three and two when a peculiar mix-up took place. The next delivery to Shuba, the fourth ball, was a high, wild pitch that got away from Bob Scheffing, the Cub catcher, and careened against the backstop. Somehow it got into Barlick's head that the ball had been ticked, and his instantaneous reflex was to stick his hand into his jacket pocket and start to hand Scheffing a new ball. This gesture had the effect of paralyzing Scheffing for a moment or two. "Say, he didn't foul that ball!" Scheffing suddenly said. "No, no, he didn't," Barlick blurted, snapping out of his lapse. Scheffing then took off after the ball, but before he could make a play, Shuba had pulled into second base.

Barlick collected himself. He ordered Shuba to return to first. He walked to the Brooklyn dugout, frankly described his lapse to Manager Shotton, and explained that he was sending Shuba back to first because, in his judgment, Shuba would not have been able to have advanced beyond first if his lapse had not deprived Scheffing of his normal chance to retrieve the ball. Shotton countered angrily that Brooklyn would protest the game. "O.K.," Barlick answered, "protest it." He then explained his reasons for his decision to the park announcer who in turn relayed it to the patrons over the public-announcement system.

As it turned out, the Dodgers won that game 9–3 and the incident died a natural death. The tough ones don't always bury themselves so conveniently, though. Midway in the 1951 season, for example, Ford Frick, then president of the National League, instructed his umpires to enforce with strictness the balk rule which calls for the pitcher to come to a full stop before delivering the ball. Working a Dodger-Cardinal game on the heels of this order, Barlick cautioned the opposing pitchers to make certain to adhere to this ruling. "That afternoon I had to call three balks on Max Lanier," Barlick remembers. "The last one, in the eighth inning, sent a runner to second, and a single drove him in with the run that won the ball game. Calling those balks didn't give me any pleasure. That was my duty. The gratitude I got was a newspaper column from a syndicated writer claiming that umpires were ruining baseball and that Barlick especially was a big ham-and-egger. That burned me. I wish there was some way that the public could look over my character and that columnist's character and let them decide for themselves who's the ham-and-egger."

Barlick today is almost totally oblivious to the noise from the stands, much in the way that a man who has lived for a stretch at the seaside no longer hears the roar of the ocean. At the same time, Barlick would not object in the least if the public developed a more accurate estimate of the work that he and his colleagues turn in, which he considers to be, all in all, of very high quality. A short time ago a New York newspaperman who was preparing a Sunday feature on umpires asked Barlick to enumerate a few of his beefs against the fans. "I don't have any," Barlick answered briskly. "As a matter of fact, I think the fans are terrific. It's you sports writers who tell them all umpires are bums. Whenever you want to stir up a controversy, you pick on umpires as the perfect target, the sitting duck. That's what discourages college men from entering the profession."

Barlick is both pleased and displeased when the fans who meet him off the field invariably express great astonishment on finding that he looks like a young high-school football coach and is a person of innate politeness and considerable charm. "I don't know what they expect," he confessed to a friend, "but I guess umpires are supposed to be gorillas—old gorillas creaking on our last legs. A couple of years ago, to give you an illustration, my wife went into Stick's department store in St. Louis to buy one of those triangular chairs. When she gave her name and address to the salesgirl, the girl started to smile as if she recognized the name. 'Al Barlick,' she says to my wife. 'Why you must be the umpire's daughter.' "

According to Dave Grote of National League headquarters, there are today about 50,000 umpires spread throughout the country who officiate sand-lot, high-school, college, and semipro games. Five hundred more officiate in the minor leagues. The best thirty-two reach the majors. Since the lot of the umpire is traditionally not a happy one, why is it that a man voluntarily goes into it? Most of the time, it is because the individual has been identified with baseball as a player and, loving the game, wants to continue in it in some capacity after his playing days are over. This is the reason why eleven of the current sixteen National League umpires chose their precarious profession. The rest got into it by accident. Barlick, for instance, turned to umpiring as a means of making some money when his family was the victim of a prolonged strike in the Illinois coal mines.

Barlick, who is of German-Austrian-Yugoslav extraction, was born in Springfield, Illinois, in 1915, the fifth and youngest son of John and Louise Barlick. The Barlick homestead stood (and still stands) on East Sangamon Avenue, a mile beyond the city limits and ten blocks from the 265-foot-deep bituminous mine called Peabody #59, where Mr. Barlick and, in time, his sons worked. It was Mr. Barlick's intention that Al should stay out of the pits. Mining was no life if you could find an easier one—some occupation, for example, where you didn't enter the mine shaft when it was still dark in the early morning and emerge into the dark some eight hours later, as the Barlick men did in the winter months. When Al finished his first two years of high school, he was encouraged to enter the Civilian Conservation Corps. He spent a six-month stretch in Washington State and another six months in the forests of Wisconsin. When Joe, the second oldest son, died in 1933, Al came home to work in the mines. He was eighteen at the time. Mr. Barlick was what is known as a "digger" and Al went along as his father's helper, classified as a "loader."

The Barlick boys played quite a lot of baseball but, oddly enough, the game that developed Al's orientation toward umpiring was a back-yard time killer he devised with a friend, Pat Ciotti. It was a two-man game. The batter was equipped with a flat board and the pitcher stood twenty-five feet away and tossed kernels of corn, mixing up his "curves" (the large flat kernels from the big ears, which sailed crazily when you snapped your wrist) with his "fast balls" (the round nubbin kernels, which went fairly straight). The pitcher also acted as umpire. In Ciotti's opinion, Al called balls and strikes with all the snap and crackle of an honest-to-goodness ump. One afternoon in the spring of 1935 when Ciotti was standing around a local diamond waiting for a Municipal League game to begin, he happened to overhear a conversation in which Jack Rossiter, who ran the league, was desperately inquiring where he could find an umpire. Ciotti butted right in. He knew just the guy.

Barlick was out in the garden hoeing tomatoes when Pat arrived with Rossiter. "I told Mr. Rossiter that I'd never umpired a game before and didn't think I could handle it," Barlick remembers. "Pat kept on insisting, 'Go on, Al, you can do it.' Finally I gave in. The way the Muny League operated, there was only one umpire to a game. You called them from behind the pitcher's mound, which wasn't easy, I found. After a couple of innings, though, my nervousness started to wear off and I felt comfortable out there. What I had to do, I decided right then, was to make every possible effort to be correct at any cost. Then I wouldn't have to worry."

The following season the Municipal League moved its games into the ball park previously used by Springfield's disbanded Three-I League team. Barlick umpired three nights a week, at a dollar a night, grateful for this opportunity since the mines were closed down and the men in the Barlick family had to depend on odd jobs to make ends meet. That August, Rossiter received an urgent call from a friend of his, Joe Bertil, the president of the Class D North East Arkansas League. One of the league's regular umpires had become ill, and Bertil wanted to know if Rossiter could send him a replacement to finish out the last four weeks of the season. Barlick accepted the invitation without hesitation and hitchhiked to Paragould, Arkansas, where the league made its headquarters. "I was the greenest kid you ever saw," Barlick has said. "I'd never been out of the county before. You know, when I ate in restaurants on the way to Paragould, so help me, I thought that guy A La Carte owned all the restaurants in the country."

Barlick was paid only $75 for his month in the North East Arkansas League but he had made the big step. He was in organized baseball and out of the mines. One of his brothers, Frank, later left the mines to work for the Illinois Power Company. Peabody #59 was shut down, apparently for good, but the other two Barlick boys still mine for a living, Lou in Farmersville and John, Jr., in Pana. John Barlick, Sr., retired after fifty years as a miner, and today, at seventy-eight, he draws a pension of $100 a month plus his social security and tends a ten-acre farm. Since breaking into baseball at Paragould, Al has returned to the mines only once. Three winters ago he went back into the pits during the off-season as a means of keeping in good physical shape. "There's nothing like baseball, but coal mining, in the type of mines we work in, isn't as bad as most people think," Barlick recently told a fellow umpire. "If I ever discover that I don't have the respect of the players, I'm prepared to go back to mining."

Barlick's rapid climb to the majors was once described as a combination of superior umpiring by Barlick and unsolicited letters of recommendation by his bosses. After watching Barlick's work in his league, for example, Joe Bertil wrote to Dan Hill, the president of Class B Piedmont League, to inform him that he had a young umpire who was ready for faster company. Barlick was instructed to report to Hill at Durham, North Carolina, the day before the 1937 season opened. He was an apple-cheeked twenty-two at the time, and he looked no older.

"I think you're a little too young for our league," Hill told Barlick after scrutinizing him. "I'm afraid I'm going to have to send you home. How old are you anyhow?"

Barlick replied with as much conviction as he could muster that he was twenty-six. "Look, Mr. Hill," he added, "I don't claim I can umpire in your league, but I left a pretty good job to come here. Just give me a tryout, for three weeks, and then if my work doesn't come up to your standards, I'll go home with satisfaction."

Barlick passed his trial period with plenty to spare, and Hill assigned him a regular partner, John "Botts" Crowley. Crowley was a Notre Dame graduate with a Master's degree in English. He was a natural teacher. "It was Botts who made me acquire the ability to think out baseball situations," Barlick says. "We'd be traveling from one game to another in his car and I'd ask Botts about some decision he'd made or some ruling. 'There's a rule book in the glove compartment,' he'd say. 'Look it up yourself, Al.' After I'd read the rule, he'd ask me to explain the meaning of the rule and why it was put in the book. If there's anyone in baseball who's been good to me, it was Botts. He not only taught me the game, he taught me the few table manners I have today." Botts Crowley went up to the International League shortly afterward and then decided to devote all his time to the sporting goods company for which he had worked during the off-seasons.

Umpiring in the Piedmont League required exhausting all-night auto trips after each series—the longest one was the 600-mile haul between Norfolk, Virginia, and Asheville, North Carolina—and the salary was not heady. During Barlick's first year he received $150 a month and a monthly expense account of $10, to cover cleaning bills for his uniforms, but no allowance for traveling or living expenses. The next year he was upped to a basic $175 a month. In his second year, however, his work came to the attention of Bill Carpenter, the supervisor of umpires for the International League, who took an option on Barlick's services for the next baseball season, 1939. The International League, a Class AA circuit, farmed him out for the first three months of that season to the Class A Eastern League, and then, having inspected him at close range, promoted him to the International. This is roughly the system by which an umpire moves up the ladder of organized baseball—the Class A and AA leagues reach down into the lower-rated minor leagues, and the majors in turn scout the A and AA leagues.

During his half season in the Eastern League, Barlick ran into the roughest rhubarb of his career. In the first game of a double-header at Scranton between Scranton and Albany,

he was umpiring on bases, working the third-base line. In the
fifth inning, a Scranton batter smashed a hot ground ball
down the line. Punching his right hand toward foul territory,
Barlick called it foul. Out of the dugout, with blood in his
eye, rushed the Scranton manager, Nemo Liebold. It was a
fair ball, Liebold protested; the Albany third baseman had
touched it with his glove when it was still in fair territory.
No, he hadn't, Barlick answered. The ball had shot foul
before reaching the bag and no one had touched it. Liebold
grew red at the neck. He began to resort to a more colorful
vocabulary, attacking Barlick personally with what is termed
in the trade "profane and abusive language." Barlick's reply
was to eject Liebold from the game.

Before quitting the field, Liebold, a talented rabble-rouser
with a home crowd to work on, succeeded in transplanting
his anger among the Scranton partisans. They rode Barlick
hard the rest of the game. The second game had hardly got
under way—Barlick was calling them at first base—when he
and Liebold clashed on another decision. Egged on by the
stands, Liebold tore at Barlick with all the vituperation at his
command. Barlick warned him that unless he stopped these
tactics immediately, he would throw him out of this game,
too.

"If you do, I'll incite a riot," Liebold threatened.

"You're out of this game. You're gone," Barlick snapped.
"Incite a riot."

Liebold nearly did. He whipped the Scranton fans up to
reach such a fury that they raged at Barlick without letup,
inning after inning, that they would get him after the game
—and they meant it. In the seventh inning, Rabbit Maranville, who was managing Albany, walked over to Barlick and
told him not to worry. "After the game, stay right where you
are," Maranville counseled. "We'll take care of you." The
moment the final put-out was made, Maranville and the entire Albany squad sprinted out to Barlick before the crowd

could get to him and formed a circle around the umpire. Each player carried a bat in his hand. When the crowd began to disperse, the Albany players convoyed Barlick to the safety of the umpire's dressing room.

Experiences like this, quite understandably, leave a lasting mark on an umpire's temperament. In Al Barlick's case, they have burned into him an intransigent unforgivingness toward managers and players who incite or threaten physical violence in the heat of anger and come around the next day with a glib smile and a handshake. Barlick's one serious fracas during his year and a half in the International League, for example, almost got totally out of hand when the first baseman of the Rochester Red Wings went berserk. Barlick coldly spurned the player's peace offerings the following day. "The damage was done last night," he said in explaining his attitude to a club official. "The apology can't fix it. The apology isn't any good today."

The situation which provoked this aftermath was as bizarre as they come in baseball. This was the setting. In mid-September, with a week to go in the 1940 pennant race, Rochester, fighting to hold onto first place, met the Montreal Royals who were scrapping for fourth and a berth in the play-offs. Montreal led 5–2 with Rochester batting in the top of the ninth. With two down and the bases loaded, Ray Mueller sliced a sharp drive down the right-field line. Two runs scored and George Fallon, representing the tying run, rounded third and headed for home. The play at the plate was close. Barlick, after waiting the necessary moment to make sure the Montreal catcher had held the ball, called the runner out. As far as Barlick was concerned, that was the third out and the ball game was over, 5–4.

Then strange things began to happen. The Montreal pitcher, backing up the play, spied a loose ball in the cloud of dust. He picked it up and fired it to third, trying to catch Mueller as he slid into that bag. Thereupon both teams rushed the umpires, Barlick in particular. Barlick stood his ground on his decision but he was completely baffled—he knew the Montreal catcher had not dropped the ball, but where did the ball come from that the pitcher had thrown to third? The mystery of "the extra ball" was cleared up the following day by Fallon, the base runner who was thrown out at the plate. As he lay sprawled on the ground, Fallon explained, perhaps a bit tardily, that he looked up and saw the extra ball jump out of Barlick's jacket pocket. The extra ball had been jolted out of the pocket by the extra-strenuous motion of Barlick's right hand as he made the "out" signal on the crucial play.

It was an embarrassing situation for Barlick and, to prevent its reoccurring, he has ever since carried a maximum of four balls in his jacket pocket, though most umpires carry five or six. In retrospect, Barlick can now enjoy the farcical aspects of that mix-up, but after the game he felt very low. He reported what had happened, to the best of his knowledge, in a night letter to the president of the league, Frank Shaughnessy. He braced himself for a demotion, at the least a reprimand. Shaughnessy telephoned him the following day. They discussed the incident and then Shaughnessy told him he had news for him. The National League, he said, had just sent through a call requesting Barlick to report for duty at once, to fill in for Bill Klem who had injured his leg.

Barlick took the next train to New York. In a delighted daze, he walked to the Piccadilly Hotel where Klem, then the unofficial chief of umpires for the National League, made his home during the baseball season. Barlick was met in the hotel lobby, as Shaughnessy had told him he would be, by Lee Ballanfant, a slight, friendly man from Dallas, then in his fifth season as a National League umpire. Ballanfant had been assigned by the league to be the rookie's partner.

"Have you ever met the Old Man?" Ballanfant asked. Barlick said he hadn't. (Barlick, incidentally, had been scouted not by Klem but by another National League veteran, Ernie "You Can't Do-oo-oo-oo That" Quigley.) "Well," Ballanfant continued in his soft Texas drawl, "I think we ought to go up and see the Old Man. He'd probably like to have a talk with you."

Klem in 1940 was in his middle sixties, nearing the end of a historic career in which, almost singlehandedly, he had transformed the umpire from a quaking target for anybody's derision into a comparatively respected guardian of order. He greeted Barlick and Ballanfant at the door of his suite, attired in a white woolen night robe that almost touched the floor. He was wearing wooden clogs, and his legs and arms were covered with a powder solution. This powder was one of his methods for dealing with the chronic skin irritation which the Old Man recognized as his nervous reaction to the strain of umpiring.

"William," Ballanfant said to the Old Man, "I want you to meet my new partner, Al Barlick."

"What did you say your name was?" Klem roared in his oratorical manner. He habitually spoke as if he was addressing an entire ball park if not the Roman Senate.

"Al Barlick," Barlick said.

"Where did you come from?" the Old Man roared on.

"The International League, sir."

Klem twisted his head so that it faced the opposite wall, then slowly swept it toward Barlick, and, as he did so, bellowed, "I never heard of you."

"I don't doubt that, Mr. Klem," Barlick said.

Klem then asked him a few questions about baseball and umpiring situations. The interview was terminated shortly after this, since Ballanfant and Barlick were due to leave for an assignment in Philadelphia. Somehow, in this brief conversation, Klem learned all he needed to know to size up Barlick to his complete satisfaction. "Even then you could see that he knew the answer to every problem that could arise on the field," Klem said later, explaining his instant confidence in Barlick. "And there was a love of baseball in him, too."

The first big league game that Al Barlick ever saw, he umpired—he worked on the bases the day Johnny Vander Meer beat the Phillies to sew up the Reds' second consecutive pennant. He made his first start as plate umpire on a Ladies' Day. "After every pitch, the girls'd be screaming their heads off," Ballanfant says, recalling Barlick's debut. "I didn't know if it was the way he called balls and strikes, 'cause he was such a loud guy. Turned out that every time he bent over to call a pitch, they could see he'd split the seat of his trousers." When the first inning was over, Barlick hastily changed into Ballanfant's extra pair, and the ladies settled down.

Barlick was twenty-five at the time of this trial period, one of the youngest umpires ever summoned to the majors and one of the most determined to succeed. He has never forgotten the kindness certain players showed him during this pressureful stretch. Ike Pearson was one. "Ike was pitching for the Phillies and Bill Atwood was catching him, on one of my first games behind the plate," Barlick remembers. "I called one of Ike's pitches a ball, and Atwood held the ball on me. That's one way a catcher shows an umpire he didn't like the call—holding the ball a good while before throwing it back to the pitcher. 'Leave him alone. That ball was low,' Ike hollered to Atwood. Spud Davis—there's another fellow who helped me out. Spud was catching for the Pirates then, I think. Anyhow I called a close pitch a ball and, being tense and nervous, I thought I'd better explain why. 'That ball was inside,' I added. 'You don't have to give me your reasons, young man,' Spud told me very nicely."

Despite his jitters, Barlick performed impressively enough the last two weeks of the season to be offered a regular contract for 1941 by President Frick. As for Klem, the more he saw of Barlick's work that September, the surer he was that the ex-miner had the stuff of which great umpires are made. Klem had a lengthy chat with Barlick after one of the last games. "Son, this is a hard business you're getting into," the Old Man said. "Nobody likes an umpire. At least half of the world hates you all the time. There're going to be some mighty lonely and heartbreaking nights when you get home after a tough day of wrangling and booing. So get yourself a pal. Get someone you can tell your troubles to when the other half of the world is against you. I know what it means. I have a wonderful and devoted wife."

"Suppose I scout around and find the right girl, Mr. Klem, and then she calls me out at first base?"

"My boy," Klem said heartily as he slapped Barlick on the shoulder, "always remember that it takes three outs to retire your side."

When Barlick reported to Klem the next training season, he was able to inform the Old Man that he had acted upon his advice. In February he had married Jennie Marie Leffell, a girl from Indiana, with whom he had been going for several years.

That season, 1941, was Klem's thirty-seventh and last as an active campaigner. Regarding Barlick as his prize protégé, he worked more games with him than with the other members of the staff. The next year Klem went into semiretirement as Chief of Staff of National League Umpires. Over the years a deep and enduring bond of friendship and respect grew up between the two, without their being entirely aware of it until the spring of 1946. Barlick was returning to baseball then, after serving two years with the Coast Guard, most of the time aboard a seventy-three-foot cutter. Klem's semiretirement had virtually become a full retirement. Near the end of the training season in Florida, Barlick made a last visit to the Old Man in his home on Venetian Causeway in Miami Beach, the house with the brass weather vane depicting Klem in the act of calling a play at the plate.

"Albert, I may never see you again," the Old Man said as he walked Barlick to his car. "I want you to do me a favor. I want you to help any umpire you possibly can. I know I have helped many who have been good fellows. I know I have helped some others who were not good fellows. But regardless of whether they are good fellows or bad fellows, don't let it enter your mind. Help them, because when you help them, you are helping baseball." Barlick has made this the core of his credo.

Since his return to baseball after the war, Barlick, despite his youth, has been regarded as one of the game's veteran pros. The "Barlick style" has also become the model for most young men entering the profession—the continuous hustle, the vigorous call, the clear and decisive hand signal, and the willingness to listen to all legitimate kicks but the insistence upon being respected at all times. When a "television manager" plays to his audience and tries to make a travesty of the game, the Barlick style recommends one step forward to douse the act right off the reel.

At thirty-eight, Barlick is still the third youngest umpire in the National League—the average age of the present staff is forty-six—but he ranks sixth in seniority, behind Bill Stewart, Babe Pinelli, Lee Ballanfant, Larry Goetz, and Lou Jorda. Salaries range from $6,000 for a newcomer to a $15,000 top. Barlick is about two-thirds of the way up the ladder, seniority being a principal determinant. Umpires assigned to officiate All-Star Games are rewarded with a large bundle of prestige, but a man who works a World Series as a regular receives $2,500 and an alternate receives $1,000. These amount to periodic bonuses since World Series assignments are parceled out among the staff on a precise rotation basis. National League umpires are paid traveling and living expenses—their allowance, for some reason or other, is $600 less than in the American League—and they benefit from an excellent forced-savings pension plan. Each month the league withholds $100 of an umpire's salary and matches it with another $100.

If you have the temperament for the job and the ability to make the majors, umpiring is not a bad-paying profession, particularly when you take into account that the salary, like a player's, covers not an entire year but the seven-month-long baseball season. Between October and March, when spring training begins, an umpire can supplement his yearly take through some other activity. Jocko Conlan, for example, runs a flower shop in Chicago, and Dusty Boggess does promotional work for a motor line in Shreveport. A sizable percentage officiate other sports, and Bill Stewart in 1938 managed the Chicago Blackhawks hockey team to a world's championship. Barlick has undertaken a variety of off-season jobs, ranging from administrative work for the Illinois Veterans Bureau to physical labor on his friends' farms. He usually plans one hunting trip, but for the most part he sticks around home. This is quite understandable when you consider that an umpire has no real private life during the baseball season and is lucky when the schedule allows him to dart home for a quick one-day reunion with his family. The Barlicks have two daughters, Marlene, ten, and Kathleen, nine. They have never watched their father work a big league game, and Barlick frequently wonders what their reaction would be if they happened to attend a game in which he was at the heart of a rhubarb.

At home before each new season begins, Barlick assembles his regalia. The most expensive items are one blue serge plate-suit and two base-suits of the same material, which cost $75 each at Schwartz Brothers in Cincinnati, the Brooks Brothers of the umpiring world. A plate-suit—the trousers and jacket are both cut more generously—generally lasts Barlick two seasons, a base-suit about four. The league supplies each umpire, free of charge, with two lightweight summer uniforms of tropical worsted. The accessories, which each individual umpire provides, include one mask (about $18), good for four or five seasons' wear; one pair of shin guards ($15), repadded every two years; one pair of plate-shoes, with metal toe-and-instep guards ($30); one pair of base-shoes ($22.50); a half-dozen plate caps for each season (at $3 each), short-billed to fit under the mask; two base-caps; two black ties; six white shirts; one indicator ($25), which, as a rule, holds out for about five years. In the American League the plate umpire wears an inflated protector over his coat; he stands almost erect and directly behind the catcher. In the National League style, developed by Klem, the umpire practically interposes himself between the batter and the catcher, leaning over the catcher's shoulder on the batter's side of the plate. He weaves in and out with each pitch. Since a big protector would be awkward, he wears a smaller, uninflated snug-fitting protector of tough fiber-composition under his coat. "It really doesn't make any difference what kind of protector you wear," Barlick believes. "If a fellow can umpire, he can umpire with a washtub in front of him." Barlick, incidentally, feels there is little or no basis for the old inside-baseball dictum that the National League tends to call the controversial knee-high pitch a strike where the American calls it a ball.

The hardest month for an umpire is September. He has been away from home for six months, traveling continuously. The daily pressure has worn him down, and the critical, pennant-deciding games lie ahead. Last September one of Barlick's easier stretches was a series of three night games in Philadelphia, in midmonth, between the Cards and the Phillies. These teams were contending for third place, and if the series had somewhat the aspect of a recuperation period for Barlick, it was only in contrast to "The Battle of the Bean-Balls" between the Dodgers and the Giants which he had worked just previously.

Barlick traveled by train to Philadelphia with his old friend and colleague, Lee Ballanfant, who had also been given the Giant-Dodger series as a special assignment. On their train ride they hashed over, intermittently, some of the episodes in that series, in particular the fifth game in which Larry Jansen, the Giants' pitcher, was summarily ejected from the game after hitting a Brooklyn batter with a pitch. Jansen had been fined $25 by President Giles, but the fine had been remitted at the request of the umpires. Jansen is known to them as a co-operative player and a nice guy. In the umpires' unanimous judgment, Larry had merely been following his manager's orders. On the other hand, the umpires felt that Durocher, who was fined $200 and suspended for three days for his part in the brawling, had gotten off perhaps too lightly. "As a general rule, players aren't out to make trouble unless the manager wants it that way," Barlick frequently states. "Did you ever see any good parents who had lousy kids?"

Because Giles was present in person for the Giant-Dodger series, the umpires conferred directly with him on their problems after the games. The usual channels for reporting to headquarters are a bit different. At the finish of a game from which he has ejected a player, a coach, or a manager, the umpire writes a report of the incident and mails it special delivery airmail to league headquarters in Cincinnati. Most ejections are provoked by a player's use of "profane and abusive language." This language must necessarily be cited oath for oath, and, as a result, these reports rank among the fruitiest reading presently available in the English language. "Dear Mr. Giles," a typical umpire's report will start, "Yesterday I ejected———in the fifth inning of the——— game because he used profane and abusive language. I have been called all kinds of a so-and-so in my time but not what he called me. He called me a gutless so-and-so, a choking so-and-so, a so-and-so so-and-so . . ." and so on into that

realm where even Hemingway fears to tread. Barlick's reports
are sometimes written with such indignation that his pen
actually shakes with his rage. "Our hands are tied like a
wooden Indian," he has written more than once when he
has felt a manager or player has gone way out of bounds and
merits a come-uppance much stiffer than a token fine or
brief suspension.

In the event the rhubarb was a complicated one, Giles
sometimes will request separate reports from all four umpires. At other times he telephones umpires for more details,
or he will phone the management of the team that is involved and ask for its side of the story. In his office in
Cincinnati, Giles has a recording machine installed beside
his desk. It is his practice to record all telephone conversations pertaining to the causes and effects of a major fracas.
He then calls in his assistant, Fred Fleig, the league's supervisor of umpires. After weighing the complete evidence to
the best of their ability, they decide on whether the player
or manager merits a fine or suspension, or both, or neither,
and if so, how much and how long.

At the Penn-Sheraton Hotel in Philadelphia, Ballanfant
and Barlick rejoined their regular partners, Augie Donatelli
and Tom Gorman. This quartet comprised team number
four in an experiment conducted last season by Giles. He divided his sixteen umpires into four teams of four, the idea
being that a permanent team would in time operate far more
smoothly as a unit than four umpires thrown together for
a series or two and then broken up. The results were uneven.
There were some good teams and some not so good teams.
Team number four was perhaps the happiest combination,
able at their work and a harmonious blend of personalities—
Ballanfant, dry-humored and mature; Barlick, the hard-
driving perfectionist; Donatelli, talkative and merry, from
western Pennsylvania, a former Air Force tail-gunner who

spent fifteen months in a German prisoner-of-war camp, now in his third year as a National League umpire; and Gorman, a brawny, quiet, respectful sophomore umpire, a native of the Bronx, a pitcher with the Giants in 1940, and at thirty-two the youngest arbiter in the league. In their bantering moods around a hotel lobby or in a dressing room, Ballanfant is "Judge" to his partners, Gorman is "The Kid," and Barlick and Donatelli confusingly refer to each other as "Moose."

It is a very helpful circumstance if umpires get along, for their profession dictates that they spend an immense amount of time in their own company. In the best interests of baseball, they are directed to choose hotels, like the Penn-Sheraton, where the ball teams do not stop. An umpire must be impartial, and familiarity might hamper his objectivity. There is nothing wrong if an umpire and a player who are friends have a meal or a drink together, and many of them do, but close or continued fraternization is taboo. Since their conduct is always subject to public scrutiny and gossip, most umpires avoid the glitter spots, drink very moderately, and usually make it beer. In Philadelphia, for example, the favorite after-the-game relaxation spot of team number four is a quiet German restaurant called Rucker's.

Barlick worked the first game of the series at Philadelphia at second base, went to first base for the second game, and moved behind the plate for the third and last game. It is conventional for umpires to rotate clockwise around the diamond, each man acting as plate umpire every fourth game. Umpiring behind the plate is, of course, the real workout. In an average game the four umpires make from 240 to 260 decisions, and the man calling balls and strikes makes 220 of them. Barlick eats light before a game in which he is scheduled to work behind the plate. The last day at Philadelphia, for instance, he limited himself to a bowl of thick vegetable soup late in the afternoon. The game was set for eight P.M.

That evening the members of team number four arrived at Shibe Park an hour before game time, their usual practice. They went immediately to the umpires' dressing room beneath the stands and fell automatically into their pregame division of duties. Ballanfant, who had umpired at the plate the night before, set off on "police duty"—positioning himself in the stands while the teams were practicing to make sure there was no undue fraternizing between the opposing players. Barlick, as plate umpire, had the job of taking the gloss off five dozen new baseballs, which the home team provides for each game. Standing at the sink, he moistened some black dirt enclosed in an old coffee tin, spread a little dirt over his fingers and his palms, and massaged the cover of each new ball for ten seconds or so until the shine was off.

As the game time approached, Barlick became increasingly talkative, a habit of his when he is about to work a game as plate umpire. He swept through a series of dialect stories and some quick imitations of the mannerisms of Cardinal and Phillies pitchers. He was oddly silent for a minute. "Moose," he then called over to Donatelli, "bientôt finie, la guerre." This was the sentence—"The war will soon be over"—with which an old Frenchman in Donatelli's prisoner-of-war camp optimistically greeted him each morning. Team number four adopted it as its motto. It was never more applicable than in September when it seemed that the season would never end.

Five minutes before eight, team number four left the dressing room and moved onto the field. As is the custom, the third-base umpire—Ballanfant this night—carted the ball bag and turned it over to the ball boy. Barlick picked up a copy of each team's starting line-up, tossed a rosin bag out to the mound, loosened up with a few deep knee bends, filled each pocket with four baseballs, gave the catcher a ball, adjusted his mask, cleared his throat and his indicator, and, at the stroke of eight, cried "Play ball!" The first pitch by Robin Roberts, on the mound for the Phillies, was over the heart of the plate. Barlick made a big lunging stride toward the first-base pavilion, shot out his right arm and jabbed his index finger in the direction of the stands, and boomed "Stee-ruck-huh." A responsive chuckle and buzz swept around the ball park.

Like all good umpires, Barlick is a "pattern-caller." His method is to call strike one with a step to the right; he whirls, strides, and thrusts to the left on strike two; he punches straight toward the sky on strike three. On balls, he makes no body movements, just growls the call. Like all good umpires, Barlick is also a rhythm-caller. As the pitcher is about to release the ball, he leans forward in a crouch between the catcher and the batter, then rocks back with the pitch. "When you miss a pitch—that is, you're pretty sure you called it right but you didn't follow it the way you know is natural for you—you don't think about how the players or the fans reacted, you think about where you went wrong in your rhythm," Barlick says. "You ask yourself, 'Did I come up too quick on that low pitch? Did I swing back too soon and miss the angle?' You bear down extra hard to get back into the rhythm so you see the pitch the way you like to see it."

Before each pitch, Barlick sets his eyes at the same level as the batter's shoulders. If the ball crosses the plate higher than his eyes, Barlick knows it is a ball—above the strike zone, which is between the batter's shoulders and his knees. Low pitches are more difficult, and the knee-high curve is the hardest of all.

The game, which Roberts and the Phillies eventually won 3–2, proceeded without incident until the first of the ninth. There were no interference or obstruction plays—the most ticklish of all "situation calls." There was no kicking on balls and strikes, and neither team had any provocation for riding Barlick or giving him "the blind-man act." This is one of the most humorous (except to the umpire) of all baseball customs: one or two players on the team which "wuz robbed" by the ump walk up and down their dugout, using a bat as a cane and groping blindly for the wall with the other hand.

In the top of the ninth, however, there was a mild blowup. The rally the Cards were trying to mount fizzled when Peanuts Lowery, with a two and two count, tried to check his swing on a high pitch; he ticked the ball and the catcher held it for the third strike. When Barlick called him out, Lowery began to jump up and down like an angry child, insisting he had not broken his wrists on the swing. Barlick ripped off his mask and, raising his voice so that it at least matched Lowery's in volume, rasped back at him, " Look, it doesn't matter whether you broke your wrists or not. You foul-tipped it. The catcher held it. You're out. You've no beef." Sensing that he was making no headway, Lowery looked for assistance to Manager Stanky, coaching at third.

Stanky walked peaceably to the plate but, upon arrival, his neck shot out like a turtle's and, pumping his head from side to side, he took up the argument with his celebrated pugnacity. Barlick took a step forward. He repeated his decision and his reasons for it. "You've no grounds for an argument," he summarized as he pointed to third base and told Stanky to get back to his position. Stanky did so after jawing for ten seconds more, and that was the end of the set-to. Another out, and the game was over.

There is always a little face-saving involved in blowups like this one. No manager or player wants the crowd to think he is being cowed by an umpire any more than an umpire enjoys being made to look ridiculous. Being human, an umpire will usually take a little more from a player or manager who doesn't try to show him up publicly. Luke Appling, for one, used to get away with some very vitriolic remarks at bat because he was smart enough to spit them out poker-faced as he rubbed dirt on his hands between pitches or removed a speck of dirt from his eye, looking for all the world like a law-abiding citizen. Sometimes—not too often—it happens the other way round. Taunted by the fans to get after an umpire, a manager will charge toward "the villain" with beetled brow. Then, while pretending to be giving him a bellyful, he will actually be asking him what he thinks of the traffic situation in Detroit. Being a direct man, Barlick is usually impatient to can the vaudeville and get on with the game.

The final Phillies-Cards game had been one of those modern baseball miracles: a game completed in under two hours. Barlick, Ballanfant, and Donatelli were thus enabled to shower and dress at a leisurely pace and still catch the eleven o'clock train for New York. Gorman, the fourth partner, was driving to New York, where he makes his home, with his wife. The following afternoon team number four was scheduled to officiate the first of a two-game series at the Polo Grounds between the Giants and the Reds; then over to Brooklyn for two games; then up to Boston. It is customary for umpires to receive their assignments six days in advance.

Donatelli, Ballanfant, and Barlick found a table in the train's club car and ordered beers and ham-and-swiss sandwiches. Barlick was in fairly buoyant spirits. He was delighted that his partners congratulated him on calling "a real good game" because he had thought it had been one of his best.

"The only pitches that really bothered me were those three in a row to Roberts last time he batted," Barlick said.

"The two fast balls on the outside corner and the curve just inside," Ballanfant remembered out loud. "I saw them that way."

"I thought you had 'em, Moose." Donatelli smiled at Barlick in corroboration.

The conversation drifted into a review of the game, then into lapidary reflections on the arduousness of their trade. "Moose," Barlick said to Donatelli, "did I ever tell you about the trapped-ball play I had at Chicago? The Judge knows this one, but I think this was before you came up. Anyhow, it was at Wrigley Field, about four years ago. The Cubs and the Cards. The Cubs ahead, 3–2. Two outs in the top of the ninth. A man on first, Diering. Nelson batting. Got it? O.K. Nelson hits a looping liner to left-center. I'm on third. I run out as far as I can to cover the play, way out. Pafko— he's in center—reaches down and across, backhand, for the ball, just as it's about to fall in. He doesn't get it. He traps it, covers it up, rolls over, and starts running in with the ball like he's caught it. I make the "no" sign immediately. I make it again. Pafko disregards it. He keeps running in with the ball as if the game's over. Diering scores from first. Nelson's around third. When Pafko finally throws, he hits Nelson on the back and Nelson scores the winning run. You can imagine how those Cubs came at me."

"Rough. Ooh, a rough one," Donatelli groaned sympathetically.

"I told that Charley Grimm," Barlick continued, worked up now and reliving the episode, "I told that Charley Grimm, 'Charley, I call 'em as I see 'em and I let the chips fall where they may.' Moose, no one will ever convince me that Pafko caught that ball, not even Andy Pafko, who's a very fine boy, because I saw that ball on the ground."

A moment later Barlick left the table to check on the suitcases and the umpires' large equipment cases.

"That old Moose," Donatelli said to Ballanfant, "he really gives it all he's got."

"All the time," Ballanfant nodded. "That boy's not just a good umpire. He's a great umpire, the same way Stan Musial's a great ballplayer." Ballanfant then gave Barlick the highest compliment one umpire can give another. "From what I've seen the twenty-eight years I've been in this business," he said with finality, "Barlick is in the same class with Klem, and those two are in a class by themselves."

THE LURE OF GOLF

In the eight years since this essay was written, the heart of the game of golf has, not surprisingly, altered little if at all. At the same time, there have been some interesting changes in our manner of approaching the game in America, and these might be briefly noted:

1. The electric golf cart, which was in its infancy in 1953, has now become a permanent part of the golf scene. Men who are perfectly capable of walking 18 or 36 holes a day sometimes go an entire year without playing a single hole on foot. The day is at hand, unquestionably, when progressive clubs will provide the equivalent of the old Wampus Babies to drive these carts, and golf will then become an even more popular diversion and a somewhat harder game.

2. The base of the golf pyramid has continued to broaden. In the old days you hesitated to recommend golf to people whose co-ordination you knew to be faulty, for you felt that they would become chagrined by their enduring inability to break 120 and would rue the day they ever took up the game. Well, today among the new thousands who have embraced golf, there are countless addicts, middle-aged women in particular, who play their nine holes between 65 and 75, hit no shots well and never will, and tell you with unabashed enthusiasm what a wonderful game it is,

even better than skee-ball. I would have thought that one needed to hit the semblance of a good shot every other round at least to take to golf, but apparently I was wrong. I was wrong also about Paul Anka, the flo-thru teabag, and wedgies.

3. In the last few years televised golf, both live coverage of the major tournaments and filmed series offering weekly matches between leading professionals, has spread the gospel far and wide. The filmed shows have had quite a few virtues but at least as many flaws, foremostly, perhaps, the introduction of a synthetic un-golfy jargon by some of the announcers. While this has been going on, the public, in a different direction, has also gradually become much more aware of the peculiar patois, almost a foreign tongue, in which the young professionals on the tour communicate. As a result one sometimes meets up these days with ardent golf fans who, having digested both the stilted TV elocution and the tour slang in equal parts, give out with a bizarre hybrid language which sounds something like this: "At the end of seven holes I was leading my opponent by four shots, 35 to 39, and, man, I guarantee I was hitting it a ton on that track. However, on hole number eight, a short hole with a par of 3 which can be reached in one shot from the tee, my veteran opponent stroked his ball onto the clipped surface of the green, and your boy, what does he do? He takes the pipe and chilly-dips it right onto the beach—a real fried egg." We must be sure and leave behind a Rosetta Stone for future generations.

O NE OF SPORT'S OLDEST STORIES concerns the golfer who threw his clubs into the sea after a painfully bad round and almost drowned trying to rescue them. That particular golfer happened to be a Scotsman, which adds a certain amount of relish to the story, but it is also irrelevant. Of all the games man has devised, supposedly for his enjoyment, golf is in a class by itself in the anguish it inflicts. For each good reason a golfer can cite (after a fine round) why it is the most satisfying of games, he knows there are at least two equally good reasons for giving it up for good. Few ever do it. Golf has been played for about eight centuries now. In its modern form—that is, since the feather-stuffed ball was replaced by the gutta-percha—it is just about 100 years old. Over that period, golfers have continuously counseled their nongolfing friends that the game is a pernicious, habit-forming drug and that a man is better off not to touch the stuff. The result has been that golf's popularity has kept on expanding and the game is now played by 10,000,000 in every corner of the globe. You might as well tell a fellow not to have anything to do with pretty girls.

As if life in mid-century United States were not sufficiently conducive to strain and frustration, 5,000,000 of the world's 10,000,000 golfers are Americans. This represents an astounding growth considering that in 1888 there were less than a dozen golfers in the country—most of them the charter members of the St. Andrews Golf Club of Yonkers, N. Y., the first permanent golf club organized in the United States. As late as 1913 there were only 350,000 American golfers, at the turn of the Twenties scarcely 1,000,000. Then the rush began and it has been continuing ever since. Today, to take care of the horde, there are approximately 5,000 golf courses: 3,000-odd private courses, over 1,200 daily-fee courses, and some 800 municipal-, county-, or state-operated courses generally lumped together with fee courses as "public links." (Technically speaking, a links or linksland is a geographic term of British origin, denoting the sandy deposits along a coast line built up over the years by the ebb and flow of the tides. This distinction between a golf links and other types of courses has long been ignored, and today a links has become, in the vernacular, synonymous with any acreage on which golf is played.) Our 5,000 courses are spread over the entire country. Nevada has eight. For the most part, however, they are congregated where the population is thickest, and one of the most fantastic and yet characteristic aerial views of America is the multiplicity of courses, each with its clearly

defined fairways and its kidney-shaped traps around the
greens, that the traveler sees as his plane approaches any
sizable city.

It is customarily recognized, I think—even among men
who are devoted to sailing, tennis, huntin'-shootin'-fishin',
or other participant sports—that the most dedicated fol-
lower of these diversions never becomes quite as intensely
and hopelessly embroiled as does the man whom golf takes
up. When you ask most golfers why this is so, they are of very
little help. They fall back on the fifty-year-old cliché about
being "bitten by the golf bug" and then each rattles on about
how bad his particular case is, like kids proudly comparing
the size of mosquito bites.

There are a few contemplative golfers who have attempted
to analyze why the golf virus hits a man so hard. The game's
singular fascination, in their consensus, rests on the fact that
while you play against par, against your opponent, against
the topography, and against the elements, in golf, as in no
other sport, *your principal opponent is yourself*. No one
touches the golfer's ball but the golfer himself. If you slice
your approach with your five iron into a luxurious patch of
brier, you cannot slink out of the responsibility for a rotten
shot by turning to your adversary, as you can in tennis, and
exclaiming, "Beautiful forehand, Reg!" Nor can you alibi
out in the other direction with the muffled insinuation that
something your partner did accounts for your seemingly
poor showing. Nobody else sliced that ball into the rough.
Furthermore, since you get no second serve, no third strike,
no fourth down, you're stuck with it. On the other hand,
when you recover neatly from the brier patch and hole your
slippery twenty-foot putt for a par, nobody else had a hand
in it either. All the glory of the accomplishment rests
squarely on the shoulders of the guy who best appreciates
your colossal skill.

While man's battle against himself is undoubtedly at the

heart of golf's abiding appeal, there are a number of subsidiary reasons for the game's acceptance by its wide and varie-
gated following. The setting in which it is played is, for most
golfers, one of the most wonderful things about it. Were it
not for the good greensward of the golf course, many hard-
pressed American males, their lives increasingly tethered by
the rites of city living, might never get any farther back to
nature than growing chives in the window box of their apartment. Golfers never really lose their awareness of the natural
beauties of a golf course—the freshness of the air in the
morning when the dew is heavy on the striped greens, the
pungent quietness in the evenings when the crickets start up
and the setting sun makes the fairways ahead seem lusher
than velvet. Veteran golfers breathe in these sensuous
charms, but they don't talk much about them. They view
them as part of the obvious bounty of golf. They are annoyed
rather than diverted when some golfer-come-lately begins to
rhapsodize on the scene like some self-elected Tennyson.
"This is golf, man!" the veteran golfer is apt to snarl on these
trying occasions. "What did you expect to find out here? A
bowling alley?"

Very few golfers ever get to that stage of nature-loving
where they can identify any flora other than grass, dande-
lions, and occasionally poison ivy. This is understandable.
Trying to hit their shots correctly is too absorbing an occupation to admit any avocations. You will find, with few exceptions, that any seasoned golfer who suddenly exhibits an
intimate knowledge of agronomy is deep in the throes of
some concealed discomfiture. At the course where I grew up,
our leading expert on the various grass strains was not the
greenkeeper but an aging boy wonder whose game had long
gone sour and who could no longer break 85 except when he
played by himself. He persisted, however, in regarding himself as a 74 golfer, and this made a knowledge of grasses a
must. "I don't see how you fellows can putt on this Merion

blue grass," he would groan in exasperation, his hands on his hips, his eyes fixed captiously on the green, after he had jabbed a three-foot putt a foot off line. "Creeping bent, that's the only grass a man with a delicate touch can putt on," he would continue. "The whole course has gone to pot. You know that spoon shot of mine that looked smothered? I hit it perfectly, really, but you can't get a ball up in the air from these fescue and redtop fairways. I ask you: how are you expected to play golf on a lousy pasture?"

Every enthusiast of the game, though, is a golf-course architect as well as a golfer. He knows exactly where each hole falls short of championship quality: the green on the first is located in the wrong spot; the trap to the right of the second green improperly penalizes a well-played shot; the third hole should not be a dog-leg; the fourth (a straightaway par five) should be a dog-leg par four; and so on, with infinitely more detail and passion. If he were chairman of the Green Committee with a free hand and the necessary funds, he'd know what had to be added and what had to come out to change his course into a testing but fair examination in golf—"which, after all, Harry, is the idea of this game, in case you've forgotten."

What this golfer-architect would end up by doing, should he ever come to power as head of the Green Committee, would be to remodel the course so that it compensated as perfectly as possible for his own peculiar and habitual short-comings as a player. This is no wild assumption. Chairmen of the Green Committee—the men elected or appointed to watch over the golf course—have historically watched over themselves. For example, when the chairman happens to be a short hitter, all those traps out by the 200-yard marker are suddenly condemned as unfit for human habitation, filled in, and turfed over. Show me, as the old saying goes, the Green Committee chairman who hasn't chopped at least five strokes off his score, and I'll show you a very angry man.

This purposeful myopia among amateur course designers goes back to an old pro at the business, Charles Blair Macdonald, who flourished just before the turn of the century as our first official National Amateur champion and as the designer of the nation's first eighteen-hole course, at the Chicago Golf Club in Wheaton, Illinois. Macdonald laid out the course so that the holes marched clockwise around the perimeter of the club's plot. The golfer who hooked on any hole ended up in heavy rough, and if he hooked quite badly, his ball shot off the course and out of bounds and he was penalized loss of stroke and distance. Old Charley, of course, never hooked. He had a fine grooved slicy swing, and when he sliced, there was always ample room out there on the right to take good care of his ball. The old boy was unbeatable on his home course for years!

Golf is unique among the "active sports" in that a man can be lacking in youth, brawn, speed of foot, suppleness of muscle, clearness of eye, and the other athletic virtues and still be a pretty fair golfer. This is certainly one of golf's attractions, this fact that it is a game which a man, or a woman, can carry through life. In Gene Sarazen's opinion, a golfer with good health and a sound swing should be able to play with his competence little diminished until he is sixty-five.

There is no debating, though, that the younger a person is when he takes up golf, the easier it is for him to develop a correct and rhythmic swing. The golf swing is not a facile natural movement (like batting a baseball) so much as it is a disciplined exercise in co-ordination—what Ben Hogan calls "muscle memory." Nonetheless, a man can take up the game with some expectation of attaining a reasonable proficiency at an age when it is no longer safe to indulge in contact or team sports. The same sanguine prospect applies for a man who was never conspicuously good at games and has no athletic prime to be past. The classic example is

Walter Travis who decided to become a golfer when he was thirty-five, and four years later—in 1900—captured the first of his three National Amateur Championships.

A Travis comes along once a century, and most men who start golf after thirty, or who begin to concentrate on the game around that age, are not fools enough to think they can duplicate Travis' miracle. It is the rare golfer, nevertheless, be he novice or old-timer, who can resign himself to the unflattering reality that he is no better than his usual score. In golf, the score is the prime consideration, whatever a man may profess to the contrary. Golfers periodically sound off about how they really don't care about their scores; all they want to do is hit the ball well, they'll settle for that. In translation this means that the speaker has been chipping and putting poorly, or is in the throes of some such score-defeating malaise, and hasn't much confidence of getting his touch back for a while.

That Ol' Debbil Score, for some abstruse reason, makes double-talk experts out of men who ordinarily have their feet on the ground, and it hatches not only more liars per capita than any other sport (not excluding fishing) but also the most implausible liars in the world. The fish that got away is one thing, but there is no rational accounting for the otherwise solid citizen who, frankly in front of your gaze, plays nine shots to get his ball into the hole and, when asked what his score was, says, "Six, dammit." The game, in some mysterious way, must have a direct pipeline to man's pride.

It can be truthfully stated, I think, that outscoring his opponent does wonders for a golfer's morale, but what really sets him up on a cloud is outscoring himself. To illustrate— once or twice a year a golfer who regularly shoots between 95 and 100 will come onto one of those days when he can do no wrong and will score an 88, no putts conceded other than the usual "gimmes" under a foot and a half. As far as that golfer is concerned, he is an 88 shooter. Those rounds between 95 and 100 to which he immediately returns are all "off-rounds," he is not shooting his game, his game is 88. A player can have his hot streaks in football or basketball or any other sport, but after the inevitable letdown sets in, most men are not too stubborn about admitting that they were playing over their heads. Golfers are a race apart. They are all convinced that they habitually play "under their heads."

There is something about the nature of the game, too, that eternally deludes the golfer into believing that he is on the verge of "coming into his own" and that if he corrects one tiny movement—the way he bends his left knee or the position of his right thumb—then his swing will overnight become a vision of beauty and even-par rounds will be no trouble at all. He begins to dream about how he will phrase his acceptance speech after winning the National Open. This is what makes golf such a humbling game. It looks to be the easiest of sports but it is in fact the hardest to play consistently well. Quite frequently, the very moment a golfer thinks he has mastered the critical technique is the precise moment when he discovers he cannot hit any shot. He wobbles off the course buried beneath such a mountain of powerlessness that he seriously doubts if he will be able to drive his automobile home and negotiate the difficult coordinative feat of climbing the front stairs.

In their pursuit of lower scores and higher self-esteem, American golfers invest prodigally in foolproof accessories, the latest models in clubs, "stroke-saving" home-practice equipment—more aids to success than for all other sports rolled together. There is nothing wrong in this, as any good pro with a well-stocked shop will tell them. In the view of many responsible critics, however, American golfers, in their obsession with lower scores at any price, have gone too far and done themselves and the game a considerable disservice over the last twenty years. They have successfully pressured

Green Committees to soften up our courses to that lamentable degree where a golfer is often no worse off after a mishit shot than after a superb one. Greens are overwatered so that a half-topped niblick will stick. Overhanging lips have been removed from traps so that a man can scramble out with a putter. Roughs, above all, have been domesticated to where they are often indistinguishable from the fairways.

This mollycoddling of the heart of the game has produced lower scores, all right, and also a new breed of golfers who have forgotten that much of the game's satisfaction results from dealing resourcefully with the hazards. And with the weather, too, it might be added. On a recent trip to Britain, a young friend of mine, who had grown up with the idea that only a cloudless, windless day was fit for golf, walked onto the first tee at Sandwich on such a day and was staggered when his English host declared that it was disappointingly poor weather for golf. "The course will be dull today," the Englishman added apologetically. "There's hardly any wind for us to contend with."

The outstanding difference in the attitudes of Britain and America, the world's two great golfing communities, is, very probably, the Britisher's zest for subduing the authentic hazards and battling the elements. He is a more accomplished bad-weather golfer than his American counterpart, not simply because his native island provides him with such a fine supply of bad weather, but also because the top-heavy percentage of British courses, including those not on the seaside, have the general characteristics of links. The typical fairways in Britain are not tree-lined, as are ours, and the wind rampages unopposed across the exposed holes and becomes the major hazard. In the opinion of Henry Longhurst, the celebrated "golf correspondent" of the *London Sunday Times*, the American pro's minutely detailed, synchromeshed type of swing could have evolved only in a country where golf is a warm-weather game and not the all-weather sport it is in Britain, where there is no "south" to head for in winter. Bundled up in two sweaters, a strong wind making perfect balance impossible, even the most talented British pro, in the cold months, must forgo the niceties of what Mr. Longhurst calls "the shirt-sleeve swing."

(Incidentally, it might be mentioned that Mr. Longhurst —along with such other British golf writers as the incomparable Bernard Darwin and Sam McKinlay, plus our own Grantland Rice and the late O. B. Keeler—has given golf a vitality in print that is probably superior to that enjoyed by any other popular game.)

British golfers play their rounds at a much faster pace than we do, a distinction that is also true of other European golfers, South American golfers, African golfers, Asiatic golfers, and aged Australian golfers with blisters. It is undeniable: the American, Speed's own child, is a tortoise on the golf course. Where it was once possible to play eighteen holes on a Saturday afternoon or Sunday morning in three and a half hours, now you are doing handsomely if you get around in under five. Our courses are clogged by new players who are polite as all get-out but are never ready to play when it is their shot and by veterans who grew up in the era when caddies were plentiful and have never learned how to watch and mark a shot themselves, which they must when a caddie cart is carrying their bag. Above all, traffic on our courses bogs down because our golfers (of all degrees of skill) have taken to overstudying their shots in imitation of our professional stars who, before playing each stroke, do everything but telephone the American Geographic Society for a report on the green ahead.

Golf is certainly not the only participation sport which offers release and relaxation, but golfers are convinced that golf does it best. In what other game, they ask, are the pleasures of sociability interwoven so naturally with the pleasures of an athletic contest? The rhythm of golf is unique. After a man gets into it—and always assuming that he is playing well enough so that golf acts as a counterirritant to the pressures of the outside world and not as a positive irritation in itself—it becomes second nature for him to slide effortlessly from a conversation with the members of his foursome into the concentration necessary to play his stroke and then to resume the conversation as if there had been no interruption at all. "Hit your shot—I'll finish the story afterwards" is a remark that occurs with such usualness, as a friendly foursome makes its way around the course, that a golfer is hardly conscious of hearing it or saying it. Contrast this camaraderie with the grim silence that overtakes competitors in other sports which are played in a purportedly affable atmosphere. Conversational exchanges on a tennis court, for instance, often begin and end with one word: "Shot!" This is an abbreviated form of "Good shot!" If a player uses the entire expression, he is classified as gabby. Besides, he is wantonly expending his wind.

Golfers talk a lot, and they talk very well as a rule. Out in the privacy of the course, invigorated by the sweet air and the spring of the turf, a man opens up. He speaks his mind candidly on almost any subject. Things strike him humorously, including himself. With so little premium placed on formal politeness, he becomes, if not precisely "a boy again," as some golfers like to think of themselves, at least a pretty outward-going fellow. As long as a golfer doesn't misuse the privilege of self-expression in the company of his golfing cronies he is free, after making some stupid error, to vent his infuriation by cursing, sulking, criticizing the condition of the course, and slamming his clubs into the ground or throwing them at any handy tree. In the outside world, this spontaneous petulance would be held against a man. Not so among his golfing friends. They have been in the same position; they understand.

True companionship flourishes on a golf course as it does in few other climes, and because it does, it is only to be expected that this boon should be abused. The most skillful offenders—well enough known to have become accepted as a permanent part of American folklore—are the country-club businessmen, the salesmen who have discovered that they can nail their man much more easily out on the golf course, where his guard is down, than in his office. If the salesman possesses a tournament-quality golf game, it helps immeasurably. Every golfer admires a well-hit shot—the fluid swing, the crispness with which the clubhead makes contact with the ball, the ever-delightful sensation of watching the ball streak for the pin, brake itself neatly on the green, and then bobble toward the hole "as if it had eyes." If you're going to have to buy from someone, you might as well give your business to a guy who can treat you to a succession of first-class golf shots. A seasoned golfing salesman knows when to win, when to come out all even, and when to fall apart at the seams and absorb a valuable thrashing. For many a golfer's money, one of the unsung classics of American art is the cartoon, executed in the '20s, depicting the "star salesman" out on the practice green practicing missing his short putts.

The fine fabric of golf is also frequently tugged to the ripping point by golfers who are not above deliberately "using" the social relationships the game affords as their chief tactic for winning their matches. A sprinkling of these "natural competitors" can be found at almost every golf club. Most of them have long since stopped trying to improve their own games, for they discover early that a surer road to victory is helping the other fellow to lose. It is easy in golf. Your opponent is always within conversational range.

At a club in my home town there was a golfer of this victory-first disposition who, whenever his opponent or opponents happened to be playing well, would pretend complete lack of interest in the outcome of the match. "How can anyone concentrate on a simply gorgeous day like this?" he would babble in a dreamy cadence. "I just can't take the

game seriously when I'm out with you fellows—you're too
much fun to be with," he would sigh with affecting wistful-
ness, or, sometimes, it would be something on the order of
"What a fool I am not to play more of these lazy rounds
when no one gives a damn if he wins or loses." This fellow
would hack away at you with sweet talk until he made you
feel like an out-and-out boor for wanting to play your best
game. Then, having lulled you into a deep torpor, he would
be all business, concede not even an eight-inch putt, become extremely technical about the rules, and relax not for a
second until he had the match safely tucked away. Walter
Hagen, the granddaddy of all tactical golfers, used to resort to
a variation of this technique when he found himself trailing
a hopeful young rival in a tournament. "My, you're hitting
the ball beautifully!" Walter would purr, all admiration.
"After you win this title, kid, you and I will go on an exhibition tour together." The young man's head would start to
spin with dreams of fame and glory, his concentration would
weaken, Hagen would pull the match out, and then, of
course, there was no more talk of that exhibition tour together.

The ways by which victory-bent golfers attempt to throw
their opponents off their games are as innumerable as the
facets of human nature. Learning how to combat or ignore
them is an essential part of learning to play the game, as
basic as keeping your head down. A few years ago when
Stephen Potter, an Englishman, published his book *Gamesmanship*, subtitled "The Art of Winning Games Without
Actually Cheating," golfers' reactions to Mr. Potter's elaboration of "ploys," "gambits," and other devices for conquer-
ing a superior opponent were drastically different from the
reaction of nongolfing readers. This latter group looked upon
Mr. Potter as a creative man with the gift of humorous invention. Golfers, however, were inclined to view him as a
reporter who had submitted a survey on a field of old and
common knowledge, and they checked his findings in the

same let's-see-how-well-he's-done-it spirit with which a Ver-
monter would read a treatise on how to make maple sugar.

The recognition of gamesmanship, by any name, is as old
as golf, and books on the subject are almost as old. Around
the turn of the century Horace Hutchinson, an early British
Amateur champion, published *Hints on the Game of Golf.*
Here are a few typical passages from the section called "Hints
to Golfers of Riper Years."

*If your adversary is badly bunkered, there is no rule against
your standing over him and counting his strokes aloud, with
increasing gusto as their number mounts up; but it will be a
wise precaution to arm yourself with a niblick before doing
so, so as to meet him on equal terms.*

*If your adversary is a hole or two down, there is no serious
cause for alarm in his complaining of a severely sprained
wrist, or an acute pain resembling lumbago which checks his
swing. Should he happen to win the next hole, these symp-
toms in all probability will become less troublesome.*

And gamiest of all:

*If you find yourself being outplayed by the excellent iron
approaches of your adversary, it is sometimes a good plan to
say to him, in a tone of friendly interest, "Really you are
playing your iron wonderfully well today—better than I ever
saw you play it before. Can you account for it in any way?"
This is likely to promote a slight nervousness when he next
takes his iron in his hand; and this nervousness is likely, if the
match is at all a close one, to be of considerable service to
you. There is no rule to prevent your doing this; only after a
time will people stop playing with you.*

The most difficult rounds in golf, it follows, are those you
play with strangers. If you do not open yourself to their per-

sonalities, you deny yourself half the flavor of golfing. And if you do expose yourself, you render yourself vulnerable to the artifices of a possible "natural competitor." The sharpest illustration that comes to mind is the story of two middle-aged golfers I know, a doctor and a laundryman, who fled the winter in Massachusetts and drove to Pinehurst. On the first tee of the number two course they were informed by the starter that only foursomes were being sent out onto the crowded course and were subsequently introduced to two men from Ohio who were in the same boat. The four jovially but warily went about the business of arranging "a little match—to make things more interesting." Since each of the four described his usual game as being between 90 and 95, a four-ball match for "dollar Nassaus" was agreed on, the two Ohioans to oppose the two Massachusetts men on even terms. The doctor won the first hole with a par. Shooting way over his head, he won the second with a birdie, the third with a par, and the fourth with another birdie. He had never been so "hot" before and kept apologizing to his opponents and assuring them his streak couldn't last. En route to the fifth tee, the two New Englanders overheard one of the Ohioans growl in grim disgust to his partner, "A ninety-five golfer and he's two under par! Why, I'll bet that lying shyster isn't even a doctor!"

When the charms of golf are listed, a priority consideration must be given to the game's uniqueness in not being played on a field or court of specified dimensions with set regulation appointments. Each golf course possesses its own distinct and recognizable character. On a first-rate course, every hole—or almost every hole—has its own especial character. When a golfer speaks of the third at Augusta, the fifteenth at North Berwick, the sixteenth at Oakland Hills, the eighth at Pebble Beach, the fifth at Mildenhall, or the thirteenth at Myrtle Beach, in his mind's eye is an image every bit as individual and defined as the face of a friend. The traveling golfer is always bumping into new faces or renewing old acquaintances, and both experiences can be tremendously enjoyable.

The more a golfer travels, the clearer it becomes that, though each golf course has a separate personality, there is an inescapable sameness to practically all nineteenth holes. Antigolf men have the nineteenth hole in mind when they call golf "the hoof-and-mouth disease," their point being that after a golfer hoofs his eighteen holes, he comes in and tells you about his round at length and boringly. This charge is not entirely true. At the nineteenth hole, men talk at length and boringly on a wide variety of subjects.

Another golfing hazard to be avoided as sedulously as the bar is the country-club dance. Whether it is a good thing or a bad thing, it is a fact that golf in the United States always has had overly strong social connotations. A man may own a Cadillac and send his son to the right prep school, his wife may be active in the right charity drives, and he may have all the other hallmarks of success, but he really hasn't made the grade unless he belongs to the right country club. Once he has "made" it, there are times when he wonders if it was worth all the huffing and puffing, and the club dance is one of the times he is most conscious of the Marquandary he is in. It is understood at most club dances that anything goes— you confide in people how much you have always liked them, you carefully explain to other people why you had previously thought they were uppish, you discuss in a very frank way what's wrong with the social setup in the community and at the club, and, furthermore, to make these points stick, you show these people how democratic and carefree and uninhibited you can be. Life can be pretty exhausting when the proper thing is to be conventionally improper.

The more a golfer travels, the clearer it also becomes to him that the breadth of golf's popularity arises from the wondrous flexibility of the game. A man can play golf any way he wants to. Or, to put it the other way round, the matrix of golf is so all-encompassing that people of the most utterly different personalities are convinced that golf is *the* game which best gives them what they hope to find in a game.

Every club has not only its gamesmen but also its suprasportsmen who are addicted to golf because of the incomparable opportunities it presents for demonstrating how self-controlled and gallant they can be under circumstances which would shatter the poise of weaker men, such as D'Artagnan and the Scarlet Pimpernel . . . it has its technical watchdogs who are devoted to golf because no other game can fulfill quite so well their fondness for protocol or offer them as many rules to be wrangled over . . . its loners, introverts given to brooding and endless practice, who gravitate to golf because it is one game a man can play and enjoy without an opponent or a partner . . . its Hemingway types who still burn with the old desire to best their buddies at physical prowess and who, when they edge into the thirties, find the golf course one of the last safe fields of combat left to them . . . its intellectuals who are crazy about golf since no other sport affords them the opportunity for deep-purple theorizing as does this game in which a stationary ball is hit from a stationary stance . . . its gamblers who find the game ideal for arranging twenty-seven or so different bets that can be decided simultaneously . . . its dressers who see in golf the chance they have always wanted to express their colorful personalities, which they do by wearing chartreuse-and-borsch-colored slacks, plaid berets, and sports shirts depicting a Pacific island volcano in the process of eruption . . . its lovers of power who need not be reminded when they bash out a 200-yard drive, a commonplace achievement in golf, that they hit that ball farther than Babe Ruth's mightiest home run . . . its misogynists who revere the locker room as one of the last strongholds of all-male companionship, and its chasers who like their drinks with a woman on the side and can usually find a very pretty one on the veranda.

The wonder is that only 5,000,000 Americans are golfers.

ON THE VERANDA
WITH
JAMES MICHAEL CURLEY

This article appeared in December 1958, not long after Mayor Curley's death. An era passed away when he did. Since he was loved, he was mourned, but since he was also an institution connoting gaiety and a mischievous wink at the somber, there was little lamentation in the air around Boston as people recalled his unique personality and methods of operation. In fact, a wonderfully right joke started to go the rounds when, shortly after Mayor Curley's death, Archbishop Cushing was elevated to Cardinal. "Imagine that," so went the jest, "Jim Curley has been up in heaven only a matter of days and look what the man's accomplished already!"

FEW THINGS bring on recollection of times long unremembered as surely as an obituary notice does. Recently, for example, shortly after I had read of the death of James Michael Curley, many times the mayor of Boston and "the last of the old-time big-city political bosses," I found that my mind would not stay focused on the immediate matters at hand and kept darting back over the years to the middle 1920s when I knew Curley well.

Ours was a summertime friendship. In the years following

the close of World War I, my family used to spend the summers at Nantasket, a beach about twenty miles from the
Boston area. From Nantasket the men could commute to
work quite easily, and this, as we kids saw it, was an advantage
in more ways than one: they weren't stuck at the beach day
after day with nothing to do as we were. I realize it sounds
arch or contrived to say this, but life was terribly boring. I
think the main trouble was that Nantasket was too good a
bathing beach. The waves came pounding in and broke beautifully the whole uninterrupted curving length from Hull
Hill at one end down to Paragon Park at the other. It was
this very excellence of the surf that hampered a kid's style.
There was no boating at all. I remember one or two live-it-up
guys, who would have been of college age, fooling around
with a kayak for a brief time, but that was it.

What you did was go in swimming a couple of times a day
(an hour after you finished eating); you broad-jumped (both
running and standing) on that in-between stretch of sand
that was half wet and half dry, firm enough to jump from and
soft enough so you didn't sting your feet when you landed;
you strung out a few kids' games like tag or ringaleevo (local
pronunciation) in which the best hiding place was the grass,
about three or four feet high, that covered the short strip of
natural duneland between the houses on Beach Avenue and
the beginning of the beach; you fooled around with a little
croquet or "ran the bases," neither of which was any fun
unless it involved some guy you hated and could handle or
some girl you secretly liked; you watched the ships sailing by
miles away on the distant horizon of the ocean, and occasionally the New York boat was late; and the rest of the time you
spent desperately trying to work up some excitement over
things that had long ceased to be exciting, like crawling
under the verandas of the houses and, on your hands and
knees, exploring those sections which were not built on
cement foundations, or seeing how far you could walk with-

out losing your balance on the cement sea walls which bordered the various plots.

In the midst of this drab torpor there loomed one shining citadel of vitality—Mayor Curley. When he was around, the pace picked up and life suddenly became quite enjoyable. For example, he annually got the summer off to a bang-up start on Fourth of July Eve with a display of fireworks that lasted almost two hours and ended with some really sensational stuff, "bombs" which burst two or three times in the air and skyrockets which outdid anybody else's skyrockets, partly because a crew of workmen spent the afternoon and early evening setting them up for maximum performance. Mayor Curley did things in a big way. When the hurdy-gurdy man with the monkey came around, our fathers customarily gave the man only enough money for him to crank out one or two selections before he tipped his hat and the monkey tipped his and they went on their way. Mayor Curley must have given him a fortune, for on Fourth of July Eve he played continuous music for two hours, and throughout the summer he presented other long evening concerts in the graveled parking space in front of the mayor's stucco house.

There were other if less spectacular ways in which Mayor Curley's presence irradiated the monotony of the summer with a helpful splash of glamour. He and Mrs. Curley didn't entertain too often, but when they had a dinner party the guests dressed like nobody else who hit the beach; the men wore tuxedos or white jackets and the women were all dolled up and carried fans or feathers. These guests arrived in the biggest, sleekest cars of the era, and each Marmon or Peerless required long and appreciative study from us and a drawn-out consultation with its chauffeur. Sometimes, when someone came in a Rolls-Royce, our loyalty was pushed close to the breaking point, but we always managed to conclude that no car was quite in a class with Mayor Curley's own Pierce-

Arrow and that no other chauffeur was really as skillful a driver as the mayor's. As for Mayor Curley himself, whether he was mayor, governor, or out of office, he always remained Mayor Curley for us, or, more exactly, he remained Mayorcurley, a phrase as indivisible as damyankee.

I would not be reminiscing about the mayor, however, if there had not been an intimate core to our relationship. We talked a lot together, practically every night except when he had company for supper. The Curleys lived next door to us, and it was my habit, and that of many of the other kids, to set out for the Curleys' veranda after finishing supper. It was a large screened-in veranda set higher than most of the others on Beach Avenue, at the top of a steep flight of stairs banked with boxes of blue hydrangeas. The wicker chairs there were wide and comfortable, and if, upon my arrival, I saw through the front window that the Curleys were still in the dining room, I plunked myself familiarly in a chair and took my ease, breathing in the stiff whiff of the geraniums in the flower boxes and listening to the tinkle those Chinese strips of glass made when the breeze stirred them. Ostensibly I was waiting for Paul and Leo, the Curley boys my age, to come out, but really I was waiting for the mayor.

I suppose that today, if I were trying to explain Mayor Curley's charm and appeal, I would come up with something on the order of "he liked people" or "he understood kids" or some such behavior-motivation analysis striking like a sword to the heart of the matter. These would be correct, but I think it would be more correct simply to say that we found him a very interesting man. There were occasional nights when he was tired or preoccupied, but almost invariably he was in expansive good humor when he arrived on the veranda after coffee, a strong-smelling cigar in his mouth. Before you knew it he was telling you something interesting. I can't remember him talking politics ever. He talked about the leading entertainers of the day (like Will Rogers), about travel, about books ("I would advise you, if you are going to read

Sax Rohmer's *Dr. Fu Manchu* at night, to keep all the lights in your room blazing"), about history, about the movies (Douglas Fairbanks in *The Thief of Bagdad* was so good, in his estimation, that he refused to discuss it for fear of ruining the enjoyment of the people who hadn't yet seen it), and above and beyond all other subjects he talked sports.

His stories were far more dramatic than those that appeared in the sports pages. Most of them were sketches of the high points in the careers of extraordinary stars we had heard very little about, if we had heard anything at all: Louis (Chief) Sockalexis, the full-blooded Penobscot Indian who had played the outfield for the old Cleveland National League team; Heinie Groh, the Giant infielder who had fashioned his distinctive bottle-shaped bat to help him cure his weakness in hitting the curve ball; Jim Thorpe and the Carlisle Indians and the year Carlisle beat Harvard by tucking the football under the back of one of the player's jerseys and achieving such total deception that the player walked unmolested until he was out in the clear and then sprinted the rest of the way to the goal without a soul near him; Harry Wills, who the mayor described as "the one man Dempsey was afraid to fight" but who Dempsey could probably beat "now that Wills has grown old and his bones have developed the brittleness of age." The mayor liked a good mouth-filling word like Sockalexis or Paavo Nurmi or Adolfo Luque or Paulino Uzcudun, though I think he was happiest of all when expounding the virtues of Eppa Jeptha Rixey, the tall Virginian who pitched for the Reds. "Eppa Jeptha Rixey," he would proclaim sonorously. "He is a superb control pitcher, this Eppa Jeptha Rixey, and you must tell your father to take you to the ball park when Cincinnati next comes to town, so you can see Eppa . . . Jeptha . . . Rixey"—this last intoned oratorically like a man reading the inscription on an important Roman ruin.

The mayor's stories were so deeply fascinating that after more than one session—in which he had related the exploits

of Lord Burghley, Roger Peckinpaugh, Joie Ray, Frank
Gotch, Suzanne Lenglen, Battling Siki, Loren Murchison,
Iron Man McGinnity, Gertrude Ederle, or Walter Hagen—
I harbored the suspicion that he was just making things up
or at least going far beyond the facts, but I inevitably found
I was wrong about this. He was simply attracted to the colorful and knew how to transmit his enthusiasm, and that is
why, as he opened new and gleaming vistas in the world of
sport to us kids, he created in us an enthusiasm on the same
wave length as his own.

Mayor Curley's love of sport was not just wide-ranging, it
could also be extremely detailed. When I learned much later
in my life that one of his prime vote-getting techniques was
satiric attacks on the Boston Brahmins, I was astonished, for
few men ever followed Harvard track (which was first-class)
more closely. One summer when the combined Oxford and
Cambridge teams came over for a dual meet with Harvard
and Yale, we had examined the probabilities so minutely during our sessions on the veranda that we had even concluded
who would pick up third place in each event. I have never
been that close to track and field since, and I look back with
amazement at the depth of our knowledge. I do not know
for a fact but I have an idea that part of the mayor's addiction
to track and field was the result of his friendship with Arthur
Duffey, then a sportswriter for the *Boston Post*, who had set
a new world's record (9⅗ seconds) for the 100-yard dash in
1902. Duffey was a fairly frequent visitor to Nantasket, and
he had something of the mayor's elicitory friendliness. During one chat with him I remember feeling on such confiden-
tial terms that I told him I was a fairly fast runner but was
slow off the mark and wondered what I could do to improve
this. "I will tell you," he said, and in such a way that I felt
he was going to divulge some secret, like shutting your eyes
or sucking in your breath, that only a world's record holder
could know. "The secret," Mr. Duffey went on, "is to practice starts. Get out there and practice, practice, practice."

You should never talk to children that way. They are not ready for the facts of life.

These sessions on the veranda had a rambling form, like the *Jack Paar Show*, but occasionally an educative strain in Mayor Curley's personality would enter a dominant phase and he would conduct a question-and-answer bee to see how much of what he was telling us was sinking in. At other times, although I don't think it was consciously set up, he would use the interrogative as a means of introducing a new figure of importance.

"All right, then," he said one such evening as he tilted himself to the rest position in a rocker, "who would you say was the world's greatest all-round athlete?"

We told him that was easy. Jim Thorpe. He had talked about him on several evenings.

"No, I am not thinking of Thorpe," the mayor said. "I am thinking of a man who more currently has claim to being America's greatest all-round athlete."

A couple of limping nominations followed of men who played two sports. Seeing we were off the track, the mayor waved a hand through the cigar smoke in the gesture of "Cease." "Harold Osborn. Haven't I ever mentioned Harold Osborn?" he asked. We told him we had never heard the name before and that we never ran across it on the sports page.

"No, you wouldn't at that," he said meditatively. "No, you hear about Harold Osborn only every fourth year when the Olympics come round. Who is Harold Osborn? He has held our national decathlon championship more times than any other man. And what is the decathlon? Well, it comes from the Greeks. It is a cluster of ten events. . . ." And so on and into a ten-minute disquisition on the decathlon.

One evening while our usual after-dinner group was sitting around, learning, perhaps, that Harry Greb fashioned his ring name by spelling his real name, Berg, backward, or that in one World Series game McGraw instructed his pitcher to throw the next one in the dirt to Babe Ruth, the mayor suddenly stopped the conversation by asking who was the girl on the beach turning the cartwheels. We told him it was only Margaret McCarthy; she was a girl about our age. "Only Margaret McCarthy," the mayor repeated with telling emphasis. "Well, I'll let you boys in on something. You can go where you like, to the stage shows at B. F. Keith's or to gymnastic exhibitions in Great Britain or on the European continent, and I very much doubt if you will see trained acrobats performing more graceful cartwheels than only Margaret McCarthy." He need say no more. We looked again at Margaret on the beach and we could see now that she turned beautiful cartwheels.

My, the mayor could be persuasive when he turned it on! The Curleys had a player piano and some wonderful rolls to go with it, among them "Oh, Katerina," "Love Nest," "Valencia," "Chérie, Chérie, Je T'Aime" (which we decoded as being French for "Cherie, Cherie, you're tame"). One roll I never went for, though, was a mournful ballad whose title I forget but which ended, roughly, with these lines:

> The days can't all be sunny
> For skies are not always blue.
> When the day is done
> I'm glad to be alone
> At peace with the world
> And the evening with you.

I should correct that earlier statement: I never went for that number until one evening when, just as the roll was finishing, the mayor called out to his son who was tending the piano, "Leo, stick that on again. That's a most beautiful tune. I could listen to it endlessly." I don't know quite how the change came about, because I was certain the mayor was wrong about that song, but within a matter of days I found I was beginning to appreciate that it possessed a certain melancholy sweetness that had somehow previously eluded me.

For a man who followed sports with his avidness, Mayor Curley was not conspicuous for his pursuit of physical exercise. He was well into his fifties then and his "bay window," though less majestic than William Howard Taft's, had long been a prominent and permanent part of his personal landscape, and it probably held him back. He contented himself, at any rate, with swimming and golf. The most remarkable aspect of his swimming was the amount of time it took him to cover the 75 to 250 yards (depending on whether the tide was in or out) from his house to the water. Accompanied by his constant cigar, he would start walking across the gravel in his clogs and red-and-blue-striped bathing suit and pause for half a dozen or more unhurried conversations—one with his chauffeur, one with Mrs. Curley (after retracing his steps back to the house), one (as he started forth again) with a neighbor's handy man, a few with his neighbors who suddenly would spring out of the beach grass, and a closing few with the Curley nursemaid and whoever else happened to be gathered around his umbrella. He obviously preferred conversation to the water, for after diving into (or, more accurately, falling into) two or three breaking waves and executing four or five yards in the Australian crawl (which meant he kept his face in the water), he would come striding slowly out of the ocean.

His golf swing, which he practiced now and then on the lawn, wasn't bad, and I could believe Paul and Leo when they told me he sometimes broke 100 and sometimes drove close to 180 yards. One spring when he formally opened the year's play on the Franklin Park municipal course, the newspaper accounts had his drive off the first tee whistling through the air like a bullet and coming to rest 225 yards down the fairway. I believed in Mayor Curley, but there are some points past which your credulity simply will not budge, and I was convinced the newspapers must have made him out to be a better golfer than he was because he was a celebrity. Since that day I have had a hard time altering my suspicion of these things despite the fact that I have once or twice witnessed a celebrity play within seven shots of what was publicized as his average score.

As I say, these things happened years ago and are part of the past I commune with hardly at all. When I was eleven I began going to camp in the summers, and my friendship with Mayor Curley went on the inactive list. Then, around 1932 or thereabouts, they gave up their Nantasket place, and not long afterward we gave up ours. I never saw him again until the autumn of 1956. During that long interim I had to modify my boyhood estimate of Mayor Curley somewhat, for I had necessarily become aware of some of the less admirable facets of his political techniques, and these naturally clashed with the relatively idealist concepts of government which are the scars of a liberal education. When he was indicted in the 1940s for using the mails to defraud, found guilty and sent to jail, I felt very bad. He was a better man than that—an old-time amoral political boss who had outlived his era, yes, but an essentially corrupt man, no. I remember discussing the whole enigmatic problem with my sister Git and at length agreeing that, bizarrely, the only thing we would not wish to do for Mayor Curley was vote for him.

In the autumn of 1956, when I did see him again, the occasion was a Stevenson dinner in Boston during the election campaign, which I attended with a group that included Git. I thought the mayor looked exceedingly well. I had expected to see a very aged man with the patina of someone stepping out of another century, but, aside from his hair being considerably grayer and his gait a shade more shuffling, he was hardly changed. As he was approaching the microphone to begin his address, the thought suddenly flashed through my mind that I had never heard him speak publicly before. That, of course, had been what he had been famous for—his speeches in which, it was said, he combined the rolling periods of the born orator with down-to-earth humor and a flair for storytelling. Well, his gifts as a speaker had probably been exaggerated, too, I said to myself preparatively, and, after all, the old boy was now over eighty. I hoped he wouldn't acquit himself too badly.

There was no need for these qualms. Mayor Curley could speak—and then some. He had, in fact, far greater artistry than anyone had claimed for him. The deep voice had the fiber and vigor of youth. His fluidity was astounding. He spoke without notes but there was never once the hint of groping for a word or an inflection. It all came out like a river. But what was really remarkable about the man was his timing. He was like Bob Hope in the way he would deliberately race ahead of his audience, wait for them to catch up with a humorous remark, and then, just as the laughter or applause began, he would embellish his first phrase with another crack and, at the right split second when the audience caught up with that one, he would be off and running again. A little later on he would let the audience rush past him and, standing still, as it were, cap the pause with a serious, slow-paced declaration he punched so hard it ricocheted off the chandeliers.

All I can remember of the content of his speech is one small segment, a rather typical one, fortunately. "If these were the old days," he said with a resonant wink, "I would advise you on election day to vote early and vote often. However, it has become apparent that times have become sadly altered and I must content myself with urging you to vote early."

This led him into a story about one pre-World War I

mayoralty campaign in which he was not the candidate but
was in charge of getting out the vote for the Democratic
party. On election day one of his most faithful disciples,
Mike Shea, a man who had fairly recently come over from
Ireland and was employed on the city's construction projects,
cast twenty-four ballots for the successful Democratic candidate. "Not too long after this," Curley went on, "Mike Shea
came to me and told me he had lost his job with the city. I
promised him he would be back on the payroll within the
week, and I headed straight for City Hall and an audience
with the new mayor.

"'Now listen, Jim,' the mayor roared at me when I had
hardly so much as got my foot inside his office, 'if it's about
Mike Shea, forget it. There's no job for that man, and nothing you say will change my mind.'

"'All right, your honor,' I replied to him. 'But in the interests of the party I think I should remind you that you
enjoyed a very small majority in this last election in which
Mike Shea voted for you twenty-four times. Consider this:
in the next election he may vote against you.'"

Mayor Curley vanished from the dais immediately after
finishing his speech, and so, although I had thought of going
up to say hello, I never did get to. I am sorry I didn't. For
all my reservations about his approach to statesmanship, as
I had grown older I had come to value the lasting pleasures
that had resulted, and would continue to, for all of us who
had sat around with him on the veranda and had been
touched by his zest and the ubiquity of his interest—particularly in the world of sport. Furthermore, as I was getting
old enough to realize, the people one gets to know in boyhood are in a special category. Your friendship for them rests
on the very simple basis of whether you like them and like
being with them, and since there are no secondary purposes
involved, you seem to see them wholly and directly and your
understanding lasts a lifetime.

ABOUT THE AUTHOR

HERBERT WARREN WIND picked the subject of golf for his freshman thesis a quarter of a century ago at Yale, and he has been writing about it with such distinction ever since that he is today known as this country's most perceptive and brilliant golf writer. Bobby Jones called his The Story of American Golf "truly monumental," and in a later comment on Wind's writing he said: "Herb Wind is a fine, sensitive writer on the game whose works range from essays of the most accurately appreciative kind to some of the finest golf reporting I have ever read."

Because golf has been his major sport devotion, it is somewhat less well known that Herb Wind is an equally splendid writer about all sports. This present collection of a sampling of his best magazine work over the past fifteen years on all sports topics, plus the long, previously unpublished preface about the era itself, attests this fact better than any extravagant claims that could be made about him.

Mr. Wind, a native of Brockton, Massachusetts, makes his home in New York.